A Korean History for International Readers

A Korean History
for International Readers

Written by The Association of Korean History Teachers

What Do Koreans Talk About Their Own History and Culture?

휴머니스트

How can we talk about
Korean history to non-Korean readers?

To Korean history teachers, the time we discuss past events with students while dreaming for a better tomorrow is the moment that we feel fulfilled. Although we are discouraged with the reality in which schools are situated, there are more cases where we feel joyful by being able to connect with the students. We also think that history should be alive in the students' life, so we endeavor to teach it to be a meaningful lesson for them.

Korean history teachers teach both Korean and World History classes across disciplines. In other words, we attempt to understand Korean history in the context of world history, thus having the advantage to prospect Korean history in relation to other nations' history. This allows us to have a more appropriate discussion of Korean history with non-Koreans. Also, history teachers are disciplined to talk and teach Korean history with language that is easily understood amongst students and therefore have an advantage to write Korean history in a way so anyone can comprehend it. It has been 6 years since we started writing this book which has such merits, and finally it is time to publish it.

This book attempted to explore Korean history without bias for non-Korean readers in the international community. Of course, it was written not only for non-Koreans but also for Koreans. As the subtitle indicates in its question, 'What do Koreans talk about their own history and culture?' this book should be first read by the Koreans who play a key role in forming their history. We, Koreans, should understand our own history to introduce our history to others, because when we know the diverse historical experiences of Koreans that affected the Korean life and culture and their influence on other cultures, we could talk about our history. Thus, this book asked and answers the questions on how Koreans should tell their history.

This book was published in two versions: Korean and English. We expect that many Koreans read this volume in Korean and English versions together and talk about it with many foreigners. We wish Korean readers to have the opportunity to review Korean history from an outsider's view and to offer different cultures a deeper look into the internal aspects of the Korean people. We also desire that this book would contribute to idealizing a better future by suggesting deliberate discussions to introspect on modern day Korea.

The Korean version is suitable for those who are searching for ways to explain Korean history to foreingers. We also recommend it for those who have a foreign friend, or those who have frequent meetings with culturally different individuals, or those who are planning to travel abroad. The English version was specifically geared towards giving a comprehensive outlook for foreigners who simply want to learn more about Korean history.

This book was designed a bit differently compared to previous Korean history books. First of all, a chronological table of world events is presented on the first page of each chapter to show what was happening in other parts of the globe while events were unfolding in Korea. Also, the section of ⟨Korea in the world, The world in Korea⟩ shows how the world and Korea are related to each other. ⟨Historical Sites⟩ introduces cultural assets representing Korea and its significant historical sites, and ⟨Life and Culture⟩ tries to reveal various historical imprints that have accumulated over the years to be embodied into the life and culture of Koreans today.

We deliberately described Korean history for both foreigners and Koreans to understand it with ease while designing the flow of history to be clearly shown. Instead of just describing historical events and facts, we provided a number of maps and visual materials with detailed explanations to entice readers' understanding the contexts. In addition, we emphasized significant figures who led the nation in every period of time with further details regarding the characters.

This volume talks about the history of Koreans from the beginning when they first appeared on the Korean Peninsula to forming a unification of national and cultural identities. Particularly, it reviews modern and contemporary Korean history that accomplished both democratic and economic successes that other third world countries little accomplished. Therefore, readers can meet those Koreans who created a history with hope having overcome the fluctuating contemporary Korean history of the Korean War and the tragic division of the country.

Although we put a lot of time and effort to write and publish this book, we are still afraid of its insufficient work. Nonetheless, we decided to publish this book to introduce Korean history to the international society with more appropriate interpretations. We hope this book can be an inspiration for more Korean history books to be published in other languages.

There are many history teachers who participated in designing and planning this book from the start. Also, the Humanist Publishing Group Inc. largely contributed to publishing it by taking its duty as a publisher into consideration. Much gratitude and respect is owed to these contributors who have made this book possible.

Nov. 2010
The Association of Korean History Teachers

Hoping to get closer to each other through Korean history

Are you ever reminded of any images or words when you hear about Korea? Or have you ever had a chance to talk about Korea with your friends?

Korea has a long history, and therefore it has cultivated diverse cultures over many years. The diverse experiences of Koreans and their culture that have long been accumulated are significant parts of the world history. We believe this book, *A Korean History for International Readers*, would contribute to studying the world history by introducing Korean history to the world.

This book is a historical text that covers Korean history from its foundation to the modern era. It especially deals with pre-modern societies of Korea in detail. Despite its long history, life in its society and its culture are rarely spoken of outsides the peninsula.

Rather than arranging the historical events chronologically, this book focuses more on the details of the historical events by questioning how the diverse experiences that Koreans had affected their life and culture and what influences that culture had on constructing Korean history. This is the reason why we publish this book, although there are already numerous books introducing Korean history. Readers could realize what Koreans have endured and how it lead to their position in the world today. It also mentions their moral values and what they believe is right or wrong.

This book was written by the Association of Korean History Teachers, a major representative of history professionals. Up until now, this association has published alternative text books on Korean and world history to reform its education. In addition, it has published many research papers that cover theories of an alternative history educational process. Although this book is written by two teachers, it is the product of many minds.

History teachers try to grab the interest of students towards an unfamiliar past by speaking in their language. This book was written based on that experience that history teachers have had while attempting to bridge the gap with their students. Looking at Korea in the past and the present, we have written this book as a reminder of what is possible for the future. We did our best to compose it for readers who are unfamiliar or unaware of Korea and its history, in hopes to bring them one step closer to understanding Korea.

Thus, this book differs from any other general history books in that it organizes narrative methods to be read easily and allows readers to feel closer to Korea by using various maps and picture materials. Readers could learn cultural assets, customs, and formalities that all symbolize the lifestyle of Koreans. Also, it introduces historical sites where significant events occurred with vivid photography. Moreover, it describes in detail many important figures whom Koreans respect as their role-models.

It has been already 6 years since we began to prepare this book, and this journey has come to end. It's not a simple task to fully understand what is familiar to us when looking from another perspective. It is said, "A Journey is the experience where I meet another one of myself at strange places". We hope those readers who read this book could meet another part of themselves by being able to relate to the historical journey of Korea.

Nov. 2010
The Association of Korean History Teachers

Contents

VIII Various Attempts for Changes 1650~1862

IX Joseon at a Turning Point 1863~1896

Korea and Koreans, Who are they?

Koreans, the first people who utilized movable metal type printing

Korean ancestors were the first to invent and use movable metal type printing in the world. This happened in the Goryeo Dynasty (918~1392) about 200 years before Johannes Gutenberg in Germany printed the copies of the Bible with such movable metal type printing. Among the printed materials that still remain today, *Jikji*, which was printed during the Goryeo Dynasty, is the earliest book of its kind.

Prior to this printing technique, woodblock printing prevailed during the Shilla Dynasty (B.C. 57~A.D. 935), which was used to print *Mugujeongwangdaidaranigyeong*, the oldest woodblock print material known to exist. Amazingly, the elaborate and delicate woodblocks that were made in the Goryeo Dynasty for producing multi-copies of the sutras are still functional today.

Not only did Korea have such a well developed printing system, but is also a culturally rich nation that has left its mark and legacy throughout its history. However, such cultural accomplishments are not widely known. Korea lies between China, with a long history of civilization, and Japan, which has risen to a technologically advanced nation in the modern era. For this reason, Korean history is frequently examined through the perspectives of these two powerful neighbors, and thereby often evaluated unfairly.

One race divided into South and North

The Southern part of the Korean Peninsula is now the Republic of Korea (South Korea), while the Northern part is the Democratic People's Republic of Korea (North Korea). The people of both South and North wish for reunification even though they have competed with each other ever since their division over 60 years ago. This is because they had lived together under one nation for over 1,000 years and shared common experiences like fighting for liberty under foreign occupation.

South Korea has a population of approximately 50 million and land of roughly 99,000km^2, while the North has about 24 million people and 120,000km^2 of land. The total population of both South and North together are a bit more than that of Britain or France, and a little less than that of Germany. The total land area combined is close to that

of Britain. Most parts of the country lie in the temperate climate, so the people settled and lived in one place to farm. South Korea has more plain farm areas ranking at 3rd place with its population density of 490 people per km² than North Korea. The Korean Peninsula was governed by a united people from the very beginning and had relationships with neighboring countries; meanwhile there were no massive migrations that often have occurred in other countries.

Korean Peninsula, linking the continent and ocean

Japan is located east of Korea, whereas west of Korea is China. Japan and Korea are narrowly separated by the Korean Strait. Koreans may travel to the mainland China both via land and sea routes.

All the previous dynasties that once emerged in the Korean Peninsula existed as a member of Northeast Asia. Especially, the earlier kingdoms of old Korea survived constant battles against China or the nomads who lived on the prairies of China. When the Korean Peninsula was thrown into turmoil during the unification war in the 7th century, China and Japan were also involved. In the 13th century the Mongolian invasion of Goryeo was followed by the invasion of allied armies of Mongol-Goryeo upon Japan. Furthermore, both Japanese invasions of Korea in the 16th century and 19th century turned into international wars on the Korean Peninsula. Also, the Korean War of 1950, which was caused by the division of the Korean Peninsula, was another international war.

Korea is located at the center of the sea that China and Japan also share, and its routes to the continent and the seas are open. So it has often been at the center of international turmoil or sometimes Korea has developed its culture cooperating with the world and became the starting point toward the world. Korea has also sought for absorbing foreign cultures and expanding its influence in the world while maintaining an independent policitical community and forming a unique cultural identity.

In the Pre-modern era Koreans adopted diversified cultures from China, but from the 19th century they were able to absorb Western cultures through Japan and America. There was once a time that under the name of modernization Western cultures overwhelmed

the traditional values. Even though the process of resisting and struggling against outside influences persisted, Koreans eventually became more accepting of foreign cultures. This clash of civilizations has left a diversified cultural heritage along with its long history, and contributed to forming a land where many different religions co-exist in harmony.

Korea is standing at the center of the tide of globalization, just like many other countries. Perhaps they may contribute to making these waves move along. Many Koreans inquire the following questions to themselves: "How are the Koreans viewed in the world?" "What does something like Korean or something global mean?"

'The Land of Morning Calm', or 'Dynamic Korea'

About one hundred years ago a foreign visitor, Griffis, William Elliot (1843~1928) described Korea as a "Corea, The Hermit Nation." (1882) Perhaps what he wanted to express was of its standing aloof from the secular interests and seeking its own value. Another foreigner Percival Lowell (1855~1913) also gave a nickname to Korea "The Land of Morning Calm." (1886) It seems likely that it was derived from 'Joseon', the name of the dynasty at that time, which stands for 'fresh morning'.

However, Joseon was neither a hidden country nor a country that appeared out of nowhere. Though Joseon was a new experience to those visitors, Joseon had been interacting with other countries in its region, forming a historic community for a long time.

Many foreigners happen to imagine Korea with a negative connotation such as the Korean War, a divided nation, and the land with nuclear threats. Perhaps, this reflects the last half century of suffering endured by its people. The minds of many Korean adults of the older generation were occupied by this kind of negative correlation that had been inscribed in their younger ages.

Today, it is no longer possible to see Korea with the same viewpoint presented to the eyes of the foreigners in the 19th century. Korea failed to maintain its sovereignty in the beginning of the 20th century, then experienced a civil war and poverty while being divided soon after being liberated from the Japanese occupation. However, in the latter half of the 20th century Koreans made spectacular improvements in a relatively short time grasp-

ing the attention of the world. Its brilliant economic development has made it possible for Koreans to be recognized as one of the top ten largest trading nations. And Koreans have accomplished a democratic nation after overthrowing fascism of Imperial Japan and despotism of military regimes.

So the younger generation of Korea paints a portrait of its society with the images that are quite different from those of their parents. Instead of picturing the gloomy nation that their parents had imaged, they are reminded that Korea is a dynamic nation that has accomplished successful industrialization and democracy in the last half century when it took over a few centuries in the Western world. Foreigners have contradictory images on depicting Koreans; likewise, there are differences between generations, regions and classes when Koreans portray their own self images. The modern Korean history is the co-existing history in which positive and negative impacts were integrated at various levels.

Koreans who are dreaming their future reunification

Koreans have optimistic prospects on their promising future. They believe they will be able to overcome any kind of difficulties, and even the unification of the two Koreas seems to be not far off. Perhaps Koreans learned a lesson from their history that their ancestors never relinquished their heritage and identity even when their culture was at the brink of destruction.

For more than 1,300 years Koreans have formed communal societies in the Korean Peninsula that used the Korean language. In the 7th century, Shilla united the middle and southern regions of the peninsula and already recognized that they were unique and different from the Chinese and Japanese kingdoms. In the 13th century, people of Goryeo acknowledged that they were a homogeneous people from a common ancestry. Since then, for several hundred years Korea had not been divided, so Koreans' recognition of the homogeneous identity grew stronger. This feeling of unity was a critical factor that inspired a revolutionary movement to fight and protect their homeland from the Japanese invasion, and that keeps them optimistic about reunification in the future, though they are currently divided.

Koreans, who are they? Let's take a step to meet them!

B.C. 500000 ~ B.C. 1C

B.C. 500000
Stone tools, which were used by the humans who lived in this period of time were unearthed at the Geomeunmorudonggul (cave).

B.C. 50000
A human bone fossil, which is believed to have belonged to a person at the age of 35, was discovered at the Seungrisandonggul (cave).

B.C. 8000
Polished stone tools and pottery, which were used by the humans who lived in this period, were unearthed at Jeju-do (Is.). From this evidence we may assume that the Neolithic Period began around 10,000 years ago.

B.C. 4000
Agricultural production began in numerous regions throughout the Korean Peninsula. The beginning of agricultural production brought stability to the settlements and also led to fast social changes.

B.C. 3200
Sumerian civilization was formed.

B.C. 2333
According to *Samgukyusa* (Memorabilia of the Three Kingdoms), Dangun founded Gojoseon in B.C. 2333. This was the first state that ever emerged in the Korean Peninsula and Manchuria.

B.C. 6C
Persia united the Orient.

B.C. 4C
While Gojoseon was developing into a kingdom, it assimilated political authorities in its vicinities. It conflicted with Yan China, which was established by the people of the Chinese Han race.

B.C. 221
Qin united China.

B.C. 109~108
Having resisted Han's invasion for more than a year, Gojoseon was finally defeated. Nonetheless, the command posts established by Han China came to face fierce resistance from the Gojoseon people.

B.C. 1C
Upon the fall of Gojoseon, various states including Buyeo and Goguryeo emerged in the Korean Peninsula and several regions of Manchuria.

I The Beginning of the Korean History

In the Neolithic Age, a large population based upon agriculture settled inside the Korean Peninsula and its surrounding areas. New groups of people came here every now and then, and some of them occasionally moved to Japan, yet most of them settled down here. Descendants of these people are related to the Koreans today. They founded Gojoseon with an advanced farming culture. Gojoseon developed into an independent entity, and later both negotiated and conflicted with the dynasties in China. Koreans today consider Gojoseon as the very first state of Korea.

Danyang Geumgul The oldest Paleolithic relics of Korea were unearthed inside the Geumgul of the Danyang area in the Chungcheongbuk-do province. Several fossil layers, from the Paleolithic Age to the Bronze Era, were also discovered at this cave.

Prehistoric Culture of the Korean Peninsula and the Historic Periods

The lands in the vicinities of the Korean Peninsula changed several times since the emergence of human beings upon it. The East Sea was originally a lake, and people were able to walk across the Yellow Sea. Considering the land's such configurations in the past, some fossils may very well be found inside the Korean Peninsula, like fossils of the humans who are believed to have lived in the southern part of China about 1,800,000 years ago, or of the Homo erectus (also called Peijing-men) figures.

The tools that may have been used by people of the Korean Peninsula around the time of the Peijing-men were unearthed inside the peninsula. Crude tools seem to have been made by cracking stone. They show us what the lives of the people back then were like: living with a lot of difficulties to prepare food. And they also show how a new era was ushered in overcoming the obstacles of nature.

The Neolithic Era began in the Korean Peninsula about ten thousand years ago. Around 4000 B.C., Koreans settled down to farm. When their lives were settled upon farming, and livestock farming was stabilized as well, political communities were formed to unite those who were scattered across the region.

Joseon was the first nation that emerged in the northwestern part of the Korean Peninsula. With its emergence, the first chapter of the history of the Korean people was opened.

Stone Hatchet
One of the most representative remains from the early Paleolithic Era.

The Seungrisan Man

The front of lower jawbone

The side of a skull

The Yeokpo Child
A human bone fossil 100 thousands year old was unearthed in the vicinity of Pyeongyang.

Mandal Man

The side of lower jawbone

B.C. 4000000	B.C. 3000000	B.C. 1000000	B.C. 100000	B.C. 50000
Australopithecus	Homo habilis	Homo erectus	Homo sapiens	Homo sapiens sapiens

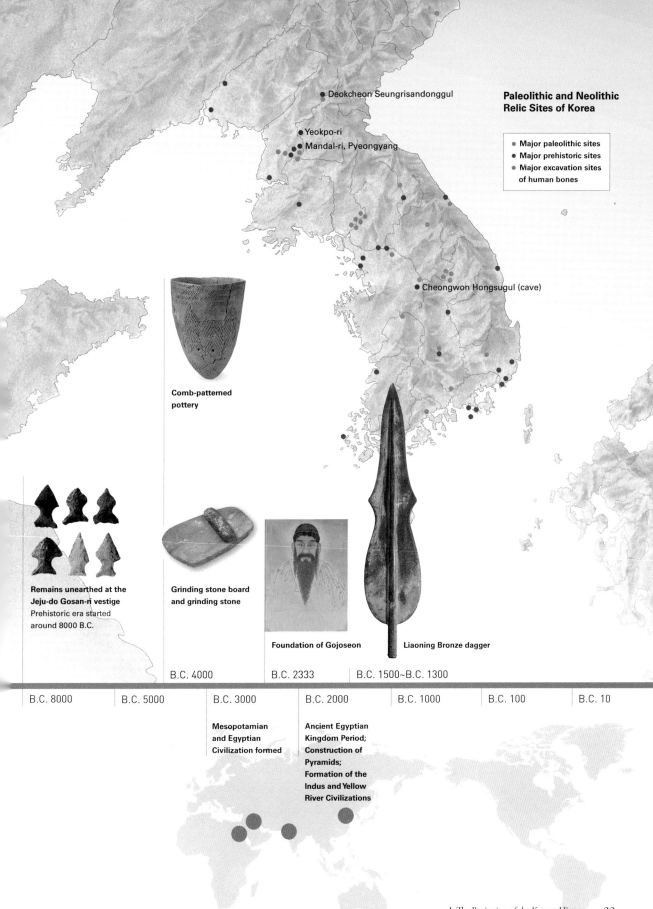

Paleolithic and Neolithic Relic Sites of Korea

- Deokcheon Seungrisandonggul
- Yeokpo-ri
- Mandal-ri, Pyeongyang
- Cheongwon Hongsugul (cave)

- ● Major paleolithic sites
- ● Major prehistoric sites
- ● Major excavation sites of human bones

Comb-patterned pottery

Remains unearthed at the Jeju-do Gosan-ri vestige
Prehistoric era started around 8000 B.C.

Grinding stone board and grinding stone

Foundation of Gojoseon

Liaoning Bronze dagger

B.C. 4000   B.C. 2333   B.C. 1500~B.C. 1300

B.C. 8000   B.C. 5000   B.C. 3000   B.C. 2000   B.C. 1000   B.C. 100   B.C. 10

Mesopotamian and Egyptian Civilization formed

Ancient Egyptian Kingdom Period; Construction of Pyramids; Formation of the Indus and Yellow River Civilizations

1

Since When Did the Existence of Man Begin on the Korean Peninsula?

Neolithic remains found all over the Korean Peninsula

The Hangang (R.) which is quite a large river, flows across Seoul, the capital of South Korea. Located along the banks of the Hangang in this overcrowded modern city are large and small prehistoric settlement sites. "Amsa-dong," which is located at the eastern tip of Seoul, is widely known as one of these Neolithic sites.

Today we are able to visit and observe the nine 'pit dwellings' that provide evidence of prehistoric human activities in the region. Various tools used by the prehistoric inhabitants near the Hangang are exhibited at the pavilion of "Amsa-dong." Judging from the tools, fashioned by ground stones and bones as well as clay potteries, we can trace back to the farming and fishing life of a communal society that settled along the banks of the Hangang thousands of years ago.

It is common to find such prehistoric remains like "Amsa-dong" throughout Korea, and these show

Excavating a scene at the Amsa-dong prehistoric settlement
This prehistoric settlement had been buried for a long time due to floods. However, it has been unearthed through several excavations since the 1960s. Pit dwellings dated to be around 4000 to 3000 B.C. along with numerous necessities such as potteries, stone axes, stone spearheads, stone scrapers as well as farming tools like stone sickles and plowshares, were all discovered.

that many people used to live all over the Korean Peninsula in the Neolithic Period. These Neolithic people were settlers and are regarded as direct fore-fathers of the present Korean civilization.

The origin of the Korean people

People began to live in the Korean Peninsula from the Paleolithic Period. Inside Geomeunmorudonggul, which is located near Pyeongyang, the capital of North Korea, stone tools struck off from larger stone and likely to be more than 500,000 years old were found. And in Beijing, an area not so far from this cave, the bones of a 700,000-year-old Homo erectus were excavated, clearly revealing that cave men had resided in the land of Korea long before the Neolithic Period.

Through the center of the Korean Peninsula flows the Imjingang (R.) which goes into the Yellow Sea. At an archaeological site half way up the river, stone axes ("Jumeogdoki") were discovered at Yeoncheon's Jeongok-ri area for the first time in Asia. Human bones that must have belonged to the people who lived in the same period when stone axes were made were found near Pyeongyang. If so, could we infer that these people were the Neolithic men who once lived in the Korean Peninsula? It's just too early to

Hand axe found at Jeongok-ri, Yeoncheon-gun, Gyeonggi-do province
This tool was called "hand axe" because of its small size which allowed people to grab it easily. They had been only discovered in the areas of Africa and Europe, but after they were unearthed here, such assumption had to be changed. More than 3,000 pieces of stone tools have been unearthed at this prehistoric site, since 1978.

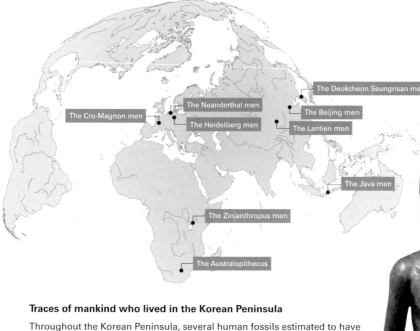

Traces of mankind who lived in the Korean Peninsula

Throughout the Korean Peninsula, several human fossils estimated to have belonged to one of the humans who lived in the same time period with the Cro-Magnon (Homo sapiens sapiens) men were unearthed. Tools used by the people who are also believed to have lived in a similar time period with the 'Beijing men' have occasionally been found as well. The picture on the right shows a restored figure from a human fossil that seems to have been from a human who lived around 40,000 years ago on the Korean Peninsula. His age must have been around five. This child was named as the "Heungsu-Ahi", as the name of the person who discovered it was Kim Heung-su.

make such a conclusion.

The remains discovered in "Geomeunmorudonggul," provide evidence of the existence of tropical animals in the Korean Peninsula. The bones of hyenas and rhinoceroes estimated to be about 500,000 years old were discovered in that cave. Interestingly, fossils of animals that might have lived only in the cold region are commonly found in Korea.

These findings may be explained by the weather changes that occurred in the Paleolithic Era, which alternated between glacial periods and interglacial periods. Due to sea level changes, the landmass of the Korean Peninsula changed significantly in the subsequent periods. Earlier human beings who depended on hunting, picking, and gathering would have frequently moved searching for food due to weather changes. They seem to have covered an incredible amount of distance. It is generally believed that these Paleolithic inhabitants of the Korean Peninsula were not directly related ancestors of the Korean people today.

Farming allows people to settle down

About fourteen thousands years ago, the last Ice Age came. And about ten thousands years ago the earth's climate began to warm up again. The earth's landscape came to feature its current shape, and the Korean Peninsula came to have four clearly distinguishable seasons. The number of acicular trees dropped during this period, and broadleaf trees flourished instead. Large animals that used to live in the cold weather disappeared, whereas small and swift animals such as wild boars and deer burgeoned across the region.

As the climate changed, many of the prehistoric humans must have moved to other areas. Yet, there were many others who adapted to the environmental changes by using advanced tools. Perhaps it was them or other groups of people who migrated to the Korean Peninsula later that contributed to the opening of the Neolithic Era in which clay pots were made to store or process food, and ground stone tools were used.

Changes in the environment and the advancement in skills had great influence upon the lifestyles of these earlier inhabitants. As broadleaf trees prevailed, acorns were soon added to their food resources. Also, their skills for gathering clams and fishing were refined. Yet, in the end it was the farming skills that ultimately brought a dramatic turn to their lifestyle.

The scorched grains found at Bongsan of Hwanghae-do province, show that the Korean people used to farm around 4000 B.C. And there are many other sites throughout the Korean Peninsula where various kinds of farm-

Neolithic farming tools
The item at the top is a 'Galpan,' which was used in peeling or grinding grains. The middle one is a plowshare used in plowing. The bottom one is a stone sickle used in cutting ears off the grain. The Neolithic Period in the Korean Peninsula can be traced back to B.C. 80C. Various tools and pieces of pottery were unearthed from Jeju-do, located in the South Sea.

ing tools have been discovered.

People cultivated farming lands at the riversides or set fire upon hills. Using stone plows they softened the soil and spread seeds, and using stone sickles they harvested. Not only did farming become a major way of producing food for the Neolithic men, but also let them build secured settlements. Usually, ten or more shelters formed a clan community, and several communities constituted a tribe. At the time, there were no classes between the poor and the rich. As productivity was not so high, all the grains harvested were equally shared among members, and important matters were discussed through meetings. Also, the women were not discriminated against. Moving toward the end of the Neolithic Period, these early farming communities changed. Development of farming skills increased productivities, which in turn enlarged the gap between the rich and the poor. As a result, the equality within the society was disrupted.

Comb-patterned Clay Pots

The most well known Neolithic clay pottery is the comb-patterned pottery, which has comb-like designs on the surface. Interestingly enough, some similarly patterned potteries have been found in regions from North Europe to Siberia. European Archaeologists called these potteries "Kammkeramik," which also means 'comb-patterned potteries.' Comb-patterned potteries were commonly used between B.C. 40C and B.C. 10C, and during this time period people lived in the vicinity of the rivers and streams, hunting and fishing. The clay culture of the Korean Peninsula along with those of the Northeast region of China and Siberia, feature similar forms of pottery. Their origin differs from the clay pottery culture of the Yellow River basin, where the mainstream Chinese civilization was formed.

Comb-patterned clay pot at Amsa-dong, Seoul
This clay pot, unearthed near the Hangang was created approximately between B.C. 40C and B.C. 30C.

Japanese "Jomon" clay pot
"Jomon Period" refers to the Neolithic Period in Japan. The most well known clay artifact of the time is the 'Jomon clay pot,' which has a straw-rope pattern designed on the surface.

Siberian comb-patterned clay pot

2

Koreans Found Gojoseon: the First Kingdom of the Korean Peninsula

Korea, and its name "Korea and Joseon"

North Korea and South Korea are currently called the Democratic People's Republic of Korea (DPRK) and the Republic of Korea (ROK) respectively. Though both names have the word "Korea" in them, the North Koreans identify themselves with the term "Joseon," while South Koreans call their country with the title "Daehanminguk."■ The origin of the name Joseon can be found from "Gojoseon (Old Joseon),"■■ from which the North Koreans claim their ancestry. "Han" in the name of South Korea means that they are the successor of "The Daehan Empire (Empire of the Great Han)" and also the Korean Provisional Government which was set up (in exile) inside China in the 1910s. However, the first historical record of "Han" appeared when a king of Gojoseon moved southbound and became "the King of Han" in the early 2nd century B.C. Based on this information, we can see that either "Joseon" or "Han," with which the Koreans identify themselves, originated from "Gojoseon."

■ **Daehanminguk** "Daehan" and "Taehan" were once used to call the Great Korean Empire.

■■ **Gojoseon** Its original name was Joseon. However, in order to distinguish it from the other Joseon established in 1392, the prefix "Go (old)" was attached to "Joseon."

Cheomseongdan (altar)
It is recorded in a book from the 15th century that this was the place where Dangun built Cheomseongdan to perform rituals meant for Heaven. We can see that Koreans have commemorated Dangun's foundation of Gojoseon for a very long time. As the Olympic torch is lighted in Greece, today the torches that would be used in the opening ceremonies for national sports events in South Korea are all lighted here.

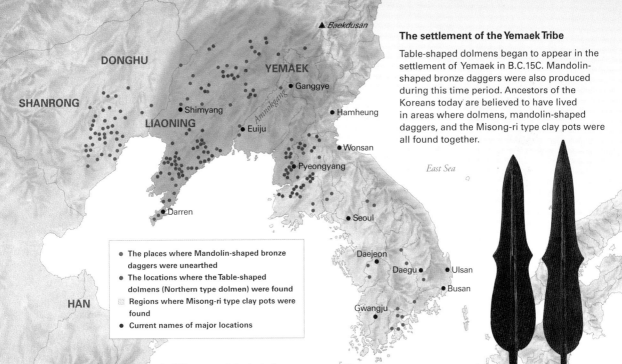

DONGHU

SHANRONG

YEMAEK
● Ganggye

● Shimyang
LIAONING
● Euiju
Amnokgang
● Hamheung

● Wonsan

● Pyeongyang

▲ Baekdusan

East Sea

● Darren

● Seoul

HAN

Daejeon
Daegu ● ● Ulsan
● Busan

Gwangju

- ● The places where Mandolin-shaped bronze daggers were unearthed
- ● The locations where the Table-shaped dolmens (Northern type dolmen) were found
- Regions where Misong-ri type clay pots were found
- ● Current names of major locations

The settlement of the Yemaek Tribe

Table-shaped dolmens began to appear in the settlement of Yemaek in B.C.15C. Mandolin-shaped bronze daggers were also produced during this time period. Ancestors of the Koreans today are believed to have lived in areas where dolmens, mandolin-shaped daggers, and the Misong-ri type clay pots were all found together.

Mandolin-shaped bronze daggers
These daggers are named "Mandolin-shaped bronze daggers" due to their mandolin-like shape. As many of these daggers have been found in the Liaoning area of China, they are also called as "Liaoning-style bronze daggers." In terms of shape, they are quite different from the bronze daggers made in China.

Misong-ri clay pot
Clay pots from the Bronze Era without any particular patterns. Approximately 20 or 30 centimeters high. Usual colors include taupe, dark-taupe, and red-taupe. Because many clay pots of this kind were found in Misong-ri of the Euiju region located at the lower reaches of the Amnokgang, they are called as 'Misong-ri type clay pots.'

To the Korean people "Gojoseon" is their first state, and Dangunwanggeom is accepted as their common forefather. So South Koreans celebrate the National Foundation Day, October 3rd, as a national holiday. Some South Koreans even continue to use the "Dangi" calendar, which begins with the year that Dangun established the nation (2333 B.C.). A religion which worships Dangunwanggeom was created as well.

However, there have been various theories regarding the beginning of Old Joseon and its process of development. Fortunately, a Chinese book "Gwanja" written in B.C. 7C described that Gojoseon was located 8,000 li units (a distance that equals 3,200km) away from Qi. According to this book, we can presume that Gojoseon was formed at least prior to B.C. 7C.

Gojoseon was founded on agriculture

The term "Joseon" sparsely appears in Chinese records. According to them, the west side of Gojoseon was occupied by the tribes named "Shanrong and Donghu," while the east side was occupied by the "Yemaek" people. Gojoseon was established by the latter, the Yemaek tribe. This tribe settled down and began farming around B.C. 40C and used bronze-based tools beginning from the 15th through 13th century B.C. When farming skills were advanced, farming replaced gathering as their main source of livelihood.

As agriculture turned out to be a significant method in food supplying, men rose to dominant positions of leadership. Women's social status also started to decline. The gap between the poor and the rich continued to

A portrait of Dangun
The story of Dangun's foundation of Gojoseon was recorded in *Samgukyusa* written by Il-yeon in the 13th century. Dangun has always been considered as the symbol of Korean independence, especially at times when the Korean people suffered from foreign invasions.

expand as well. Eventually, conflicts among tribes waged to obtain more wealth came to break out frequently. Either individuals or groups defeated in competition became possessions of the victorious. Appeared was a distinction between the ones who governed and the ones who were governed, and such distinction led to the birth of social classes. Technological advantages generated by using bronze-based instruments resulted in more diversity, not to mention more gaps among classes and tribes. The large dolmens found in the Yemaek region are proofs to the authority and power possessed by political leaders who used to rule either small or large communities composed of several tribes. The legend of Dangun's foundation of Gojoseon is recorded in *Samgukyusa* (Memorabilia of the Three Kingdoms), which contributes to understanding the fact that Gojoseon was indeed an advanced agricultural society.

Gojoseon's development and its becoming a representative power of the Yemaek race

Between the 5th and 3rd centuries B.C., drastic political changes occurred in the northern region of the Korean Peninsula and the northeast region of China. In China, various states of the Han race competed with each other to achieve unification. And on the north side of the Great Wall of China, the nomads called Donghu and Shanrong organized large and small political power groups. In the meantime, in the land of Yemaek, several states coexisted with each other, and Gojoseon was one of them.

As the Chinese Han race moved toward east, Gojoseon continued its growth assimilating states near its border and developed into a confederate kingdom that ruled neighboring small states since B.C. 4C. However, its power eventually weakened by on-going confrontations with Chinese states like Yin. With repeated competitions and compromises ensuing, Gojoseon decided to accept and embrace the advanced civilization of the Han race,

Gojoseon's territories, and its battle against Han in the latter half of the 2nd century B.C.

Gojoseon became a power that represented the Yemaek tribes, and in the 2nd century B.C. it extended its authority over the southern and middle regions of the Korean Peninsula. Han attempted to disrupt the inner-dynamics of the Yemaek tribes, and after mobilizing a large number of troops, it also invaded Gojoseon, which defended itself for more than a year.

▨ Gojoseon territories	○ Important geological
➡ Gojoseon's attack	locations of the time
➡ Han's attack	● Important geological
★ Battle fields	locations of today

HAN   *Liao*

Yoyang (Yangpyeong)

7,000 naval soldiers under Yang

● Dengzhou

● Naeju

including Chinese letters. Gojoseon achieved political and social developments under the centralized authority and power of the king.

In B.C. 2C, Gojoseon of the Wanggeomseong fortress (today's Pyeongyang) established itself as the power representing the Yemaek tribes. It built its own economy and enhanced its military power, with iron-based tools and weapons they devised. Gojoseon came to control trade traffics between China and other Yemaek areas, and tap into them as well.

Confrontation between Han China and Gojoseon

As Gojoseon seized power, the Han Dynasty that had united China revealed its intentions and started to threaten the Gojoseon borders. In fear of being killed, several tribes of the confederate Gojoseon surrendered their land and people to China, instead of resisting the incoming Chinese army.

Gojoseon's authority was challenged by various opponents, and it was also invaded by 50,000 troops of Wu Ti of the Han China (B.C.109). Wu Ti succeeded in uniting all the remaining kingdoms in China, and he pushed the powerful nomad tribe Xiongnu all the way up to the outside of the Great Wall of China. Then those Chinese troops invaded Gojoseon. At first, Gojoseon stood its ground for a year. The Gojoseon soldiers continued to defeat the invaders and their reinforcements as well. However, a prolonged war caused certain disruptions to occur inside Gojoseon. People started to call for ending the war.

Internal conflicts led to the fall of the capital city, and shortly after that Gojoseon fell as well in 108 B.C. After the war, Chinese invaders left, but not before they established commanderies here and there to rule the Gojoseon region from remote. Then, all the Chinese commanders who led the invasion were punished upon their return to China, and because the Gojoseon people continued to fight even after the war ended, the Chinese commanderies were also dismantled in a not so distant future.

Sehyeong Bronze Daggers
Because their shape is thin and long, they are called "Sehyeong Bronze Daggers." These daggers are only found inside the Korean Peninsula. So they are also called "Korean style daggers." They were the next generation of the Mandolin-shaped bronze daggers.

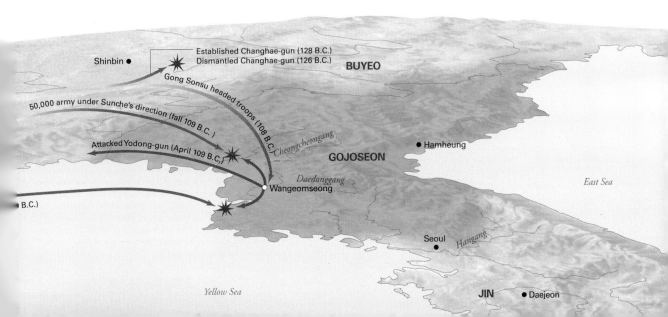

3

Developments of Several Ancient Kingdoms, in the South and North of the Korean Peninsula

The time when Myeongdojeon was used

In 1927, several iron-based artifacts of unknown origins and functions were discovered in the Yongyeon area of the Pyeonganbuk-do province. The most interesting one found in this ruin which belonged to the 3rd century B.C. was a sword-shaped item with the letter "Myeong (明)" inscribed upon its surface. There were several of them. They had a hole at the center so one could hang them with a string. Archaeologists soon concluded that they must have served as some kind of currency.

This item was called Myeongdojeon, a currency which was used in the Chinese Yan and Qi dynasties. Today they are found all over the region that belonged to Gojoseon, and that means that Gojoseon was in active trade engagements with Yan. This is also supported by Chinese records, as they say that in the 7th century B.C. Gojoseon had an active trade partnership with Qi, and that the Cheoksan region in the Shandong Peninsula was an important port for the Qi Dynasty. Later, many states were established in the southern region of the Korean Peninsula as well. They produced a substantial amount of iron which they traded with not only Japan but also other countries in the north. One of the reasons that Han China invaded Gojoseon in the first place must have been Gojoseon's taking initiatives in international trades.

The Cheongcheongang (R.), main trading route of Gojoseon
Large amount of Myeongdojeon pieces were found in the vicinities of Beijing, which was the capital of the Yan Dynasty. Yet another large amount of them were found in areas near the middle stream of the Cheongcheongang. They were also found in areas such as Shandong (central area of the State of Qi), the outskirts of Beijing, the east side of Yoha (Liohuh), and near the middle stream of the Daedonggang (R.). From this, we can extrapolate the overall scale of the trade network that existed among Gojoseon, Yan, and Qi.

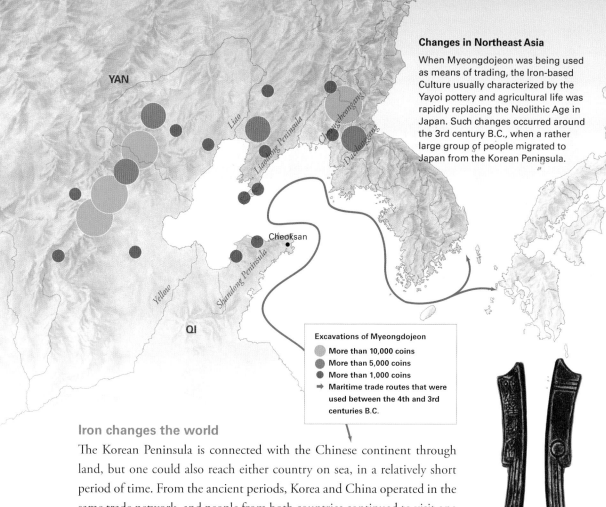

Changes in Northeast Asia

When Myeongdojeon was being used as means of trading, the Iron-based Culture usually characterized by the Yayoi pottery and agricultural life was rapidly replacing the Neolithic Age in Japan. Such changes occurred around the 3rd century B.C., when a rather large group of people migrated to Japan from the Korean Peninsula.

YAN

Liao

Liaodong Peninsula

Changcheongang

Daedonggang

Cheoksan

Yellow

Shandong Peninsula

QI

Excavations of Myeongdojeon

⬤ More than 10,000 coins
◐ More than 5,000 coins
⬤ More than 1,000 coins
➡ Maritime trade routes that were used between the 4th and 3rd centuries B.C.

Iron changes the world

The Korean Peninsula is connected with the Chinese continent through land, but one could also reach either country on sea, in a relatively short period of time. From the ancient periods, Korea and China operated in the same trade network, and people from both countries continued to visit one another.

In the Gojoseon region, Myeongdojeon is often discovered along with some iron tools, which included agricultural utensils, mechanical tools, and weapons such as spears and swords. Lumps of iron chipped from a larger one, probably to make other iron tools were also found with these tools. These are all solid evidences which prove the fact that iron was widely used in the Korean Peninsula at the time.

Between the 4th and 2nd centuries B.C. in Northeast Asia, large groups of people were always on the move, fleeing from the on-going wars waged for unification inside China. And even after unification, they still could not settle as they had to evade all the smaller internal battles going on as well. Many of them moved to the region which used to belong to the late Gojoseon, and some of them moved southbound even further, spreading the culture of using items made from iron as they progressed.

Iron literally changed the world. The iron-based agricultural utensils replaced the existing ones that were made of wood and stone. The cutting-edge technology also contributed to producing more diverse and more ef-

Myeongdojeon
Currency that was used in Yan and Qi China.

Yayoi pottery
This clay pot was produced between 300 B.C. and 300 A.D. during the Yayoi Age of Japan. It was discovered in the Kitakyushu area.

ficient weapons. As a result, agricultural productivity and military tactics were refined and advanced. Meanwhile, the gap between the poor and the rich widened drastically, and tribes that took advantage of channels through which they accessed the merits of iron expanded their own influence rather rapidly by integrating less skillful tribes around them into their realm. Going through a similar procedure, Gojoseon developed into a powerful political force in the first place and was able to battle the mighty Han Dynasty for more than a year.

Jin, Buyeo and many other states established inside the Korean Peninsula after the days of Gojoseon

Around the 2nd century B.C., Gojoseon expanded its territories by uniting the political forces of Yemaek. By blocking other political forces from trading with China directly, and instead relaying their trade traffics with each other for them, Gojoseon was able to fully exploit the merits of international trading.

Around this time, a state called Jin was founded in the south of Gojoseon, the middle and southern parts of the Korean Peninsula. Around the 10th century B.C. a bronze-based culture was introduced to the region, and soon followed by an iron-based culture, showing a similar rate of development with the northern regions. Development of productivity and social classes progressed steadily, and by the time around the 3rd century B.C. several states came to existence in this area. These states appointed the king of Mogjiguk as their representative and established a relationship with the Han Dynasty.

In the north of Gojoseon there was Buyeo, in the basin of the Songhua River. Its economy was based on farming and animal breeding. In its west

Remains excavated at Songguk-ri, Buyeo area
There is a city named Buyeo in the southwest region of the Korean Peninsula. Buyeo was the last capital of Baekje. Baekje once considered itself the successor of Buyeo, as we can see from the title "Nambuyeo (South Buyeo)," which they used to refer to themselves. In Buyeo, a bronze-based culture based upon farming was formed in the 10th century B.C. This picture shows the remains of the Bronze Era: a bronze sword, stone arrowhead, stone knife and jade, which were all unearthed at Songguk-ri in Buyeo.

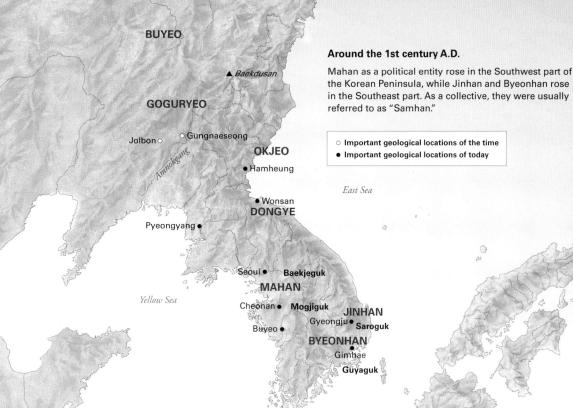

BUYEO

▲ Baekdusan

GOGURYEO

Jolbon ○   ○ Gungnaeseong

OKJEO

● Hamheung

Amnokgang

East Sea

● Wonsan

DONGYE

Pyeongyang ●

Seoul ●   Baekjeguk

MAHAN

Cheonan ●   Mogjiguk

JINHAN

Gyeongju ● Saroguk

Buyeo ●

BYEONHAN

Gimhae ●

Guyaguk

Yellow Sea

side there were the nomad tribes. Buyeo maintained a close relationship with the Chinese Han-race kingdoms, yet had a hostile one with the nomad tribes.

After Gojoseon collapsed, there were some significant changes that struck the region. People who lived in the center of Gojoseon moved south, evading the invasions of the Han forces. People who stayed continued to resist the Han invaders and developed a new political force.

Thus, around the 1st century B.C., several political powers came to existence. In the north, Goguryeo, Okjeo, and Dongye arose in addition to Buyeo, and in the south, small and large states formed political alliances such as Mahan, Jinhan, and Byeonhan.

The states in the north grew and developed, in the midst of confrontations with the ever-advancing Chinese forces. Sometimes they had to negotiate and make compromises, and such efforts helped them develop as well. Goguryeo was the prime example.

Among 54 internal states of Mahan, Baekje rose above all else, as did Saro and Guya inside Jinhan and Byeonhan respectively. These were the central powers that would develop into Baekje, Shilla, and Gaya, states that all played a pivotal role in the ancient history of Korea.

The Largest Dolmen Kingdom in the World

Large stone monuments just like Stonehenge in England or stone statues in the Easter Island of Chile are also found in the regions where the ancestors of the Koreans resided. They are either dolmens or monoliths. The most frequently discovered ones are the dolmens. They feature different shapes from one another in various regions. Yet, they are all believed to have been erected between the 15th and 10th centuries B.C., and they continued to appear all over the Korean Peninsula and Manchuria up until the 2nd century A.D.

The dolmens constructed in the north side of Korea resemble large tables. And other dolmens concentrated in the central and southern regions of Korea look like square-shaped game boards. Assuming that dolmens were built to bury people who held significant importance, and considering the ancient people's ideas that the deceased would take care of their offsprings, we can imagine them being used as stone tombs or altars for religious services.

Quite impressively, Korea has the most dolmens in the world. Some of them are of tremendous historical significance, and added to that they are beautiful as well. In the year 2000, sectors of dolmens inside Gochang, Hwasun, and Ganghwa areas were designated and declared as part of the World Cultural Heritages.

Monolith
Numerous monoliths were erected with dolmens during the Bronze Era. The monolith shown in this picture is located in Songbong-ri of the Euncheon-gun area inside the Hwanghae-do province.

Hwasun Dolmen Park in Jeollanam-do

A place where a heavy concentration of dolmens was discovered. This Hwasun Dolmen Park is now registered as part of the World Cultural Heritages.

North-style Dolmen (above) and South-style Dolmen (below)

Among the dolmens discovered inside Korea and its vicinity, there are North-style dolmens that look like round tables, and South-style dolmens that look like Chinese play tables. The former ones have a chamber upon the surface, while the latter ones have a chamber beneath it.

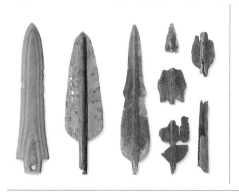

Things found with dolmens

Many artifacts which show us the life style of the time were discovered from dolmens. These are the items discovered inside the dolmen chambers: from the left to the right, there are a stone knife and a Mandolin-shaped bronze dagger, personal ornaments made of jade, and red polished pottery.

Ritual Ceremony to God

"Always in May, after sowing is finished in the field, Koreans perform a ritual ceremony. Many people gather around, dance, sing, and drink many days and nights. In October, when harvest is over, they celebrate in the same way." – *Samgukji* (Records of Three Kingdoms)

This is a story from a Chinese source named *Samgukji*. It describes how people in the central and southern parts of the Korean Peninsula lived around the 1st century. The words such as "Dongmaeng" and "Mucheon" appear in Goguryeo and Dongye sections of that book. These words referred to a harvest festival, a ritual of thanksgiving that was usually held in Goguryeo and Dongye in October. Just as such events which were observed in the south, all the events in the north also had people gather around, prepare a memorial service for the ancestors, and hold a banquet and a festival. The Buyeo people also had a similar custom, but they performed their rituals as their hunting season began. "In December, all people of the nation gathered together to give thanks to heaven."

"Chuseok" is considered to be the most important holiday in Korea, and on this day, August 15th of the lunar calendar, people celebrate the harvests of the year. On "Chuseok," Koreans cook rice with new grains, brew liquor, and perform a ritual to thank their ancestors with newly harvested fruits and foods. Those who left their home town return, and all the family members scattered around the country get together in a long time. It is also an opportunity for the family to get together and pay respect to the heaven and their ancestors altogether.

■ 'October' and 'December' mentioned here are the lunar calendar months. Even today, Koreans commemorate New Year day and Chuseok by the lunar calendar.

Holiday customs

In Korea, populations are concentrated in large cities, and always a few days before Chuseok, the roads are over-crowded with people returning to their homes for the Chuseok holiday; people make jokes, naming the unending trail of southbound traffic "the great migration." They reunite with their family members and relatives whom they haven't seen for a long time. And they conduct rituals and care for their ancestors' graves together.

❶ A memorial service for the ancestors
❷ An express bus terminal crowded with people heading for their hometowns
❸ Making Songpyeon
❹ Family paying respect to their ancestors' graves

B.C. 1C ~ A.D. 700

B.C. 57
Samguksagi (History of the Three Kingdoms), which is the oldest
historical record in Korea that remains today, documents that Shilla,
Goguryeo, and Baekje were founded in B.C. 57, B.C. 37, and B.C.
18 respectively. However, it is a more general opinion that Goguryeo
emerged earlier than Shilla and Baekje.

A.D. 260
Baekje established its own official rank system which distinguished
sixteen rank positions with different official uniform colors. The rank
system indicates that an institution for ruling was being formed.

313
Rome officially authorized Christianity.

372
Buddhism was authorized in Goguryeo. In 384, Baekje authorized
Buddhism, and then Buddism was introduced to Shilla as well.

391~413
King Gwanggaetowang of Goguryeo unified the region of Manchuria
and formed a great kingdom, and began to expand his power to the
middle section of the Korean Peninsula.

427
King Jangsuwang of Goguryeo moved the capital to Pyeongyang.
Pyeongyang was located at the center of the old territory of Gojoseon.

540~576
Under the leadership of King Jinheungwang, Shilla achieved quite a
development. Such development was large enough to push Shilla into
a dominant position in the war for unification.

610
Muhammad established the religion of Islam.

612
The Sui emperor invaded Goguryeo with 1,130,000 troops.
The Goguryeo people defeated them under the leadership of Eulji
Mundeok.

645
The Goguryeo people defeated the large troops of Tang led by Emperor
Taizong, one of the most magnificent kings in Chinese history.

The Beginning of the Three Kingdoms Period

Goguryeo, Baekje, and Shilla, which all emerged in the 1st century B.C. grew into centralized kingdoms between the 4th and 5th centuries. Goguryeo, which developed itself in the wake of constant confrontations with the northern tribes, overcame several invasions of the united kingdoms of China as well. Baekje arose in the southwest and transported its advanced culture to Japan. Shilla at the southeast expanded its power after the 6th century and became a leading power which later unified the three kingdoms. By exchanging its culture with neighboring countries, each of these kingdoms developed its own unique culture.

Onyeosanseong This mountain fortress, located at Huanrun, Lioningseong in China, was the center of Goguryeo when it was first established (B.C. 37~ A.D. 3).

Formation of the East Asian Culture Block

As powerful, united kingdoms appeared in China, a unique political system called 'Appellation and Tribute' relationship was formed between the powerful kingdom of China and its neighboring states. A Chinese emperor vested official posts or titles to the rulers of the neighbor countries, and in turn, those rulers sent envoys to the emperor with tributes. The price for the tributes was always paid, and exchanges of envoys were arranged through mutual agreements.

This particular relationship contributed to the stabilization of the region. Economic and cultural exchanges, either official or unofficial, became more active between countries.

The East Asian region came to share various cultural elements. People used Chinese characters in their daily lives. Chinese-style governing spread throughout the region through Confucian scriptures and Chinese history books. Buddhist scriptures from India were also translated into Chinese characters and were introduced to the neighboring countries. Through such process East Asian countries formed a cultural block, sharing Chinese letters, political ideals of Confucianism, Chinese political system, and the Buddhist culture.

China

Chinese character

Characters inscribed on bones and tortoise carapace
The early Chinese life using letters can be traced from characters inscribed upon bones and tortoise carapace. During the days of Qin and Han dynasties, the Chinese letters were formed in a unified fashion. "Hanja" refers to 'the letters of the Han race or the Han Empire.' "Ganjache," which is a letter style that displays a simplified form of the individual original characters, has been in use in China since the 1950s.

Vietnam

Chu Nom

Chu Nom
Vietnamese used the Chinese letters as well. However, 'Chu Nom,' designed to describe Vietnamese pronunciation using Chinese sounds or utilizing the Chinese letters' meaning, was put to use since the 13th century. From the beginning of the 20th century, they began to use Roman letters instead of either Chinese letters or Chu Nom.

History of Vietnam's Fall
History of Vietnam's Fall was published in Shanghai, China, in September 1905. This book recorded the dialogues between Phan Boi Chau (1867~1940), a Vietnamese nationalist and Liang Qi Chao (1873~1929), a Chinese political reformist during the ending days of the Qing Dynasty. Soon after this book was introduced to Korea, it attracted and intrigued many Koreans. Phan Boi Chau most admired An Jung-geun (1879~1910), a young Korean man who assassinated Ito Hirobumi (1841~1909, the first Prime Minister of Japan) who led the invasion of Korea. These four men, An Jung-geun, Liang Qi Chao, Phan Boi Chau and Ito Hirobumi never met each other. Given an opportunity, they would have continued to communicate with each other through letters. If so, their psychological distance would have been much closer than that between the Koreans and the Japanese, or the Chinese and the Vietnamese today.

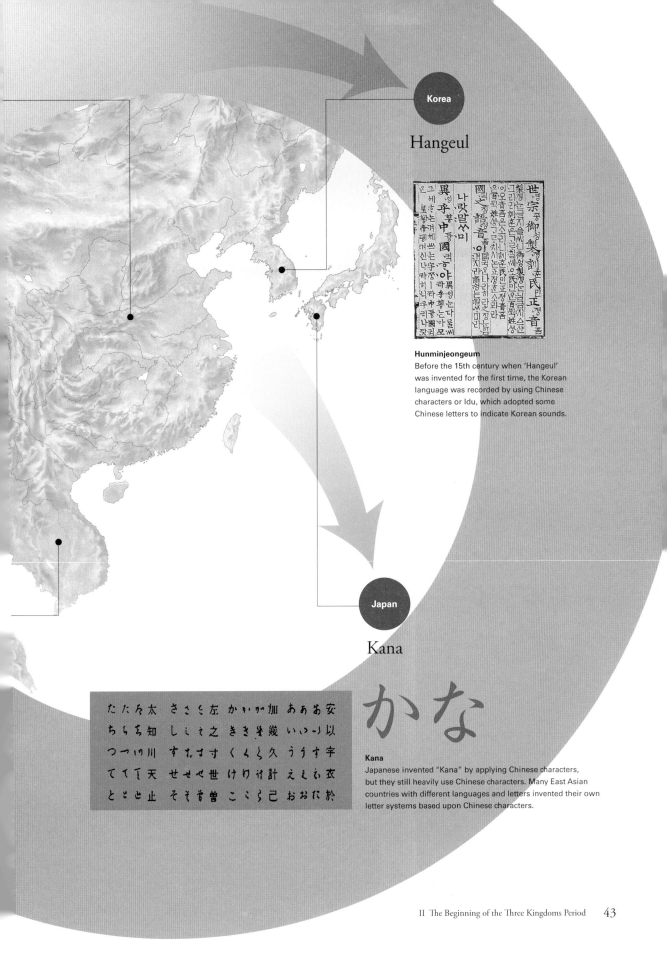

Hangeul

Hunminjeongeum
Before the 15th century when 'Hangeul' was invented for the first time, the Korean language was recorded by using Chinese characters or Idu, which adopted some Chinese letters to indicate Korean sounds.

Kana

Kana
Japanese invented "Kana" by applying Chinese characters, but they still heavily use Chinese characters. Many East Asian countries with different languages and letters invented their own letter systems based upon Chinese characters.

1

The Formation of the Three Kingdoms: Goguryeo, Baekje, and Shilla

Buyeo and Goguryeo fight for power in the northern region of Korea

After Gojoseon collapsed, Buyeo became the No.1 power among the political forces of Yemaek. Buyeo had already been exchanging active trades with China, while advancing agriculture and farming as well. Around the first century B.C. Buyeo developed into a kingdom and continued to grow as a powerful state.

Still, Goguryeo remained a threat to Buyeo. Goguryeo, which originated from inside Buyeo, was established by Jumong in 37 B.C. in the Amnokgang basin. It continued to assimilate minor tribes around it. In an attempt to take control of the prairies near Buyeo and Han China, Goguryeo confronted both of them.

The conflicts between Buyeo and Goguryeo became more complicated as they came in contact with the nomads in the west, not to mention with Han China, which was striving to expand its influence to the east. While clashes continued between Goguryeo and Buyeo or Goguryeo and Han China due to Goguryeo's ambition to obtain wider fertile regions, China and Buyeo managed to maintain a friendly relationship.

Gold crown
A gold crown, discovered inside one of the tombs of the Gyeongju area, shows well developed craftsmanship.

Daereungwon
In Gyeongju, which had been the capital of Shilla for a thousand years, there are 23 tombs of kings, queens and noble men. The picture shows large scale tombs that were built between the 4th and 5th centuries. Bodies were placed along with grave goods inside wooden coffins, and then the coffins were covered with a number of stones. After that, soil was piled over the stones in a shape of a hill. Numerous remains that show us an impressive culture, such as gold crowns, were unearthed from these tombs.

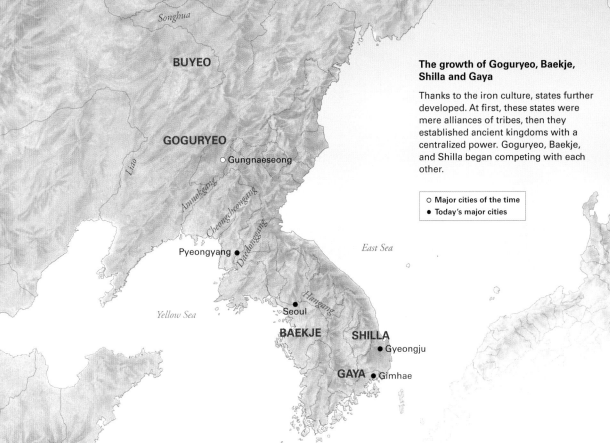

Baekje, Shilla and Gaya

As Buyeo and Goguryeo were struggling for territory in the north of the Korean Peninsula, in the central and southern areas Baekje, Shilla, and Gaya rose to power.

In 18 B.C. Baekje, which was established earlier by those from Goguryeo emerged in the vicinity of today's Seoul as a confederated kingdom which incorporated various walled-town states of Mahan. During the 3rd century it expanded its borders and grew large enough to occupy the entire Hangang region.

In the same time, the Shilla Kingdom, which would literally last for a millenium (57 B.C.~935 A.D.), was formed in Gyeongju in the southeast side of the Korean Peninsula. In this area, many states called as the Jinhan Alliance were established and prospered around the B.C. 2nd~A.D. 1st centuries. Then the Saro state, which emerged in Gyeongju, developed into a leading force by assimilating surrounding political powers.

Also, in the west side of the Nakdonggang (R.) which passes through the southeast part of the Korean Peninsula, there was the Gaya Alliance of six allied states led by the central state of Guya (Geumgwangaya). These people were able to advance their skills of cultivation and farming, using iron utensils. With natural resources at their disposal, the six states continued to grow. This area produced substantial amounts of iron as well, and the state of Guya established at the Gimhae area became the trade center dealing with the northwest region of the Korean Peninsula, and Japan as well.

Aristocrats, slaves and free peasants

The emergence of dominant powers led to the assimilation of small political forces. Some states yielded to centralized powers without conflict, yet most of them were dominated by force and forced to relinquish their own authority. The treatment of local residents who were assimilated into more powerful states varied to a certain degree, mainly by the policy of integration. The heads of factions who surrendered without a fight were incorporated into dominant positions inside the central government, and the local residents of those factions were not harshly discriminated against. Yet, the residents of the areas or factions that were conquered by wars were treated very much differently. Many free peasants were captured and taken as slaves to serve the occupants. In some cases, even the whole population was treated like slaves.

In the meantime, disputes and conflicts continued in the inside of the unified center. Through campaigns, leaders were able to accumulate power and expand their land, while a majority of peasants continued to suffer from constant wars and heavy taxes. Thus, the peasant class was being shoved into poverty.

Eventually, differentiated treatments of certain local regions and differences among certain groups of people, all gave birth to a hierarchical so-

Susan-ri Mural Painting (Restored graphics)
This mural painting of Goguryeo depicts the aristocratic members going on a picnic. At the left of this picture, there are actors who are fooling around, and the slaves are holding an umbrella for the nobles. Also, the nobles are drawn largely, while the slaves are described in small sizes. We can see that this painting attempted to exhibit different social statuses. The commoners constituted the largest portion of the population. However, the Korean slavery system was quite different from that of the western world, as most slaves were allowed to live in family.

cial structure that was composed of classes such as aristocrats, independent peasants, and slaves. Most of the aristocrats were either officials who developed a kinship with the king or chieftains of the conquered states. They enjoyed political and financial privileges as a dominant class. On the other hand, a majority of the people were peasants who engaged in farming and they were levied heavy taxes. And at the bottom of the foodchain, there were either privately owned slaves or collectives of slaves that belonged to the state.

The fall of Buyeo and Gaya

Buyeo, which made spectacular development while competing with Goguryeo, was eventually destroyed by the attacks of nomad tribes from the west. In the 4th century, its capital was turned to ruins and more than fifty thousand people were captured and taken away from their homes. Later, the royal lineage of Buyeo resurrected, but soon it was merged into Goguryeo.

The collapse of Gaya also showed a similar process. Geumgwangaya, which led the Gaya Alliance for a long time, suffered a large defeat by the allied forces of Goguryeo and Shilla, and could barely maintain its state, at the end of the 4th century and the early of the 5th century. Without such leadership, the Gaya Alliance was dismantled and various Gaya states strayed away from each other.

The struggles and confrontations of the five states narrowed down to conflicts among the remaining three kingdoms. Goguryeo was in the north, while Baekje and Shilla were in the south. Hence the so-called 'Era of the Three Kingdoms' began.

The Gaya Potteries

In the regions that belonged to Gaya which was located in the south of the Korean Peninsula, quite a few remains were unearthed, and they show us the fact that this area was actively engaged in a variety of exchanges with Japan. For example, the clay potteries of Gaya show a lot of similarities to those of Japan. Some Japanese historians argue that Gaya was the ancient Japan's ground of activity. Some North Korean scholars claim that the states in the Korean Peninsula established their own sub-states inside Japan. Most scholars agree that there were quite a few exchanges in both regions; however, they consider these two opinions as groundless, due to lack of evidence.

Gaya pottery

Japan potteries

2

Competitions Become Intense Among the Three Kingdoms

Goguryeo drives out the Han Chinese presence

In the beginning of the 4th century, the Korean Peninsula and Manchuria were in turmoil. In the north of the Korean Peninsula, nomad tribes grew more powerful, while Goguryeo and Baekje were ready to extend their territories after enhancing their own governmental systems.

China achieved unification at the end of the 3rd century, but came to face internal disturbances in the 4th century. The Han race also lost its control over its garrisons along the border, and the nomads established their own independent state. Goguryeo's attacks upon Han people who remained in the old terrain of Gojoseon further complicated matters for them.

In 311, Goguryeo expanded its territory all the way to the basins of the Amnokgang, and between 313 and 314 it seized power throughout the northwest region of the Korean Peninsula, the realm of the late Gojoseon. The Liaotung area was occupied by the Seonbi tribe who have their root in the Mongol prairie, and Goguryeo's confrontations with the nomad states at the east of the Liao began. Han China found itself no more staying in the game.

Confrontations between Baekje and Goguryeo

While Goguryeo was confronting the Seonbi tribe, Baekje grew remarkably in the Hangang area. By the end of the 3rd century, Baekje took control of the middle part of the Korean Peninsula to the point that they expanded their borders and came in direct contact with Goguryeo.

Goguryeo's expansion policy toward the south became an enormous threat to Baekje which had

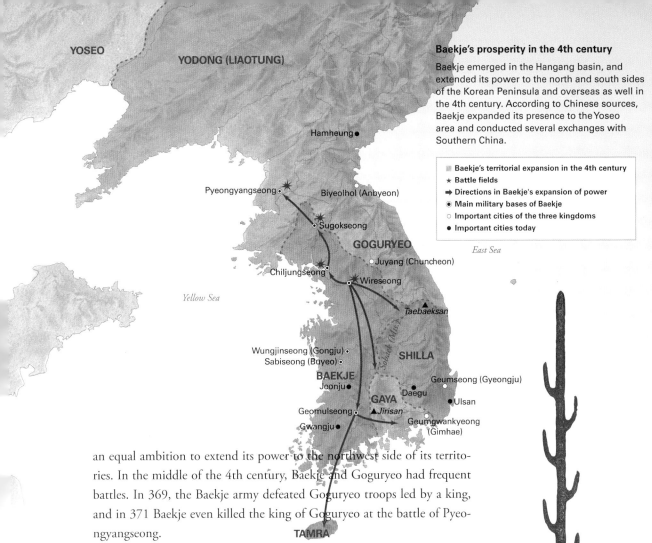

YOSEO

YODONG (LIAOTUNG)

Hamheung●

Pyeongyangseong

Biyeolhol (Anbyeon)

Sugokseong

GOGURYEO

East Sea

Juyang (Chuncheon)

Chiljungseong

Wireseong

Yellow Sea

Taebaeksan

Wungjinseong (Gongju)
Sabiseong (Buyeo)

SHILLA

BAEKJE
Jeonju●

Geumseong (Gyeongju)

Daegu

●Ulsan

GAYA ▲*Jirisan*

Geomulseong

Geumgwankyeong (Gimhae)

Gwangju●

TAMRA

an equal ambition to extend its power to the northwest side of its territories. In the middle of the 4th century, Baekje and Goguryeo had frequent battles. In 369, the Baekje army defeated Goguryeo troops led by a king, and in 371 Baekje even killed the king of Goguryeo at the battle of Pyeongyangseong.

With its triumphs in the north of territory, Baekje turned its attention to the southwest, even reaching out to Tamraguk in Jeju-do. Its presence became a threat to several states inside Gaya, located between Shilla and Baekje.

And Baekje also stretched its influence overseas. With its advanced navigational skills Baekje actively engaged in trades with various areas of China. Baekje dispatched delegations to Japan and had maritime trades with it. Meanwhile, by continuously accepting the advanced governing system and Buddhism from China, Baekje came to establish a strong, centralized ruling power, and thus strengthened authorities of its royal family.

Overcoming crises, Goguryeo develops into a great empire

Goguryeo was battling two enemies at the same time, one in the south and the other in the north. Yet, even in such crisis, Goguryeo also reconstructed

Chiljido
A spear-like sword, approximately 74cm in length. Including its main branch it has seven branches, with three of them on each side, so it has been called "Chiljido." On this sword there are 61 letters inscribed, stating that it was created as a gift, and then bestowed from Baekje to Japan. However, conflicting arguments have been suggested concerning the nature of this gift presentation. Japanese claim that it was given as a tributary to their king, whereas Koreans argue that it was a simple gift of friendship.

◀ **Janggunchong**
32m in width, and 12.5m in height. The tomb has a nickname, "the pyramid of Asia," and is also called "Janggunchong" due to its mammoth scale. This tomb is known as King Jangsuwang's burial ground. There are more than 10,000 stone tombs inside the Gungnaeseong area (Jiahn, Jilinseong in China) where Janggunchong is located.

Goguryeo's expansion of power, and its prosperity in the 5th century

Between the 4th and 6th centuries, when the Northwest nomad tribes were moving toward the Yellow River, drastic changes were in progress in terms of the political dynamics of northern China. Goguryeo united the Manchurian region by utilizing international power shifts to its favor. It became the supreme power in the Northeast Asian region, and in the 5th century it entered an era of prosperity.

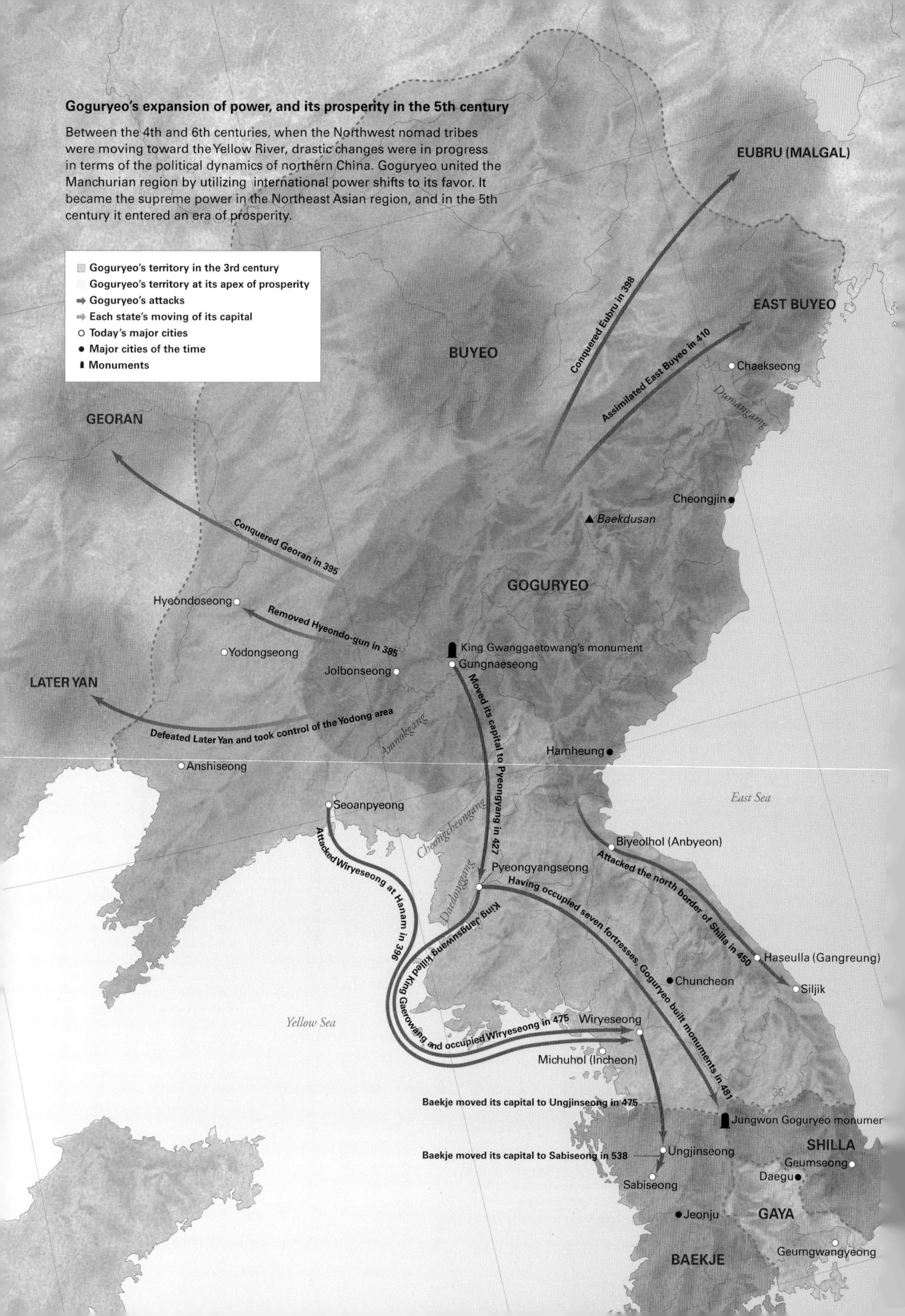

Legend:
- Goguryeo's territory in the 3rd century
- Goguryeo's territory at its apex of prosperity
- → Goguryeo's attacks
- → Each state's moving of its capital
- ○ Today's major cities
- ● Major cities of the time
- Monuments

EUBRU (MALGAL)

Conquered Eubru in 398

EAST BUYEO

BUYEO

Assimilated East Buyeo in 410

Chaekseong

Dumangang

GEORAN

Cheongjin

▲ Baekdusan

Conquered Georan in 395

GOGURYEO

Hyeondoseong

Removed Hyeondo-gun in 385

Yodongseong

Jolbonseong

King Gwanggaetowang's monument
Gungnaeseong

LATER YAN

Moved its capital to Pyeongyang in 427

Defeated Later Yan and took control of the Yodong area

Amnokgang

Hamheung

Anshiseong

East Sea

Seoanpyeong

Biyeolhol (Anbyeon)

Cheongcheongang

Attacked the north border of Shilla in 450

Attacked Wiryeseong at Hanam in 396

Pyeongyangseong

Daedonggang

Having occupied seven fortresses, Goguryeo built monuments in 481

Haseulla (Gangreung)

Chuncheon

Siljik

Yellow Sea

King Jangsuwang killed King Gaerowang and occupied Wiryeseong in 475

Wiryeseong

Michuhol (Incheon)

Baekje moved its capital to Ungjinseong in 475

Jungwon Goguryeo monumer

SHILLA

Geumseong

Baekje moved its capital to Sabiseong in 538

Ungjinseong

Daegu

Sabiseong

Jeonju

GAYA

BAEKJE

Geumgwangyeong

its nation by reinforcing a centralized ruling power, adopting the political ruling system of China, and implementing educational institutes to raise and train political administrators. During the reign of King Gwanggaetowang (391~412), Goguryeo triumphed in its conflicts with Baekje in the south and the nomads in the north. Thus, a great empire was established in Northeast Asia.

King Gwanggaetowang who ascended to the throne at the age of 18 led tens of thousands of infantry and cavalry soldiers in his campaign into vast areas of Manchuria and in his occupation of the long-contested Liaotung region, which used to be one of Gojoseon's central areas.

Also, Goguryeo extended its territory to the Hangang basin by defeating Baekje. In order to defend itself, Baekje allied itself with Gaya and Japan. However, when Goguryeo sent 50,000 troops to the south, Baekje lost the northern area of the Hangang. The former Gaya Alliance with Geumgwangaya in its center was forced to disband, and the king of Shilla pledged its loyalty to Goguryeo by sending hostages.

In the reign of King Jangsuwang, the successor to King Gwanggaetowang, Goguryeo flourished and prospered. King Jangsuwang moved the capital to Pyeongyang and engulfed more and more populated areas and fertile lands of the south. Goguryeo's army even attacked and occupied Baekje's capital city Hanseong, the Hanam Wiryeseong fortress, penetrating deep inside the inlands of the Hangang area.

Allied Baekje and Shilla forces confront Goguryeo

Goguryeo's aggression towards the south forced Baekje to fall into a disastrous situation. After the capital fell the king was executed by Goguryeo; Baekje moved its capital to Ungjin (today's Gongju), maintaining a wartime ruling system for survival. Shilla was also threatened by the rapidly growing power of Goguryeo.

In response to Goguryeo's southbound advance, Baekje and Shilla formed an alliance to protect themselves from Goguryeo. To ensure the amicable nature of such ties, the two countries arranged a marriage between both countries' royal families, thus they were able to protect their territories from Goguryeo's invasions. Allied with each other, the two reserved their power for another round of competitions, fighting for the hegemonic rule over the peninsula between themselves.

The Tombstone of King Gwanggaetowang
The stone monument of King Gwanggaetowang was built in 414. It features 6.14m in height. The achievements of King Gwanggaetowang, who exponentially expanded Goguryeo's territory, are inscribed upon this monument. At this time, Goguryeo recognized itself as the center of the world and demanded submissions from its annexed neighbor states. His own title indicates that he was the king who achieved a territorial expansion larger than ever.

The Royal Tomb of King Muryeongwang (above)
The features of King Muryeongwang's royal tomb show similarities to those of the brick tombs that prevailed in southern China. King Muryeongwang (501~523) centralized the Baekje Kingdom's power and actively engaged in diplomatic activities with both China and Wae (Japan). Baekje, located inside a fertile plain, flourished with an aristocratic culture.

Golden ornaments (below)
These golden ornaments were pinned to both sides of the golden crown. They were found inside the Royal Tomb of King Muryeongwang.

Ancient Tombs and Murals; Meeting the Goguryeo People 1,600 Years Ago

Tombs of Goguryeo
There are a number of ancient tombs located near the Gungnaeseong area, which served as the Goguryeo's capital until the early 5th century.
The picture is a scene of the capital, viewed from Hwandosan (Mt.).

The remains of Goguryeo show us the lives of the Goguryeo people. There are a number of ancient tombs, and from each of them a variety of drawings were found. From early on, tombs were built by piling up stone blocks. The ancient tomb Cheonchuchong was made of square-shaped stone pieces (85m in each side) piled up like staircases.

In the middle of the 4th century, another type of tombs were constructed. Appeared were Burrow Style Stone Chamber tombs, covered with soil and built with stone walls with an exit to the outside. They continued to be made until the end of Goguryeo. Ancient drawings painted upon the walls of the tombs depict the lives and visions of the people of Goguryeo.

In the beginning, they drew paintings on plaster-coated stones, but later they polished the stones' surface so that they could draw pictures upon a flat surface. Also, in earlier days, they usually depicted the lives and customs of Goguryeo people, but pictures depicting Taoist hermits and Buddhism emerged as well. Since the mid-6th century, mural paintings of hermits used to fill entire walls.

An opened view of the Burrow Style Stone Chamber tomb (Deokheung-ri Ancient Tomb, west side)

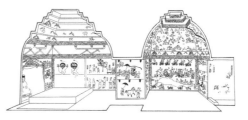

An opened view of the Burrow Style Stone Chamber tomb (Deokheung-ri Ancient Tomb, east side)

Muyongchong (tomb) Mural Painting depicting a hunting Scene
This wall painting of Goguryeo was drawn upon the north-west wall of the Muyongchong, which is now located inside Jian, China. The hunting scene is vividly depicted, like a motion picture.

Wall Painting at the First Jangcheon Tomb (partial)
The faces of Buddhist saints are drawn upon the ceiling of the south-front chamber of the First Jangcheon Tomb, located in Jian, China. As Buddhism prevailed in Goguryeo, people expressed their wishes that the Buddhist virtues could be observed in the afterlife as well, hence these wall paintings were made. It is interesting to see the faces of Buddhist saints described upon the petals of a lotus flower, a symbol of Buddhism.

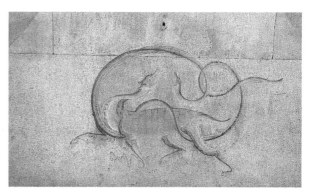

Hyeonmu on the wall of Gangseodaemyo (tomb)
This picture of a Hyeonmu is drawn upon the wall of Gangseodaemyo, located at Gangseo-gu, Nampo city of North Korea, and it reveals that Goguryeo was influenced by Taoism. Goguryeo people believed in the four imaginary animal gods that protected the four directions of the world: at the east side there was a blue dragon, west side a white tiger, south side a Jujak figure, and in the north side there was a Hyeonmu, which had a head of a snake and a body of a turtle.

3

Goguryeo's Defeat of Successive Invasions of Sui and Tang

Shilla, rise of a new power

At first, Shilla's position among the three kingdoms was rather peripheral. Yet, after accumulating power in the 4th and 5th centuries, centralizing the kings' leadership and evading Goguryeo's intrusions, Shilla significantly grew to have its own voice. In the 6th century, Shilla established a strict form of royal sovereignty, reconstructed its own bureaucratic organizations, and systemized the nation's Youth organization, which was called Hwarang. It successfully finished preparations for further development.

In the early 6th century, Shilla was able to unite all the areas of the Nakdonggang (R.) region and also assimilate the Ullreungdo (Is.) of the East Sea into its territory.

Shilla's remarkable expansion was accomplished during the reign of King Jinheungwang (reigned from 540 to 576). Shilla annexed Gaya in the south and attacked Goguryeo in the north to expand its territory to the north. Shilla also fought with Baekje in the west and occupied the vast plains sitting in the middle of the Korean Peninsula.

With a growing economy, expanded territory and increased population, Shilla quickly became the most powerful of the three kingdoms. In addition, Shilla independently developed a diplomatic relationship with China and secured yet another springboard for future victories. While Shilla basked in victory and also the spoils of war, both Baekje and Goguryeo sought revenge against Shilla.

Bukhansan (Mt.) King Jinheungwang Monument (located in Seoul)
This monument was built after Shilla became the occupant of the Hangang area. King Jinheungwang, was touring the newly conquered areas, and ordered the erection of this monument, in commemoration of his own royal tour, which must have taken place somewhere between 553 and 561. Comments that he dropped taxes levied upon the subjects and that he released the incarcerated prisoners, are inscribed upon it.

Tumultuous Northeast Asia

The race to unify all three kingdoms was also affected by outside variables. The Sui Dynasty united China, and Japan was forming a powerful, centralized nation. They had their own agendas intertwined in confrontations going on inside the Korean Peninsula. The united China wished to extend its territories, the nomads attempted to prevent further Chinese intervention, and Japan wished to trade and negotiate directly with the continent for their own benefit.

The most important factor was the united Sui. The ambitions of Sui did not stop with the unification of China, as it wished to extend its borders into the northeast of the Asian continent. Such international circumstances gave Shilla a valuable opportunity for growth, which would have otherwise suffered attacks from the powerful Goguryeo. As Shilla requested help from Sui, Sui placed military pressure on Goguryeo. In preparation of the final stretches of the war, Shilla developed close ties with Sui. Goguryeo confronted the invasion of Sui by forming an alliance with the Dolgweol, and to join them Baekje allied with Japan. In the early half of the 7th century, international warfare was gearing up between the east-west allied forces of Shilla and Sui and the north-south alliance of Goguryeo and Baekje.

A miniature of Hwangnyongsa (temple) Nine-story Pagoda
A huge wooden pagoda erected in Gyeongju effectively exhibits Shilla's own ambition for territorial and cultural expansions. According to the legend of Shilla's foundation, there was a myth concerning a construction of a Nine-story pagoda. It dictated that if people's faith in Buddha was strong enough, foreign invasions would be prevented. The magnitude of this pagoda signals the intense nature of the ongoing international conflicts of the 7th century. The pagoda was incinerated in the Mongol invasion of the 13th century, and was never reconstructed.

The political situation of the Northeast Asian region in the 7th century

As Shilla expanded its power, competition among the three kingdoms intensified more than ever. At the time, China succeeded in uniting its states and was eager to expand its territory in the northeast direction. Meanwhile, Wae constructed a centralized ruling system with a king at the center of power, and started to have exchanges with the Korean Peninsula and China.

Eulji Mundeok Memorial Coin (North Korea, issued in 2003)
Eulji Mundeok was the Goguryeo's greatest general who protected the kingdom from the Sui's invasions in 612. He successfully lured the Sui troops to Pyeongyangseong and completely destroyed them. He was also known for his talents in Chinese poetry; His poem, conveyed to Sui's general Wu Jungmun, has been passed on for generations. Eulji Mundeok is a historical figure whom both the South and North Koreans admire.

Goguryeo wins the wars against United China

Sui, which accomplished the unification of the Chinese continent, demanded submission from all the political forces at its periphery, promulgating its almighty power. However, Goguryeo, which had prospered for 600 years and maintained its independence in Northeast Asia, firmly refused Sui's order. Battle was inevitable between the demanding Sui and the stubborn Goguryeo.

The first Chinese attack on Goguryeo occurred in 598 when the first emperor of Sui, Munje (reign 581~604), was in power. While 300,000 troops crossed the Liao and attacked the outskirts of Goguryeo's territory by land, the naval forces of Sui attempted to conquer the capital of Goguryeo by penetrating Goguryeo's defenses by sea. However, Goguryeo managed to defeat Sui's soldiers and successfully drove them out of Goguryeo's borders. The Sui Dynasty came to suffer a crisis in and outside of its borders.

The second emperor of Sui, Yangje (reign 604~618), assaulted Goguryeo again with a massively mobilized troops. In 612, 1,130,000 troops led by Yangje himself invaded Goguryeo. Surprisingly, Goguryeo, with a total population of about 3.5 million, refused to surrender and resisted boldly until they demolished the invaders and drove them out of the territory once again. Another retaliatory attack of Sui followed in 614, and failed as well.

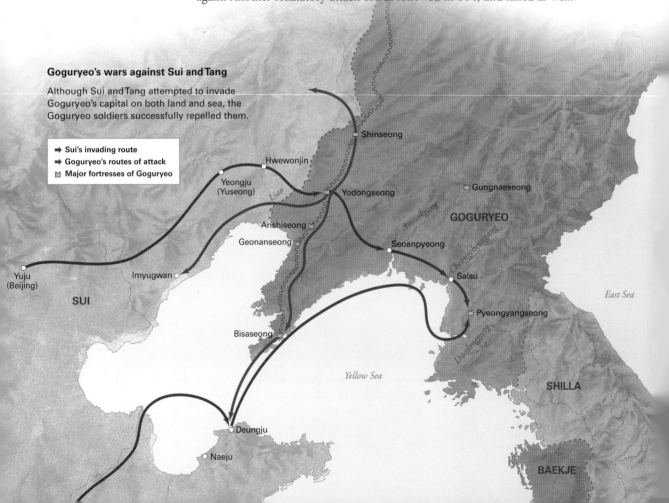

Goguryeo's wars against Sui and Tang

Although Sui and Tang attempted to invade Goguryeo's capital on both land and sea, the Goguryeo soldiers successfully repelled them.

→ Sui's invading route
→ Goguryeo's routes of attack
🏯 Major fortresses of Goguryeo

Yuju (Beijing)
SUI
Imyugwan
Yeongju (Yuseong)
Hwewonjin
Shinseong
Yodongseong
Anshiseong
Geonanseong
Seoanpyeong
Salsu
Gungnaeseong
GOGURYEO
Amnokgang
Cheongcheongang
Pyeongyangseong
Bisaseong
Daedonggang
East Sea
Yellow Sea
SHILLA
Deungju
Naeju
BAEKJE

The continent of China was again united by the Tang Dynasty (618~907), which managed to control the chaos caused after the collapse of Sui. Like its predecessor, Tang ordered Goguryeo to yield to its authority and frequently threatened Goguryeo with military force. In 645, Goguryeo was attacked by the troops of Tang led by Taizong. In the beginning of the war Goguryeo lost several fortresses, but later in the battle of the fortress of Anshiseong, Goguryeo offered furious resistance to force the Tang's troops to withdraw.

The invasions of Sui and Tang were essentially wars fighting for the hegemonic power in Northeast Asia. Sui and Tang claimed themselves to be the center of the world, whereas Goguryeo identified itself as the most powerful in the region. Goguryeo must be given some credits for its triumphs over Sui and Tang, as it made possible for Baekje and Shilla as well as itself to maintain political and cultural independence. However, consecutive battles left irreparable damage on Goguryeo, and as a result, its power weakened substantially. Also, the conflict between Goguryeo and China divided the international order in half, and opened a door for more multi-national conflicts.

Daeseongsanseong
Pyeongyang, the capital of North Korea, was not only the capital of Gojoseon but also the capital of Goguryeo in its golden years. There are countless historical remains inside Pyeongyang. This picture shows a fortress built to defend the capital.

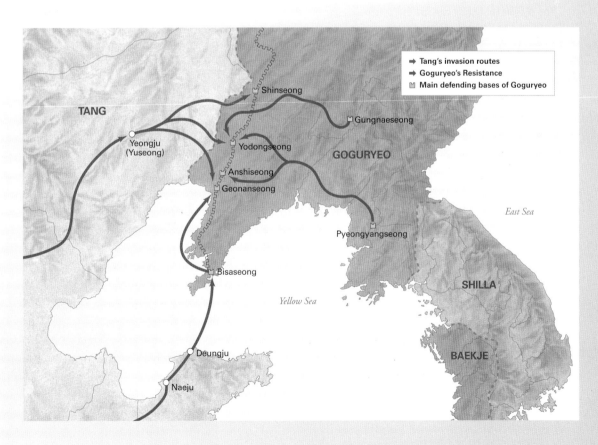

4

A Variety of Flourishing Cultures due to the Expansion of Trades

Worshipping Heaven and Earth

According to Chinese records, Goguryeo people celebrated a harvest by holding a festival every fall, and gathered together to perform a religious ceremony. And a record says, "There is a huge cave in the east of the capital of Goguryeo. They received God here and then carried out a religious ceremony at the Amnokgang which is located in the east side of the capital, where they kept their wooden statue of God." During the 5th century, on a tombstone of Goguryeo, the following lines are inscribed: "The son of the Sun and Moon, and the grandson of the water goddess Habaek, King Chumo Seong-wang (Jumong) was born in a town of North Buyeo. All people under heaven should be able to feel the holiness shining over it."

The reason that they carried out a ritual ceremony above the river under the illuminating sun must have been related to this story that the water goddess' daughter Yuhwa met the son of the Heaven God Haemosu, and conceived the founder of Goguryeo, Jumong.

Goguryeo's royal families built a number of shrines to perform ritual ceremonies for their great ancestor. They seem to have worshipped Jumong not only as their great ancestor, but also as the descendant of the Sun and Moon, as well as the offspring of Heaven and Earth.

Gukdongdaehyeol
There is a cave named "Tongcheongul," 17km away from the east of Gungnaeseong, the capital of ancient Goguryeo. The Goguryeo people held religious ceremonies called "Dongmaeng." It is said that they received God here and performed a ritual ceremony at the Amnokgang.

As farming progressed, worshipping Heaven and Earth became more important, since it was believed that heaven provided water whereas earth bore fruits and crops. Thus, rulers wished to identify themselves as a direct descendent of the heaven father and the earth mother. The legend of Shilla's foundation was also based on such ideas. The birth of Shilla's founder began with the meeting between a man from Heaven and a lady who was born near a well. In order to establish royal sovereignty the royal families made these ritual ceremonies for the heaven and earth as to reflect prestige.

The God of Sun and the God of Moon
This is a portion of a mural painting found at the fourth grave in Ohhoibun located at Jian-hyeon, China. Inside these ancient tombs from the 6th century, various figures of Taoist hermits were portrayed. Haemosu, father of the Goguryeo Dynasty's founder Jumong, was considered as the God of the Sun, while his wife (and Jumong's mother), Yuhwa, was considered as the Goddess of the Moon.

Introduction of new religions

In order to unify numerous political forces accustomed to worshipping their own distinctive gods, royal authorities needed a more powerful and persuasive ruling system with well-organized theories that would support it.

China, being a civilized country with a long history, established an empire that had a variety of legal systems and well-constructed ruling structure. When Goguryeo, Baekje, and Shilla adopted a more advanced legal governing system from China around the 4th century, they also accepted the Chinese laws and rules, along with Confucius scriptures and history books. The three kingdoms established an educational system to teach students about progressive social ideology and systems of the world.

As trades among nations became more active, the Chinese religious culture also became more known to the Korean people. As a result, many Chinese gods appeared in the three kingdom's religious culture and myth. Among these religions, Taoism, the most popular Chinese religion, became prevalent in Korean societies. And Buddhism, which originated in India, was also introduced to Goguryeo, Baekje, and Shilla. The mural paintings in Goguryeo's tombs depict such religious activities of the time.

Prosperity of Buddhism

Buddhism was accepted to support centralized power of royal authorities. In the middle of the 4th century, Buddhism was introduced to the general population. Priests from China, who were believed to harbor Buddha's holy abilities, were considered healers for the sick and prayers for the nation's wellness and prosperity. The Buddha was introduced as a powerful God

Baekje incense burner made of gold and copper
This burner was used in rituals commemorating the deceased kings. It has detailed inscription upon it which represents the ideals of Buddhism and Taoism. It is believed that this burner was made in the late 6th century. It was first made of bronze, and then plated with gold. 64cm in height, 11.8kg in weight.

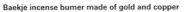

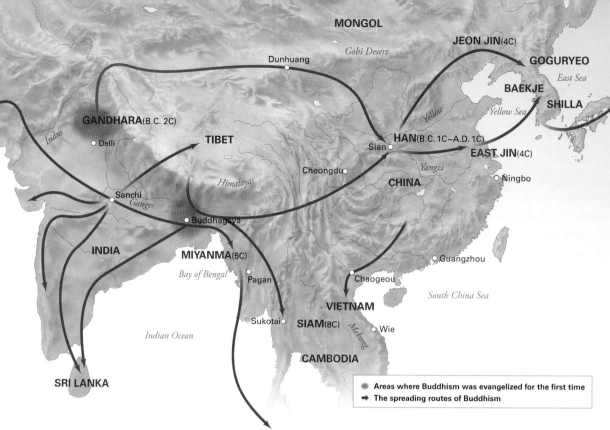

Areas where Buddhism was evangelized for the first time
➡ The spreading routes of Buddhism

Introduction of Buddhism

Buddhism was introduced to Goguryeo through the Northern route of China, and to Baekje through the Southern route of China. The Buddhism that was introduced from the Chinese was Mahayana Buddhism that worshipped Buddha as a God, and its key message was the salvation of people. Japanese Buddhist religion was introduced from Baekje and Goguryeo.

■ **Jeonryun Seongwang** This king appears in the legend of India. He was an ideal king who ruled the world by rolling the Wheels of Truth. Many people consider King Asoka who founded The Maurya Dynasty as a real Jeonryun Seongwang figure.

from a foreign land.

Buddhism was officially accepted and flourished in the three kingdoms with support of the royal authorities. Goguryeo, Baekje, and Shilla all competed in building large temples and in creating statues of the benevolent Buddha. Religious congregations of Buddhism where people prayed for the wellness of royal families required a large budget. The three kingdoms also sponsored Buddhist priests who were sent abroad to further their study of Buddhism.

In the 6th century, King Jinheungwang, the conqueror of the Hangang, identified his son as the most idealist ruler, and the Buddha of the real world, Jeonryun Seongwang.■ Also King Jinpyeongwang, the grandson of King Jinheungwang, identified himself as the father of Buddha (Jeongbanwang), and his wife adopted the same name of Lady Maya, the mother of Buddha. Based on this idea, he endowed the holiest status to his families.

However, among commoners, the gods of Heaven and Earth were still widely believed and accepted, along with totems. Since Buddhists claimed that Buddha was the almighty God, the royal families sanctified its holiness and came to identify themselves as family to the holy Buddha, claiming that their own country was indeed the kingdom of Buddha.

Active cultural exchanges between the three kingdoms and Japan

The three kingdoms, maintaining an adversarial relationship among themselves for centuries, tried to enhance their diplomatic ties with neighboring countries. Baekje, Gaya, and Shilla all invested huge amount of efforts in establishing an allied relationship with Japan. Isolated from the cultures of the continent, Japan was eager to accept and embrace more advanced cultures especially through them.

The three kingdoms and Japan not only exchanged frequent official delegations, but also had non-governmental trade activities and transactions among merchants. At times, Korean people moved to Japan in large-scale migrations, and at times Japanese troops battled with the Koreans inside the Korean Peninsula. Through such exchanges either peaceful or hostile, the culture of the three kingdoms were transmitted to Japan. Japan developed a close relationship especially with Baekje, which sent numerous scholars, priests, and technicians to convey and deliver elements of an advanced culture.

At the end of the 6th century, Japan's cultural exchanges with the three kingdoms reached its peak. As Shilla continued to expand, Baekje and Goguryeo wanted to promote friendly relationships with Japan. Meanwhile, the royal families of Japan successfully achieved centralization of their power and more rapidly embraced the advanced cultures of the continent. After Buddhism was introduced to Japan through Baekje, Buddhist arts of the three kingdoms such as statues, architectures, and paintings were transported to Japan as well.

The three kingdoms' culture widely spread throughout Japan in the late 7th century. However, when Japan began to directly dispatch its delegations to Tang, the relationship between Shilla and Japan deteriorated, and thus the nature of their cultural exchanges began to shift into a different direction.

Baekje Gwaneumsang (statue)
This Gwaneumsang located at the Horyu Temple of Nara, Japan, was made of wood, presumably in the 7th century. Its height is 210.8cm. The Horyu Temple was constructed in a style similar to that of a Baekje temple in the 7th century.

National Treasure No. 83: A Sitting Golden/Bronze Maitreya statue
This Maitreya has a head featuring a curvy mountain shape. Its inner layer was molded in bronze and then plated in gold. It was made in the Three Kingdoms Period. 93.5cm in height.

Maitreya statue in sitting posture at the Goryu Temple
This Maitreya statue in sitting posture is at the Goryu Temple of Kyoto, Japan. It was made of wood and its height is 123.5cm. The overall features are quite similar to those of the Golden/Bronze Maitreya statue, National Treasure No. 83.

Bab and Gimchi,
Stories of the Korean Dining Table

Steamed rice, referred to as "Bab," is the Koreans' staple meal. The dining table is also known as "Babsang," and upon this Babsang table rice is usually served with soup and side dishes.

In the past, millet or Indian millet served as the Koreans' main meal, but soon after rice and barley began to be cultivated, they quickly replaced their predecessors. Around the 6th century, as irrigation facilities like reservoirs were built and agricultural tools made of iron began to be widely used, rice farming showed remarkable advances. However, millet and barley still remained as significant options for food in the northern area, where dry fields instead of wet fields were better developed.

During the cold and long winter seasons, Koreans consumed their vegetables that they had been preserving in salt. Those preserved vegetables supplied not only necessary nutrients such as vitamins and minerals, but also much needed sodium to the bodies of human beings.

Dwenjang (soybean paste), full of protein and sodium, was also a very important type of food. With

---

Processes of Making Soy Sauce

❶ Steam soy beans and pound them for making soybean lumps. Hang lumps of fermented soy beans with straw strings during the winter and then allow them to continue fermenting in the air.
❷ After removing mildew on the lumps of well-fermented soy beans, soak them in salt water. ❸ After adding a lump of charcoal and red peppers, wait for between thirty and forty days until all the elements delude into the water, to make soy sauce juice.
❹ Scoop up all the soy sauce juice from the jar and then boil it until it thickens to a proper degree. ❺ After adding cooked barley with salt, mix it with sedimentary soybeans, press the paste in the jar firmly. ❻ Until the soy sauce paste well ripens, hang "the caution string" around the jar in order to well and cleanly preserve it.

bean productions active all over the Korean Peninsula and Manchurian areas, Koreans developed a habit of adding salt to fermented steamed beans to make Dwenjang paste, or dipping lumps of fermented beans in salty water to make soy sauce. At the same time, cuisines made of beans like tofu and bean sprouts had been developed early on as well.

In Buyeo and Goguryeo, a Korean meat cuisine named Maekjeok was introduced and spread. It was a sort of seasoned meat, similar to the Korean's favorite meat cuisine today, which we all know as Bulgogi. Due to the Buddhist influences and the tradition of farming, Koreans have shown a tendency of eating grains more than meat in the past, but since the 14th century, both vegetable and meat have been considered equally important in balancing people's diet.

❶ **Gimchi** The word "Gimchi" is originated from "Chimchae," which means salted vegetable. In the past it was simply preserved with salt or lees of rice liquor that were used for keeping vegetables fresh. However, as various types of seasoning began to add its flavors, many different types of Gimchi were made. Today's fermented Gimchi, mixed with ingredients such as hot peppers, green onions, garlic, pickled anchovies and other seafood, appeared only after the 18th century.
❷ **Bulgogi** These days, Koreans enjoy eating grilled Bulgogi, which is made of beef that has been set in seasoned soy sauce. When pork is used in place of beef, it is called Pork-Bulgogi. It can be eaten with meat juice dripped from the specially made Bulgogi-grill, or without juice and just grilled on the loosely interlaced grill.
❸ **Bibimbab** Bibimbab is rice mixed with fresh vegetable, seasoned wild vegetable, along with red hot paste. Because of its flavor and taste of several seasoned wild vegetable, it has become the Korean's representative menu. Another type of Bibimbab, Dolsot Bibimbab, served in a heated stone pot, also is enjoyable.

648 ~ 926

660
The allied forces of Shilla and Tang conquered Baekje in 660 and
defeated Goguryeo in 668. Restoration movements of Baekje and
Goguryeo both occurred, yet eventually failed.

676
Shilla defeated Tang forces, which attacked Shilla after the fall of
Baekje and Goguryeo. Shilla took control of the entire Baekje territory
and also part of the Goguryeo territory. The Shilla royal family were
proud that they finally unified all the three kingdoms.

698
In the old territory of Goguryeo, the Balhae Kingdom was established
under the leadership of Dae Jo-yeong, who was once a general
of Goguryeo. He claimed himself as the successor of Goguryeo.
Shilla and Balhae together opened the Era of the 'South and North
Kingdoms.'

751
The Shilla royal family and the Buddhist community began the
exquisite renovation of Bulguksa (temple), to prove Shilla was the land
of Buddha.

771
Carolos the Great Emperor unified the Franc Kingdoms.

828
Jang Bo-go who dominated the East Asian trades in the Yellow Sea
of the Korean Peninsula constructed a trading base at Cheonghaejin.

900
Gyeonhwon established New Baekje in the southwest region of
the Korean Peninsula, and the next year Gungye established New
Goguryeo in the north and middle regions. Shilla was divided into
three kingdoms once again.

907
Tang was demolished.

926
Balhae whose power had waned since the latter half of the 9th century
was demolished soon after the Georan attacks.

III Unified Shilla and Balhae in the South and North

As Shilla united Baekje and Goguryeo with itself, and Balhae emerged in the old terrain of Goguryeo, the Era of the South and North Kingdoms began. When fierce competitions among the three countries finally ended, the society was stabilized, the economy expanded, and active cultural exchanges with the outside continued.

Shilla was proud of being a Buddhist land, while Balhae, which succeeded Goguryeo, constructed a unique culture based upon a variety of Goguryeo and Tang traditions. Many merchants, scholars, and monks actively visited neighboring countries.

Munmudaewangam in the Front Sea of Gampo, near Gyeongju Inside the rock, there is an underwater tomb of King Munmuwang.

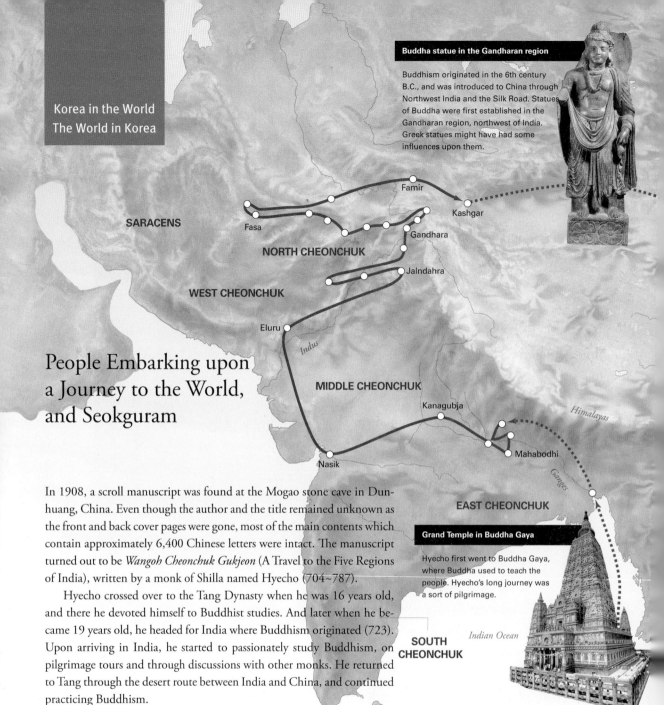

Buddha statue in the Gandharan region

Buddhism originated in the 6th century B.C., and was introduced to China through Northwest India and the Silk Road. Statues of Buddha were first established in the Gandharan region, northwest of India. Greek statues might have had some influences upon them.

SARACENS

Famir

Kashgar

Fasa

Gandhara

NORTH CHEONCHUK

Jalndahra

WEST CHEONCHUK

Eluru

Indus

MIDDLE CHEONCHUK

Kanagubja

Himalayas

Mahabodhi

Nasik

Ganges

EAST CHEONCHUK

Grand Temple in Buddha Gaya

Hyecho first went to Buddha Gaya, where Buddha used to teach the people. Hyecho's long journey was a sort of pilgrimage.

SOUTH CHEONCHUK

Indian Ocean

People Embarking upon a Journey to the World, and Seokguram

In 1908, a scroll manuscript was found at the Mogao stone cave in Dunhuang, China. Even though the author and the title remained unknown as the front and back cover pages were gone, most of the main contents which contain approximately 6,400 Chinese letters were intact. The manuscript turned out to be *Wangoh Cheonchuk Gukjeon* (A Travel to the Five Regions of India), written by a monk of Shilla named Hyecho (704~787).

Hyecho crossed over to the Tang Dynasty when he was 16 years old, and there he devoted himself to Buddhist studies. And later when he became 19 years old, he headed for India where Buddhism originated (723). Upon arriving in India, he started to passionately study Buddhism, on pilgrimage tours and through discussions with other monks. He returned to Tang through the desert route between India and China, and continued practicing Buddhism.

Although he is considered as a true cosmopolitan, he was not the only one at the time. Before him many monks travelled to India, and traces of Shilla people's life can be found in many regions of China and Japan. Also, it is not difficult to find traces of other worlds in Shilla people's life and culture as well. Mahayana Buddhism which was first established in the northwestern part of India, and the statues of Buddha in the Gandharan region which influenced the Seokguram (grotto) statue are good examples.

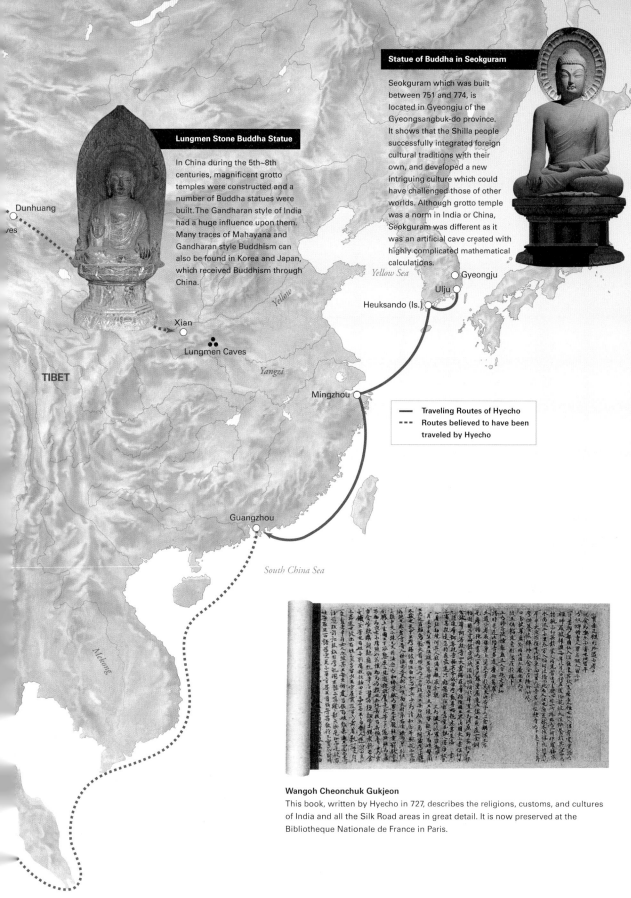

Lungmen Stone Buddha Statue

In China during the 5th~8th centuries, magnificent grotto temples were constructed and a number of Buddha statues were built. The Gandharan style of India had a huge influence upon them. Many traces of Mahayana and Gandharan style Buddhism can also be found in Korea and Japan, which received Buddhism through China.

Statue of Buddha in Seokguram

Seokguram which was built between 751 and 774, is located in Gyeongju of the Gyeongsangbuk-do province. It shows that the Shilla people successfully integrated foreign cultural traditions with their own, and developed a new intriguing culture which could have challenged those of other worlds. Although grotto temple was a norm in India or China, Seokguram was different as it was an artificial cave created with highly complicated mathematical calculations.

Dunhuang

Xian

Lungmen Caves

TIBET

Yellow

Yangzi

Yellow Sea

Heuksando (Is.)

Ulju

Gyeongju

Mingzhou

——— Traveling Routes of Hyecho
- - - Routes believed to have been traveled by Hyecho

Guangzhou

South China Sea

Mekong

Wangoh Cheonchuk Gukjeon
This book, written by Hyecho in 727, describes the religions, customs, and cultures of India and all the Silk Road areas in great detail. It is now preserved at the Bibliotheque Nationale de France in Paris.

1

Shilla Unites Baekje and Goguryeo

Shilla's agreement of military alliance with Tang

In the year of 648, Shilla dispatched delegates to Tang. Having been struggling with frequent attacks from Baekje and Goguryeo, Shilla sought for an allied relationship with Tang in order to turn the tides of war. The chief-delegate was Kim Chun-chu, who later ascended the throne and became King Taejong Muyeorwang (654~661).

Diplomatic negotiations between Shilla and Tang continued for days, and they finally agreed to organize an allied force to defeat Baekje and Goguryeo. In case of victory, Shilla agreed to occupy Baekje, and Tang was to rule Goguryeo as a remuneration. Shilla also promised that it would accept and embrace Chinese institutions and culture.

With this newly forged military alliance, Northeast Asia was embroiled in rapid changes. Baekje and Goguryeo failed to deal with these new changes effectively, and failed to reform their internal ruling systems as expected. As a result, they both had to stand alone against the allied forces of Shilla and Tang.

Kim Yu-shin (595~673)
Kim won numerous battles against Baekje and Goguryeo, and from the year of 660, he led the overall war effort for the unification of the three kingdoms. He received a posthumous title with an honorary rank of a king, 150 years after his death. It shows that he was remembered by the Shilla people for a long time. The picture is the statue of Kim Yu-shin erected in Gyeongju

Muyeorwangreung
This is the grave of King Muyeorwang who established the foundation for unification of the three kingdoms. A monument commemorating his achievements was erected in front of the tomb, yet today only the top and base sections remain.

The collapse of Baekje and Goguryeo

In 660, 50,000 soldiers from Shilla and 130,000 soldiers from Tang invaded the Baekje territory. Baekje never faced such a gigantic number of troops before, and defeat was inevitable. Although Baekje fought courageously to the very end, their capital was seized, and the Baekje king surrendered.

It was Tang's intentions to demolish Shilla as well after the surrender of Baekje. Yet, their plan was thwarted when Shilla displayed impressive determination of military resistance. Tang reluctantly put its advances on hold and concentrated upon its priority target, Goguryeo. Allied troops of Shilla and Tang attacked Goguryeo the following year. Tang's troops advanced from Goguryeo's northwest border and Shilla attacked from the south. Though Goguryeo managed to deflect numerous attacks, the circumstance became inescapably worse, as the allied forces continued their attacks.

Yeon Gaesomun, the powerful leader who led all the battles, died in 666. Without a leader, Goguryeo was plunged into internal conflicts raised over the issue of whether or not to continue fighting. Added to that, power struggle for the throne aggravated. And in the midst of such chaos, the allied army of Shilla and Tang finally succeeded in destroying Goguryeo (668).

Wars Throughout Northeast Asia in the 7th Century

Conflicts between Goguryeo and Tang, and competitions among the three kingdoms, triggered the so-called Unification War. And this war quickly developed into an international conflict, which even included the Japanese as well. In 663, a large number of Japanese troops participated in battles against the Shilla-Tang alliance, under the cause of supporting the Baekje restoration army. After defeated, Japan was concerned about possible retaliatory attacks from the alliance, so it constructed fortresses in numerous locations, and even moved its capital to another location.

The people who fought for the restoration of Baekje and Goguryeo

After the capital was seized and the king surrendered, many Baekje people were captured and forcibly relocated to Tang. And when Tang returned home, it seemed like the war was finally over.

Even after the Baekje king was taken to Tang, the Baekje people continued to fight. They instated a new king and fought the invaders. In response, Tang dispatched reinforcements to Baekje, and Shilla sent troops as well. In spite of its inferior situation in terms of military resistance, Baekje was able to maintain control over 200 castles throughout its territory.

At the request of Baekje, Wae (Japan) sent a large relief troops. In 663, 30,000 troops of Baekje-Wae allied forces confronted the Shilla and Tang armies; nevertheless, they eventually lost. Any chance for Baekje's own revival was lost as well.

Meanwhile, the resistance of the Goguryeo people was so severe that numerous battles significantly hurt the Tang troops. In response, Tang put the captured Goguryeo king in charge, but failed to suppress the Goguryeo people's resistance. And subsequent confrontations led to the creation of a new Korean dynasty inside Goguryeo's old territory. It was Balhae which in the end drove out Tang's forces.

Goryeoyeong

After the fall of Goguryeo, about 200,000 people were forcibly relocated to the border regions of Tang's territory. Though the majority of them went through tremendous suffering, a few people managed to obtain significant social positions. A Goguryeo general named Go Seon-ji led the decade-long campaign launched against the Islam dynasties over the control of the Silk Road. Another Goguryeo emigrant named Yi Jeong-gi formed an independent political force in the Santung area inside Tang's territory.

There are other records of many Baekje people being forcefully taken to Tang, after their restoration movement failed. Their fate was not that much different from that of the Goguryeo people. Some of the war refugees even went over to Japan, where they maintained their identity and traditions. This picture is of a Goryeo town, located 20km away from the north of Beijing. Goguryeo migrants used to reside here. We can see the name written clearly on the road sign (in the circle).

Shilla defeats Tang

After Goguryeo collapsed, Tang took control of its territory, as both Tang and Shilla had agreed in the beginning of their alliance. However, Tang was not satisfied with the agreement. It wanted to extend its power to Baekje too, and furthermore, it intended to rule Shilla as well. Shilla protested this blatant breach of the original agreement and sternly requested them to honor it. However, Tang continued to extend its power over the territories of Baekje and Goguryeo, and in the midst of such efforts to subjugate Baekje, Shilla had to confront Tang as well. In response, Tang either sent diplomatic missions or launched military attacks upon Shilla forces.

Since Goguryeo's collapse, Shilla continued to fight Tang, for total of eight years. Shilla defeated 200,000 soldiers of the Tang's army at the Mae-soseong fortress (today's Yeoncheon, Gyeonggi-do province), and at the same time Shilla destroyed Tang's well-trained naval forces in the Yellow Sea. With the costs for a prolonged conflict estimated to be too high, the Tang forces finally withdrew from Shilla.

Although Shilla was still concerned about further attacks from Tang or from other potential enemies like Japan, it was indeed the final winner of a war that had involved the entire Northeast Asia.

The underwater tomb of King Munmuwang
King Munmuwang who accomplished the unification of the three kingdoms ordered his people to "Melt all swords to make plows." According to records, his instruction in the will was that he wished to be cremated and buried under the East Sea in front of Gyeongju, so that he may defend Shilla as a dragon. Though he must have believed in a peaceful future, it seems that he was also concerned with possible invasions by Tang, or the allied forces of Baekje and Japan.

2

The Unified Shilla and Balhae's Occupying the South and North of the Peninsula

Shilla accomplished a unified kingdom

It was not Shilla's intention from the beginning to unify all the three kingdoms. But after it annexed Baekje and as it kept on battling Tang's advances, Shilla continued to incorporate all those refugees from Baekje and Goguryeo into the Shilla population. Shilla offered official positions to former Baekje and Goguryeo dignitaries. And the newly established unified army allowed people from all three countries to participate. Shilla extended its bureaucratic ruling system to former territories of Baekje and Goguryeo.

The Korean Peninsula finally entered an era of peace that lasted for a couple of centuries. The people of all three kingdoms came to live under a unified ruling system. Nevertheless, some discrimination against the conquered did exist. The unified Shilla had a rigid caste system in which the aristocrats in Gyeongju were the ones who came to enjoy exclusive privileges.

However, as the people of the three kingdoms continued to live together and share experiences, a homogeneity was developed among them in terms of identity. In that regard, Shilla's unification of all the three kingdoms did mark a significant turning point in the formation of the Korean race. The Shilla royal family's argument that they unified all the three kingdoms, was not far from the truth.

Regional government's ruling in the time of unified Shilla (8th, 9th centuries)

Total of nine new "Ju" units were installed throughout the Korean Peninsula, three for the old territory of Goguryeo, three for the old territory of Baekje, and three for Shilla. Also, royal family members were dispatched to newly designated local capitals which were called 'Sogyeong.'

Balhae's succession to Goguryeo

While Shilla developed a new governing system for the unified Korean Peninsula, Goguryeo people's struggles continued in Manchuria. As the resistance grew, Tang established large military bases throughout the region and relocated a number of Goguryeo people to the border areas of Tang. However, Tang's attempt to subdue the Goguryeo resistance and rule them under the laws of Tang, eventually failed.

The Goguryeo people who were forcibly relocated to Tang began a resistance movement in 696 inside the Yoseo area which was under Tang's occupation. The leader of these Goguryeo resistance fighters was Dae Jo-yeong. After defeating Tang's forces, he established Balhae (698~926) in the old territory of Goguryeo.

Dae Jo-yeong's foundation of Balhae was the final straw placed upon the already broken back of Tang's ruling in the region. Balhae reorganized the Goguryeo people throughout the region and rapidly developed into an independent kingdom.

Balhae, the dynasty that was called "Haedong Seongguk"

Balhae's foundation by the Goguryeo descendants in the old territory of Goguryeo changed the map throughout the northeast region. Tang at-

Balhae's Dongmosan (Mt.)
Dongmosan (600m above sea level) is where Dae Jo-yeong supposedly established the Balhae Kingdom. It is also called as Seongsanjasanseong fortress. It is located in Jirinseong's Dunhwa-shi area. A number of ancient tombs of Balhae are found in the northeast area, 10km away from here.

Haedong Seongguk, Balhae

In the 9th century, Balhae was immensely prospering, thanks to political stability and economic developments. At the time, Balhae's territory included the northern part of the Korean Peninsula and reached the Chinese northeast region in the west and the littoral province of Siberia in the northeast. The history of Balhae is considered as part of the Korean history by Korean historians, for the reason that it was founded by Goguryeo refugees in the old territory of Goguryeo.

On the other hand, Russia considers the history of Balhae as history of one of the Siberian region's minority tribes, the Malgals. And, because most of the past events concerning Balhae occurred inside regions that currently belong to the Chinese territory today, the Chinese claim that the history of Balhae should be considered as an exclusive chapter of the Chinese history. Chinese historians in fact have claimed that all the historical events that occurred in the current territories of China fall in the category of Chinese history; for this reason, they consider Balhae as a regional government of the Tang Dynasty.

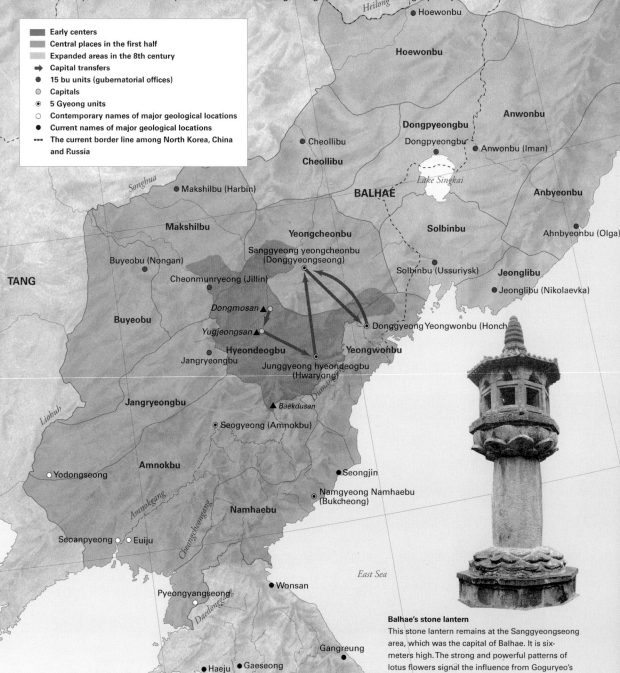

■	Early centers
■	Central places in the first half
■	Expanded areas in the 8th century
➡	Capital transfers
●	15 bu units (gubernatorial offices)
○	Capitals
◉	5 Gyeong units
○	Contemporary names of major geological locations
●	Current names of major geological locations
---	The current border line among North Korea, China and Russia

Heilong

Hoewonbu

Hoewonbu

Anwonbu

Dongpyeongbu
Dongpyeongbu

Anwonbu (Iman)

Cheollibu

Cheollibu

BALHAE

Lake Singkai

Anbyeonbu

Songhua

Makshilbu (Harbin)

Solbinbu

Ahnbyeonbu (Olga)

Makshilbu

Yeongcheonbu

Sanggyeong yeongcheonbu
(Donggyeongseong)

Solbinbu (Ussuriysk)

Jeonglibu

Buyeobu (Nongan)

Jeonglibu (Nikolaevka)

Cheonmunryeong (Jillin)

TANG

Buyeobu

Dongmosan ▲ ○

Yugjeongsan ▲

Donggyeong Yeongwonbu (Honch

Hyeondeogbu

Yeongwonbu

Jangryeongbu

Junggyeong hyeondeogbu
(Hwaryong)

Liohub

Jangryeongbu

▲ Baekdusan

Amnokgang

◉ Seogyeong (Amnokbu)

○ Yodongseong

Amnokbu

● Seongjin

◉ Namgyeong Namhaebu
(Bukcheong)

Cheongcheongang

Namhaebu

Seoanpyeong ○ ─ ○ Euiju

East Sea

Pyeongyangseong ○

● Wonsan

Daedonggang

Gangreung

● Haeju ● Gaeseong

Yellow Sea

SHILLA

Balhae's stone lantern
This stone lantern remains at the Sanggyeongseong area, which was the capital of Balhae. It is six-meters high. The strong and powerful patterns of lotus flowers signal the influence from Goguryeo's Buddhist traditions.

tempted to attack Balhae by taking sides with the Malgal tribes in the north of Balhae. Pursuing an amicable relationship with Tang, Shilla also sided with Tang and assumed a hostile position against Balhae. But they were never successful. In 732, the allied forces of Shilla and Tang launched a joint attack upon Balhae, yet Balhae firmly stood on its ground. And proclaiming that it was the legitimate successor of Goguryeo, Balhae continued to expand its territory at a rapid pace, and also overcame other crises as well by developing a close relationship with the Dolgweol tribes in the north and Japan.

A Dragon Head, which was excavated at Palace Vestige No.1 of the Sanggyeongseong area
It was unearthed at the vestige of Sanggyeongseong, the capital of Balhae. Its height is 37cm.

By the middle of the 8th century, Balhae was already exhibiting remarkable advances. By adopting the Tang dynasty's ruling system to its internal governance, Balhae established a stable government and took control of a region that was even wider than the old territories of Goguryeo. The Chinese praised their achievements, by calling them with the nick name "Haedong Seongguk." ▪

▪ Haedong Seongguk means 'the most prospering country over the east sea.'

With all such developments, Tang and Shilla had no choice but to admit Balhae's sovereignty. Balhae began to send diplomatic delegates to Tang and Shilla, and Shilla also dispatched its representatives to Balhae. And, in order to promote more efficient transportations, roads connecting Balhae's capital and the border areas of Shilla were constructed. But exchanges between Balhae and Shilla were not that active, as the two kept competing with each other in order to garner Tang's exclusive support. Tang even encouraged such rivalry between the two countries, using that kind of situation to its own advantage.

Restored image of the Sanggyeongseong palace (left)
The Sanggyeongseong palace was constructed during the reign of Balhae kingdom's 3rd king Munwang. The Hwangseong structure was at the center, and many public offices and temples stood closely to each other. The design of this city was well planned. The circumference of the palace was 16km. The city perished with the fall of Balhae. Today we can only see where the palace and temples would have been standing. The overall design of this city was modelled after the Tang Dynasty's Janganseong capital.

Restored image of the Heian Castle in Japan (right)
In the 8th century, the internationally acclaimed Tang culture spread to its neighboring states. Tang capital Jangan's features inspired the capitals of Balhae and Japan.

3

The Remarkable Development of a Buddhist Culture

Shilla and Balhae's expanding their views toward the world

Although Shilla continued to battle the Tang dynasty for many years, the Shilla people also studied and embraced the Chinese governing system. Shilla's authorities intended to establish a centralized power, and the administrative ruling system and legal codes of China had considerable influences upon the bureaucratic governance of Shilla.

Civilian contacts with Tang were also very active. The Chinese civilization was internationally recognized, and Tang's reputation attracted people from all over the world. In order to study the advanced Tang society, many Shilla students went over there, and countless merchants visited Tang for trade purposes. Some of them chose to take a permanent residence there. Also, there were some Shilla travelers who did not stop at visiting Tang. They left for India, West and Central Asia in search of a new world.

Balhae too actively engaged itself in foreign relationships. Since the middle of the 8th century, Balhae sent more than 60 separate official delegations to Tang. It enthusiastically embraced Tang's culture

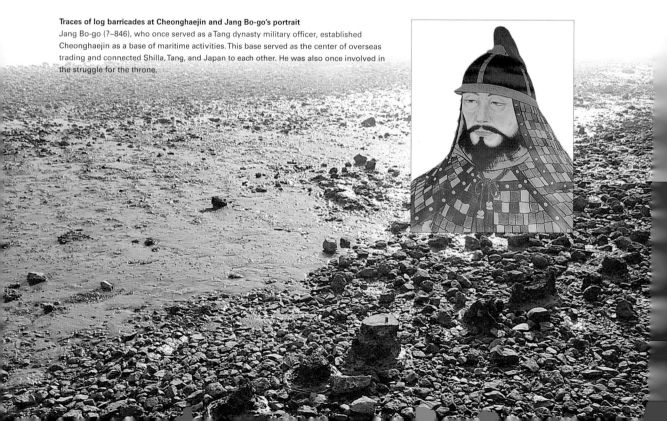

Traces of log barricades at Cheonghaejin and Jang Bo-go's portrait
Jang Bo-go (?~846), who once served as a Tang dynasty military officer, established Cheonghaejin as a base of maritime activities. This base served as the center of overseas trading and connected Shilla, Tang, and Japan to each other. He was also once involved in the struggle for the throne.

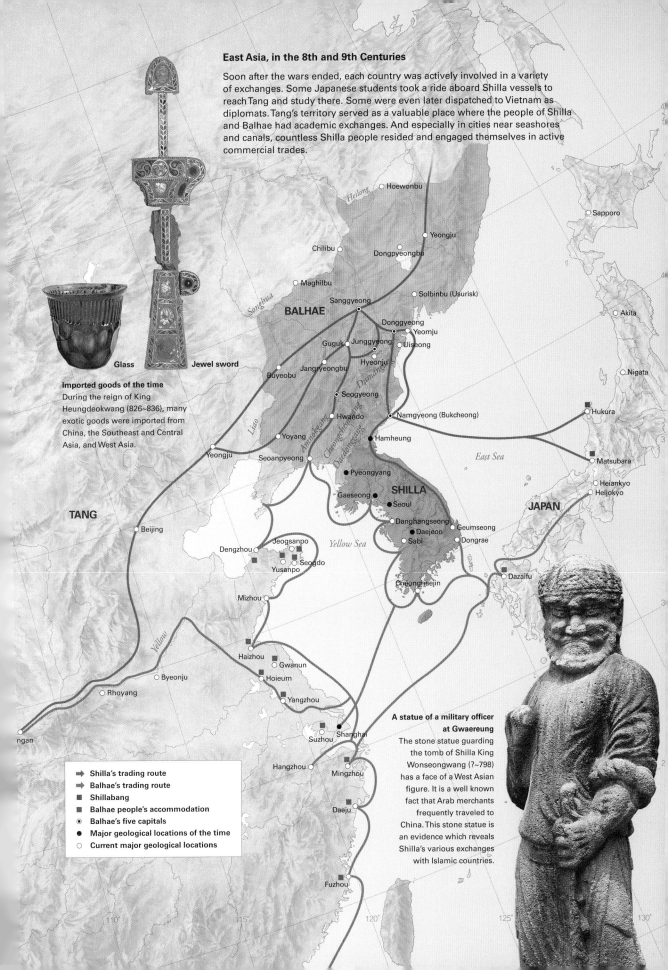

East Asia, in the 8th and 9th Centuries

Soon after the wars ended, each country was actively involved in a variety of exchanges. Some Japanese students took a ride aboard Shilla vessels to reach Tang and study there. Some were even later dispatched to Vietnam as diplomats. Tang's territory served as a valuable place where the people of Shilla and Balhae had academic exchanges. And especially in cities near seashores and canals, countless Shilla people resided and engaged themselves in active commercial trades.

Glass

Jewel sword

Imported goods of the time
During the reign of King Heungdeokwang (826~836), many exotic goods were imported from China, the Southeast and Central Asia, and West Asia.

A statue of a military officer at Gwaereung
The stone statue guarding the tomb of Shilla King Wonseongwang (?~798) has a face of a West Asian figure. It is a well known fact that Arab merchants frequently traveled to China. This stone statue is an evidence which reveals Shilla's various exchanges with Islamic countries.

TANG

BALHAE

SHILLA

JAPAN

Hoewonbu
Yeongju
Chilibu
Dongpyeongbu
Maghilbu
Solbinbu (Usurisk)
Akita
Sanggyeong
Donggyeong
Yeomju
Guguk
Junggyeong
Uiseong
Nigata
Buyeobu
Jangryeongbu
Hyeonju
Seogyeong
Hwando
Namgyeong (Bukcheong)
Yoyang
Seoanpyeong
Hamheung
Hukura
Yeongju
Pyeongyang
East Sea
Gaeseong
Seoul
Matsubara
Beijing
Danghangseong
Daejeon
Geumseong
Heiankyo
Sabi
Dongrae
Heijokyo
Dengzhou
Jeogsanpo
Yellow Sea
Yusanpo
Seogdo
Cheonghaejin
Dazaifu
Mizhou
Haizhou
Gwanun
Hoieum
Yangzhou
Byeonju
Rhoyang
Suzhou
Shanghai
ngan
Hangzhou
Mingzhou
Daeju
Fuzhou

Heilong
Songhua
Liao
Annoksang
Cheongcheongang
Damangang
Dadonggang
Yellow

➡ Shilla's trading route
➡ Balhae's trading route
■ Shillabang
■ Balhae people's accommodation
⊙ Balhae's five capitals
● Major geological locations of the time
○ Current major geological locations

and learned many things about the Tang's advanced administration system. Many students studied in Tang, and some of them successfully passed the Chinese state examination held for foreigners, just as the Shilla students did.

By embracing the world's diverse ideas, historical experiences, and religious philosophies, the Shilla and Balhae people widened their cultural horizons. Especially, the Confucian ideology that formed the foundation of the Chinese governance system, and Buddhism which came to reflect Chinese lifestyle and values, proved to be quite instrumental in various social changes and developments that continued inside these two countries.

Development of Confucianism in studies and philosophies

In Shilla, there was an institution named 'Dokseosampumgwa.' It was an educational system for the civil officers of the Shilla government. Students were hired to various levels of administrative positions according to the grades they received. Gukhak, the national university of Shilla, oversaw the process. It also continued to educate officer candidates who would pledge their loyalty to the king in future services.

Acquiring an understanding of Confucian scriptures was considered a fundamental element in their education. Students who deeply understood scriptures, history, literature, and also other kinds of philosophy were highly valued and respected. Balhae also established schools to develop knowledge and ideas regarding Confucianism, history, and literature. As a result, many students who had earlier studied in Tang largely contributed to the advancement of Balhae's academics and culture.

Wonhyo (left) and Euisang (right)
Wonhyo (617~686) and Euisang (625~702) endeavored to study the Buddhist scriptures and educate the public of their meanings. Their efforts led to a new era of popular Buddhism. Many of the oldest temples we have today were built during this time period.

As the people's understanding of Confucianism and history continued to deepen, the emphasis placed upon understanding the Confucian philosophy of governing increased as well. The Chinese governing system based on Confucianism was widely introduced to Korea, and Chinese characters were adopted in renaming geological locations. Morally absolute values such as loyalty to the kings and filial piety to the parents became general values of the society.

Yet, at the same time, Shilla's noble class called "Jingol (true-bone)," was the only class that held socio-economic privileges. Members of this class occupied most of the high ranking seats inside the government. Balhae was also run by only a few aristocratic elites who were descendants of the people of Goguryeo. A bureaucratic ruling system with the king at the center continued hiring governmental officials according to their abilities, yet the power of the nobility was still being passed down to following generations.

Budo
'Budo pagoda' 'refers to pagodas where the monks' 'sari' remains were preserved. They are also called as 'Seungtab.' The picture is a Budo pagoda that contains the 'sari' remains of Monk Doeui Seonsa. It is located at the Jinjeonsa (temple) in the Gangwon-do province.

Buddhism becomes the people's religion

At the time, Buddhism had more influences upon the people's lives than Confucianism. Confucianism was of interest to a few powerful politicians, while Buddhism was a religion for all classes of people.

Buddhism was first introduced to the royal family members and the aristocracy class, and in the 7th century it became a popular religion among the people. The royal family held magnificent rituals wishing for peace and prosperity. The Buddha was considered as an almighty God, and worshipped by all classes. People came to believe that by merely pledging that

Pagodas of Unified Shilla and Balhae
Pagodas were a sort of tombs made to preserve the 'sari' remains that came from the body of Buddha. Because the Buddha was considered as an eternal being, pagodas were also believed as his residences. The left is the Shilla Dynasty's Gameunsatab (pagoda), and the right is the Balhae Kingdom's Yeonggwangtab (pagoda).

Seokguram
From this grotto, we can see the delicate architectural technique and outstanding engraving skills of the Shilla people in the 8th century. In this artificially created stone cave, the Buddha statue, several guardian deities, practitioners, and the Inwang statue were all realistically engraved. This grotto is located on the ridge of Tohamsan (Mt.) at the east side of Gyeongju, the capital of Shilla.

"I believe in Buddha and will rely upon him." one would be saved. They also believed that the Buddhist Goddess of Mercy would bring them good fortune before they die and leave this existence. Buddhism's growing popularity was also due to the contributions of some monks such as Wonhyo and Euisang, who dedicated themselves to helping people by sharing their pains and woes.

Buddhism was a religion that interpreted death and life in a philosophical context. And there have always been questions like "What was my prior life like?" or "What can we expect in the next one?" or "What would be the most desirable life?" or "What are the mysteries of life and death?" or "How can a true understanding be reached while going through a cycle of reincarnation?" Numerous Buddhist scriptures that were introduced to Korea were studied. There have been serious discussions in pursuit of the true nature of the genuine teachings of Sakyamuni.

Flourishing Buddhist art

As the royal family and aristocrats actively absorbed Buddhism into their society, Buddhism became the religion of the people and it initiated the development of a Buddhist art. Most of the renowned temples in Korea, as well as cultural treasures of Buddhism, were constructed during this time period.

Gyeongju, the old capital city of Unified Shilla, is full of cultural treasures of Buddhist origin. Also in Sanggyeongseong, the capital of Balhae, many artistic pieces of Buddhist items such as big stone lamps have been found. Bulguksa and Seokguram are the representative historical remains of Gyeongju, a city where we can experience the artistic spirit of the Shilla people.

Double Statues of a Sitting Buddha
Since two Buddha figures are sitting together, this statue is called "Yibulbyeongjwasang." Next to this pair of Buddha figures, the female Buddha figures and monks can be seen. These statues reflect the influence from the Goguryeo Buddhism in the 7th century, which was based upon the Beobhwa Sutra Buddhist scripture that worshipped Buddha and Dabo. This statue was excavated at Jirinseong, which used to be the center of Balhae, and is currently in custody of the Tokyo University of Japan. We can see that the Buddhist beliefs of Goguryeo were transmitted to Balhae. The height of this stone statue is 29cm.

Bulguksa,
a Temple in the Land of Buddha

The Buddhist followers of Shilla believed that Shilla had been a land of Buddha for a very long time. The belief that the world in which they lived was the chosen land for Buddhism, and the idea to develop that land into a most idealistic nation for Buddha, is generally called the idea of 'Bulgukto (Land of the Buddhist Nation).'

Bulguksa, the greatest Buddhist temple of Shilla, was first built in the 6th century during King Beob-heungwang's reign. He officially authorized Buddhism as the Shilla dynasty's national religion and encouraged the people to believe in Buddhism. Later in the 8th century, when the cultural prosperity and self-confidence of the Shilla people reached its apex, Bulguksa underwent an extensive reconstruction.

Inside the Bulguksa, there are three figures of Buddha enshrined. One is Sakyamuni who came to this world to enlighten the people, another is the Amitabha who would save the people by leading them into Nirvana, and the third is Birosana who serves as the light of truth.

Panoramic display of the Bulguksa's features
In order to meet Sakyamuni Buddha of the real world, one must cross the 'cloud bridges' that were called 'Baegungyo (White Cloud Bridge)' and 'Cheogungyo (Blue Cloud Bridge)' at the right side. And in order to meet the Amitabha Buddha, one must pass 'Chilbogyo (Seven Treasure Bridge)' and 'Yeonhwagyo (Lotus Flower Bridge)' at the left side.

Bulguksa site

Bulguk-sa was constructed on the ridge of Tohamsan east of Gyeongju, alongside Seokguram. Its original size was much larger, yet many sections and structures were lost in wars during subsequent periods. The largest structure in this picture is the main temple. The building on its right side is the Paradise building where Amitabha Buddha was enshrined.

❶ Iljumun Entering the temple through this gate, practitioners should be ready to obtain awakening by cleansing themselves of the suffering and troubles from daily life, and by thinking about Buddha's teachings, before standing before Buddha.

❷ Cheonwangmun When believers pass through this gate, they meet the four Devas (heaven guards). They are symbolic figures who would keep the believers from the turbulence of mind when practicing.

❸ Yeonhwagyo, Chilbogyo These are stairways to the Paradise Building, and lotus flowers are inscribed on it.

❹ Cheogungyo, Baegungyo The stairways where blue clouds and white clouds stay. It is a passage way, leading to 'heaven', which is represented by the Main building (Daeungjeon; 'Daeung' indicates Buddha).

❺ Buddha (Sakyamuni) Buddha is enshrined in the Main building, located at the center of the temple.

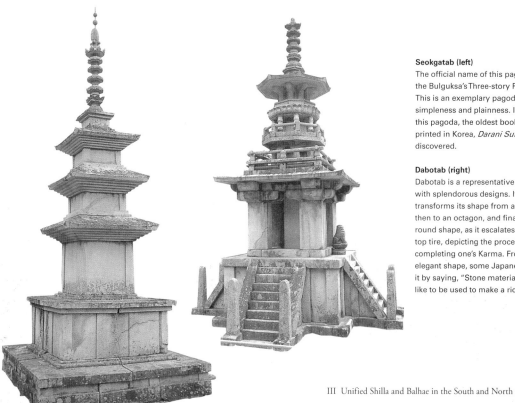

Seokgatab (left)

The official name of this pagoda is the Bulguksa's Three-story Pagoda. This is an exemplary pagoda featuring simpleness and plainness. Inside this pagoda, the oldest book ever printed in Korea, *Darani Sutra,* was discovered.

Dabotab (right)

Dabotab is a representative pagoda with splendorous designs. It transforms its shape from a square, then to an octagon, and finally to a round shape, as it escalates to the top tire, depicting the process of completing one's Karma. From this elegant shape, some Japanese praised it by saying, "Stone material seems like to be used to make a rice cake."

4

The Decline of the South and North Kingdoms Era

Thriving capital; starving people

When the king mounted the Weolsangru (tower) to have a look at the city of Geumseong (Gyeongju), he saw crowded residences and heard songs coming out of those houses. He asked his subjects, "Is it true that people nowadays usually build their roofs with tiles instead of straws, and that they prepare their meals with charcoal and not wood?" In response, a subject named Mingong answered, "Yes, I heard so, Your Highness."
– *Samguksagi*

We can see that at the time in Shilla many houses were built with tiled-roofs, and used charcoal instead of wood in order to produce less smoke when cooking and heating. However, not everyone was able to have such luxuries.

Sonsun had a child, who often took away the meals that Sonsun prepared for his mother. Unable to bear the child's misbehavior, Sonsun and his wife took the child to a nearby mountain, intending to bury the child in a pit. While digging, they found a stone bell. And when they struck the bell, the bell produced marvelous sounds.
– *Samgukyusa*

The characters who appear in this story were from Geumseong as well.

Juryeonggu
This is a dice made with 14 sides. It was excavated from Anabji (pond), and total of 14 game penalties for certain moves are instructed on each side. The height is 4.8cm.

Anabji
Anabji is the royal park (pond) where an artificial pond and small islands were established to plant exotic flowers and raise rare animals, to be enjoyed by the people. The pavilion seen in a distance is Imhae-jeon, a place where royal families and nobles frequently had banquets.

Power struggles inside the nobility class intensified

At the time, there were more than one million people living inside the Geumseong capital city, yet the prosperity of the country was only reflected in the lives of the nobles. In a strictly hierarchical social system, only the members of the nobility class had opportunities that led to higher positions in the government, and with those positions, they expanded their own private lands and enjoyed services from a large number of slaves (Nobi workers). With their multiplying wealth, they also purchased a large quantity of foreign goods and luxury items.

However, it was the peasants who occupied the largest portion of the population. Because their overall productivity was still quite low, commoners were not able to escape poverty, in spite of their long hours of labor. In order to collect taxes more efficiently, Shilla performed a census research and surveyed the number of individuals and households throughout the country, the size of land units owned by individual peasants, the number of farm animals owned by them, and also certain special products that were being generated in respective regions.

The tax burden was too harsh and eventually pushed the peasantry population into poverty, yet the aristocrats continued to exploit the people. They continued to do so, as the domestic demand for luxury items drastically increased due to the ever expanding popularity of profitable foreign trades, and as competitions among the nobles intensified in their pursuit of political power.

In 780, King Hyegongwang was assassinated, soon after one of his distant relatives seized the throne. Major struggles for power among the no-

Survey report on Shilla villages
From Jeongchangwon (Shosoin), a Japanese storage facility where royal treasures were preserved, this survey report was discovered in 1933. The economic details and the overall size of an individual village, and information regarding the tax administration of the 7th century, are recorded in this document.

Succession chart
Due to conflicts among nobles that broke out when a new royal family was established in 780, the throne in this period was rarely passed to the sitting king's son. In many occasions, even the kings who fought their way to the throne could not keep it that long. The nobles' struggle for the royal throne brought extreme divisions to the Shilla society.

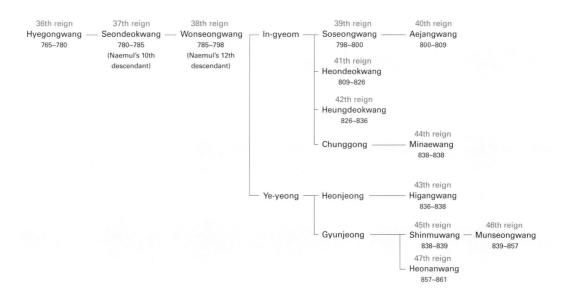

Choi Chi-won (857~?)
Choi Chi-won was a Shilla noble. He studied in Tang and later passed the state examination. He served the Tang Dynasty as an official for many years. Upon his return to Shilla, he stood up for a political reform, but when it was met with strong resistance from other nobles, he had to withdraw from his official position. He was well known for his literary talent and achievements, and left several outstanding pieces of writing.

Castle of gentry
The gentry who appeared in the ending days of Shilla governed farmers independently and built their own fortresses, in order to keep their territories independent, and they also possessed a number of troops. There were also a number of aristocrats who owned vast lands and private soldiers. However, the Shilla society in general did not turn into the type of feudalism that prevailed in Europe and Japan. Instead, all these gentries and aristocratic figures used to support more powerful nobles, and later they participated as volunteers in establishing a new united kingdom in Korea. The homogeneity level shared by the Korean people at the time in terms of history and culture was already high enough, and that prevented the arrival of another period of divided kingdoms. This picture is the Gyeonhwon-seong fortress that was built by Gyeonhwon, which is located in the Sangju city of the Gyeongsangbuk-do province.

bles had begun. And ever since then, the fight for the throne continued for 155 years. In that time period, about twenty members of the royal family claimed the throne.

The nobles routinely exploited peasants in order to acquire resources that would help them win the competitions with the others. Unable to withstand all the suffering any longer, the people staged revolts and resistance. And in the wake of all those power struggles, the authority of the king and the government in general eventually collapsed. The powers of the gentry class arose. They challenged the king's authority and formed a new wave of political forces.

The collapse of Shilla, a new beginning

Kim Heon-chang, a member of the nobility class, staged a revolt in the western region of Shilla in 822. Such revolt was not to kill the sitting king and to seize the throne himself. Yet, he proclaimed that a new kingdom should be founded and replace the declining Shilla. 16 years later, a general named Jang Bo-go, who was the leader of the most prominent maritime force ever formed in the Korean sea, defeated the king's army and endorsed a new king for the reign.

Yet, neither Kim nor Jang was successful in establishing a new kingdom. It was only in the middle of the 9th century when the government lost control over the local provinces. In remote areas distant from the capital, numerous figures of the gentry class called "Hojok" ruled their own peasants independently and attempted to seize opportunities to build their own realms of influence that were free from the king. Meanwhile, wealthy individuals who accumulated profits through maritime trade activities, and the military officers in local regions also showed similar ambitions.

The central government struggled to fix certain problems and reform its society, not to mention control such civil unrest, yet their efforts ultimately failed. Reformers were forced to leave the government, by the more conser-

vative nobles who wished to protect their prerogatives and privileges.

In the meantime, Buddhist beliefs continued to challenge the authorities of the aristocrats, by claiming that anyone could be a Buddha by having an enlightenment. Also, spreading rumors had it that Shilla's fortune had finally run out and a new kingdom would eventually emerge to replace Shilla before long. A new order was already on the horizon.

Collapse of Balhae

In 926 Balhae, the great nation of the north, collapsed with the invasion of the Georan tribes, the nomads who resided in the Mongolian plateaus. The invasion started in December 925, and in January the next year the war between Balhae and Georan already ended. Balhae fell in a mere month, ending its 230 years of history. Georan historians described the fall of Balhae in a sentence that says, "Our ancestors won without a fight."

However, it is impossible to verify the validity of this description since no reliable records remain today. Another speculation is that there might have been a natural disaster, such as volcanic eruptions that eventually resulted in Georan's victory. However, another record of Georan states that "They (the invading Georan forces) took advantage of the division and dissension between the Balhae people." We can also consider for a variable the lives the common villagers led, which was quite different from the life inside the Sanggyeongseong capital, in terms of size and extravagance. With such kind of internal polarizations, confronting a new mighty rising force might have been a fatal blow that broke the camel's back.

After the fall of Balhae, many refugees moved to the south, and through these emigrants, Balhae's history and culture were incorporated into the Korean history. However, the Balhae people who were forcibly relocated to other regions, and many others who were grounded in the old territory of Balhae became more and more alienated from the history of the South as time went on.

Dae Jo-yeong
After the fall of Balhae, the center of old Balhae turned into ruins. And there remains no history book written by the Balhae people today. A majority of Koreans today believe that Balhae succeeded Goguryeo, and that a large number of Balhae people merged with the Goryeo population. This led to the belief that the history of Balhae is part of the Korean history as well. This poster is made to advertise the TV drama "Dae Jo-yeong" that was on the air between 2006 and 2007.

The traces of Sanggyeongseong
Sanggyeongseong was the capital city of Balhae. In this place, traces of seven palaces and several temples were discovered. Although the individual palaces and the Balhae Kingdom in general all disappeared into history, the positioning of stones in places where palaces used to be, lets us know that there must have been some magnificently big structures standing here.

A bone container with a shape of a tile-roofed house
Chinese used to cover their roof with clay tiles. Such technique dates back to somewhere prior to the beginning of the 15th century B.C. and around the 1st century, clay tiles were widely used in China. Tile roofs first appeared in Korea at the beginning of the 1st century. This is a container in which bones were restfully placed after the cremation of a dead body. It was excavated from Bukun-dong at Gyeongju.

Tile-roofed Houses, Straw-roofed Houses, and Ondol and Wooden Floors

In the 8th century, Geumseong (Gyeongju) was a city well-designed, in a squared shape resembling a Chinese chess board. The life in Gyeongju is depicted as follows; "In this city, many houses were decorated with gold. There were so many temples positioned throughout the capital, like stars scattered in the sky shining at night. Pagodas stood side by side, in a fashion resembling a flock of wild geese flying somewhere." (*Samguksagi*) Sources also state that most of the houses in Gyeongju had tile roofs.

However, not all houses in Geumseong were covered with tiles. The lower class people who couldn't afford to pay the cost of expensive tiles, used straws to cover their roof because they were easy to secure during harvest seasons. Even until the 1960s most houses in this country were made with straw-covered roofs. Regardless of the type of roof, all houses installed the Ondol heating system and a wooden floor called 'Maru.' Floors for rooms were equipped with Ondol. A foreigner who visited Korea in the early 20th century joked that "Koreans all accustomed themselves to baking their bodies like hot bread every night." Koreans indeed warmed themselves in winter using heated stones which increased the temperature of a room. Meanwhile, wood floors were laid to connect rooms, or to extend the fringe of the exterior of a room. The openness of the main floor was designed to facilitate air ventilation and maintain a pleasurable temperature in hot summer days.

Ondol is a heating system which originated in the north, while wood flooring was used in houses of the south. When the three kingdoms were unified, cultural exchanges became active. As a result, the Maru originating from the south and the Ondol from the north merged with each other and became essential components of Korean traditional houses.

❶❷ Tile-roofed house and straw-roofed house Most Korean traditional houses are either tile-roofed or straw-roofed houses. Only the rich lived in a tile-roofed house. **❸ Tiles** During the Three Kingdoms Period, tile-roofed houses were common. Tiles were made of baked clay, and round-shaped "male" tiles and flat-shaped "female" tiles were laid on the roof in an alternating fashion. The row-closing tile is called "Magsae," and the end section of a male tile was called 'Sumagsae' while the end section of a female tile was called 'Ammagsae.' **❹ Ondol and 'Maru'** The climate of Korea is characterized as 'continental,' which has hot summers and cold winters. Ondol and a wooden floor called Maru, were very effective devices in fighting hot and cold weathers. Thus the Korean traditional house, "Hanok," is commonly equipped with an Ondol system and a Maru floor.

A miniature of a cooking fireplace
On the fireplace a large iron pot is placed. It was used to boil water or cook food. This picture is a recreated model of a fireplace that is believed to have been used during the Goguryeo period. It clearly shows the structure of the fireplace, the ondol system, and the chimney. This was excavated in Unsan, Pyeonganbuk-do province. The length is 66.7cm.

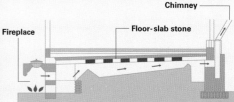

Ondol structure
Ondol heats the stone laid underneath a room's floor, as the fire hole causes heated stones to emit warmth into the room. Through the burrows which were laid underneath the stones, the heat and smoke were able to travel and exit through the chimney.

Korean traditional kitchen

900 ~ 1135

918
Wang Geon, a leader of regional power near Gaeseong, established the
Goryeo Kingdom and claimed himself as the successor of Goguryeo.

936
The period of division finally ended, as Goryeo united Shilla and
New Baekje. Goryeo welcomed the Balhae refugees and extended its
territory to the north.

958
Goryeo adopted the state [civil] examination system of China, and the
era of acknowledging not only one's heritage but also one's individual
abilities began.

962
Otto the Great was crowned as an emperor of the Holy Roman
Empire.

992
Gukjagam, which was the equivalent to a national university today, was
established. And aside from Confucian scriptures, literature, technology
and foreign language were taught and learned here as well.

993
Georan [Khitan] attacked Goryeo three times beginning this year, but
Goryeo successfully defeated them.

1037
Seljuk Turks established.

1086
"The First Edition of Great Collection of Buddhist Sutra (scriptures)"
was published, with various Buddhist scriptures collected and classified,
alongside studies of them as well. It was printed with woodblocks.

1127
Chin occupied the north of China. North Sung was demolished.

IV Emergence of a United Power Named Goryeo

The foundation of Goryeo, and the unification of the Later Three Kingdoms, was a process of constructing a new dynastic ruling system, a new political authority and a more liberal society. Goryeo adopted the state [civil] examination system that selected officials through testing, and enhanced its educational system as well. Goryeo implemented the existing diplomacy, acknowledging the confrontational situations between the Han race of China and northern tribes in the vicinity. The Goryeo people also endeavored to embrace new ideas and import commercial goods through active interactions and economic exchanges. A number of Arabian merchants visited Goryeo, and through them the world came to know Goryeo, under the name of 'Corea.'

Goryeo's Seonggyungwan university at Gaeseong This is the Seonggyungwan university building, located in Gaeseong. Outstanding Confucian scholars and countless reformist officials were trained here. It was rebuilt in the 17th century, and today, the building is being used as the "Goryeo Museum."

The Byeokrannaru Ferry Dock and Gaegyeong, the Imperial Capital of Goryeo

LIAO

There is an interesting story inside a book which contains songs that were sung during the Goryeo Dynasty Period. There was a foreign merchant from the Sung Dynasty of China who often visited Goryeo and docked at the Yeseonggang (R.) port. One day he happened to meet a beautiful woman. The man could not leave Goryeo without her, so he went to her husband and offered him a bet, of which the winner would take all the merchant's money and not to mention the female. The merchant won the bet, leaving the husband behind to sing a sad song upon parting with his wife.

Gaegyeong, the center of the Goryeo Dynasty, was regarded as the imperial capital where the Goryeo emperor resided. It was a well designed city and had over half a million population. The wealthy population of nobility made this region the most frequented market place in the entire country.

The Byeokrannaru ferry dock, located at the entrance to Gaegyeong, became the most thriving international harbor in the country. Many Goryeo people who were to visit China embarked upon their journeys here, and many foreign merchants came to Goryeo through the port. There were many shops in every corner of the streets on the way to Gaegyeong, and many foreigners resided there as well.

Major products of Goryeo
From left to right: lacquer ware products inlaid with mother-of-pearl material featuring chrysanthemum patterns, a three-drawer chest with Dangcho (a creeper plant) patterns, a vase with bird patterns, and a blue celadon incense burner with carved patterns of seven treasures.

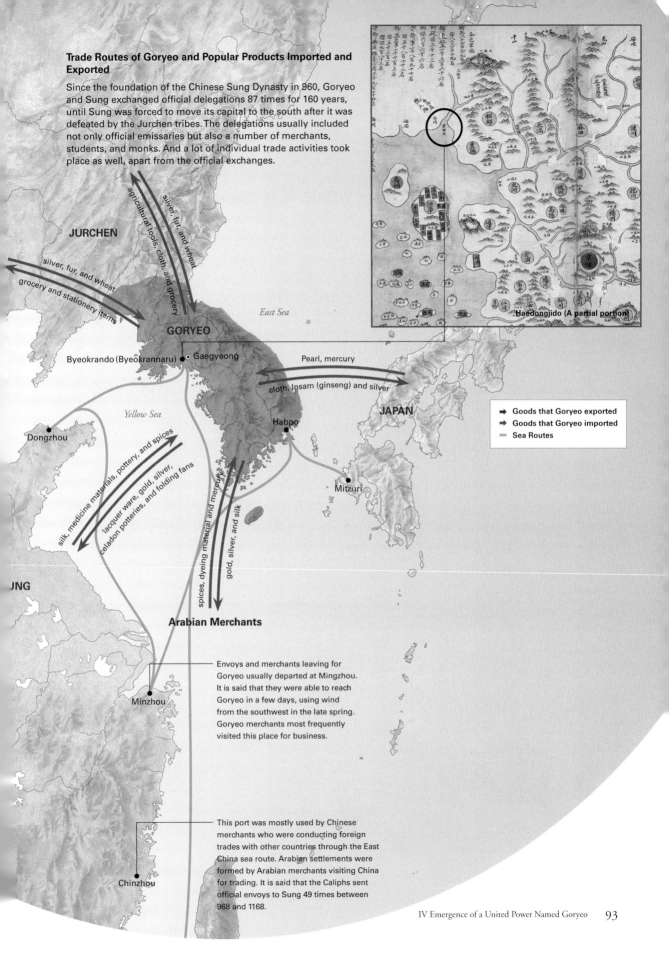

Trade Routes of Goryeo and Popular Products Imported and Exported

Since the foundation of the Chinese Sung Dynasty in 960, Goryeo and Sung exchanged official delegations 87 times for 160 years, until Sung was forced to move its capital to the south after it was defeated by the Jurchen tribes. The delegations usually included not only official emissaries but also a number of merchants, students, and monks. And a lot of individual trade activities took place as well, apart from the official exchanges.

Haedongjido (A partial portion)

JURCHEN

silver, fur, and wheat

grocery and stationery items

agricultural tools, cloth, and grocery

silver, fur, and wheat

East Sea

GORYEO

Byeokrando (Byeokrannaru) ● Gaegyeong

Pearl, mercury

cloth, Insam (ginseng) and silver

JAPAN

Yellow Sea

Dongzhou

Habpo

silk, medicine materials, pottery, and spices

lacquer ware, gold, silver, celadon potteries, and folding fans

spices, dyeing material and mercury

gold, silver, and silk

Mitzuri

➡ Goods that Goryeo exported
➡ Goods that Goryeo imported
— Sea Routes

Arabian Merchants

Envoys and merchants leaving for Goryeo usually departed at Mingzhou. It is said that they were able to reach Goryeo in a few days, using wind from the southwest in the late spring. Goryeo merchants most frequently visited this place for business.

Minzhou

This port was mostly used by Chinese merchants who were conducting foreign trades with other countries through the East China sea route. Arabian settlements were formed by Arabian merchants visiting China for trading. It is said that the Caliphs sent official envoys to Sung 49 times between 968 and 1168.

Chinzhou

JNG

1

Goryeo Unites the Later Three Kingdoms

Opening of the Later Three Kingdoms Period

As the local gentry (Hojok) became powerful and also independent from the central government, the fundamental structure of Shilla continued to be dismantled. Most of the local gentry were integrated and assimilated into the powerful leadership of a few selected local influentials. Among these political forces, Gyeonhwon (867~935) and Gungye (?~918) grew strong and established a new state.

Gyeonhwon and Gungye all claimed that Shilla treated the people of old Baekje and Goguryeo unfairly and that central governmental officials had been exploiting the entire population ever since the unification. So, as a natural conclusion, they began to call for the restoration of Baekje and Goguryeo. They named their nations as "New Baekje" (Hu-Baekje) and "New Goguryeo" (Hu-Goguryeo, later called as 'Taebong') respectively, and promised their followers that they would eliminate practices of discrimination that had continued against local regions. Especially Gungye, who claimed himself as the Maitreya Buddha, gained huge popularity, and promised to open a new world for the people in suffering. Yet, Wang Geon, who later became the founder of the Goryeo Dynasty (918~1392), drove him out. Wang Geon proclaimed himself and the Goryeo Dynasty as the successor of Goguryeo, and promised to reform the tax system. United Shilla, no longer able to hold its country and people together, had

Wanggeonreung
Wang Geon (877~943), the dynasty founder of Goryeo, was a gentry that dominated the area of Songak (today's Gaeseong). Alongside Gungye, he formed the foundation of the "New Goguryeo (later to be called 'Taebong')." This photo shows Wang Geon's tomb, the royal mausoleum that still remains at Gaeseong. Only a few Goryeo tombs including this one have been preserved.

to witness the Era of the Later Three Kingdoms unfold and proceed.

Gyeonhwon and Wang Geon's struggles for unification

Shilla was too weak to maintain its power, while New Baekje led by Gyeonhwon and Goryeo led by Wang Geon gradually grew and expanded their influence. Frequent military clashes were inevitable.

They fought furiously with each other, both intending to reunite the Korean Peninsula under their own regime. Gyeonhwon, for more than one occasion, swore that he would recover all territories of Goguryeo by advancing to the Daedonggang. Wang Geon also occasionally pledged to his followers that he would be the king of the unified kingdom, who would rule the Korean Peninsula.

Such passions to unite all of its opponents were distinguishably different from the mentality of Baekje, Goguryeo and Shilla, as none of them was ambitious enough to consider the others as its subject to be subdued and united. It had been 200 years since Shilla's unification of Baekje and Goguryeo, and the people were already accustomed to a life under a unified regime, a life in a unified country, and most importantly, a culture among a unified people.

Indeed, Goryeo considered absorbing Balhae in the north as its next step toward a complete unification. Unlike Shilla which considered Balhae as its rival, the Goryeo people considered Balhae as another successor of Goguryeo, and viewed it as a kin country. After Balhae collapsed, Goryeo welcomed its refugees and angrily confronted Georan which demolished Balhae, revealing Goryeo's own intentions to recover the lands of Goguryeo.

Goryeo's unification of the Later Three Kingdoms

The struggle for reunification between New Baekje and Goryeo did not take long. Gyeonhwon's oldest son betrayed his own father and seized the throne, pushing New Baekje into an internal conflict. To save his life, Gyeonhwon escaped, headed for Goryeo and asked Wang Geon for help. Not before long, Goryeo invaded New Baekje and crippled it beyond repairs.

The victory of Goryeo was the result of Wang Geon's decades of efforts to unite the country. Perhaps it was destined to be so. Gyeonhwon and Gungye both advocated a powerful monarchy. On the other hand, Wang Geon treated the local gentry well and

Goryeo's Gold-plated Bronze Grand Pagoda
This gold-plated bronze pagoda seems to have been originally built with seven tiers, and it is well-known for its grandiose size: the currently remaining part, total of five tiers, is 155cm in height. We believe it was built at Gaetaesa (temple), which was built to celebrate Goryeo's reunification of the country.

Mireukjeon at Geumsansa (temple)
The reunification war was in a sense triggered by the people's resistance against the wrong doings of the central authority. At the time, in Shilla the idea of a Mireuk Buddha bringing about a new era for the people was widely circulating. The picture shows the Mireukjeon hall at Geumsansa, which served as the center for such Mireuk belief. This place is not too far from Wansan, the capital of New Baekje. Gyeonhwon was detained in this temple by his own son. He escaped there and fled to Goryeo.

therefore acquired their support. He also avoided unnecessary frictions by not only acknowledging the privileges of the local gentry, but also offering them official positions inside the central government. Yet at the same time, Wang Geon firmly established a royal authority, by reinforcing the alliance with the gentry families by bestowing his last name "Wang" to them. And by encouraging marriages between the gentry families and the royal family, he made local influentials essentially an extension of the royal family.

The fact that Wang Geon himself had been leading one of the gentry factions helped him garner support from the local gentry community. The gentries expected Wang Geon to understand their demands and to provide opportunities to them, instead of only giving it to a few aristocratic families inside the capital. In response to the tyrannical ruling of the previous governments, the people chose Wang Geon as their leader, in hopes that their lives would be improved.

Wang Geon freed those who had been wrongfully forced into slavery. He also lowered taxes to one-tenth of the harvest and prohibited plundering committed by the local authorities. As a result, he managed to receive great support from the peasantry population.

In 935, Goryeo finally accepted the voluntary surrender of Shilla, a kingdom that lasted for nearly a thousand years. When Wang Geon attacked New Baekje in 936, the reunification war ended.

This war was more than about being Goryeo's mere expansion of its territory. The peasants resisted unjust exploitation, and the gentries stood up to oppose discriminations. The unification was a realization of the people's own wishes, hoping for a safer, more equal and secured society.

Although discrimination and unfair exploitations were not totally wiped out, Goryeo's reunification of the Korean Peninsula ultimately contributed to constructing a society more open and equal than ever before.

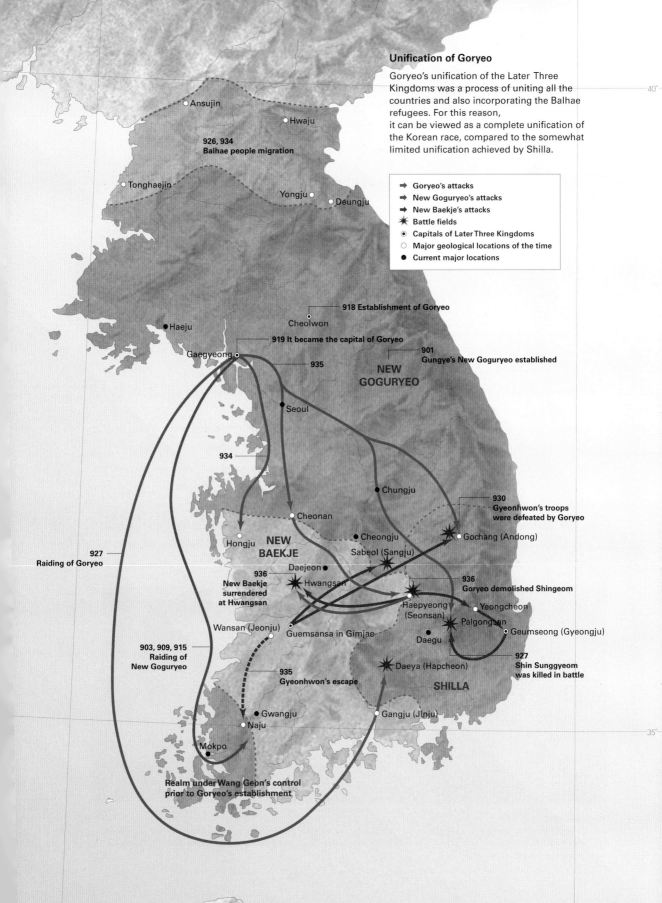

Unification of Goryeo

Goryeo's unification of the Later Three Kingdoms was a process of uniting all the countries and also incorporating the Balhae refugees. For this reason, it can be viewed as a complete unification of the Korean race, compared to the somewhat limited unification achieved by Shilla.

➡ Goryeo's attacks
➡ New Goguryeo's attacks
➡ New Baekje's attacks
✳ Battle fields
◉ Capitals of Later Three Kingdoms
○ Major geological locations of the time
● Current major locations

○ Ansujin

○ Hwaju

926, 934
Balhae people migration

○ Tonghaejin

Yongju ○   ○ Deungju

918 Establishment of Goryeo
Cheolwon ◉

919 It became the capital of Goryeo
● Haeju

Gaegyeong ◉
935

NEW GOGURYEO

901
Gungye's New Goguryeo established

● Seoul

934

● Chungju

○ Cheonan

930
Gyeonhwon's troops
were defeated by Goryeo

○ Hongju

NEW BAEKJE

● Cheongju   ○ Gochang (Andong)

Sabeol (Sangju) ○

927
Raiding of Goryeo

936
New Baekje
surrendered
at Hwangsan

Daejeon ●
✳ Hwangsan

936
Goryeo demolished Shingeom

Haepyeong
(Seonsan) ○

○ Yeongcheon
Palgongsan ✳

Wansan (Jeonju) ◉
○ Guemsansa in Gimjae

● Daegu   ◉ Geumseong (Gyeongju)

903, 909, 915
Raiding of
New Goguryeo

935
Gyeonhwon's escape

✳ Daeya (Hapcheon)

927
Shin Sunggyeom
was killed in battle

SHILLA

● Gwangju   ○ Gangju (Jinju)
○ Naju

● Mokpo

Realm under Wang Geon's control
prior to Goryeo's establishment

TAMRA

2

Goryeo Adopts the Civil Service Examination, and Develops a Bureaucratic Ruling System

The three Choi's in the final days of Shilla and the beginning of Goryeo

Towards the end of Shilla, there were three famous men who carried the family name "Choi." They were Choi Chi-won, Choi Seung-wu, and Choi Eon-wi. All three were respected by the people as renowned scholars of the time. They already earned their reputation when they were studying in China. They all rose to high positions inside the government as well after having passed the civil service examination held for foreigners residing in China. Quite naturally, the news of their returning home was of people's special interest at that time.

However, none of them were able to successfully join the decision making process concerning governmental affairs during their stay home. It was because Shilla still maintained the "Jingol (True bones)" class system, in which only those of certain blood lines were appointed to high ranking offices. The above-mentioned people's knowledge and experiences were never duly recognized by the central government of Shilla, and thus, the things that they could do were severely limited.

So after failing in political reforms, Choi Chi-won disappeared into the mountains and became a hermit. Choi Seung-wu left Shilla and joined Gyeonhwon's New Baekje. And Choi Eon-wi, who had

Hongpae in the Goryeo period
This is a certificate that shows someone has passed the civil officer examination. On a piece of red paper, the name and rank of the person who passed the test are recorded. During the Goryeo period, this Hongpae certificate was issued to represent the honor of the family that had a son who passed the examination.

remained as a low ranking official, was only able to do things that he wished, after Shilla collapsed and Goryeo emerged.

Choi Eon-wi later contributed to the task of constructing a ruling system for the new dynasty. Goryeo's reformation of the ruling system provided an opportunity to many intellectuals from Shilla, whose paths had literally been blocked due to the rigid social class system.

The educational institution, and the civil officer examination system of Goryeo

Gukjagam
- Yuhakbu (The Confucian Studies Dept.)
- Gisulhakbu (The Technology Dept.)

Mungwa
- Jesulgwa
- Myeonggyeonggwa → High ranking officials

Jabgwa → Technicians

Gukjagam, and the civil officer examination system
In the Gukjagam university, Confucian scriptures, historical texts, and literature were taught at the department of Confucian Studies, and teaching of laws, mathematics, medicine and foreign language was provided at the department of Technology. Examinations for both departments were held separately; those who wanted to be a civil officer applied to the Literary Exam (Mungwa), and people who were willing to be a technician applied to Miscellaneous Exam (Jabgwa). The former department tested the students' fluency in Chinese and knowledge in Confucian scriptures.

Adoption of new official employment system

Shilla's division and Goryeo's reunification can be interpreted as a process of new leaders' struggling to form a more advanced country.

The country was not to be ruled by merely a king and a few nobles. Local gentry figures who contributed to the war efforts of reuniting the country actively involved themselves in political affairs of the government. Quite a large number of these gentry figures were recognized with their achievements and were named meritorious vassals, and some others were able to receive important governmental seats for merely being members of the gentry families. And they all maintained their privileges in the areas they had been ruling.

Yet at the end of the 10th century, a new bureaucratic system of hiring officers via civil service examinations was adopted from China, and the political dynamics throughout the country started to shift accordingly. This

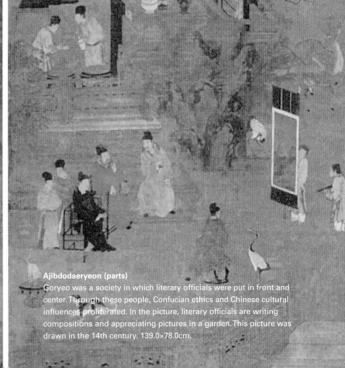

Ajibdodaeryeon (parts)
Goryeo was a society in which literary officials were put in front and center. Through these people, Confucian ethics and Chinese cultural influences proliferated. In the picture, literary officials are writing compositions and appreciating pictures in a garden. This picture was drawn in the 14th century. 139.0×78.0cm.

new examination system, which provided opportunities to eligible officials who had passed the civil service examination, changed the overall atmosphere of the society that was accustomed to the idea of bequeathing social positions as a matter of course.

As the civil service examinations were implemented inside the Goryeo society, one's abilities were more and more acknowledged in selecting officer candidates. The opportunities were still limited, yet Goryeo's ruling system was different from its predecessors. Even the aristocrats had to serve in a governmental seat in order to maintain their privileges, and the civil service examination was the most important step in becoming an officer of the government.

Goryeo forms the foundation for a ruling system that will last for 1,000 years

Shilla's ruling system was controlled by a small number of royal family members, until it was replaced by a new governing system of Goryeo. The reformers who led such transformation were scholars who had once studied in Tang China, or who had received systematic education. Based on profound understanding of Chinese history and Confucianism, which provided philosophical background for the new ruling system, Goryeo established the foundations of a new ruling system that would last for the next 1,000 years.

The organization of Goryeo's central government which began reforms

Goryeo's ruling system
The central governing system was greatly influenced by the system of three chancelleries and six boards of the Chinese Tang Dynasty. High-ranking officials reached agreements through debates and discussions and carried them out by assigning tasks to the six boards according to their specialties. This system was maintained during the Joseon dynasty period as well. The origin of the Six Boards can be found in a Confucian scripture, the "Analects of Confucian Practice (Jurye)."

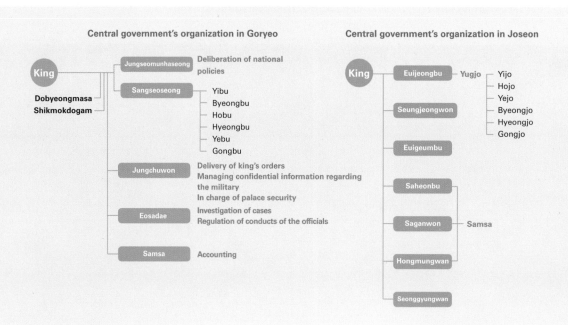

at the end of the 10th century was operated by various bodies: Chancellery for State Affairs which evaluated performance and made policies; many special departments and administrative offices which oversaw and undertook the execution of such decisions and policies, and monitors which supervised government officials and inspected their wrong doings as well as work results. Although the Goryeo governing system granted kings of absolute power and considered them as sacred persons serving the will of heaven, it also emphasized the moral duty of kings and the obligation of the officers to guide kings to righteous paths.

As Goryeo adopted the Chinese governing and legal system, there was a constant urge to change its customs into forms more suitable for embracing Confucianism. However, there were others who argued that they should preserve their unique heritages and emphasize their own traditions. Nevertheless, Buddhism became even more influential to the Goryeo society, due to the support of the royal family and a considerable number of monks who participated in government affairs as king's advisers. It was also common to find officers who believed in Taoism. Fungshui which believed that geomantic factors affected the fates of people, Totems, and Shamanism were prevailing ideas that affected the people's daily lives. So, while discussions regarding full employment of Chinese cultural aspects were actively in progress, diverse cultures and religions also coexisted harmoniously with the others inside the Goryeo society.

Euicheon (1055~1101)

Euicheon was the fourth son of King Munjong. He became a monk at the age of 11. He studied various Buddhist scriptures in Sung China, and embraced the world of Buddhism. All his life he tried to merge the Zen school and non-Zen school together, and he is well known for establishing the "Haedong cheontaejong" school, as part of such efforts.

Yeongtongsa (temple) at Gaeseong

The temples of Goryeo were places where kings and aristocratic figures paid a visit to pray for their wishes. The nobles built their own private temples in numerous places. It is believed that there were more than 300 temples around Gaegyeong. Yeongtong-sa was built during the reign of King Hyeonjong (1027), and right here Daegak Guksa Euicheon founded the Cheontaejong school. This site was once lost to fire, but in 2005 it was restored as seen in the picture.

Blue Celadon and Porcelain Expositions

Inlaid Blue Celadon vase with patterns of cranes flying the sky through white clouds 12th century, 42.1cm in height.

The mysterious blue tone of the Goryeo celadon, resembling the color of a clear blue sky when all clouds are gone after rain, signifies the Koreans' pride in their aesthetics of purity and loftiness. Celadon was first made in China, during the days of the Han Dynasty, and they quickly became popular items eagerly sought for and immensely enjoyed throughout not only East Asia but also around the globe. From the term in English that refers to celadon, "China," we can guess it was China where Blue Celadon was first made.

Koreans manufactured their own Blue Celadon around the 9th and 10th centuries when Shilla was replaced by Goryeo. By the 11th and 12th centuries, the Korean Blue Celadon received huge recognition with its gracious lines, magnificent color, and unique designs.

During the 12th and 13th centuries, the Goryeo celadon artists created a unique type of celadon, namely the "Sanggam Blue Celadon." It used

Porcelain Expositions
The Korean people, whose ceramic culture came to gain a worldwide reputation already in the past, annually hold "Porcelain Expositions," so that people not only from Korea but also from many other countries can experience and appreciate a variety of fine porcelain products.

Melon-shaped celadon vase
12th century, 22.7cm in height.

Grayish blue-powdered celadon (Buncheongsagi porcelain) with patterns of peony vines
15th century, 45.0cm in height.

White Celadon vase
15~16th century, 36.2cm in height.

the method of engraving patterns upon the surface. With all patterns in place, those engraved gaps were filled with another type of clay, and the porcelain was baked one more time. There were various designs including a flock of cranes soaring high in the blue sky through white clouds.

With the decline of the Goryeo Dynasty, the age of Blue Celadon ended as well. Yet, porcelain-related skills of the Korean people prevailed and led to a new era which witnessed the invention of Buncheong Celadon, White Celadon, and Cheonghwa White Celadon. Until the 16th century, Korea and China were the only countries that could produce celadon.

Celadon Cultures of Korea, China, and Japan in the 17th Century

From the 9th century and through the 17th, Korea was a leading porcelain maker alongside China. Yet at the end of the 16th century, when Japan invaded Korea, they captured many porcelain artists in order to advance their own clayware culture. Since then, the porcelain industry in Japan began to prosper, and from the 18th century, with its colorful fine porcelain products, Japan aggressively exported porcelain products to Europe and surpassed China.

White pot with blue-lined patterns of clouds and a dragon
Korea, 17th century, 36cm in height.

Dish with patterns of Pomegranate
Japan, 17th century, 30cm in diameter.

Bottle with patterns of plants, grass, insects, flowers, and birds
China, between the 16th and 17th century, 55.3cm in height.

3

Northeast Asia in Turmoil: Goryeo Employs Practical Diplomacy

Policy enhancements in centralizing power

While Goryeo reunited the Korean Peninsula, its northwestern region was undergoing a turbulent time. After the collapse of the powerful Tang Dynasty (618~907), nomad tribes established independent kingdoms in the northern prairie and continued to compete with each other to extend their territory toward the fertile farming lands in the south.

The Liao Dynasty in the east side of the Mongol plateau and the Tungustic people who inhabited areas adjacent to the Silk Road were representative cases of such nomad tribes. Especially Liao, which had earlier demolished Balhae, advanced toward east and did not hesitate to confront Sung China. It also attacked the northeast side of Goryeo. Liao's annexation of Balhae and its battles with Sung certainly alarmed Goryeo, as we can see from the military system employed in Goryeo's early days. Goryeo's reconstruction of its own ruling system at this juncture was not a coincidental turn of events. Goryeo established a military base at the city of Pyeongyang and constructed numerous military facilities along the northern border to prepare itself from the nomads' invasion. A powerful army was trained under the king's leadership, and at the same time the policies of the central government incorporated the political power and influences of the gentries as well.

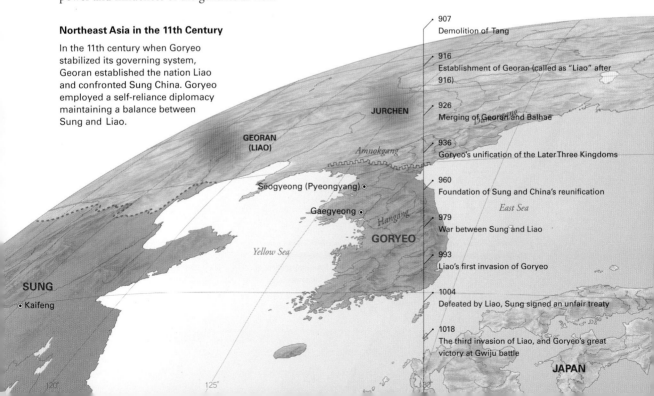

Northeast Asia in the 11th Century

In the 11th century when Goryeo stabilized its governing system, Georan established the nation Liao and confronted Sung China. Goryeo employed a self-reliance diplomacy maintaining a balance between Sung and Liao.

907
Demolition of Tang

916
Establishment of Georan (called as "Liao" after 916)

926
Merging of Georan and Balhae

936
Goryeo's unification of the Later Three Kingdoms

960
Foundation of Sung and China's reunification

979
War between Sung and Liao

993
Liao's first invasion of Goryeo

1004
Defeated by Liao, Sung signed an unfair treaty

1018
The third invasion of Liao, and Goryeo's great victory at Gwiju battle

Goryeo battles with Liao for 30 years

It was 993, when 800,000 the Liao troops invaded Goryeo for the first time. Such attack was staged as Liao was worried that the allied forces of Goryeo and Sung might later turn into a larger threat.

While Goryeo struggled to fight against a massive army, it also attempted to end the war through diplomatic channels. Liao requested the return of the old territories of Goguryeo that Goryeo was occupying. However, Seo Hi refuted that since Goryeo was the successor of Goguryeo, a considerable amount of Liao's own land should be turned over to Goryeo.

Negotiation was accomplished without much difficulties. A peaceful relation with Liao was established, and Goryeo managed to extend its territory to the north. Seo Hi succeeded in turning this national crisis into a great opportunity to restore the old territory of Goguryeo.

After the first conflict with Liao, Goryeo maintained a peaceful attitude for the moment. Goryeo also continued political and economical exchanges with Sung China. Sung too wanted to get military support from Goryeo and maintain more frequent exchanges with Goryeo.

In the meantime, Liao, far from being content with Goryeo's friendly relationship with Sung, invaded Goryeo with 400,000 troops in 1010 and 100,000 troops in 1018 respectively. The Goryeo military firmly defended the country from Liao's attacks. Especially in the third battle of 1018, Goryeo annihilated the invaders, and thus achieving a great victory.

Goryeo, a dynasty ruled by an Emperor

Goryeo spent most of the 11th century defending itself from Liao, and in the 12th century it confronted the Jurchen. For quite some time, the Jurchen had been developing its power over Manchuria, as well as an ambition to conquer the agricultural regions. Goryeo and Sung China were determined to confront it.

The Jin dynasty of Jurchen attempted to dominate Goryeo before it confronted Sung. Though Goryeo had to make a promise that it would not ally itself with Sung against Jin, Goryeo did not succumb to Jin's coercion to terminate its diplomatic relationship with Sung entirely. Sung was eager to maintain an alliance with Goryeo, and in turn Goryeo was willing to have cultural and economical exchanges with Sung. And of course, exchanges between Goryeo and

Dragon-engraved bronze Buddhist bell
This bell was made between the 12th and 13th centuries. A figure of a dragon, a symbol of the king, is elaborately engraved upon the hanging section at the top. 40cm in height, and 26.4cm in diameter (bottom).

Jin continued as well.

Maintaining a balance in the triangular relation with Jin and Sung, Goryeo established an independent, yet highly practical diplomatic policy. The Goryeo people believed that they were living in a uniquely civilized society that was quite different from China. Goryeo's kings identified themselves as emperors, and called their princes "wang (king)." They also named the capital as "the City of Emperors," and adopted titles and customs of the Chinese emperors in their ruling system.

Goryeo is introduced as "Corea" to the world

As international relations stabilized, the cultural and economical exchanges among Goryeo, Sung, and Liao became even more frequent and active. The capital of Goryeo, Gaegyeong, was always crowded with delegates from Sung and Liao while Goryeo's diplomats were sent to those two dynasties as well. Since Goryeo admired Sung's culture so much, they pursued that particular relationship more vigorously. A large number of merchants, students, and monks were sent to Sung over sea. And many traders from Southeast Asia and the Arabic world visited Gaegyeong.

Goryeo mostly exported gold, silver, ginseng, and lacquerware while importing silk, books, and herbs from Sung. From the Arabian merchants, the Goryeo people purchased mercury and spices.

Some of the foreign merchants even took permanent residence inside

Miniature restoration of the Goryeo palace
This miniature model is a representation of the Goryeo palace that was built in 919 and burned to the ground in 1361. In 1945, the location of this palace was discovered at the southern foot of Songaksan (Mt.) in Gaeseong, and based upon the vestige, the palace's old features were restored in a miniaturized scale.

Gaegyeong. They opened stores and engaged themselves in more vigorous business activities. Byeokrannaru which was always frequented by a large contingent of foreign merchants developed into an international port, and the Gaegyeong capital shaped up as a cosmopolitan city. Through such progress, Goryeo's name began to spread throughout the world, and the Europeans began to call it "Corea (Goryeo)," ■ which is the previous term to the current name "Korea."

■ Two different spellings, Corea and Korea, have been used to spell the name Korea. Corea seems to have come from the word "Kao-li," which appears in West Asian books of the 14th century. Later, in the middle of the 16th century, more frequent usages of 'Core' or 'Corea' are found in European travel journals and navigation maps. 'Korea' was mostly used in English-speaking countries around the end of the 19th century.

Boats and Vessels in the Goryeo Period

Both transportation of collected taxes and International trades were made through the sea route. Records from the 10th century confirm that 300-ton class warships were already made back then. In the 13th century, when the allied forces of Goryeo and Mongol invaded Japan, the vessels are described to have been large enough for even horses to run on the ship. According to records, total of 900 ships of that size were all constructed in merely four months. Goryeo technicians also installed canons on their ships, for the first time in Korea.

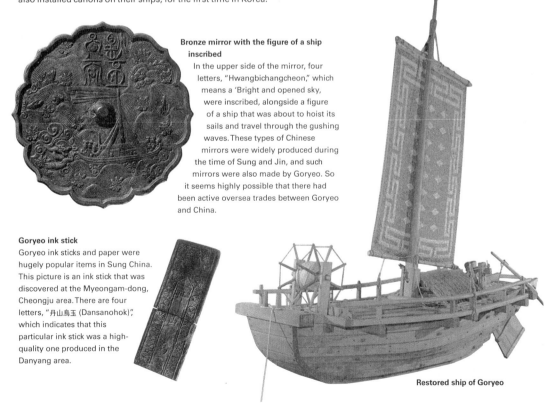

Bronze mirror with the figure of a ship inscribed
In the upper side of the mirror, four letters, "Hwangbichangcheon," which means a 'Bright and opened sky, were inscribed, alongside a figure of a ship that was about to hoist its sails and travel through the gushing waves. These types of Chinese mirrors were widely produced during the time of Sung and Jin, and such mirrors were also made by Goryeo. So it seems highly possible that there had been active oversea trades between Goryeo and China.

Goryeo ink stick
Goryeo ink sticks and paper were hugely popular items in Sung China. This picture is an ink stick that was discovered at the Myeongam-dong, Cheongju area. There are four letters, "丹山烏玉 (Dansanohok)", which indicates that this particular ink stick was a high-quality one produced in the Danyang area.

Restored ship of Goryeo

Goryeo Believed in Buddha and Respected Confucius

The summer is gone, and we are already in the middle of autumn, yet we still thirst for rain. Is it because I have not led the people properly, or is this due to my lack of ability as a king? Did I judge properly, and ordered punishments and awards suitably? When I first began to govern, I opened the prison doors and freed prisoners, avoided staying in a luxurious palace, reduced the number of dishes on my dining table, and prayed to mother nature with all my heart. But still it isn't raining, and the drought is getting worse. Due to my lack of virtue to govern my people, they came to suffer this severe drought. So I would like to express my concern for farming, by opening a public event for the elderly people. – *Goryeosa* (The History of Goryeo)

Stellar observatory near the palace
This is the Goryeo stellar observatory, which was located in the west side of the emperor's palace at Gaeseong. A three-square-meter stone board is placed on the top of the three-meter stone pillars. It is presumed that there was originally a stone handrail placed upon it. Interpreting the Heaven's order correctly and informing the people of it was considered to be an important duty of the king.

This story is from a section inside *Goryeosa*, which recorded an event of 991. Whenever a king moaned over a difficult time, he repented all his mistakes or wrong doings, and then swore reformation in his future admi-nistration. Such stories are from the Chinese classic *Seogyeong*.

This book suggests the principle of Confucian governing, and describes the king as "the subject who received the power to connect Heaven and people by carrying out the principles of Heaven." It also depicts the king to be having responsibility and obligation to use his power for the sake of his own people's happiness. It is also said, "If a king cannot accomplish this duty, Heaven will warn him through various natural disasters." From this story, we can tell that the Goryeo people considered every natural phenomenon as 'incidents' that were caused for a specific reason. Also, this forced the kings to reevaluate their own actions and find out what they were doing wrong or against the principle of Heaven.

Based on *Goryeosa*, we can tell that diverse rituals were performed at the time in order to pray for rain. Buddhist monks led such praying events at temples, while Taoist practitioners prayed for rain through their religious ceremonies called "Jaecho". They also prayed for rain at renowned mountains and rivers.

In Goryeo there was a saying, "At home is Buddha and outside is Confucius." This indicates that though the theoretical foundation of the political administration was based upon Confucianism, the people were in no way reluctant to worship Buddhism. There was also another saying which dictated that in order to rule the dynasty in balance, the three ideologies, Confucianism, Buddhism and Taoism, should be in place like a pot with three legs. The Goryeo people believed practicing Confucianism would be beneficial for the country with all its Chinese cultural aspects, yet they also respected their own traditions. They indeed had an open attitude toward alternative ideas.

Mireukhasaenggyeong Byeonsangdo (above)
A king and officials worshipping a stone statue of Maitreya can be seen in the picture. 14th century, 176.0×91.0cm.

The Picture of Constellation on the ceiling of the Gongminwangreung mausoleum (below)
In the time of Goryeo, ritual ceremonies that worshipped Heaven and constellations were common practices. Such ceremonies were called "Jaecho." The Dipper was especially the most representative object to be worshipped.

◀ **Village shrine**
Goryeo was a society of multiple religions. Not only did Confucianism, Buddhism and Taoism co-exist, but also folk beliefs had its prevalence. In every village and community there was a guarding god, and accordingly there was a worshipping shrine ("Seonghwang") as well. In the Goryeo society, people also relied upon the superstitious power of the female shamans, and they also believed that famous mountains and rivers had a spiritual power. The picture shows a village shrine, an indicator of prevailing superstitious beliefs.

1135 ~ 1380

1145
Kim Bu-shik completed writing *Samguksagi* which is the oldest book of Korean history remaining today. This book is essential in studying the ancient history of Korea.

1170
Military generals eliminated many civilian officers and took power. Since then, military despotism continued for over a hundred years.

1206
Genghis Khan united the Mongols.

1231
Mongol invaded Goryeo. Goryeo suffered total of six Mongol invasions ever since.

1270
Goryeo made a treaty agreement with Mongol and began to suffer foreign intervention for over 80 years.

1279
The Chinese South Sung Dynasty was demolished.

1285
Il-yeon authored *Samgukyusa*. He introduced various religions and cultures of Three Kingdoms, and especially the history of Gojoseon in this book.

1308
The national university changed its name to Seonggyungwan, and Confucian education was enhanced. Around this time Neo-Confucianism ("Seongrihak") has been widely introduced.

1337
In Europe, the Hundred Years War began(~1453).

1351
King Gongminwang ascended the throne. He successfully carried out a movement to regain Goryeo's independence confronting the Yuan Dynasty.

1377
Jikji was printed with movable metal printing types of Goryeo.

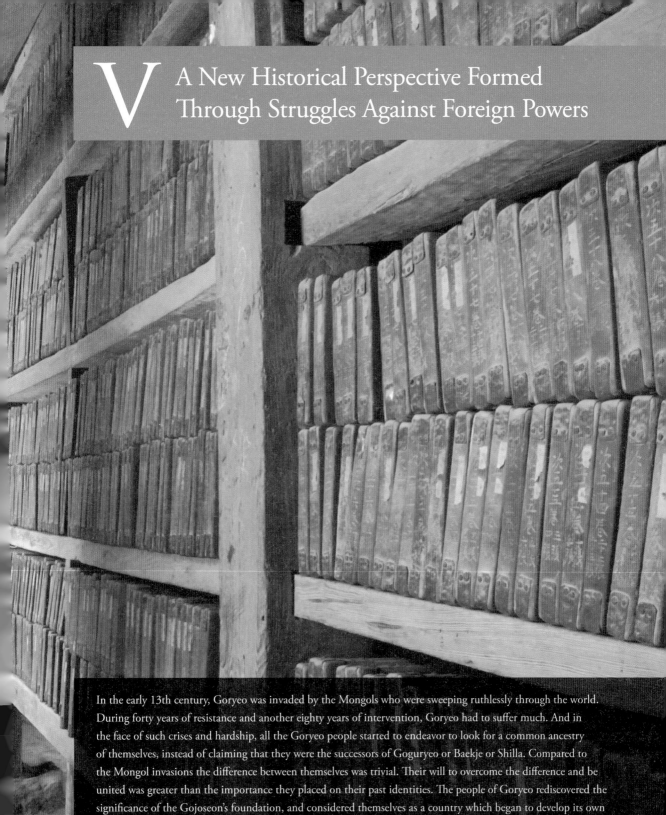

V A New Historical Perspective Formed Through Struggles Against Foreign Powers

In the early 13th century, Goryeo was invaded by the Mongols who were sweeping ruthlessly through the world. During forty years of resistance and another eighty years of intervention, Goryeo had to suffer much. And in the face of such crises and hardship, all the Goryeo people started to endeavor to look for a common ancestry of themselves, instead of claiming that they were the successors of Goguryeo or Baekje or Shilla. Compared to the Mongol invasions the difference between themselves was trivial. Their will to overcome the difference and be united was greater than the importance they placed on their past identities. The people of Goryeo rediscovered the significance of the Gojoseon's foundation, and considered themselves as a country which began to develop its own culture as early as China and its culture.

The Gyeongpango storage facility where the "Tripitaka Koreana" is preserved While struggling against the Mongol, the Goryeo people created woodblocks to print the Buddhist scriptures so that they could overcome their own difficulties with the help and power of Buddha. The picture is the Gyeongpango storage facility at Gyeongsangnam-do province's Hapcheon Haeinsa (temple), which was designed to preserve the woodblocks from being deformed for over 800 years.

Cultural Exchanges Between Goryeo and the Mongol Empire

Genghis Khan established the Mongol Empire after unifying various nomadic tribes in 1206. His troops, the Mongol invasion force, literally swept through Eurasia. Goryeo as well had to suffer such invasions for about 40 years, and continued to resist it desperately. The Eurasian continent became one under the Mongolian order, and Goryeo became part of such order while retaining a level of independence.

The residents of the Eurasian continent shared such order through exchanges. The capital of the Yuan Empire became the main hub of international activities which connected many cities throughout the world. In this capital, a variety of cultures came in contact and blended with each other, while diverse people of different faces and backgrounds closely associated with each other. The Goryeo people corroborated this trend as well while maintaining its own culture, and accordingly, Yuan's tradition also spread over to Goryeo.

"Mongolpung (Mongol Style)" and "Goryeoyang (Goryeo Fashions)"

Various foreign cultures were introduced to Goryeo through the country's active exchanges with Yuan. Mongolian clothes and Mongolian hair-style featuring the so-called "Mongolpung" were in fashion, and new words that came from the Mongolian language appeared in Korean vocabulary too. A new genre of art appeared as well when religious traditions of Mongol were introduced to the Goryeo society. And in the meantime, exchanges between the two countries showed not one but two directions. As we can see from the word "Goryeoyang," cultural aspects that displayed 'styles' of Goryeo prevailed in Beijing as well.

Jokduri and Yeonji
Jokduri, a crown-like headpiece that Korean brides used to wear in wedding ceremonies, actually originated from the outdoor hats used by Mongolian women. The custom of Yeonji, a red dot make-up put upon the bride's cheeks, also originated from Mongolian customs.

Black Sea

Caspian Sea

Aral Sea

Indus

Arabian Sea

YL

Cotton

Mun Ik-jeom, who was dispatched to Yuan as an official emissary, brought back some seeds of cotton to Goryeo upon his return. After succeeding in cultivating cotton, he happened to meet a monk from Mongolia and was able to learn from him how to make threads and how to weave cloth. Cotton textiles which came to be widely produced in Joseon were one of the most favorite merchandises that the Japanese were eager to purchase.

Sojugori (Soju Distiller)

Soju, the Koreans' most favorite liquor, came from Yuan. Soju was produced by a method of distilling that the Mongol people learned from West Asian habitants during their invasion of West Asia. Then it was introduced to Koreans while the Mongol troops were stationed inside Goryeo.

The Gyeongcheonsa (temple) Pagoda

It is a ten-tier stone pagoda built in 1348. At the time, there were active Buddhist exchanges between Goryeo and Yuan. Due to such influences, the pagoda shows distinctive features which set itself apart from other more traditional pagodas. Its height is 13.5m.

● Kharakorum

JAPAN

● Gaegyeong
GORYEO

Yellow

Yangzi

East China Sea

Himalayas

South China Sea

1

"Liberate the Slaves of Samhan!"

The sad story of Jungmijeong

> Jungmijeong was a gorgeous pavilion of the Goryeo Dynasty. …When it was under construction, people who were constructing it had to bring their own lunch to work. However, there was a man who was too poor to bring his own lunch, so others shared their lunch with him. One day his wife came to see him and said, "Please share this food with the other workers." Perplexed, the husband asked, "How did you get this? Did you have an affair with another man? Or did you steal it?" When her angry husband demanded an answer, the poor wife answered, "Who would want such an ugly woman like me? And do I have a nerve to steal something from others? I sold my long hair to buy this." She unveiled her hair to show her husband. He couldn't eat the meal, for his throat was choking with sorrow. His colleagues were also moved to tears, at the couple's tragic poverty. *— Goryeosajeolyo*

Peasants were obligated to pay one tenth of their harvest as a tax, and their special local products as well. They were also required to provide free labor for construction projects of the government. Agricultural productivity was so low at the time that the peasants had to suffer a meager living. When a lean year came, their entire lives were threatened.

However, the life of slaves, who were at the bottom of the food chain and social hierarchy, was even

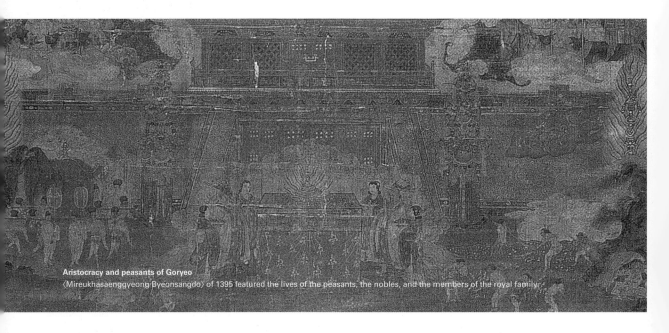

Aristocracy and peasants of Goryeo
〈Mireukhasaenggyeong Byeonsangdo〉 of 1395 featured the lives of the peasants, the nobles, and the members of the royal family.

more terrible than that of the peasants. While some of them inherited their slave status, others voluntarily became slaves to feed themselves and escape starvation. They were all poorly treated as a human being. The poor were always required to pay sacrifice for the comfortable lives of the kings and vassals.

Trembling aristocracy

In the 11th century, the society of Goryeo was stabilized, and peaceful time continued. And in that process, a few powerful families gradually monopolized power and wealth.

While the nobles residing in the capital enjoyed luxurious lives, the window of opportunities for the local officials to be promoted to an official position in the central government became narrower. While the positions and status of the literary officers became more and more stabilized, the importance of the role and functions of the military officers were neglected and disdained. Accordingly, the monopoly of power by a small number of civil officers resulted in an increase in corruption and exploitations of the people.

In 1135, influential characters of Seogyeong, the second largest city of the country (Today's Pyeongyang) staged an insurrection demanding a political reform and the moving of the capital to Seogyeong. Under the slogan of overthrowing the central power, a number of people participated in the revolt, and this resistance prevailed in the northwest area of Goryeo for over an entire year.

Royal family
High-ranking officials

Middle Class
Low-ranking officials, Seori and Hyangri clerks, Namban figures, low-ranking army officers

Yangin
Baekjeong figures, peasants, merchants and hand-manufacturers (residents of Hyang, So, and Bugok)

The lowest class
Slaves, Hwacheok, Jincheok, Jaein figures

The Goryeo Dynasty class system
In Goryeo, switching one's social class was a little more lenient, even though the nobles maintained their privileges by holding official positions in the government. The class system of Goryeo was more 'open' than that of Shilla. However, there were many people who were regarded as personal properties of other individuals or the government.

Statues of literary and military officers at the Gongminwangreung mausoleum
There were two types of high-ranking officers in Goryeo and Joseon dynasties. Literary officers who studied Confucian scriptures, history, literature were responsible for legislating and implementing laws. On the other hand, military officers were in charge of commanding the army. In Goryeo and Joseon societies, where Confucian ethics were emphasized in politics, literary officers were always at the center of power, and it was almost impossible for the military officers to rise to the highest echelon of the government.

In 1170 a military uprising by those who suffered from discrimination challenged the existing social order. Military officers killed many literary officers, seized power, and dethroned the king. Many low-ranking officers and soldiers also participated in revolting against those in power, as they as well had been exploited by the state.

100 years of the military regime

After the revolt of the military, the Goryeo society was in chaos, and the leaders of the military fought among themselves for power. Revolts against the military broke out in many areas as well.

Although a military ruling system was established, neither "decentralization" nor 'feudalism' that appeared in the Middle Ages of Europe was formed in Goryeo. Goryeo maintained a central government with the king at its center. And ongoing wars with foreign countries hindered such development of feudalism.

The military officers maintained power by training their private army and holding exclusive authority over official appointments. However, the royal Wang lineage prevailed, and the overall institutions of governance (including the class system) remained unchanged.

As power became important virtues, the road to opportunities of elevating one's social position was widely open, especially for those who were not born into noble families. Transfers between classes were more active than any other time periods. Even a soldier who had risen to an official position from a slave class could succeed in becoming the most powerful man in the government.

Popular uprisings for reform

In the 12th century, repetitive power struggles resulted in the weakening of the central political authority. The people who had long suffered unfairness and discrimination finally protested to change the world and reform the society, being encouraged with the social atmosphere that encouraged active shifts in class.

After the 1170s, numerous revolts occurred all over the Goryeo society. Some rebels executed the local officers in protest of exploitations and heavy taxation. Others raided into the central government in an accusation of resorting to discriminating practices. Especially the slaves who suffered most at the bottom of the social hierarchical order were determined to die with

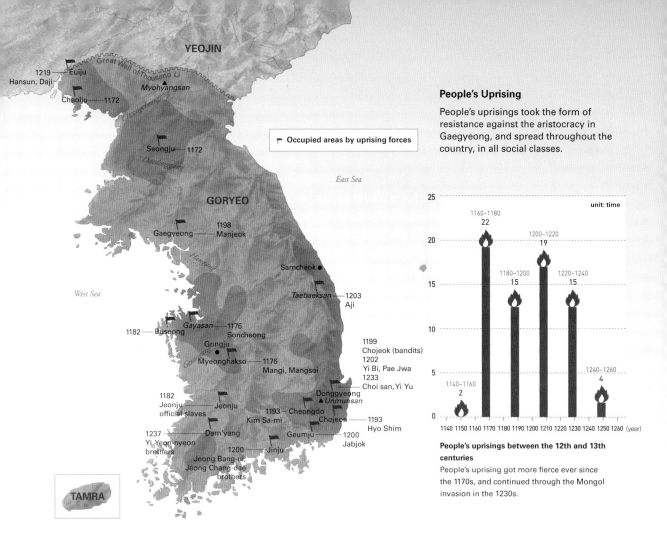

1219
Hansun, Daji — Euiju

Great Wall of Thousand Li

Myohyangsan

Cheolju — 1172

Seongju — 1172

Occupied areas by uprising forces

East Sea

GORYEO

1198
Gaegyeong — Manjeok

Samcheok ●

Taebaeksan — 1203
Aji

West Sea

Gayasan — 1176
1182 — Buseong
Soncheong
Gongju ●
Myeonghakso — 1176
Mangi, Mangsoi

1199
Chojeok (bandits)
1202
Yi Bi, Pae Jwa
1233
Choi san, Yi Yu

Donggyeong
▲ *Unmunsan*
1182
Jeonju — Jeonju
official slaves
1193 — Cheongdo
Kim Sa-mi
Chojeon — 1193
Hyo Shim
1237 — Dam'yang
Yi Yeon-nyeon
brothers
Geumju
1200 — Jinju
1200
Jabjok
Jeong Bang-ui,
Jeong Chang-dae
brothers

TAMRA

People's Uprising

People's uprisings took the form of resistance against the aristocracy in Gaegyeong, and spread throughout the country, in all social classes.

25

unit: time

1160~1180
22

1200~1220
19
20

1180~1200   1220~1240
15   15
15

1199

10

5

1140~1160   1240~1260
2   4
0

1140 1150 1160 1170 1180 1190 1200 1210 1220 1230 1240 1250 1260 (year)

People's uprisings between the 12th and 13th centuries
People's uprising got more fierce ever since the 1170s, and continued through the Mongol invasion in the 1230s.

honor rather than surrender in disgrace; "Are these emperors and aristocrats as well as generals and ministers born into power because their blood is different from that of the common people? ... Let us get rid of this unfair social hierarchy in the Korean Peninsula!" Manjeok screamed, as he ruthlessly attacked the capital Gaegyeong.

At the center of the old territories of Shilla and Baekje, "Restoration" movements emerged. Those who were involved in this movement refused to acknowledge the legitimacy in Goryeo's foundation. The exclusive political system that was only favoring the aristocracy residing in the capital, resulted in this defiance.

The people's rebellion ended in failure. But their attacks against those in power contributed to a certain level to narrowing the social gap between classes and reducing the exploitations and taxation.

2

Development of a New Historical Perspective

Samguksagi and Samgukyusa

Current studies of ancient Korean history greatly depend on two important historical records. *Samguk-sagi* compiled by Kim Bu-shik in the middle of the 12th century, and *Samgukyusa* authored by Il-yeon in the end of the 13th century.

These two history books dealt with stories of the three kingdoms, Goguryeo, Baekje, and Shilla. However, the focuses of these books are quite different from each other; the former was written with the belief that historical studies should contribute to accomplishing Confucian virtues, while the latter more emphasized Buddhism and 'miscellaneous' traditions. Also, while the former placed more value on depicting the history of the three kingdoms, the latter described the history of Balhae with details, and also the legend of Gojoseon's foundation.

What would have been the reason for all these different focuses? The Goryeo people must have become desperate to find their own origin and identities, and expanded their quest to not only the area of historical facts but also to the realms of myths.

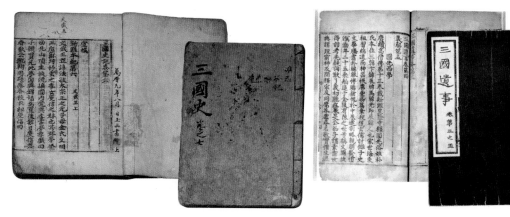

Samguksagi (left) and Samgukyusa (right)
Samguksagi was written by a renowned Confucian scholar. It is the most representative history book in Korea ever written by one, and it was an authentic history book that adopted the format of the Chinese ones. On the other hand, *Samgukyusa* was written in a more liberal form and style, and it intended to 'supplement' and 'complement' the contents of the previous 'orthodox' history books. The former rests more on factual accounts, while the latter shows a tendency of highlighting certain mystical portions of the history.

The Mongolian invasions

Goryeo suffered the terrible Mongolian invasion for about half a century before Il-yeon authored *Samgukyusa*. Although the people of Goryeo resisted the Mongolian advances at various fortresses located along Goryeo's northern border, the Mongol troops circumvented it and demanded surrender by besieging the capital. The military regime surrendered to the powerful Mongolian cavalry.

The war seemed to have ended. However, the Mongols' unreasonable terms agitated the Goryeo people, so they finally moved the capital to Ganghwado (Is.), determined to continue fighting against the Mongols. So the Mongols invaded Goryeo again. Many Goryeo people were brutally killed, plundered, and were also relocated to the Mongol territory and forced to become slaves.

People had to fight for their own lives. They never hesitated to fight in such desperate situations when death was certain. Although in many cases civilians and soldiers were entirely massacred, there were other battles as well where people accomplished legendary triumphs.

The Mongol invasion of East Asia

In the early 13th century, after the Mongols united their tribes, they established a grand empire that extended from the prairies of their home territory to the farming lands of many regions. Jin (Jurchen) Dynasty and Chinese Sung Dynasty were invaded, and so were Goryeo and Japan.

1206
Unification of the Mongols

1219~1225
Mongol expeditions to West Asia and Central Asia

1231
Mongol's first invasion of Goryeo

1236
The Mongols demolished the united European army at Poland

1259
Goryeo and the Mongols signed a peace treaty

1274
The first Mongol invasion of Japan

1281
The second Mongol invasion of Japan

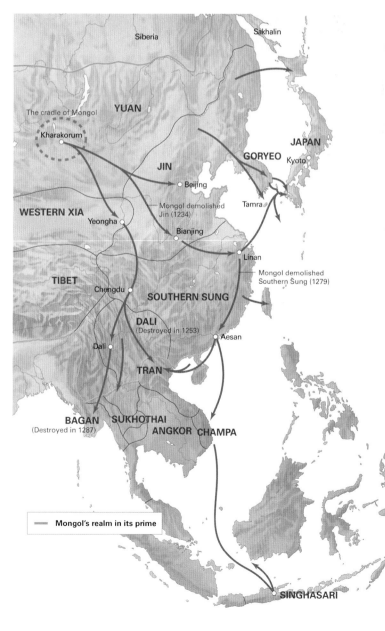

Mongol's realm in its prime

Especially in the battles of Cheoinseong and Chungjuseong, the lowborn people who had been discriminated against for a long time, crushed the Mongol troops and forced them to withdraw.

Continuing torment

In 1259, Goryeo and the Mongols agreed to a ceasefire. The new "Yuan" Emperor Qubilai Khan promised Goryeo that he would respect its independence. With the assistance of the Mongols, the Goryeo royal family returned to Gaegyeong.

However, not all the Goryeo people agreed on the treaty. Especially the military which had been in power for the last hundred years strongly protested. So, the newly organized Goryeo army, allied with the Yuan military troops, had to suppress them.

And then, the Goryeo society entered a new and more difficult period. Yuan requested Goryeo's assistance in their preparation of the Japanese campaign, and many Goryeo people were mobilized into unendurable working conditions. Yuan also took control of a large region inside Goryeo and ordered a variety of tributes to be annually submitted. They even demanded young girls to be delivered as gifts known as 'Gongnyeo.'

Yuan's promise of guaranteeing the independence of Goryeo was often breached and violated. Many attempts were made to assimilate Goryeo into Yuan's territory, and many of the kings were put in the throne, then forced to descend from it, in a repetitive fashion, at the will and mercy of the Yuan government.

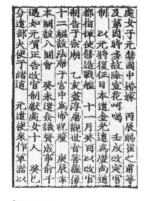

Gongnyeo
Mongol's requests for Gongnyeo females that continued for decades ultimately changed the marriage custom of Goryeo. To avoid being drafted as a Gongnyeo figure, formed in the ending days of the Goryeo Dynasty was a custom of 'early marriage,' in which young girls aged only 13 or 14 would be married to boys aged merely 9 or 10. This picture shows references to Gongnyeo figures from inside *Goryeosa* (The History of Goryeo).

Monggoseubraehwoesa
Goryeo was forced to mobilize its army and assist Yuan's invasion of Japan. In 1274 and 1281, allied forces of Goryeo and Yuan army attacked the Kyushu area of Japan. However, due to a sudden storm that developed on the sea, they had to return to Goryeo, and the allied forces lost a majority of their soldiers in the process. This Japanese picture depicts a battle in which Japanese soldiers are fighting the Mongol troops.

Such hardship and suffering certainly had its toll upon the Goryeo people. They came to form a different perspective on their identity and history.

The aftermath of the Mongol war

Gojoseon and its founder "Dangun" were never fully recognized in Kim Bu-shik's *Samguksagi*. At the time, most of the people still identified themselves as the descendants of the three kingdoms, Shilla, Baekje, and Goguryeo respectively. The "Restoration" movement to reconstruct Shilla and Baekje persisted, while the royal family of Goryeo claimed themselves as the successors of Goguryeo. However, in the process of confronting Yuan invasions, the people of Goryeo came to drop their ideas of bearing distinctive historical lineages, realizing that such difference was a trivial one in the presence of the Mongols' invasion. They also realized that only by overcoming those differences they would be able to withstand the Mongols' attacks.

Samgukyusa from the 1280s acknowledged Dangun's foundation of Gojoseon as the beginning of their own history, and presented a new perspective which considered all the descendants of the three kingdoms as the offspring of Gojoseon.

Finally, 600 years after Shilla's unification of the Korean Peninsula, all the people residing in it came to identify themselves as members of a homogenous race. Apparently, the name "Joseon," the dynasty which succeeded Goryeo was not chosen by accident.

Yi Je-hyeon and Mun Ik-jeom

In Daedo, the capital of Yuan (today's Beijing), a variety of languages were used. At the time, the Korean Peninsula's relationship with China was more than amicable. A number of Goryeo people resided in the capital, and many Mongol people established permanent settlements inside Goryeo as well.

Yi Je-hyeon visited a number of places in Yuan while spending many years at the Daedo capital. Although he experienced the mainstream of Yuan's culture, he also tried to maintain the identity of Goryeo, which had a language and culture distinctly different from those of Yuan. Through active interactions he introduced Neo-Confucianism developed by Southern Sung scholars to Goryeo. Many Goryeo officials who served the government in its ending days learned from Yi's lectures.

Mun Ik-jeom was a secretary who accompanied the Goryeo envoy dispatched to Yuan. Having been wrongly accused, he was exiled to the border of Yuan. When he was released from exile, he secretly brought several cotton seeds on his way back home. He succeeded in cultivating cotton despite of many difficulties, and he contributed to the devising of a cotton thread and the building of a spinning wheel with the help of a Mongol monk. His efforts enabled a huge leap of improvement in the Korean people's clothes.

Yi Je-hyeon (1287~1367)

Mun Ik-jeom (1329~1398)

Jikji, and the Museum of Archaic Printing

Before printing techniques were ever invented, people had to copy books with their own hands. However, the innovation of printing skills removed such inconveniences.

In the early days, woodblock printing skills were used. First they inscribed one or two pages of contents, or even contents from an entire scroll, and then used those woodblocks to produce multiple copies. Although they were very helpful, it was not easy to carve all the letters on the block. In cases of producing only 20 to 30 copies, handwriting was more effective and efficient.

Printing skills were dramatically advanced, thanks to the invention of the movable metal type printing. People used them in publishing books by assembling them and then arranging them, according to the content of the books. It was always convenient to print book with movable metal types, regardless of the number of copies printed.

Koreans used woodblocks in the middle of the 8th century, and the first book printed with a movable metal type in Korea came out in the 13th century. The Korean Buddhist scripture *Jikji* is the oldest work remaining today printed with movable metal types in 1377. As a collection of Buddhist scriptures and teachings, it was printed at Heungdeoksa (temple) in Cheongju, where now the Museum of Archaic Printing is offering exhibitions of the ancient times' printing process.

Goryeo's metal types of Chinese letters, "顚 (Jeon)"(left) and "復 (Bok)"(right)

Jikji Printing blocks (woodblocks), and a photographed edition
Jikji was published by a monk named Baegun (1298~1374) in 1372, and it is currently in custody of the National Library of France.

The Tripitaka woodblock [Tripitaka Koreana at the Haeinsa (Temple)]
Tripitaka Koreana is a collection of Buddhist books that organized and categorized Buddhist scriptures in order. This collection of Buddhist books included not only the Buddhist scriptures in Goryeo but also those in China and Japan. This accomplishment was made possible due to the advancement of research methods and also a spectacular printing technology. Two pages of contents were carved upon a single piece of woodblock. Total of 81,258 pieces of woodblock were created for this Tripitaka, and they contain approximately 52,000,000 individual letters. Goryeo people's religious passion to repel the Mongol troops with the power of Buddha contributed to the production of this Tripitaka. It has already been designated as a World Heritage, along with the storage facility where it has been preserved.

The Process of Printing with Movable Metal Types

Woodblock printing was of course an extremely convenient way to print books. However, when only a limited number of copies were needed, printing by metal movable types proved to be more efficient. They were used by temples or the government engaged in printing projects. Unfortunately, the employment of this technique was not able to spark wide distribution of knowledge throughout the general population.

❶ Selecting the letter [character] model
❷ Pasting the model on a wooden block
❸ Carving letters
❹ Making a brass frame

❺ Pouring boiled iron
❻ Completed metal types
❼ Typesetting [composition, arrangement]
❽ Printing

3

Rise of the Reformers Dreaming of a New World

King Gongminwang raises the flag against Yuan

In 1351, the emperor of Yuan decided to bestow the throne of Goryeo to King Gongminwang. Having resided in Yuan for 10 years, King Gongminwang returned to Goryeo with his wife, a princess of Yuan.

Four years later, a delegate came from his father-in-law's country. Yuan requested him to send Goryeo's army to repress numerous revolts in Yuan, placing King Gongminwang in a dilemma. He did not want to send his army, but he was concerned about Yuan's probable response as well. And during his 10 years of residence in Yuan, he clearly witnessed that civil frustration and resistance against the Yuan government was getting stronger.

Nevertheless, he was not able to turn down Yuan's demands. Such demands only made it clear for King Gongminwang that the Yuan government's power was indeed waning. In the following year, he began to lead a resistance movement against Yuan. He abolished Yuan's liaison offices which were built to intervene in domestic political affairs of Goryeo. He also attacked the Yuan army bases located at the north to recover the northeastern area where Yuan used to rule directly for 100 years. Then he also banned the customs of Mongol from being used in Goryeo.

Cheonsan Daeryeobdo
It is believed that King Gongminwang drew this picture of hunting himself. It signifies Goryeo's close relationship with the Mongol empire and shows the hunting characters' hair style as well, which featured the Mongolian, braided hair style that was in fashion at the time.

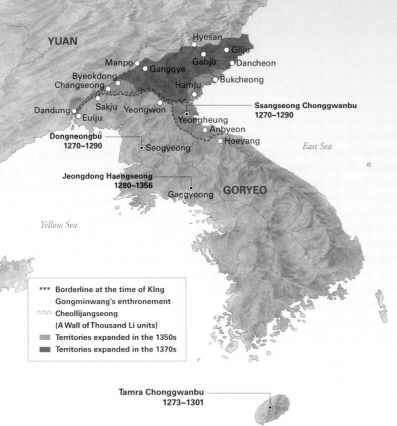

YUAN

Hyesan
Gilju
Manpo Gabju Dancheon
Ganggye
Byeokdong Bukcheong
Changseong Hamju
Dandung Sakju Yeongwon **Ssangseong Chonggwanbu**
Euiju **1270~1290**
Yeongheung
Dongneongbu Anbyeon
1270~1290 Hoeyang *East Sea*
Seogyeong

Jeongdong Haengseong
1280~1356
Gaegyeong **GORYEO**

Yellow Sea

```
•••  Borderline at the time of KIng
     Gongminwang's enthronement
∿∿  Cheollijangseong
     (A Wall of Thousand Li units)
▓▓  Territories expanded in the 1350s
██  Territories expanded in the 1370s
```

Tamra Chonggwanbu
1273~1301

King Gongminwang's recovery of Goryeo's old territories

Although the Mongols approved Goryeo's maintaining of its independence, they still intervened in internal affairs of Goryeo by establishing the Jeongdong Haengseong provincial government, and they also took direct control of some areas inside Goryeo territory. Dongnyeongbu in Seogyeong, Ssangseong Chonggwanbu headquarters at Yeongheung, and the Tamra Chonggwanbu headquarters at Jeju-do (Is.), were all associated with such intentions and ruling. Dongnyeongbu and Tamra Chonggwanbu were dismantled not before long, and the regions were returned to Goryeo, but it took one hundred years until Ssangseong Chonggwanbu was returned to Goryeo, as a result of King Gongminwang's preemptive strike. It was also this time when the family of Yi Seong-gye, who later became the founding king of Joseon, began to earn a countrywide reputation, for his cooperation with the efforts of the Goryeo government.

Yuan angrily opposed these actions and dispatched an army to replace the king. However, King Gongminwang eliminated powerful nobles who were in alliance with Yuan and triumphed against the invaders. Finally, he terminated Yuan's interventions in the internal affairs of Goryeo, which had lasted for over 80 years.

Trembling reforms; continuous invasions from the Red Turban rebels and Japanese marauders

Having succeeded in pushing Yuan back to the north, King Gongmin-wang was determined to reform the economic and social systems of Goryeo. For the last 80 years, under the pressure of Yuan, the society of Goryeo had become severely corrupted. Only those who were favored by Yuan were able to hold power and privileges. Many nobles and officials showed little concern about the lives of their own people, and instead concentrated their energies on keeping Yuan content. Gradually, more and more land was seized by the powerful, and the peasants who lost their source of income

JURCHEN

Euiju
Gwiju
Seonju
Anju
Hwaju
Gangdong
Deungju
Seogyeong (Pyeongyang)
Tongju

Cheollijangseong

Dancheon

Hamheung

GORYEO

Gaegyeong
Ganghwa
Namgyeong (Seoul)

Hangang

East Sea

Yellow Sea

Uljin

Geumgang
Hongsan
**1376
Choi Yeong defeated
Japanese marauders**
Hansan

Nakdonggang

Hwangsan
**1380
Yi Seong-gye exterminated
Japanese marauders**

Youngsangang

Naju
Jangheung
Goseong

Tsushima Island

Invasion of the Japanese marauders

The plundering of the Wae marauders began in the 1350s, and between the 1370s and 80s it pushed Goryeo into a serious crisis. Their bases were located either at the Tsushima Island or in the west coast of Japan. Invasions took various forms, with either a fleet of 500 ships or more than 1,500 cavalries.

➡ Invasion routes of the Red Turban rebels
➡ Invasion routes of the Japanese marauders

Daejanggunpo (a cannon)
This cannon used gun powder, and was necessary to stop the Japanese marauders on sea. This particular cannon was developed by Choi Mu-seon (1325~1395).

fell into slavery. As a result, the number of tax payers, as well as the available number of soldiers, was drastically reduced. People's lives became as barren as the land they toiled, while the national treasury was draining empty.

King Gongminwang targetted the nobles who owned vast lands and an army of slaves, forcing them to return their land to its original owners and to liberate those who were unjustifiably enslaved. At the front line of these reforms was a monk named Shin Don. As the land and slave survey was activated by the officers of Jeonminbyeonjeongdogam, a number of people praised him saying "A sage was born," and dreamt of the emergence of a new world. Yet, the resistance of the conservative base was still greater than the power of the reformers.

Continuous foreign invasions were also a hindrance to the reforms. Hundreds of thousands of Red Turban bandits from China raided the territory of Goryeo twice and plundered everything in sight, while the Wae (Japanese) pirates waged their attacks along the south coast of Goryeo to a serious degree. Numerous acts of pillaging deteriorated the coastal regions to rubble. As the sea route transportation of items collected as tax became difficult, the government's finance had to suffer serious shortage.

Those dreaming of reforms

Unfortunately, in the end King Gongminwang was assassinated. After his death, reforms of the Goryeo society were discouraged to the point that dismantling of farm lands and renovation of the slave class no longer showed any progress. Meanwhile, the Chinese Han race established the Ming Dynasty and unified China driving out Yuan to the Mongolian Plateau. However, there were still some conservatives who argued that Goryeo needed to enforce its political relationship with Yuan as before. Moreover, Wae's raids increased to the extent of being a threat to the entire country.

Suweol Gwaneumdo
This paint depicting the Buddhist Goddess of Mercy, is a symbol of splendid and delicate style of the noble society of Goryeo. It was drawn in 1310. 419.5×254.2cm.

The new bureaucratic class, the literati class who had implemented active reforms during the reign of King Gongminwang, once again tried to reform the Goryeo society.

Most of the literati figures were small and medium size land owners, and they suggested reconstruction of the society based on Neo-Confucianism, while criticizing the corruption of the temples and the principles of Buddhism. The literati stood at the forefront of reforming the government, asserting that politics should serve the people instead of being used to satisfy the greed of powerful families.

However, the power of nobles was so strong that several attempts failed to accomplish meaningful reforms. Each and every time, the leaders of these reforms had to undergo severe hardships.

The Meaning of Buddhism to Koreans

On April 8th of the lunar calendar, Buddhist temples in Korea are crowded with many worshippers celebrating the birthday of Sakyamuni. They wish for a brighter world by lighting a number of Lotus lamps, commemorating the day on which Buddha was enlightened.

Buddha awakened the people, as the Lotus lamps brighten the darkness. Believers wish to obtain wisdom which would direct their minds toward a righteous path. Just like beautiful lotus flowers which bloom from a pond filled with filthy water, the people long to come out vibrant in this world.

In the capital Gaegyeong, there were more than three hundred Buddhist temples. Every year, people in Gaegyeong crafted a number of Lotus lamps and walked around the pagoda, praying for hope and wisdom that would bring enlightenment to their lives. The ceremonious "Yeondeunghoe" occasion, the festival of lotus-shaped lanterns, began in the 6th century, and continues even today. It was considered one of the most important holiday celebrations by the people of Goryeo. The custom of lighting lanterns

Songgwangsa
Jinul (1158~1210), the most renowned Buddhist monk who lived in the latter half period of Goryeo, founded the Jogyejong school at this temple. Now Jogyejong is regarded as the representative Buddhist denomination in Korea. Sixteen Guksa masters who served as teachers to the king were trained here. This formidable temple of Goryeo has a number of designated national treasures.

❶ Roof-tile carved with wishes A new temple is usually constructed with tiles, on which letters wishing for good health and accomplishments are written or inscribed.
❷ Buddha's Birthday It is the most meaningful and joyful day for Buddhists. This day is designated as a national holiday, on which public offices and civilian facilities are closed.
❸ Yeondeung Procession Before and after the Buddha's birthday, a variety of ceremonies are held: every temple hangs Yeondeung lamps (Lotus-shaped paper lamps), and a group of citizens and Buddhists participate in parades with those lamps.
❹ Tabdori Pagoda is considered as a home where Buddha stayed after his death. People make wishes and memorize his teachings, while circling around a pagoda.

originally came from the Indians who used them as lights for their gods.

Today about 53% of Koreans are religious and 26% of them are Buddhists. Roman Catholics and Protestants combined, the percentage of Christians are about the same as Buddhists.

However, Buddhism has been more meaningful and influential to the Koreans than accredited. About 60% of the nationally acknowledged cultural heritages are Buddhist artifacts. The influence of Buddhism on the mind and culture of Koreans is magnificent.

1380 ~ 1474

1392
Yi Seong-gye, who was a military general defending the frontier, ascended the throne and changed the name of the country from Goryeo to Joseon.

1394
The new dynasty decided Hanyang (today's Seoul) as its new capital, and constructed a city designed to uphold Confucian ideology in philosophical terms.

1404
Japanese shogun Yoshimitsu, serving in the capacity of a king, sent an envoy to Joseon. After this occasion, a diplomatic relationship between governments was established.

1405~1433
A large fleet of Ming forces led by Zheng He successfully navigated seven times to the South China Sea and the Indian Ocean.

1434~1450
In the area south of Dumangang (R.), six military outposts ('Jin' units) were constructed. It was approximately this time when the border line of today's Korea was determined.

1444
With previous examinations of heavenly bodies' movements, and after having studied the calendars of China and the Islamic world, the Joseon government published the first calendar of its own, that reflected the reality and environment of Joseon.

1446
Hangeul was announced as the official letters of Joseon. It provided the Korean people with opportunities to overcome certain handicaps that were generated from the difference between the Joseon and Chinese languages.

1453
The Ottoman Empire occupied Constantinople.

1474
Continuous efforts to establish a comprehensive law code of the country finally bore fruit by the completion of *Gyeongguk daejeon*. Joseon was finally equipped with a legal framework necessary for a law-governed Confucian country.

VI Rise of a New Dynasty, Joseon: The Beginning of New Traditions

Yi Seong-gye, who was a general guarding the frontier, and Jeong Do-jeon, who was a mere low-ranking officer that came from a local province, served at the center of the efforts to establish a new dynasty. The new regime seized political power, and formed a philosophy which considered people as its foundation, and they pledged that politics should be designed for the benefit of the people. The new capital Hanyang was constructed to bring the Confucian ideology to the real world. Today's border line of Korea composed of the Dumangang and Amnokgang lines was formed around this period. An identity as a people who had shared the same history and political fate was developed, and the people came to distinguish themselves from other countries based upon such developments. Independent calendars and the Koreans' own letter system were created as well.

The Geunjeongjeon hall at Gyeongbokgung (palace) This is the place where coronations of kings or other dynastic ceremonies were held or conducted.

Korean's First Calendar, Chiljeongsan

The Gregorian calendar that is used worldwide today was first developed by Pope Gregory XIII in 1582, and Korea has been using it since 1896.

Yet long ago, Koreans used a calendar borrowed from China. Such calendar was not able to precisely forecast the movements of heavenly bodies such as solar or lunar eclipses because the latitude and longitude of Korea are different from those of China.

So, *Chiljeongsan* was published in 1442 (the 25th year of King Sejong's reign). By calculating the "Chiljeong" figures (Sun, Moon, Mercury, Venus, Mars, Jupiter, and Saturn), this calendric book was able to forecast solar or lunar eclipses and the changes of weather as well. We can see that the Koreans were finally able to invent their own calendar.

Before this, only China and the Islamic world were able to invent a complex calendric system like those of today. Yet with the understanding of both Chinese and Islamic calendars, and the results from long observations of heavenly bodies, the Koreans were able to create *Chiljeongsan* on their own. Various observation facilities established in the 15th century are also the pride of all Korean people.

Ilseongjeongshieui
This instrument was invented in 1437 to measure time, based upon observations of the Sun in the daytime and stars at night.

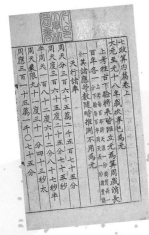

Chiljeongsan
While the Chinese calendar was based upon movements of heavenly bodies observed from the perspective of China (Beijing), *Chiljeongsan* was based upon the latitude of Hanyang, the capital of the Joseon Dynasty.

Cheonsangyeolchabunya Jido

This is a star map carved in stone. It was made during King Taejo's reign. It is 122.8cm in width and 200.9cm in height. It shows the picture of a constellation in the upper section. The people's perspective on the cosmos at the time, the origin of the celestial map, and the list of officers who contributed to the creation of this map, are recorded at the bottom section of the map.

Angbuilgu

It was a concave sundial that was invented in 1434, and it was used for a long time since its invention.

Honcheoneui

It was invented in 1443 to observe the movements of Sun, Moon, and stars.

1

Joseon Designates Hanyang as the Capital for a New Dynasty

The meeting of Yi Seong-gye and Jeong Do-jeon

While a group of young governmental officials armed with understanding of Neo-Confucian ideology were dreaming of a series of reform, there was another group of people that were expanding its political influence and power, namely the military. In order to protect its territory from invasions, the central government endowed officer positions to influential local figures and allowed them to train private forces of their own.

As a result, many of the local gentries were able to obtain officer positions in the military and created large private armies under their control. The most representative example was Yi Seong-gye in the northeast region, who was a military general that exhibited remarkable talents and was also extremely triumphant in numerous battles.

Yi Seong-gye achieved extraordinary victories. Yet in terms of his political career he was held back because of his origin, being a character from the border areas. It was Jeong Do-jeon (1337~1398) who joined Yi Seong-gye and pursued an overall reform. Jeong Do-jeon was a newcomer to the government, and he had been exiled by the conservative power group inside the government.

Yi Seong-gye (1335~1408)
He was a representative of a local power established in the region of today's Hamheung area. He owned an army of private soldiers, and earned the admiration of the people as he played a pivotal role in repulsing the Japanese marauders and the Red Turban rebels. He later founded the Joseon Dyasty and ascended the throne, yet due to the struggles that broke out among his own sons, he had to retire from the throne rather early.

Hamheung Palace
Yi Seong-gye returned to his hometown Hamheung upon his withdrawal from his own throne. The picture is his palace located in Hamheung.

Under the leadership of these two men, the military and the literati joined forces. They came to forge an impressive presence, not to mention a bigger power. Finally in 1388, Yi Seong-gye refused to follow a direct order from the king who ordered Yi to attack the Liaodong region. On his way there, he decided to turn his soldiers around, and upon his return to the capital, he succeeded in seizing power and taking control of the government. Through the land reforms, he confiscated agricultural estates held by the old nobles and thus demolishing their economic base. Though they resisted such reforms, they could not stand up against the strength of the military, or against the people's support for such reforms.

The new dynasty is named Joseon, and the capital is moved to Hanyang

In 1392, which was the 475th year since the foundation of Goryeo by Wang Geon, the leaders of the reform enthroned Yi Seong-gye as their new king.

Yi Seong-gye (King Taejo, reigned from 1392 to 1398) proclaimed his royal enthronement and renamed his dynasty "Joseon." He named it so in order to proclaim that the new dynasty was a proud successor to Gojoseon, and that the history of the Korean Peninsula was as long as that of

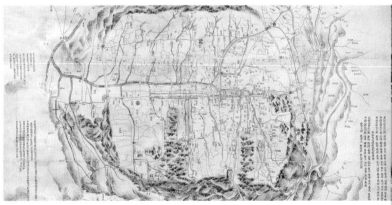

Doseongdo

In front of Bukhansan (Mt.) a palace was constructed. At the right side of the palace were the altars for the Land God and the Crop God, and at its left an ancestral shrine was built for the royal family members. Also, fortresses surrounded the capital, and all the main gates that led to the capital were named after specific Confucian concepts. At these places, the kings vowed the implementation of new policies which would reflect Confucian values, and they would also ask the gods and ancestors to protect the dynasty and its subjects.

❶ **Sajikdan** Sajikdan is the place where the god of land and the god of crops were worshiped. The picture is the view of the altar, in Seoul.

❷ **Gyeongbokgung** This palace was built as an official palace for the king. The picture shows Geunjeongjeon, the palace restored in the 19th century, 300 years after it was incinerated in war during the 16th century.

❸ **Jongmyo** This is the place where the royal family tablets were preserved and memorial rituals were conducted. It is also designated as a World Cultural Heritage.

❹ **Sadaemun (The Great Four Gates)** These four gates were named according to Confucian ethics. The picture on the bottom shows the Sungryemun gate at the south, which means "holding high ethics." There were also Heunginjimun in the east, Doneuimun in the west, and Sukjeongmun in the north.

the Chinese. He also did so to let it be known to other countries that the Koreans had always believed in Confucian philosophies and upheld them as dynastic values. Many shrines were built to worship Dangun who was the founder of Gojoseon, and Gija who was a king of the 'Late' Gojoseon and proclaimed to have accomplished an idealistic ruling of Korea based on Confucianism.

Upon its foundation, Joseon moved its capital to Hanyang, which is the current capital of Korea. It was located at the center of the country, and was quite advantageous in terms of transportation convenience on both sea and land. Thus, the new capital was constructed here with a specific design, so that it could display and transmit the new ruling ideology of the new dynasty to the rest of the country.

From Buddhism to Confucianism

The first Joseon king Yi Seong-gye and his son King Taejong (reigned from 1400 to 1418) established the basis of the Joseon Dynasty so that the Joseon society would thrive for the next five hundred years. That basis was a set of Confucian ideas.

The ideas of Confucianism required people to show absolute loyalty to their king, as it was believed that "A king is a representative of the heaven." However, the political ethics of Confucianism also emphasized the significance of a king's morality in his ruling of the people; "People are the foundation of a dynasty, therefore a king must do his best to be ethical and respectable when ruling them." Not only the king's absolute authority and divinity but also his duties and moral obligations were emphasized.

The Confucian ideology was reflected upon various systems and insti-

Seonggyungwan
The officials who were well versed in Confucian virtues and values, governed the people according to Confucian ideals. Seonggyungwan was a national university located only in the capital. However, there were secondary educational institutions located throughout the country. Education was the most important duty of the local officials. The picture is Seonggyungwan, which is currently located in Seoul. There still remains a place for rituals, as well as class rooms and residences for teachers and students.

Gyeonggukdaejeon
In 1474, the Joseon Dynasty Law Code *Gyeonggukdaejeon* was finally completed. It integrated all the laws and rules that had been practiced in the ending days of the Goryeo Dynasty and the early days of Joseon. All the legal clauses were organized into six categories including administrative law and criminal law. These law codes were maintained through generations. Indeed, Joseon was a country that was ruled by the principles of laws.

tutions. The rights of the government officials to express their opinions were ensured, and the council sessions of the officials were also granted with a high level of autonomy and discretion. At the same time, new governmental offices were established to check and balance the behaviors of the king and the vassals.

In order to teach and research Confucian scriptures and history, educational facilities were newly organized throughout the country. Policies designed to spread Confucian ethics to the public were continuously promoted. And such process was accompanied by the act of disenfranchising Buddhism. Buddhist doctrines were opposed and criticised. The Joseon government dismantled many temples all over the country and restrained the monks' activities. The cultural transition to Confucianism was inevitable. Yet, overall Buddhism managed to prevail as the people's most basic religion and continued to govern their spiritual lives.

Nosangalhyeondo
Yangbans were the landlords and governmental officials who enjoyed many social privileges. The commoners who occupied the majority of the population engaged in farming and commercial activities and were obligated to pay all kinds of taxes and report for military duties as well. The lowborn class including "Nobi" slaves (servants actually) was treated inhumanely. Another new class called "Jungin" which was a newly formed class, was composed of low-ranking office clerks. They were in some cases also the descendants of Yangban figures but were born as a child of illegitimate wives and females. This picture was drawn by Kim Deuk-shin (1754~1822). In this picture a couple from the peasant class is lowering their heads as they met a Yangban figure. It shows us the hierarchical class structure of the Joseon society.

Yangban rules the Confucian society

The elites were recruited to the government through the civil service examination. Among three fields of examination for the civil officials, the military officers, and technicians, the exam for civil officials was considered to be the most important.

Whoever wished to be promoted had to study Confucian scriptures and Chinese history to meet the level of proficiency in Chinese characters. According to test requirements, anyone, except the slaves, were eligible to take the test. However, commoners who lacked wealth did not have enough resources to prepare for the exam. In essence, the exam was mostly meant for members of the upper, wealthy class. In addition, as time went on only a handful of descendants of governmental officers could manage to apply. Consequently, the civil service exam became a secured way for the prestigious class to become governmental officials. The so-called "Yangban" class was formed.

The children of Yangban houses received an education to serve in governmental posts in the future. They were educated to study and act upon the teachings of Confucianism. They called themselves "Sadaebu (Scholar-official)," and had pride in advising the king properly and guiding the people appropriately.

The Annals of the Joseon Dynasty

Joseonwangjosillok (The Annals of the Joseon Dynasty)
History books named "Sillok," can be seen in other countries like China, Japan, and Vietnam. However, few annals were published with such huge and large volumes, and under such strict regulations like Joseon's. *Joseonwangjosillok* was registered as a World Cultural Heritage in Records, by UNESCO in 1997.

In the Joseon Dynasty, there was always an official whose job was to follow and monitor the king. He slept in the room adjacent to where the king slept, and he attended every meeting the king held. The king could not go hunting or meet a person secretly without the presence of this official.

Total of eight officials, relatively low-ranking ones whose grades ranged from Jeong 7th to Jeong 9th, were called "Sagwan," and in rotation they observed and recorded all the details of daily events that involved the king, things that the king said, and things that happened to him. The authority and confidentiality of these officials were

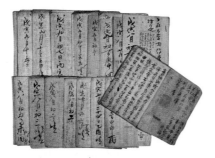

A Sacho material containing records of King Injo's reign (author unknown)
This picture shows a 'Gajang Sacho' material which was a Sacho material created in 1638 (16th year of King Injo's reign), and preserved at the historian's house. 'Gajang' means that this Sacho material was created at home. The historian who called it a day could return home and must have written things that he monitored at the office in a more quieter environment. The author's comments upon certain events are also inserted here and there.

Compact Disks of Joseonwangjosillok
In 1996, the entirety of *Joseonwangjosillok* was translated in Korean and then digitalized (digitally rendered). From the year of 2007, the original contents in Chinese, its translated version in Korean and the original images are all available for free on the Internet. The homepage of *Joseonwangjosillok* can be viewed at *sillok.history.go.kr*.

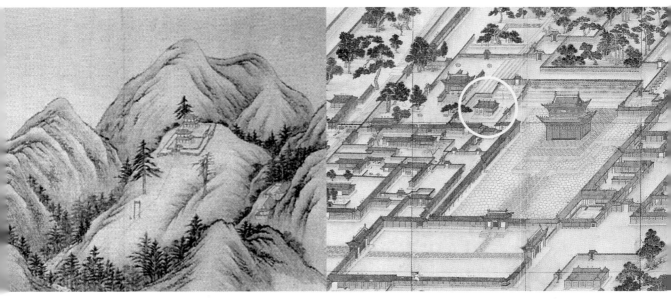

Odaesan History Archive for Joseonwangjosillok
The Annals were completed and then for preservation were moved to facilities located deep inside the mountains to avoid being destroyed during wartime. This picture is the Archive facility which was constructed in the rugged mountainous areas of Odaesan (Mt.). It was drawn by Kim Hong-do in 1788.

Gweolnaegaksa (part of Donggweoldo)
Historians always stayed near the king's office. The picture shows the Changdeokgung (palace) in the 1820s. Historians in charge of documenting historical events used to work at a building (indicated inside the circle) right next to the Injeongjeon (hall) where the official functions of the government were conducted.

guaranteed by the system, and their work was not to be intervened or interrupted by others. The drafts created by them were called 'Sacho.' Even the king was not allowed to read those drafts, and the compilation process only began after the king's death.

When the king passed away, the highest ranking governmental official would be appointed as the chief historical compiler. A research team would collect all the drafts and relevant supporting materials, select important records with historical significance, and organize them in a chronological order. The finished product was usually called 'Sillok,' which means annals.

These "Annals" were created under strict regulations and protocols. Total of five sets were published. One set was kept in the king's palace, and the rest of them were stored in special repositories located in remote mountains far from the capital, in order to avoid possible damages in a disaster. Although only four copies were made in the beginning, when three sets out of four were incinerated during the war with the Japanese in the 1590s, Joseon began to make five copies to prevent the same problem.

The Annals of the Joseon Dynasty features a most magnificent scale, as it is a record of all the events that occurred over 472 years, from the reign of King Taejo to the reign of the 25th King Cheoljong (1392~1863). It consists of 1,893 volumes and 888 books (total of 64 million Chinese characters).

The Annals of Joseon was allowed to be read in only special occasions. But if it was so, why did they put such a tremendous amount of effort into recording their own history? And why would such efforts have continued throughout the history of Joseon? The people of Joseon must have thought it was very important to live a life that would not be shameful to their own descendants.

2

Joseon's Expansion of Its Northern Border to the Amnokgang and the Dumangang

Joseon and Ming maintain a Tributary-Investiture relationship

The year of 1434 was a significant one for Joseon because it succeeded in extending its territory all the way up to the Dumangang. In the "Annals," the volume containing records of the 16th year of King Sejong's reign described this event in details. The year also indicates the 9th year of the Seondeok era, which was during the reign of Ming Emperor Seonjong.

It was only at the end of the 19th century that Koreans began to use the western calendar that uses years like "1434." Nevertheless, such practice was only institutionalized after 1962. Both fashions were used until the 1890s.

Joseon sent its gifts with envoys to the emperor of Ming several times a year. In return, Ming offered their own gifts to Joseon taking the amount of the gifts that came from Joseon into consideration. Also, when a new king was enthroned in Joseon, Joseon always notified Ming and received an investiture to officially crown the king. Joseon also used the Ming Dynasty calendar. This kind of a relationship could be described as a 'Tributary-Investiture' relationship. However, such relationship was only titular, and the emperors of Ming rarely intervened in the internal affairs of Joseon. Joseon was proud of its history and tradition which in their eyes were by no means inferior to those of Ming China. Although they tried to avoid war at all costs, they were also ready to resist any kind of wrongful treatments from Ming.

Sungnyeongjeon shrine at Pyeongyang
Sungnyeongjeon was a shrine which was built to worship the legendary character Gija, who contributed to the establishment of Confucianism's foundation. Gija was believed as a predecessor to Confucius, and was believed to have brought a civilized culture to Korea in the past. For this reason, the Joseon scholar-officials considered their land as another central area where Confucianism developed.

Six Jin
Onseong
Gyeongwon
Jongseong
Gyeongheung
Hweoryeong
Buryeong

JURCHEN

Dumangang

Four Gun
Baekdusan
Yeoyeon
Wuye
Jaseong
Muchang

Amnokgang

Hamgyeong-do

⊙ Hamheung-bu

MING

Pyeongan-do

East Sea

Pyeongyang-bu ⊙

JOSEON

Gangwon-do

Hwanghae-do

⊙ Gaeseong-bu
Gyeonggi-do
⊙ Hanseong-bu

Gyeongsang-do

Yellow Sea

Chungcheong-do

⊙ Gyeongju-bu

JAPAN

⊙ Jeonju-bu

Jeolla-do

Joseon's Territories (borders) in the 15th Century

Soon after Ming was founded, it sent out envoys to other countries and tried to establish new foreign relationships with them based upon tributes and investitures. Once such a relation was built, Ming provided them with favors in terms of foreign trades by issuing official trading permits to them. Japan also agreed to engage in such relationships which indicates that Japan as well submitted to the order of East Asia which was newly established with Ming at the center.

Four Gun units and Six Jin units

Four Gun units and Six Jin units were administrative districts and military facilities newly established to bring cultivation and security to the northern regions of the Korean Peninsula. Four administrative districts were installed at the midstream of the Amnokgang to encourage the people's relocation to the area from the south, while six military facilities were built in the midstream and lower areas of the Dumangang to secure the Joseon borders in the north.

Joseon expands its northern border

Even after they established such an amicable relationship, there were a few crises between the two countries that were so intense that it almost broke out into a war.

Conflicts had arisen regarding the control over Manchuria, which was quite distant from Ming. Joseon, the successor of Goryeo, yearned to recover the land of its ancestors. Needless to say, Ming also sternly proclaimed that all Yuan's territories belonged to Ming.

Integrating the south-bound Jurchen tribes into the Joseon population without provoking Ming had been the ultimate goal of Joseon for a long time. In 1434, the 16th year of King Sejong's reign, Joseon openly deplored the plundering committed by the Jurchens near the Dumangang, and proclaimed a war against them, saying "We should not withdraw a step from the land of Joseon that was given to us from our ancestors."

For 16 years ever since, the people of Joseon continued to cultivate farms near the border line and built fortresses to secure their land along the Am-

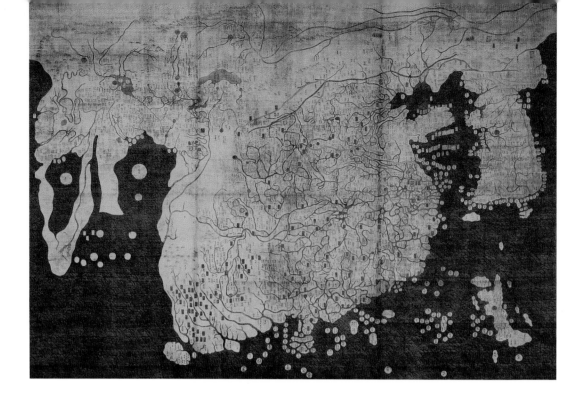

Honilgangriyeokdaegukdo Jido (1402)
This map managed to integrate contents of all available maps at the time, which had been made in numerous countries. It was indeed a spectacular achievement. This map contains names of more than 100 European places and 35 African locations. Interestingly enough, the size of Joseon was drawn four times larger than that of Japan.

nokgang. It was also at that time when the border lines between Josoen and China were finally established.

However, establishing fortresses and dispatching armies were simply not enough for the Joseon people to secure their land and stabilize their lives. Therefore, the central government decided to relocate large groups of people to the remote region, not only from its vicinities but also from distant regions such as the southern part of the Korean Peninsula.

To encourage migration, the government offered free farm land and reduction of taxes for a certain period of time. However, it was a heavy burden for the settlers to cultivate new farming lands along the frontier, therefore the migration project failed to accomplish its anticipated goals. In order to achieve the goal it had in mind, the government often had to force the people to move and resettle in that area.

Due to abrasive environments, the lives of earlier residents were harsh and dismal. Not only were there no actual taxation benefits given to such residents (compared to the tax rates of other regions), but also the additional burdens generated by taking shifts in defense efforts made their lives even tougher. In some cases the Jurchen marauders raided their villages and wrecked their foundation of life completely. Cultivation of the basins of the Amnokgang and the Dumangang was accomplished with great dedication and sacrifices of this early generation of migrated residents.

The people's awareness of the border lines of their country becomes evident

All those defense facilities built along the line from the Dumangang to the Amnokgang were helpful in preventing the Jurchens from entering Joseon territory without authorization. The border also contributed to the formation of the Koreans' pride of being a civilized country, so it essentially served as a psychological line distinguishing themselves from the Jurchens, whom the Joseon people considered to be 'barbaric.'

Meanwhile Joseon sternly removed the Japanese marauders from its territories in the south. Joseon also placed a great deal of effort in keeping them away from their coasts, just as did Goryeo. In 1419, Joseon's naval forces attacked the island of Tsushima where the base of the pirates was located.

As pillaging by the Japanese marauders disappeared at the coasts of Joseon, the Japanese were authorized to trade with the Joseon merchants under official terms. Although there were a few restrictions, the Japanese were allowed to visit Joseon, return to Japan, and even reside in Joseon as well.

Between the end of the 14th century and the beginning of the 15th century, the Joseon people came to distinguish themselves from the Chinese, and established their own identity different from those of the Jurchen and Wae (Japanese). The territorial boundaries of Korea were clearly confirmed with discernible coastlines and rivers.

Waegwan: a Japanese town in Joseon

Waegwando (part)

In 1404, Joseon and Japan established an official diplomatic relationship. Yoshimitsu, a Japanese Shogun, first sent a group of envoys with the authority endorsed by the Japanese king. And in return, the Joseon king also sent delegates to Japan. In the capital of Hanyang, Dongpyeonggwan was built to be used as the Japanese envoys' residence. In addition to these diplomatic exchanges, trades were made as well.

Joseon kings also developed individual relationships with Japanese feudal lords. Official titles of Joseon were given to several lords, and one of the representative examples is Tsushima beon, which had their trading with Joseon officially authorized.

At today's Busan (Busanpo), Ulsan (Yeompo) and Jinhae (Naeihpo, Jaepo), there were "Waegwan" villages, which referred to "Japanese villages". According to the record of 1494, the number of Japanese in Joseon increased to 3,105. However, there must have been more people than that. The Japanese people at the Waegwan villages sold commercial goods they brought from Japan and also purchased commodities to sell to the Japanese market. Cotton, silk, beans, and rice were popular Korean items to export to Japan, and copper, gold, wood, and pepper from Japan were favored by the Koreans.

Although the Japanese were restricted to travel outside the Waegwan villages, the Joseon people were allowed to enter the area without permission. Thus meetings between the Joseon people and Japanese became an ordinary daily activity. Through the Japanese people, the Joseon people were able to meet with another world.

This picture, which was drawn by an artist named Byeon Bak of the Dongrae region in 1783, shows the features of the Waegwan village. After the Ganghwado Treaty was signed in 1876, Japan continued to expand its influence from this area.

3

The Korean Alphabet Hangeul is Invented

Because of differences between Korean and Chinese languages...

> Since our language is not the same with the Chinese letters, our poor subjects intend to speak yet find themselves not able to fully address what they wish to say. Out of sympathy here I newly invented 28 letters, so that practicing them may convenience you in your life of everyday.

The above announcement was made when the 4th king of Joseon, Sejong invented *Hunminjeongeum*, which is now known simply as Hangeul. *Humnimjeongeum* means 'proper sounds to instruct the people.'

Because of the differences between the Joseon language and the Chinese language, the Joseon people had to endure many inconveniences and difficulties in dictating what they said, prior to the creation of the Korean alphabet. They had to borrow Chinese characters to record things spoken in Korean. In addition to that burden, the Chinese letters were very difficult for them to use and write, not only because there were so many letters in the first place, but also because the figures of individual letters were extremely complex.

Fortunately, the new 28 letters were easy enough for the people to use in writing. Instead of ideographic letters, *Hunminjeongeum* is comprised of phonetic letters, which could represent all possible sounds of

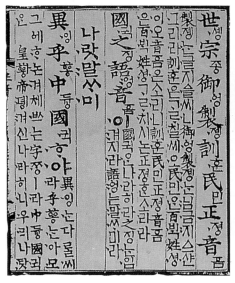

Hunminjeongeum Haeryebon
This book contains the principles that were observed in creating the Korean alphabet Hangeul, and also examples of the usage of this new letter system. Here King Sejong explains that he invented 28 letters to help his subjects. We can see that the king wished to base his ruling upon a political ideology that valued the people foremost.

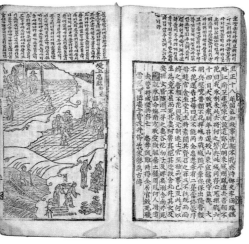

a spoken Korean by simply combining consonants and vowels. The Korean people was finally given a writing system in which sounds and letters served each other as perfect counterparts. As a result, they became able to express their mind very easily.

The new alphabet becomes widely used in Joseon

When the new letters were created, not everyone immediately welcomed them. Some bureaucrats vividly opposed utilizing these new letters, saying "Politics is to practice the teachings of Confucianism, and these new letters are nothing but a hindrance to studying Confucian texts which are already written in Chinese." Many bureaucrats despised and intentionally ignored these new letters, and soon after King Sejong died they abolished the office that was established to educate Hangeul. To the ruling class of Joseon, only the Chinese characters were considered as official letters, up until the 19th century.

However, due to its easiness and effectiveness in learning and using, the number of its users grew rapidly. At the beginning, only court ladies and low-ranking officials used Hangeul. However, it gradually spread throughout the local peasantry population and the merchant societies. Especially among many women who were excluded from the opportunities of receiving a formal education, Hangeul was used as a popular method of recording, and there arose a movement to seek ways of sharing these new letters more wildly. Since the beginning of the 16th century, the new letters prevailed and were established as the 'letters of the people.'

These new letters that could display and represent all kinds of sounds largely contributed to the development of the Korean culture. Many orally transmitted stories and songs were documented in Korean letters. Thanks to Hangeul, many great works of literature which candidly expressed the natural feelings of the Korean people in their own daily lives were created during this time. The innovation of this new letter system formed a foundation for a unique culture which was distinguishable from those of neighboring countries that used different sounds and letters.

"People are the foundation of a dynasty"

King Sejong emphasized the fact that "since people are the foundation of a dynasty, policies should be designed with the people in mind caring for their interests." Of course, his idea of "politics for the people" was not similar to a modern, democratic idea that we have today. At the time, most people were suffering from class discrimination and excessive exploitation of tax. Yet, with King Sejong's sincere intentions the exploitation was restrained to a certain degree, and with his policies the people's lives were generally enhanced.

In the early 15th century, technology continuously advanced through people's creative attempts. For dry land cultivation, new methods were developed to enable farmers to have harvests twice a year, or even three times over the course of two years. After the method of 'rice transplantation' was introduced, the 'double cropping' of rice and barley was experimented as well. Technology also advanced in areas such as porcelain production, shipbuilding, and 'movable types' printing.

Scientific research was also supported by the government. The central government supported agricultural studies by publishing books containing details regarding advanced farming, and encouraged distributing copies of

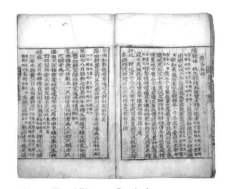

Nongsajikseol (Notes on Farming)
This book was compiled by Jeong Cho in 1429 with an order from the king. It was distributed to high-ranking officers in both the capital and local regions. In this book, farmers' experiences were recorded with details so that they could be utilized in advising and encouraging local governmental officials' agricultural policies.

Mongyudowondo (Utopia seen in Dream)
This painting depicts the story of the Prince Anpyeong's dream, who was a son of King Sejong. Policies regarding culture and art were established during the reign of King Sejong. An Gyeon, who was a painter at the Dohwaseo office (an official organization for artists), drew this painting. An artwork in 1447, with the size of 38.7×106.5cm.

those books to the peasants. Also the 'rain gauger' which could measure the exact amount of rain drops was invented for the first time around the globe and was utilized in predicting the weather. The results of such weather observation were closely reviewed by the government. At the same time, Joseon scholars created calendars, using various observation tools designed to look for celestial bodies, and with accurate observations made by such tools as well. Medical books were also published. Those books contained records of symptoms of diseases, names of herbs which were produced in the country, and the appropriate usage of those materials for the treatment of various illnesses.

The idea of the "People being the foundation of a dynasty" was not always practiced and maintained. However, the idea that policies should be designed for the people, and designed to make their lives convenient, and to take care of their lives, was deeply rooted in the Joseon society. New cultural creations based on people's lives and circumstances, such as the innovation of *Hunminjeongeum* as well as all the technological advancements, were gifts from nothing but humanism that prevailed in the 15th century Joseon.

Cheugugi (Rainfall gauger)
In 1442, a system to measure the amount of rain drops was established, and in the next year, rainfall gaugers were installed at local offices throughout the country, not to mention the capital. The picture shows the rainfall gauger that has been kept at the Seoul Meteorology Administration. The letters inscribed upon it indicate that this gauger was made in May 1770.

Joseon's Technology in the 15th Century

The Joseon technology in the 15th century was so advanced that it could actually challenge others on the international level. In the 13th and 14th centuries, the Koreans had already had active exchanges with the Yuan Empire and embraced many varieties of culture and science in the process. In the 15th century, the government managed to equip itself with a secure infrastructure in terms of politics, economy, and culture. And as a result, new technology was developed, the living styles changed, and the population increased. Yet, Confucianism at times hindered such development in terms of science and technology.

White Celadon Bowl
In the Joseon period, a large number of white celadon products were produced. They required more advanced skills than needed in creating blue celadon-ware. The white celadon bowl in the picture was made in the 15th~16th century and its height is 11.8cm.

Jagyeokru
This is a 'water clock' made by Jang Yeong-shil. All Jagyeokru units made during the reign of King Sejong are currently lost. Some of them which were made in 1536 can be found today.

Shingijeon
Shingijeon was a projectile, explosive weapon that was invented in 1451. It demonstrated a tremendous amount of destructive power, by launching a bundle of 100 arrows at once. Exceptionally powerful cannons, and iron-planted warships called "Geobukseon," (turtle ships) also appeared in this time period.

The statue of King Sejong
Korean letters greatly contributed to reducing the number of 'illiterates' in Korea. Since 1990, UNESCO has awarded the King Sejong Prize to individuals or groups throughout the world, whoever contributed to the lowering of the illiteracy rate. The prize commemorates the achievement of the great King Sejong.

Beautiful and Scientific Letters of Hangeul

Hangeul is an exceptional letter system. We all know its inventors, and the theories on which it was developed. This is a very scientific set of letters that can almost completely represent and fully display the Korean 'spoken' language. Since the 7th century, Koreans had to write down their own language with borrowed Chinese characters, and the 13th and 14th centuries were no exception. Then the innovation of Hangeul was accomplished, by absorbing various knowledge on linguistics and phonetics from numerous other countries.

Hanguel is made of phonetic letters which could denote sounds of the Korean language. In the beginning there were 28 letters; but currently only 24 letters are used: among the basic 24 letters, 10 phonemes are vowels, and 14 phonemes are consonants.

One letter is not merely placed to the next. Endlessly placing consonants and vowels to another is not possible. Instead, a consonant

The beauty of Korean letters
The Korean letters can be written in various styles, so various types of calligraphy which could effectively express the beauty of the letters were duly developed. Various products that exhibit the excellence of Korean letters are available at markets.

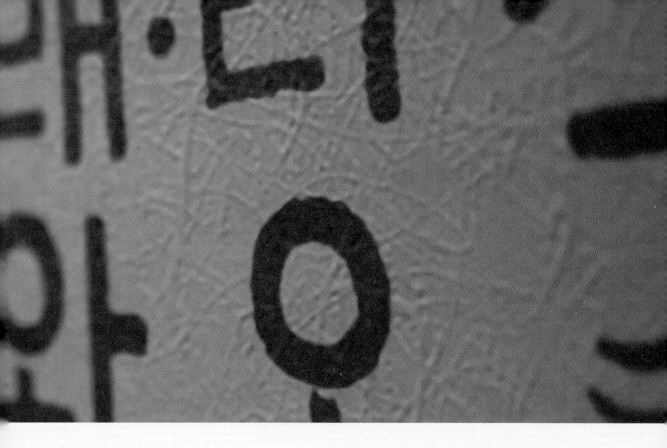

and a vowel is merged with each other, to form an individual syllable. By combining all the possible letters (syllables), which consists of 19 initial sounds, 21 middle sounds and 27 ending sounds, Koreans can possibly create or denote 10,773 (19×21×27) types of sounds overall.

Vowels
Korean phonemes and English phonetic signs

ㅏ	ㅓ	ㅗ	ㅜ	ㅡ	ㅣ	ㅐ	ㅔ	ㅚ	ㅟ
a	eo	o	u	eu	i	ae	e	oe	wi

Consonants
Korean phonemes and English phonetic signs

ㄱ	ㄴ	ㄷ	ㄹ	ㅁ	ㅂ	ㅅ	ㅇ	ㅈ	ㅊ	ㅋ	ㅌ	ㅍ	ㅎ
g	n	d	r	m	b	s	ng	j	ch	k	t	p	h
k		t	l		p								

Initial 19
Korean phonemes and English phonetic signs

ㄱ	ㄲ	ㄴ	ㄷ	ㄸ	ㄹ	ㅁ	ㅂ	ㅃ	ㅅ	ㅆ	ㅇ	ㅈ	ㅉ	ㅊ	ㅋ	ㅌ	ㅍ	ㅎ
g	kk	n	d	tt	r	m	b	pp	s	ss	ng	j	jj	ch	k	t	p	h
k			t		l		p											

Middle 21
Korean phonemes and English phonetic signs

ㅏ	ㅐ	ㅑ	ㅒ	ㅓ	ㅔ	ㅕ	ㅖ	ㅗ	ㅘ	ㅙ	ㅚ	ㅛ	ㅜ	ㅝ	ㅞ	ㅟ	ㅠ	ㅡ	ㅢ	ㅣ
a	ae	ya	yae	eo	e	yeo	ye	o	wa	wae	oe	yo	u	wo	we	wi	yu	eu	ui	i

Final 27
Korean phonemes and English phonetic signs

ㄱ	ㄲ	ㄳ	ㄴ	ㄵ	ㄶ	ㄷ	ㄹ	ㄺ	ㄻ	ㄼ	ㄽ	ㄾ	ㄿ	ㅀ	ㅁ	ㅂ	ㅄ	ㅅ	ㅆ	ㅇ	ㅈ	ㅊ	ㅋ	ㅌ	ㅍ	ㅎ
g	kk	ks	n	nj	nh	d	r	lg	lm	lp	ls	lt	lp	lh	m	b	bs	s	ss	ng	j	ch	k	t	p	h
k		k		n	n	t	l		k	m	p	ls		p	l										p	p

ㅅ + ㅔ + ㅈ + ㅗ + ㅇ = 세종
initial sounds / middle sounds / initial sounds / middle sounds / final sounds
s e j o ng = Sejong

한국 Hanguk   서울 Seoul   한겨레 hangyeore

1474 ~ 1650

1492
Columbus' fleet arrived at the West Indian Islands.

1519
Jo Gwang-jo who pursued idealistic politics based on Confucianism
was executed due to political attacks that he received from his
opponents, the privileged.

1519~1522
Magellan's fleet completed a journey around the world. Later Spain's
oversea expansion, especially in Asia, became active.

1543
Baegundong Seowon was founded. Later it developed into Sosu
Seowon. These Seowon schools contributed to spreading out
Confucian education and enhancing Yangban community's level of
autonomy.

1570
The Sarim faction was divided into Dongin (the Easterners) and Seoin
(the Westerners) factions. Since then, for a long time Joseon central
politics continued to be operated in disarray because of strife between
the factions.

1592~1598
Joseon succeeded in repelling the Japanese invaders after 7 years of
battling.

1607
Upon receiving Japan's official apology, Joseon reconciled diplomatic
relationships with Japan.

1623
King Gwanghaegun who established a 'neutral' diplomatic policy
between Ming and the Jurchen was forced to step down from power
by the Sarim faction who prioritized the loyalty to Ming above all else.

1636
The Jurchen who united the northeast area of China invaded Joseon
after establishing the Qing Dynasty.

1644
Qing raided to occupy Beijing, thus demolishing Ming.

VII The Spread of Confucian Culture

"If kings behave like a king, vassals like a vassal, parents like a parent, child like a child, society will become a wonderful place to live."

Since the 16th century, Joseon had rapidly changed and became a solid Confucian society. The Sarim figures who newly joined the central government attempted to make social reforms with policies based upon idealism truthful to the Confucian philosophy. As studies on Confucian scriptures continued, researches on rules and protocols needed in practicing Confucianism were prevalent as well. The Confucian ethics that emphasized loyalty to kings, piety to parents, and the submissiveness and sacrifice of women became the principle of daily life. While observing Qing's ruling of China whom they once regarded only as a race of barbarians, the Joseon people confirmed its own identity as the only successor of the Confucian Civilization.

Jongmyo This is the place where the ancestral tablets of members of the royal family are preserved for conducting ritual ceremonies.

Northeast Asia Engulfed in Wars

Hwacha (Shingijeongi), an anti-personnel arrow launcher

In April of 1592, 150,000 Japanese troops invaded Joseon. The Joseon soldiers fought against the Japanese troops with all their power, and the Ming Dynasty, which became concerned about its own security, dispatched a large scale of troops to confront them as well. With Ming's intervention, all three countries got involved in the war.

Japan continued to lead the battles in the beginning of the war, yet the Joseon navy seized control over the sea and inflicted heavy damages upon the Japanese naval troops.

The Japanese victories in the early phases of the war were largely due to a new weapon that Japanese troops used, which was the so-called Jochong (rifle). Jochong was introduced to Japan through Portuguese merchants, initially as a gun for sniping. But it became a deadly weapon when trained troops armed with such rifles were deployed at the front row of large infantry units.

The Joseon navy was able to win the battles with its superior cannons. The artillery of Joseon had tremendously destructive firepower and the gunshot range was much longer than that of Jochong. The advanced shipbuilding technology, which was also able to absorb the rebounding vibrations generated by artillery fire, contributed to Joseon's triumphs as well.

The seven-year war between Joseon and Japan was essentially a war which tested advanced technologies. Japan used Western battle techniques while Joseon independently developed its own technology. However, the war ended without a complete victory by either side.

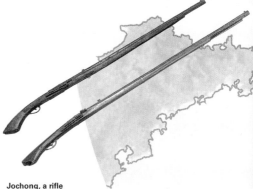

Jochong, a rifle
It was also called as a flintlock because it was fired with a lighted wick. It was introduced to Japan for the first time in 1543 and played a pivotal role in the unification war of Japan.

Panokseon, a warship with a roof
The most representative type of a naval ship was made in Joseon in 1555. This ship was designed to make soldiers climb to the roof top created above the second story, in order to allow soldiers to fight from a higher position. Ships of this design were able to sustain nearly 200 soldiers aboard. Artilleries were installed on the second story so that soldiers could shoot distant targets. When the Japanese invaded Joseon in 1592, vessels with this design, along with the famous Geobukseon ('Turtle ship') protected the Joseon sea from the Japanese invaders.

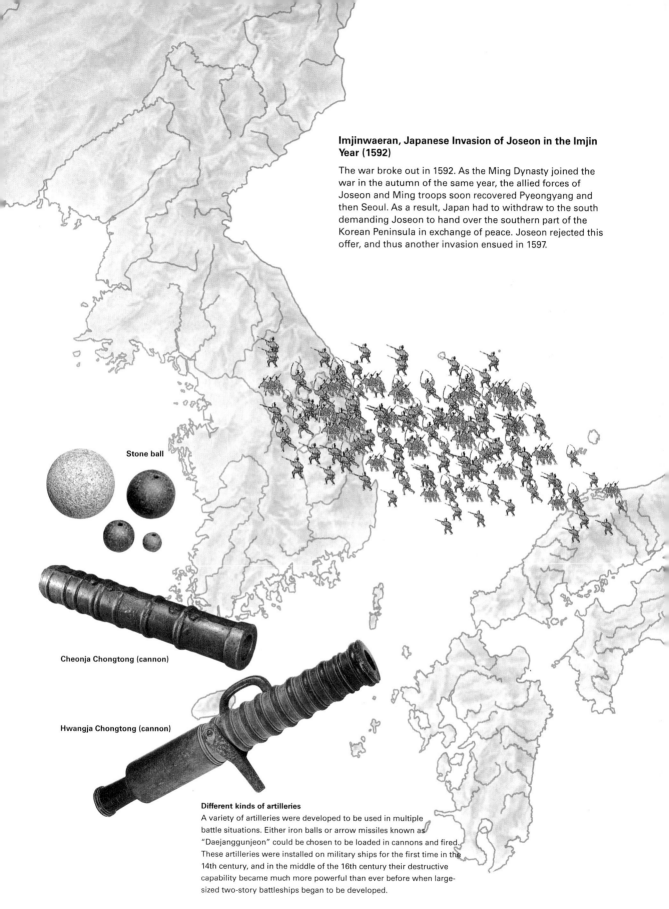

Imjinwaeran, Japanese Invasion of Joseon in the Imjin Year (1592)

The war broke out in 1592. As the Ming Dynasty joined the war in the autumn of the same year, the allied forces of Joseon and Ming troops soon recovered Pyeongyang and then Seoul. As a result, Japan had to withdraw to the south demanding Joseon to hand over the southern part of the Korean Peninsula in exchange of peace. Joseon rejected this offer, and thus another invasion ensued in 1597.

Stone ball

Cheonja Chongtong (cannon)

Hwangja Chongtong (cannon)

Different kinds of artilleries
A variety of artilleries were developed to be used in multiple battle situations. Either iron balls or arrow missiles known as "Daejanggunjeon" could be chosen to be loaded in cannons and fired. These artilleries were installed on military ships for the first time in the 14th century, and in the middle of the 16th century their destructive capability became much more powerful than ever before when large-sized two-story battleships began to be developed.

1

The Sarim Scholars, Dreaming of an Idealistic Governance Based on Neo-Confucianism

Who are the people called Sarim?

Most of the Yangban class members wished to become a governmental official, and some of them spent their entire lives preparing for the civil service exam. However, passing the exam was not the only objective for them. They believed that being able to control one's own mind instead of controling the fate of others was crucial, and that only a person who could control one's own actions and maintain order inside the family would be able to govern the country well. The task of building one's character and maintaining one's convictions was considered very important to the Yangban class, more so than being governmental officials.

The political situations in the ending days of the Goryeo Dynasty and the early days of Joseon pushed them to make several difficult decisions. Yi Seong-gye was a vassal of the Goryeo Dynasty, but founded a new dynasty of his own and ascended the throne. Later, the second eldest son of King Sejong had his own nephew put to death and became the king himself (King Sejo, reigned from 1455 to 1468). King Jungjong (reigned from 1506 to 1544) overthrew his older brother and succeeded the throne of Joseon. Some scholars cooperated in such instances and subsequently held senior positions, yet some of them were determined to resign from their posts under the name of 'not serving two kings.'

Those who decided not to join the new dynasty and its government, or opposed new kings who ascended the throne through emergency measures returned to their hometowns. They dedicated their lives to educating students and practicing Confucian ethics. Such scholars, who considered the cause of maintaining one's own integrity as an important thing above all else, were called "Sarim."

Gosagwansudo
This picture was drawn by Kang Hi-an, a painter from the early half of the Joseon Dynasty period. Using ink only, he depicted a scholar who was watching a stream while contemplating upon something. The scholar wanted to clear his mind from the burdens of life, dreaming of a life where he and the nature would eventually become one. 23.4×15.7cm.

Sarim scholoars at the government posts

In several decades after the foundation of a new dynasty, those who contributed to estatblishing the dynasty's foundation became a power group. And later, others who supported King Sejo's revolt also received a large amount of land with many slaves, so quickly became rich and powerful. Some of them even grew powerful enough to challenge the king's authority. We call them the Meritorious Elite, the "Hungupa" faction.

These Meritorious Elites, while enjoying their privilege and power, eventually became corrupted. The balance of power between the authority of the king and the influence of the vassals were shifting. In response to this change the king wanted to restrain those in power by hiring new elites. Scholars in local regions also started to argue that they should join the government and initiate reforms.

In the late 15th century, kings began to hire Sarim scholars, in an effort to carry out political reforms. During the reign of King Seongjong (reigned from 1469 to 1494), Sarim members from the Gyeongsang-do province including Kim Jong-jik were invited, and during the reign of King Jungjong, more reformers like Jo Gwang-jo joined the government. These Sarim literati dared to criticize the corruptions and wrong doings of the Meritorious Elites, and recommended the kings to study academic subjects and practice the ethics of Confucianism. Sarim scholars also asserted that public opinions should be accepted and studies of Confucianism scriptures and ethics should be encouraged.

Shimgok Seowon
This is a Seowon founded in Yongin, where Jo Gwang-jo was buried. In 1650, Jo's followers built this Seowon school to commemorate their great teacher and to foster young students. Jo Gwang-jo was recognized by his outstanding personality and intellectual brilliance. He was able to form a reformative political power with the support of King Jungjong and his followers. However, Jo Gwang-jo met heavy resistance from the "Hungupa" faction, and was executed because of his claim for idealistic policies based on Confucianism.

The Sarim political group is formed

Clashes between the Sarim reformers and the Meritorious Elites were inevitable. The kings had originally supported the Sarim reformers in order to deal with the Meritorious Elites, yet when it comes to crucial decisions the kings always sided with the Meritorious Elites instead, as they were not ready to accept all those radical changes suggested by the Sarim scholars who valued righteousness, causes, and ethical politics.

The Meritorious Elites continued to make political attacts on the Sarim newcomers without mercy. Many Sarim officials were persecuted and executed. Kim Jong-jik's body was taken out of his tomb and beheaded. Jo Gwang-jo was put to death alongside all the reformer officials whom he had invited to the government.

However, their ideals of a reformed world were widely recognized even after their death. Some Sarim scholars decided to stay in their hometowns and engaged in studies and education while others decided to apply for governmental seats in the capital more than before. The Meritorious Elites' monopoly of important posts finally began to be shaken, and accordingly, the government was opened to a wider group of people.

As more Sarim scholars joined central politics, changes were made to the overall administration of the government. They aggressively voiced their political opinions and argued the importance of practicing Confucian ideals. No one could stand against their conviction to establish Confucian ideals throughout the society. Therefore, near the end of the 16th century, either the kings or powerful vassals could no longer arbitrarily push their agendas forward without the consent of the others. Private

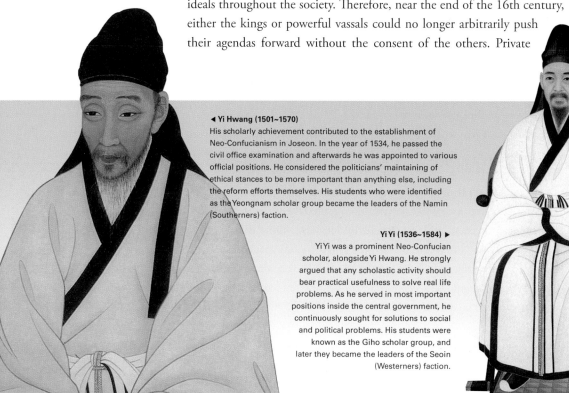

◀ Yi Hwang (1501~1570)
His scholarly achievement contributed to the establishment of Neo-Confucianism in Joseon. In the year of 1534, he passed the civil office examination and afterwards he was appointed to various official positions. He considered the politicians' maintaining of ethical stances to be more important than anything else, including the reform efforts themselves. His students who were identified as the Yeongnam scholar group became the leaders of the Namin (Southerners) faction.

Yi Yi (1536~1584) ▶
Yi Yi was a prominent Neo-Confucian scholar, alongside Yi Hwang. He strongly argued that any scholastic activity should bear practical usefulness to solve real life problems. As he served in most important positions inside the central government, he continuously sought for solutions to social and political problems. His students were known as the Giho scholar group, and later they became the leaders of the Seoin (Westerners) faction.

governance of state matters was no longer possible and gradually diminished. The significance of the public opinion was more and more recognized as time progressed.

'Easterners' and 'Westerners' are formed

As Sarim scholars began to actively participate in political affairs, research on Confucian scriptures became more vitalized. Neo-Confucianism was originally established by Zhu Xi of Sung China. Joseon scholars inherited such studies and developed those studies into a new phase. Great scholars such as Yi Hwang and Yi Yi were born. Schools were formed around these two scholars, and fervent academic debates and discussions started.

The Sarim politics considered both the scholarly pursuit of righteous governing and the practical opinions of regional communities to be important. For this reason, those who shared the same region of origin or the same academic stances tended to form political groups and factions, which were called "Bungdang." ▪

Scholars in those factions devised policies and decided priorities to implement in politics. Their growth of power was attributable to the public opinions in support of their views. The Yeongnam regional literati developed the Dongin faction (the Easterners) under the instruction of Yi Hwang, whereas the Gyeonggi and Chungcheong regional literati established the Seoin faction (the Westerners) under the scholarship of Yi Yi. The former asserted the need for improving the autonomy of local regions and the people's welfare while the latter claimed that state security could be maintained only by the wealth of a nation so its robust military system should be prioritized.

▪ **Bungdang** The term itself refers to 'political buddies.' Incumbent governmental officials and scholars currently out of office joined through these factions. These factions were scholarly in origin yet also political in nature as the members devised factions and contended with other factions over policy issues. But these factions were also established on the basis of regional relationships and academic connections, so they were very different from today's political parties in nature.

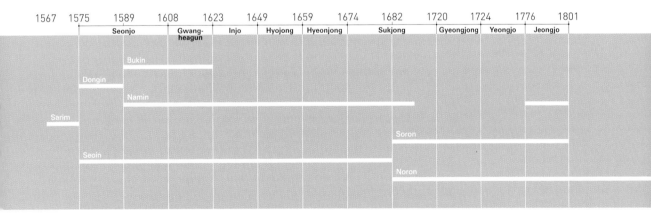

The structure of political factions (parties)

At the end of the 16th century, two factions (political parties), the Dongin faction ("Easterners") and the Seoin faction ("Westerners") emerged. Not before long the former was divided into the Bukin faction ("Northerners") and the Namin faction ("Southerners"), and at the end of the 17th century, the Seoin faction was divided into the Noron faction ("Elders") and the Soron faction ("Juniors"). Since the middle of the 17th century, the Seoin and Namin factions played a major role in the political administration.

In the 18th century, policies designed to 'alleviate' the tension and reduce conflicts between the factions were introduced. However, in the 19th century a small number of families of the Noron faction, branched out from the Seoin faction, came to monopolize power, for an extended period of time.

Dosan Seowon
Dosan Seowon was built in 1574 to commemorate the great scholar Yi Hwang, right in the place where he used to teach his students. It is located at Dosan-myeon in the Andong region, of the Gyeongsangbuk-do province.

Seowon, Where Joseon Scholars' Life Can be Found

To those literati who believed austere practice was the foundation of everything, upholding the philosophy of a respectable teacher was very important. Seowon schools functioned as a private academy, in which students engaged in extensive studies and also held memorial services for past scholars of prominence.

It was in the middle of the 16th century when Seowon schools were first established. At these schools, the Sarim scholars studied basic scriptures of Confucianism and the teachings of Chu Hsi, along with history and literature. Teachers and students, sometimes with local literati as well, used to gather at Seowon schools and contested their writing skills.

Most of the regional literati participated in the operation of Seowon schools. It was like an organization through which regional opinions would be collected and relayed to the capital. The literati cooperated with each other and established autonomous rules to govern their region, so Seowon school was usually more or less an intimidating body of authority to the peasants and the slaves.

As the Sarim factions played a pivotal role in governing, the number of Seowon schools increased, and regional and national networks of Seowon schools were organized. As a result, the power of the king and regional officials was somewhat weakened. The literati established a dominant position over the peasantry population under the justification of promotion of the Confucian culture, but later their arbitrary exploitations of peasants sometimes went too far and caused new social problems.

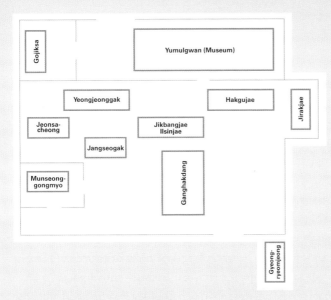

Gojiksa	Yumulgwan (Museum)		
	Yeongjeonggak	Hakgujae	Jirakjae
Jeonsa-cheong	Jikbangjae Ilsinjae		
Jangseogak			
Munseong-gongmyo	Ganghakdang		
	Gyeong-ryeomjeong		

The plan of Sosu Seowon

Sosu Seowon was the first Seowon ever built in Korea. It was built in 1543. 'Sosu' means "restoring the teachings that had long been neglected." It was constructed by the Sarim figures to facilitate Confucian education throughout the region.

Suweolru: the front gate of Dodong Seowon

This was first built as a private shrine of Kim Kweng-pil in 1568, and in 1607 it received its name "Dodong Seowon" from the King. The title harbors a certain sense of pride shared by all Korean people, because using the word 'dodong' implies a belief that "The Way of Life ("Do[Tao]") has moved and found a place to settle in the 'East (the Korean Peninsula).'" In other words, this very word signals a touch of a proud belief that Joseon, placed in the east of China, was indeed the most ideal place where the way of life can be studied and learned and cherished. This school is located at Guji-myeon in Daegu, of the Gyeongsangbuk-do province.

❶ **Munseonggongmyo** This is the place in which the portrait of An Hyang, the great scholar of Goryeo who introduced Neo-Confucianism to the Korean people for the first time, has been displayed. Rituals are performed here in honor of him.
❷ **Ganghakdang** Auditorium where scholars debated and studied together.
❸ **Hakgujae and Jirakjae** These were used as a residence hall for teachers and students.
❹ **Jangseogak** Library

2

Turmoil from the Two Wars

Japanese invasions of Joseon

In the spring of 1592, more than 150,000 Japanese troops raided the coast of Busan. Soon after they attacked the Busan fortress, Japanese troops continued forward to the Dongrae fortress. Many Joseon soldiers and commoners valiantly fought. However, soon the fortress was taken and there were almost no survivors.

The Japanese invasion, the so-called "Imjinwaeran" began like this. While the professionally trained Japanese army attacked Joseon like a storm, the unprepared Joseon troops were defeated in almost every battle during the opening phase of the war. It took only 18 days for the Japanese troops to seize the Hanyang capital. As the king of Joseon fled to the north, the whole country fell into anarchy and chaos.

In retrospect, there were indeed prior arguments claiming that Joseon should prepare for war. Joseon even once sent envoys to Japan, to obtain information regarding Japanese activities. Joseon's defeat cannot be solely blamed upon the supposedly corrupted and negligent nature of the ruling class of the time. The literati were more focused upon studying ideal politics, and the officials were concentrating their efforts in accomplishing such idealistic politics.

Nevertheless, their preparation for the war was insufficient. This is because thay believed, "When a nation becomes richer, people would become poorer. In order for the country to have a strong army, the people have to bear the suffering." Instead of getting ready to fight a war which was yet to happen, improving the people's lives was a more urgent matter to them. Such reasoning hindered them from assessing the international situations more accurately and objectively.

Dongraebu Sunjeoldo
A picture of the Dongrae people's and also the soldiers' valiant and costly struggle against the Japanese invasion force. The confrontation at the south gate, and the fortress falling down at the northeast side, can be seen in the picture. It was drawn by an artist of Dongrae, whose name was Byeon Bak, in 1760. 147×97cm.

Japan's ambition to rule East Asia

In the end of the 16th century, Japan was about to end the civil war among states, which had lasted for more than 100 years. Yet, some wanted to use the unification of the Japanese islands as a springboard for waging another war. Having succeeded the seat of Oda Nobunaga who constructed the foundation of unification, Toyotomi Hideyoshi officially disclosed his intention to invade Joseon and Ming.

Toyotomi Hideyoshi openly swore his ambition to invade the Ming Dynasty since 1585 when he seized power. In 1590, when he completed the unification of the Japanese islands, Toyotomi Hideyoshi engaged himself in active preparations for the invasion. He wanted to endow newly conquered lands to his subject warriors, and put Japan at the center of the international trade order of Asia, which had been showing exponential growth.

About this time, European merchants appeared in the sea of East Asia. The Portuguese who had participated in trading with Asia since 1498 began to trade with Japan in 1544. Not long after that, the Portuguese opened its trading ports at Macao, China. In 1570, Spain established a trading base in the Philippines and exchanged silver from its colony Mexico with Chinese silk and porcelains. In the beginning of the 17th century, Netherlands occupied Taiwan.

Invading Routes of the Japanese Troops During Imjinwaeran

The victories of the Joseon naval forces played a key role in defeating the Japanese troops, as the Joseon forces were successful in cutting off the supply lines of the Japanese troops and made them unable to continue with their inland advances. As militias were mobilized throughout the country and soon after Ming's troops joined the war as a relief force for Joseon, the Japanese troops withdrew to the southeastern coast, fearing of being isolated and pinned down in early 1593.

➡ **Primary routes of
the Japanese invasion**

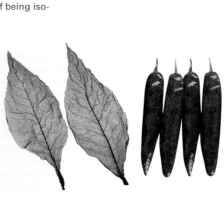

Tobacco and hot peppers

Hot peppers and tobacco which were originated in America brought considerable changes to the eating habits and life styles of the Joseon people. They were introduced to Korea around the time of Japan's invasion of Joseon. Potatoes, sweet potatoes and corns which were introduced a little later than hot peppers and tobacco were also products originated from America.

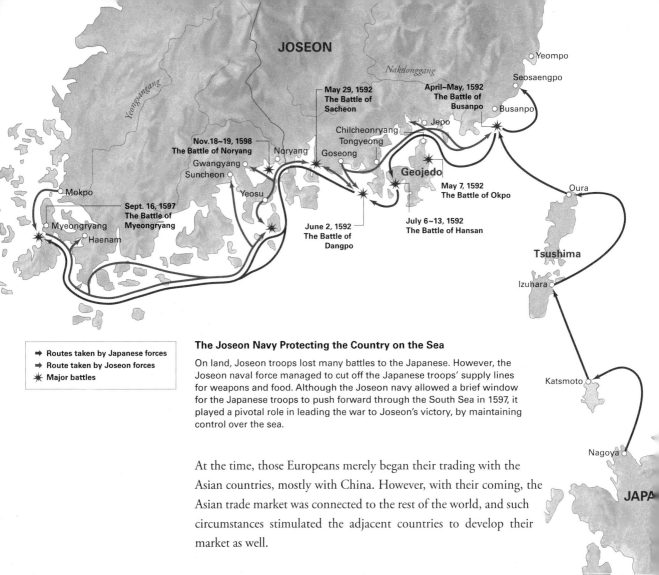

JOSEON

Nakdonggang

April~May, 1592
The Battle of
Busanpo

Yeompo
Seosaengpo
Busanpo

May 29, 1592
The Battle of
Sacheon

Jepo

Chilcheonryang
Tongyeong

Nov.18~19, 1598
The Battle of Noryang

Noryang

Goseong

Geojedo

Gwangyang

May 7, 1592
The Battle of Okpo

Suncheon

Oura

Yeosu

Yeongsangang

Mokpo

Sept. 16, 1597
The Battle of
Myeongryang

July 6~13, 1592
The Battle of Hansan

Tsushima

Myeongryang

Haenam

June 2, 1592
The Battle of
Dangpo

Izuhara

Katsmoto

Nagoya

JAPA

➡ Routes taken by Japanese forces
➡ Route taken by Joseon forces
✳ Major battles

The Joseon Navy Protecting the Country on the Sea

On land, Joseon troops lost many battles to the Japanese. However, the Joseon naval force managed to cut off the Japanese troops' supply lines for weapons and food. Although the Joseon navy allowed a brief window for the Japanese troops to push forward through the South Sea in 1597, it played a pivotal role in leading the war to Joseon's victory, by maintaining control over the sea.

At the time, those Europeans merely began their trading with the Asian countries, mostly with China. However, with their coming, the Asian trade market was connected to the rest of the world, and such circumstances stimulated the adjacent countries to develop their market as well.

The resistance of warriors aganist the Japanese invaders

Joseon was not aware of the fact that Japan had achieved unification and been preparing a war with new technology. The major reason for most of the Joseon army's early defeats was their own ignorance. But it does not mean that Joseon didn't prepare for the war at all.

When the possibility of a war was brewing in 1591, the Joseon government began selecting generals who were qualified to defend the country. Admiral Yi Sun-shin was one of them. He became the commander of the Jeolla Jwa-do naval troops. By building more powerful battle ships and organizing more naval forces, Admiral Yi carefully prepared the fight against the Japanese navy. When the war broke out, with his well-trained troops he did not lose a single battle.

Although they had been initially against the idea of making preparations for a war as such preparations would greatly burden the people, the Yang-ban Confucian literati actively endeavored to defend and preserve the local communities as a war actually broke out. They organized righteous militias throughout the country and fought against the Japanese troops.

The victories of the naval forces and the actions of the righteous militias turned the tides of war. In addition, Ming also dispatched a large contingent of troops to Joseon as a relief force, in that Ming was concerned that the war might extend over to China. Counter-attacks from the allied forces of Joseon and Ming forced the Japanese troops to withdraw to the south. And from that point, as Ming wanted to minimize their losses and the Japanese knew that they lost the initiative to defeat Ming, both parties entered negotiation's to reach an agreement upon an armistice. However, Ming found it impossible to accept the unreasonable request from Japan, which demanded that half of Joseon's terrain be placed under permanent occupation of Japan.

Yi Sun-shin (1545~1598) and Geobukseon (the turtle-shaped ironclad battleship)

He was a general, initially in charge of guarding the northern border of the country, but later he was promoted and appointed to admiralty in navy, a year prior to the breakout of Imjinwaeran. His comprehensive tactics and astute technical expertise enabled him to defeat the Japanese navy again and again. Yet unfortunately, he was killed by enemy fire during the last battle of Noryang in 1598. This picture is of the Admiral Yi Sun-shin's statue, placed at the center of the metropolitan city of Seoul.

The ship in the picture is called a "turtle ship," because its body resembled the back of a turtle and its front looked like a head of a dragon. The ironclad turtle ship in the picture is a restored model. It was designed and created based upon records which let us know that it was used as an attack ship in the battles with the Japanese invaders.

In 1597, Japan broke the ceasefire agreement and raided Joseon again. Unlike before, however, in this time Joseon was fully prepared. Being discouraged by the fierce resistance, the Japanese invaders were driven off the peninsula in 1598, and the seven-year war was ended.

Aftermath of the war

During the war, the frustration of the Joseon population continued to mount. They lost their family, they were out of food, and they had nowhere else to go. Yet most importantly, they were exposed to foreign attacks without any protection from the government. They could never forgive the king and the vassals who swiftly fled to the north at the first sign of trouble. And their rage against the looting of the so-called 'relief troops' of Ming was also on the rise.

While the Joseon leadership continued with its repair efforts, they continued to blame Japan and praise Ming, hoping that such promotions would divert the angry people's attention away from the Joseon government.

However, the progress of such efforts was quite slow, as the royal treasury had already been drained. Meanwhile, complaints grew just bigger and bigger. The Joseon government continued singing praises of Ming, as it was the only thing that they could do at the time.

Joseon enhances security of the southern border and guards the northern border

In 1603 the Tokugawa family, which had displayed a less aggressive attitude toward Joseon, seized power in Japan. It was the beginning of the Edo Shogunate period. The new power desired to reconcile with Joseon as well as Ming, because Tokugawa Ieyasu hoped to raise the international status of the Tokugawa regime by reviving international trades.

Joseon was reluctant to open trades with Japan again, naturally because of its general population's hatred against Japan. However, the exchanges of war prisoners, and the overall reconstruction efforts required negotiations between both sides. Joseon was also concerned of the mobilization of the Manchu tribes across the northern border. So Joseon finally agreed to negotiate with Japan, in the pretext of Japan's issuing an official apology.

In 1607, Joseon decided to restore its diplomatic relationship with Japan, and sent a large group of emissaries which would be called later as "Joseon Tongshinsa." Joseon also allowed the Japanese to have trading activities in-

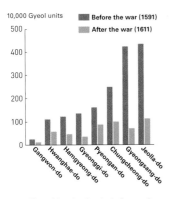

Size of farming lands, before and after Imjinwaeran
The size of taxable lands was reduced to 30% due to the aftermath of the wars.

side Joseon.

The threat from the north soon became a reality. The Jurchen, who was once willing to send its troops in support of Joseon, rose to power in Manchuria after unifying their own tribes. In 1616, the united Manchu tribes established "New Jin" (Qing, since 1636). By the year of 1618, they grew powerful enough to occupy most of the Manchurian region, and turned out to become the greatest threat ever to both Ming and Joseon.

Abolishment of "Neutral Diplomacy" and the outbreak of "Byeongjahoran"

In 1619, Ming organized an army to confront 'New Jin.' Then it requested Joseon to send its army, as a payback for Ming's sending a relief army to Joseon during the Japanese invasion of Joseon. Joseon agreed that Ming was indeed entitled to ask for the Joseon troops, but Joseon also had to avoid making a new enemy by getting involved in a conflict between Ming and New Jin. It put the Joseon government in a serious dilemma.

King Gwanghaegun (reigned from 1608 to 1623) who ascended the throne succeeding King Seonjo was very hesitant in mobilizing the Joseon army to support Ming's war. Since he went through a bloody war with the Japanese himself, he adopted a policy to remain neutral between Ming and New Jin. Although he sent the Joseon army to Ming, the Joseon forces refrained from aggressively fighting the New Jin forces. Some Joseon vassals, who had opposed King Gwanghaegun's enthronement in the first place, criticised this tactic and behavior as a 'betrayal to loyalty.'

The memebers of the Seoin faction who were estranged from the center of power during King Gwanghaegun's reign organized a revolt, under the name of maintaining 'integrity' in the relationship with Ming. They put a new king on the throne, and as a result, the neutral diplomacy policy ceased right there.

In 1627, New Jin launched its first invasion into Joseon soil, and in 1636 another attack was launched with a larger number of troops. This was an attempt to subdue Joseon before taking on Ming. New Jin had to invade Joseon first in order to prevent Joseon's support of Ming. However, it was also partly due to Joseon's new diplomatic policy which only emphasized the relationship with Ming. Joseon remained faithful to Ming, yet it failed to win the war. As a result, Joseon surrendered to Qing and had to endure a series of interventions from Qing for quite some time.

3

Establishment of a Patriarchic Family System

"From now on, Joseon is the only remaining Confucian state"

After the war with Qing ended, the Seoin faction which led the war efforts found itself in a difficult situation, as they couldn't evade the criticism that their philosophy of maintaining loyalty to Ming only resulted in an unnecessary war with — and surrender to — Qing.

Nevertheless, the majority of Sarim figures still wanted to keep their conviction of 'instead of seeking imminent profits, we should distinguish right and wrong first.' Of course, the people of the Seoin faction were the most stubborn in upholding such principle. As a result, "the idea of the northern conquest" was suggested. They argued that military expenses should be increased rather quickly so that they could launch a retaliatory strike against Qing.

The idea of the northern conquest had a powerful influence upon the Korean people during the 17th century, and it continued to do so even after the plan itself was deemed undoable as Qing became the

Site of the Mandongmyo Shrine (Gwesan, Chungcheong-buk-do province)
This shrine was built in the prospect of holding memorial services in the honor of Ming Emperor Shinjong, who helped (and supposedly "saved") Joseon during the Japanese invasion. The Seoin faction members, who continued to suggest launching a retaliatory strike against Qing ever since the end of the Byeongjahoran war, promoted the creation of this shrine.

dominant ruler of China. Such conviction stemmed from the idea that Jo-seon was the only remaining civilized state with the experiences of practicing Confucian teachings. The people of Joseon thought that they were now the only state that could be identified as the successor of Sino-Centrism,■ while Qing was nothing but a powerful barbaric nation.

And at the time, the Confucian customs were emphasized more strongly than before. The government put a lot of efforts into practicing and observing numerous dynastic rituals according to the ideals and details of Confucian-ism. Research upon the formalities of such protocols was a major concern and interest, shared not only by the royal court but also by the Sarim scholars out of office. Confucian ethics and customs spread from royal families to the Sarim figures and the general population.

■ **Sino-centrism** Confucian scholars considered the culture of the Han race of China as the center of the Confucian civilization. As Qing (Jurchen) became the ruling power of China, the Joseon scholars figured that now that center had no choice but to move over to Joseon, instead of remaining with the barbaric Qing race. So they regarded Joseon as a small version of the Confucian civilization.

Changes in marriage customs and family system

Since the 16th century, research on Neo-Confucianism became more metic-ulous and comprehensive, and the protocols to be observed in family rituals established by Chu Hsi widely spread throughout the Joseon society. The fu-nerals and rituals that embraced Buddhist formalities gradually disappeared. Social interest in ritual protocols continued to grow, so related manual books were actively published as well.

Sohak ("Elementary Studies")
This is a textbook that Chu Hsi published to educate young students with Confucian teachings during the time of Sung China. Confucian ideals were being emphasized throughout the Joseon period, thus Korean translations of the book were pub-lished in Joseon many times.

Shinhaeng
This is a picture by Kim Hong-do, which describes the bridegroom and bride heading to the bridegroom's house after the wedding ceremony that was held at the bride's house. In the early half of the Joseon period, the bridegrooms used to move into the brides' home or at least areas in the vicinity, but in subsequent periods the brides began to move into bridegrooms' home. In the picture, a man with a wooden wild goose appears. A wild goose was considered a symbolic animal that promised everlasting love. It was also considered as an animal which treated its own family with a gentle manner. 39.7×26.7cm.

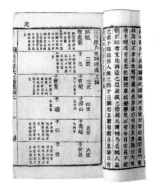

Genealogy

This is a genealogical record (a family tree book), which described the ancestral lineage of a Yangban family. Through such records, people were able to tell their own personal lineage and the boundary of one's group of relatives.

Since the 17th century, more of these records were made, because they were considered as an important indicator to one's being a Yangban figure.

Protocols were regarded as an important method to express one's disciplined mind and ethical training. Etiquettes, rules and manners for various ceremonial occasions were newly established. In order to be considered as a virtuous man, he or she was required to have "a truthful mind to practice morality." It was also advised: "Practicing morality and family ethics should be considered more important than working for the country and the government." So, a claim was made: "Prior to working for the state, one has to manage his own household in good manners first."

From the 17th century, in which the northern campaign and the "politics of protocols" were deemed the most important agendas of the government, Confucianism continued its spreading of influence, involving all areas, marriages, familial relationships, and inheritance practices.

Since this time, the previous custom of marriage which usually had the bridegroom move into the house of the bride was changed, and as a result, the bride began to move into her husbands' home. Only the oldest son was left in charge of maintaining the family and preparing memorial services for the ancestors. When there was no son to undertake such role, then a son would be invited from a relative family, so the role and status of daughters within the family became deteriorated. Women were also cast out from the property distribution process, and sons other than the oldest were also discriminated against to a certain degree. After the 17th century, it became a general practice to leave all the parents' properties only to the oldest son.

Establishment of Confucian customs throughout the Joseon society

And with all these changes, a new hierarchy structure, discriminative in nature, was created throughout the society. Women's rights were ignored, and instead their 'responsibilities' to their husbands were emphasized. There were discriminations even against younger sons.

Confucius taught that every individual should lead a life suitable to his or her position inside a family or a country. He once said "If kings behave like a king, vassals like a vassal, ... the nation will flourish." And his followers established "Five Codes of Ethics■" that carried the Confucian doctrine. With those codes, loyalty to the king's authority, filial piety to parents, and women's devotions and service to men, were the most honorably mentioned, pivotal values.

The doctrine of Confucianism spawn public notions that required sacrifice

■ **Five Codes of Ethics** These rules suggested that there are certain disciplines of behavior that are needed to be upheld in interactions between the king and vassals, fathers and sons, husbands and wives, the young and the elderly, and among friends.

of the underprivileged: between lords and slaves or landlords and tenant farmers. Such notions served as a justification for the social hierarchy. The Confucian formalities emphasized by the state in the 17th century were to stabilize the class system which established itself in the aftermath of two wars.

Since the 17th century the Confucian customs began to be upheld firmly among the Yangban class. The Yangban class who identified themselves as the privileged accepted the Confucian family system, claiming the importance of Confucian ethics. Whoever wanted to be categorized as a Yangban figure also accepted it voluntarily.

Confucianism led by the upper class seemed like the major trend of the time. However, there were many parts of the society that failed to adapt to Confucianism. Buddhism was still the people's belief, and the Confucian-styled marriage and the family system conceived by it were still not widely accepted. There were also some resistances against Confucian virtues that admitted discrimination. New religions surfaced, opposing the discrimination of sexes and classes. And people's ideas of abolishing a discriminatory society began to emerge as well.

Virtues of women in the Five Codes of Ethics
The Confucian ethics included many rules that discriminated women. The virtues of "Samjongjido" required that women were supposed to be submissive to their fathers when they were young, and upon marriage to their husbands, and after their husbands deceased then to their sons. The picture is a piece from the "Five Virtuous Behaviors (*Oryun Haengshildo*)" paintings that depicted such contents with documents and illustrations. This book was published at the king's order in 1797.

Yeolnyeomun
Joseon awarded women who dedicated their lives to their deceased husbands, by building "Yeolnyeomun," a gate to commemorate the sacrifice of a dedicated woman. Families that had such dedicated woman received numerous benefits from the government, including the reduction of taxes. However, such high demand upon women forced them to suffer unnecessary pains.

Ancestral Rituals:
Commemorating the Deceased Parents

One day in November of the year 1791, a Catholic believer named Yun Ji-chung was arrested and be-headed because he burned the tablet of his deceased mother. At the site of execution, he warned the people that to bow and worship the spirit of dead people was against God's will.

In Joseon, when parents passed away they inscribed their parents' names on a piece of wood and kept it in their house or shrine. On the annual memorial day of their parents, all family members gathered to have an ancestral ritual. They placed the wooden board on the table in early dawn and set all kinds of food on the table burning incense sticks. Also, most of the literati had a family shrine in their houses to keep such wooden tablets.

Such customs were prevalent all over Joseon after the 16th century. Research on the method and pro-cedures of ancestral rituals (memorial services) was also actively conducted. Studies on the *Zhuzijlali* (The Family Rituals of Zhu Xi) continued, and various manuals were published to explain how to perform rituals or family ceremonies appropriately. Rituals made in accordance with such formalities were upheld as the essence of the Confucian ideology. When Yun Ji-chung denied such ancestral ritual, the Joseon society had no choice but to regard his testament to be grossly defying the virtues of Confucianism.

170

Therefore, they had to refuse Christianity.

Confucian rituals are quite different from those of Buddhism, not to speak of Christianity. Worshipping is an exhibition of absolute reliance upon God, while the (Confucian) rituals are more or less like a ceremony which encourages people to have a solemn mind in commemoration of the deceased ancestors. Confucianism considers ancestors to be spiritual beings, but does not identify them as a god, so Confucianism might be considered religious in some ways, but not so much in others.

Ancestral ritual at the temple
In the Buddhist nation Goryeo, rituals were mostly held at temples. The tablets of the deceased were kept inside the temple, and it was the monks who performed the rituals. Since rituals for one's parents were held at the temple, children shared the expenses evenly, and in return they inherited assets equally among siblings.

How to Conduct Ancestral Rituals

As people's understanding of the Confucian protocols broadened, the table settings and the order of rituals came to be well-organized. However, each family had slightly different manners in actual observation of the rituals, and today they are more or less observed in a simplified format. A memorial ritual is a ceremony that commemorates the deceased ancestor by treating them with various foods. First we bring "Wipae" from the shrine in the house and place them on the table (❶). "Wipae" refers to a wooden tablet on which the name of a deceased ancestor is inscribed. As such individual shrines no longer exist in people's homes today, we now write the names of the ancestors on paper which we call "Jibang" (❷). Although the manner of table setting (❸) for the ritual varies from region to region, the basic cuisine includes cooked rice, side dishes, fruit and liquors, and they are all placed on the table. Sometimes favorite dishes that the deceased ancestor used to enjoy eating when he or she was alive are also placed on the table. By opening the door as a welcoming gesture the ritual begins, and all descendants maintain a polite, decent and reverent manner for the duration of the ritual, assuming their ancestors are indeed having a meal (❹). When the ancestors are believed to have finished their meal, family members present farewell greetings to the ancestor. When the ritual is finished, family members share the foods. This special meal is called "Eumbok," which refers to the act of receiving fortunes from ancestors blessing their descendants (❺).

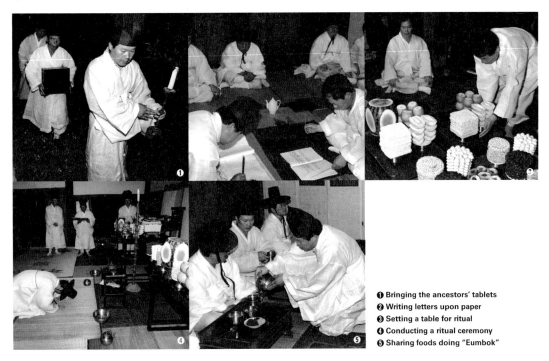

❶ Bringing the ancestors' tablets
❷ Writing letters upon paper
❸ Setting a table for ritual
❹ Conducting a ritual ceremony
❺ Sharing foods doing "Eumbok"

1650 ~ 1862

1650
King Hyojong who ascended the throne started a Northern Campaign Movement, swearing revenge upon Qing.

1669
This year the population of Seoul was surveyed as 200,000 people. Business developed fast.

1728
Yi In-jwa staged a revolt, demanding the king's withdrawal from the throne. Later a more active policy to alleviate all the confrontations among political factions inside the government was implemented.

1776~1783
America established a democratic republic based on federalism through the War of Independence.

1783
Yi Seung-hun became the first Christian in Korea after having been baptized in Qing, and soon after in Seoul a church was established.

1796
The construction of the new city Hwaseong was completed. An elegant fortress, a large scale market street, and a national farm were established.

1801
There were stern oppressions upon the progressive academic movements and the Catholic believers. Later "Sedo" Politics, with which a part of the prestigious class monopolized power, prevailed.

1811
Hong Gyeong-rae and the farmers, merchants, and miners of the Pyeongan-do province brought about a large scale insurrection to demolish the central authority.

1840~1842
Britain invaded Qing for its placing of prohibition upon opium imports. Around this time, Western fleets were occasionally spotted in Joseon's shores.

1860
Choi Je-wu founded a religious school named Donghak, and since the 1880s it quickly spread among the Korean people.

1862
Nationwide People's movements of the local communities spread out, with intentions to reform the broken-down tax system and to drive out the corrupt officers.

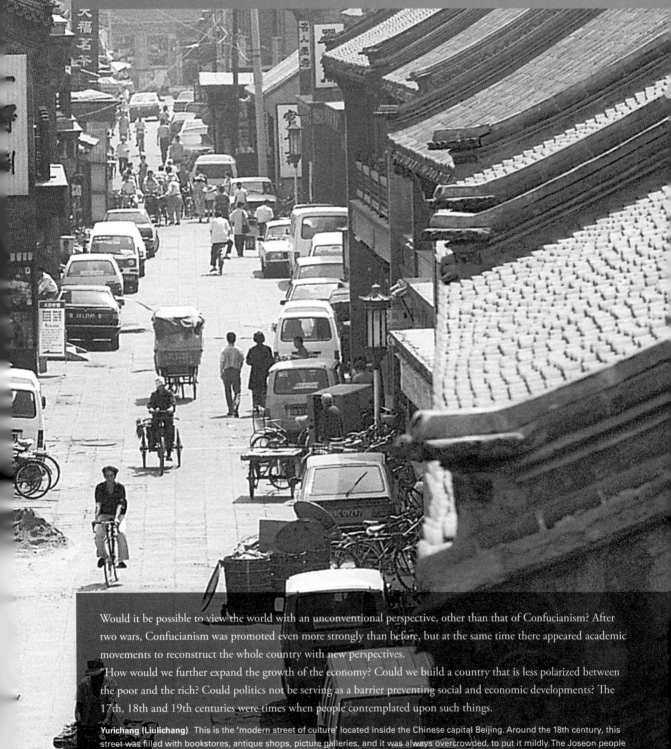

VIII Various Attempts for Changes

Would it be possible to view the world with an unconventional perspective, other than that of Confucianism? After two wars, Confucianism was promoted even more strongly than before, but at the same time there appeared academic movements to reconstruct the whole country with new perspectives.

"How would we further expand the growth of the economy? Could we build a country that is less polarized between the poor and the rich? Could politics not be serving as a barrier preventing social and economic developments? The 17th, 18th and 19th centuries were times when people contemplated upon such things.

Yurichang (Liulichang) This is the 'modern street of culture' located inside the Chinese capital Beijing. Around the 18th century, this street was filled with bookstores, antique shops, picture galleries, and it was always overcrowded, to put it mildly. The Joseon people who visited this place were able to come in contact with the new world literally.

Those Who Visited Yeongyeong (Beijing) and Edo (Tokyo)

As peaceful coexistence continued in the Northeast Asian region in the 17th, 18th and 19th centuries, the three countries (Joseon, China, Japan) maintained amicable relationships and exchanged their own culture and products with each other. Joseon dispatched envoys named "Yeon-haengsa" to Yeongyeong and sent "Tongshinsa" emissaries to Edo.

In this time period, as Joseon continued regular exchanges with Qing and Japan, the Joseon people began to meet foreigners with blue eyes for the first time. Their visits and presence prompted the Korean people to reevaluate their relationships with the outside world.

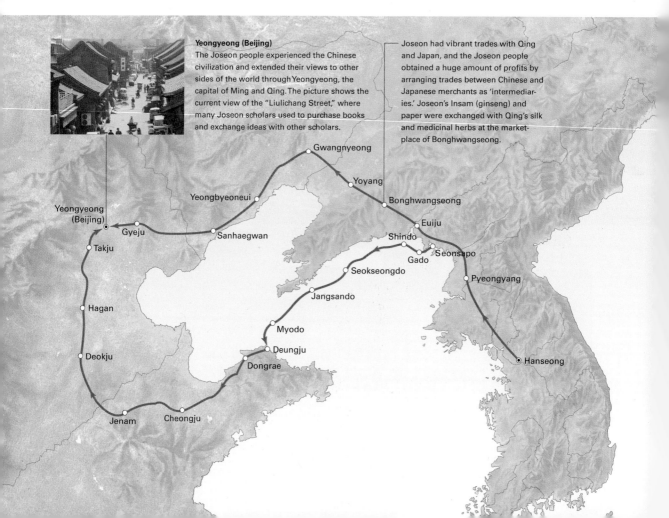

Yeongyeong (Beijing)
The Joseon people experienced the Chinese civilization and extended their views to other sides of the world through Yeongyeong, the capital of Ming and Qing. The picture shows the current view of the "Liulichang Street," where many Joseon scholars used to purchase books and exchange ideas with other scholars.

Joseon had vibrant trades with Qing and Japan, and the Joseon people obtained a huge amount of profits by arranging trades between Chinese and Japanese merchants as 'intermediaries.' Joseon's Insam (ginseng) and paper were exchanged with Qing's silk and medicinal herbs at the marketplace of Bonghwangseong.

Gwangnyeong

Yoyang

Yeongbyeoneui

Bonghwangseong

Yeongyeong (Beijing)

Euiju

Gyeju

Sanhaegwan

Shindo

Takju

Gado

Seonsapo

Seokseongdo

Pyeongyang

Jangsando

Hagan

Myodo

Deungju

Deokju

Dongrae

Hanseong

Jenam

Cheongju

Travel route of the Joseon Tongshinsa emissaries

Joseon emissaries and envoys dispatched to Japan for total of twelve times between 1607 and 1812 were called "Joseon Tongshinsa" emissaries by the Japanese people. Japanese shoguns requested Joseon to send envoys, in an attempt to raise international recognition of their leadership. On the other hand, Joseon sent the envoys with an intention to observe the internal situations of Japan, while maintaining a peaceful relationship with the Japanese people.

Waegwan

Although both Joseon and Japan employed a policy of blockading the sea, mutual exchanges between the two countries were not discontinued. There was an area arranged for Japanese residence called Waegwan established in the Dongrae area of Joseon, where roughly 500 or even 600 people from Japan stayed. Also, more than 50 trade ships visited the port every year.

Hanseong
Gwangju
Dongrae
Tsushima
Iki
Ainoshima
Nagasaki
Kaminoseki
Ushimado
Yodogawa
Osaka
Okazaki
Shizuoka
Edo (Tokyo)

— Path taken by Hamel —

The Journal of Hamel

Hendrik Hamel (?~1692), a crew member of the Dutch East India Company, drifted to the seashore of Joseon with his colleagues in 1653, on the way from Taiwan to Japan. They were detained in Joseon until 1666. "Description du *Royaume de Coree*," which was a part of "*The Journal of Hamel*," is known as the book that first introduced Joseon to Europe in details.

Picture of a parade of the Joseon Tongshinsa envoy

1

From "Bukbeol" to "Bukhak"; Expanding One's Perspective in Viewing the World

The tragic successor to the throne

Crown prince Sohyeon finally returned to Joseon in February 1645, ending a long term captivity in the capital of Qing. At the time he was 34 years old.

As King Injo (reigned from 1623 to 1650) officially surrendered to Qing in 1637, crown prince Sohyeon was taken to the Qing capital where he remained as a captive. According to the history records, everyone bitterly sobbed as the prince was about to depart Seoul.

Yet oddly enough, the records describing the crown prince's long-anticipated return to Joseon are surprisingly short. Moreover, his own father's welcome was awfully cold. All the gifts that the crown prince brought for his father from Qing disappeared without being noticed. What surprises us is that about three months later, the crown prince mysteriously died.

No one knows for sure whether there was any conspiracy or not. The government at the time was filled with voices asking for a brute retaliation against Qing. But the crown prince had a different opin-

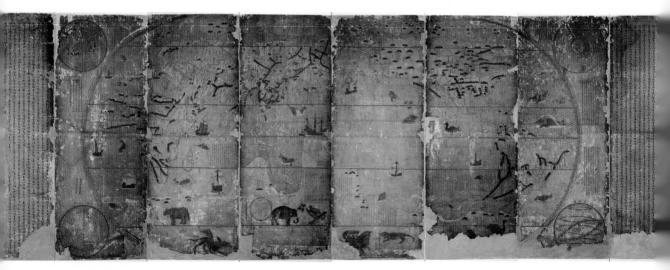

The Great Map of Ten Thousand Countries (part)
The Italian Jesuit, Mateo Ricci (1552~1610) drew this "Great Map of Ten Thousand Countries." This map was introduced to Korea through the Joseon delegates who visited Ming in 1603. This map shattered the Joseon literati's general assumption that China was the greatest country located at the center of the world.

ion and insisted that a diplomatic compromise was needed for the Joseon people. While the king and most of the officials in the government considered Qing as a barbaric race, Sohyeon believed there were many things that they could learn from the Qing people. All the things that he brought from Qing were initially bought to it from Westerners.

The crown prince's funeral was performed very humbly, and his sons and wife also faced a tragic fate. In his place, the second son of King Injo, who favored the Northern Campaign policy, ascended the throne.

Bronze globe
Among the items that crown prince Sohyeon brought from Yeongyeong in 1645, there was a bronze globe. It was called "Yeojigu," and it is assumed that a world map would have been drawn upon the globe: a map that might have been created by the Jesuit missionaries in the early 17th century. The object in the picture above is a bronze globe made during the latter half of the Joseon Dynasty period. Longitudes and latitudes are indicated in a 10-degree span, and the Tropic of Cancer and the Tropic of Capricorn are described, along with the ecliptic.

The Northern Campaign Movement hits its limit

King Hyojong (reigned from 1650 to 1659), who succeeded the throne in place of his brother, suggested a swift retaliation policy against Qing. Accordingly, the financial plan was devised. They repaired fortresses and increased the number of troops, including both cavalry and artillery units.

Yet, all these preparations for war soon became a burden to the people. Needless to say, taxes were increased. The people were frequently mobilized for military training and recruited to tasks like fortress rebuilding and weapon repairs. In the meantime, the Qing Dynasty continued to become more powerful everyday.

When King Hyojong died, the Northern Campaign Plan ("Bukbeol") disppeared with him as well. Many people still agreed with the cause, yet stabilizing the people's lives had to take priority. The task of strengthening the military system had to make ways for the task of building a social unity.

It was also argued that "Unless a true countrywide reform is implemented, the Northern Campaign Plan is just another dream." It was the claim of Yu Hyeong-won (1622~1673). He argued that land reforms that allow only people who actually cultivate lands to own lands should be implemented. He also argued that only such reforms, with the reconstruction of the class system and other tax system reforms as well, could enable the country to be strong enough to revenge against Qing.

Bangye Seodang
Bangye Yu Hyeong-won was born in Seoul and received a Confucian education. However, he never pursued a political career, and only resided in the countryside engaged in academic researches. He dreamt of a new political and social administration, contradictory to the traditional thinking of Neo-Confucianism. The picture shows his schoolhouse where he taught children in his latter years. It is located at Buan in the Jeollabuk-do province.

Land reforms, or tax reforms

Most of the governmental officials at that time were landlords. Enough study would grant them a way to an official position inside the govern-

Rice transplantation
A method of rice transplantation was developed and increased agricultural productivity of rice during the Joseon Dynasty's latter half period. Also increase in the general amount of lands per person encouraged landlords to establish larger farms.

ment, and when they retired they still had enough economic support that would allow them to maintain an affluent style of life. So naturally it was difficult for them to relate to and understand the general lives of the peasants, and the Confucian ideal society that they were thinking was actually very different from what the peasants were really hoping for.

In the latter half of the 17th century, the Northern Campaign was still being discussed, and in the meantime the problem of "landless peasants" continued to worsen. The two wars weakened the government's ability to govern the country, and as a result, the peasant class collapsed, leaving the majority of their land to the hands of a few landlords. As the royal family, the Yangban figures, and governmental officials continued to monopolize the lands, peasants were driven into severe poverty. The remaining landowners had to sell away their lands to escape starvation.

The notion that the people cultivating their own lands were required to pay taxes and report for labor services was the very premise that had sustained the Joseon society. Yet, that notion was being seriously threatened. The problem had to be addressed, not only for the upcoming Northern Campaign but also for the very survival of the dynasty.

Tax administration was the most immediate concern. The system which required people to pay local special items regardless of the economic situations (Gongnab), and the military expense that was charged only upon poor farmers (Gunpo), were two main targets of the reform.

However, as officials were all landlords it required a lot of time for a conclusion to be made. The landlords' taxes would increase, as the farmers' military expenses were reduced.

And it was also argued that tax reforms were just not enough to solve all the problems. Some suggested that the class system should be abolished and a land reform be carried out. The discussions that were initiated to address the stability of peasants' life and the Northern Campaign as well, evolved into a comprehensive discussion of reconstructing the country.

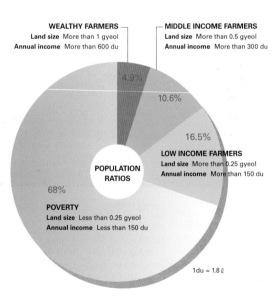

WEALTHY FARMERS
Land size More than 1 gyeol
Annual income More than 600 du

MIDDLE INCOME FARMERS
Land size More than 0.5 gyeol
Annual income More than 300 du

4.9%

10.6%

16.5%

LOW INCOME FARMERS
Land size More than 0.25 gyeol
Annual income More than 150 du

POPULATION RATIOS

68%

POVERTY
Land size Less than 0.25 gyeol
Annual income Less than 150 du

1du = 1.8 ℓ

The 17th century life of farmers at Hwein-hyeon, Chungcheong-do province

A new recognition on self and the world

The idea of "Qing is a barbaric nation, so a campaign should be launched against it" gradually changed, as the "Bukhak" idea which argued "Let us learn from the North" emerged. In the late 17th century, when diplomatic relationships with Qing stabilized, exchanges between Joseon and Qing dramatically increased. The number of delegates who visited Qing jumped, and tons of books were imported from Qing. People were sent to Qing in order to learn new technologies. International trading and commercial activities between the two countries increased exponentially. In addition to trading with Qing, trades with Japan also increased and new trading cities emerged near the border. The prosperity of urban business in Seoul became a major driving force for the commerce, and many regular markets appeared in all regions. As productivity increased, commercialization of agricultural products became typical as welll. Also, mining was developed, and there was an increase in the amount of handicraft productions.

Dramatic changes in the society was also accompanied by certain ideological changes. The development of commerce came to be considered as a positive thing. More people became interested in agricultural and handicraft production. Meanwhile, the opinion that Joseon should accept advanced studies and culture from Qing continued to gain more support.

Those who visited Qing documented what they heard and witnessed, and then informed the others. In order to embrace the studies and culture of Qing, they got their hands upon various materials through a variety of channels. Western studies and religions were widely introduced to the Joseon people, as Joseon delegates dispatched to foreign countries returned. The people's attention was also drawn to maps made by Westerners, along with books on geography, science, religion, etc.

Much efforts were made to conduct research on the history and traditions of the Joseon people themselves, essentially to further explore Joseon's cultural values. More studies of the Gojoseon history were encouraged, and efforts to examine newly found historical records and verify the authenticity of them also continued, while researches went on in areas like language and geography as well.

Therefore, in the 18th century, the Joseon people formed a new perspective other than the existing Neo-Confucian perspective to view themselves. This new perspective was armed with self-awareness and awareness of the world.

Sangpyeongtongbo
Sangpyeongtongbo is a bronze coin that was used in the latter half period of Joseon. In 1678, it was decided to be issued for countrywide circulation. The value of 400 nips of Sangpyeongtongbo was worth one "gama" of rice, and was the equivalent of one "nyang" (37.5g) of silver at the time.

Taepyeong Seongshido
'Seongshido' refers to a landscape picture of a capital city. This picture vividly shows an active aspect of the capital as the national center of commerce. According to the census of 1669, the population of Seoul was about 200,000, which was twice its population of the same city one century earlier.

2

"Let's Rebuild Joseon!"

Cheongju in March 1728

A troop of unidentified soldiers raided Cheongju in March of 1728. While the government security officers scampered around without knowing what to do to protect the city against the raiders, the city was swiftly seized by the revolting power. There were many people who supported the revolt in the city.

The head of this rebellion was Yi In-jwa (?~1728), a grandson of a high-ranking officer of the Namin faction. However, there were other rebels who also came from certain Yangban families that had been well known for generations.

Yi In-jwa occupied the city of Cheongju, and additional military activities followed inside other regions as well. Some of the regional officials of the Chungcheong-do province vowed their support to him, and some figures from the Jeolla-do province came to Cheongju to join the revolt. Also, Yangban figures from five villages of the Gyeongsang-do province captured the official administrators in their towns, and took control of local administrations.

Yi In-jwa marched towards the capital, and to justify his actions he claimed that the former king of Joseon was assassinated by the Noron faction. He also planned to replace the sitting king. However, this revolt was suppressed by the troops sent by the government in the fourth year of King Yeongjo's reign

◀ **Portrait of King Yeongjo**
King Yeongjo ascended the throne with the support of the Noron faction, succeeding King Gyeongjong who was supported by the Soron faction. At the time, the king was chosen amongst the competition of political factions, and once even his own life was threatened in the turmoil. During his reign, he pursued the "Policy of Impartiality," through which "nonaligned politics" would be implemented to appease and assuage the conflicts between members of the Noron and Soron factions.

▶ **Tangpyeong monument (Seonggyungwan, Seoul)**
The importance of an impartial employment policy (Policy of Impartiality) was inscribed upon a monument. It says that a man of virtue is the person who puts the highest value upon official affairs, and seeks harmony without organizing a group, on behalf of his personal interests.

(reigned from 1724 to 1776). It took a month plus four days for the central government to put down the uprising.

From faction-centered politics to the king-centered governance

There were many literati figures who participated in this revolt, as around the time of 1728 normal ways for them to be promoted to an official position inside the government were blocked. Provincial influentials who were not allowed to join the central government due to their relationships with certain political factions, and impoverished peasants for sure, also joined or supported the revolt.

For example, the Bukin faction was completely eliminated from the central government in the beginning of the 17th century, and the Seoin and Namin factions were left to compete against each other, until the political purge of 1694 in which the Seoin faction drove the Namin faction out of the government. Several years before Yi In-jwa's revolt, there was a brutal power struggle within the Seoin party, and the Soron faction which asserted that they should embrace the Namin members lost their power. As a result, the descendants of the Soron faction in the Seoin faction had to forfeit all hopes of rising to an official position inside the government in the future. As a result, only a few aristocrats of the Seoin faction called Noron faction, who formed the mainstream power ever since they had proposed

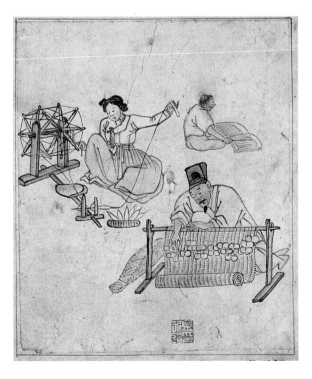

▲ **Expansion of the Yangban Class**
Between the 17th and 18th centuries, the traditional class hierarchy was destroyed. The number of Yangban figures increased, while the number of slaves sharply decreased. Yangban families with powerful lineages were still the dominant power throughout the society, yet as the number of Yangban figures increased, the meaning of the class system changed and became less significant. The picture is a "Gongmyeongcheop" which was a document that officially granted the Yangban status to commoners or slaves, who paid to buy such status.

◀ **Straw Mat Weaving**
In this picture of Kim Hong-do (1745~?), the husband is weaving a straw mat and the wife is spinning a thread wheel. The working man is wearing a hat, which indicates his Yangban status. This picture shows that the Yangban figures were no longer the symbol of wealth and power. Nonetheless, the child sitting in the back is studying to prepare for a civil office examination. Size 39.7×26.7cm.

the Northern Campaign, were able to survive the struggle. The surviving families of the Noron faction kept a wide range of Yangban figures from participating in the affairs of the official government.

The Noron faction regared the teachings of Neo-Confucianism as an absolute value. Thus, it insisted on maintaining the principles that had been upheld since the 16th century, such as the class system centered on Yangban figures, the landlord system, and political operations under theocracy upholding the nationwide spread of Confucianism.

Yi In-jwa's revolt proved that the people's opposition against the Noron faction became intense. On the other hand, the impoverished classes hoped for a new society where the class system was abolished and land distributions were equally made. They might have found more common ground with the members of the Namin faction and Soron faction who dare to challenge the doctrines of Neo-Confucianism with various reforms.

The revolt also created a new trend in politics. The Yangban figures came to conclude that political monopolies of a single faction should be restrained. There was a sense of crisis among them. More people came to believe that they should address the concerns of the people in order to sustain the dynasty that had been based upon the Yangban-centered politics.

King Yeongjo who was an excellent politician, and his grandson, King Jeongjo (reigned from 1776 to 1800) who succeeded the throne, both implemented the "Policy of Impartiality," which contributed to maintaining the balance of power among factions.

Though the factions were still recognized as legitimate bodies and the leadership of the Noron faction was not denied, official positions were opened to the Namin and Soron members as well. The royal authority became so powerful that the provincial Yangban figures who had been enjoy-

Changes made in faction Politics
From the mid-18th century, as the policy emphasizing the 'balance between factions' was implemented, the king and the family heads of powerful lineages came to play a pivotal role in the government's ruling. A system that supported theocracy disappeared, and the local Sarim figures' opinions on dynastic policies were less reflected on the central government.

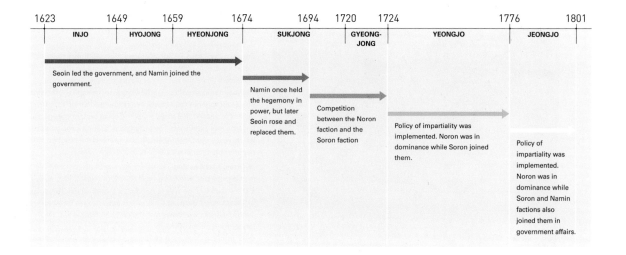

1623	1649	1659	1674	1694	1720	1724	1776	1801
INJO	HYOJONG	HYEONJONG	SUKJONG		GYEONG-JONG	YEONGJO	JEONGJO	

Seoin led the government, and Namin joined the government.

Namin once held the hegemony in power, but later Seoin rose and replaced them.

Competition between the Noron faction and the Soron faction

Policy of impartiality was implemented. Noron was in dominance while Soron joined them.

Policy of impartiality was implemented. Noron was in dominance while Soron and Namin factions also joined them in government affairs.

ing a wide range of autonomy had to submit to the bureaucratic authority. So, in a sense, the faction politics in general in which the Yangban figures' opinions had significant influence, rather came to an end.

Collapse of the faction-centered politics

The life of a literati deprived of opportunities to be appointed to an official position was no better than that of a commoner. Although many of the Yangban figures owned large lands, there were also many other aristocrats who were too poor to maintain the title of a Yangban.

To make things worse, corrupted government officials sold the title of Yangban to peasants and slaves who supported the financial needs of the government. The number of people who claimed to be Yangban figures considerably increased. Accordingly, their status was shaken, and the traditional system of Yangban governance in which they dominated low-born tenants as landlords started to break down in provincial areas. Also, the faction politics of the central government, which decided policies based on idealistic theories and the people's opinions, was also significantly weakened.

Inwangjesaekdo
Jeong Seon (1676~1759) depicted Inwangsan, as a water fog spraying the mountain after a summer shower. In the 18th century, a "Jingyeong Sansuhwa" method that depicted the landscape of Joseon with a unique technique became a trend. This picture reflects the Joseon people's cultural perspective of the time, which viewed Joseon as the new center of Confucian civilization. Size 79.2×138.2cm.

The Time of "Baekhwajebang"

King Yeongjo and King Jeongjo who claimed the royal authority's superiority to theocracy carried out several plans of their own, in order to improve the people's lives, with concessions made by the Yangban figures. The grandfather and grandson frequently went outside the palace to meet the people, to better understand their plights and to learn more of their lives in general.

King Yeongjo implemented the Gyunyeokbeop, a new tax law which alleviated the people's burden of submitting military expenses, by raising taxes on other land units. And King Jeongjo promoted more business transactions of the people by reducing privileges enjoyed by a few wealthy merchants. He also declared an emancipation of public slaves in 1801.

As more factions came to participate in political affairs in an equal fashion, various opinions and ideas surfaced as well. However, the Noron faction still maintained the majority and continued to uphold the value of Neo-Confucianism. They argued that Joseon was the only civilized world in East Asia, and they defined Western religions, Western scholarship, and other interpretations of Confucian scripts as a 'heresy'. In contrast, Namin and Soron members suggested various reform plans based on studies of the original Confucianism that came before Neo-Confucianism, and on researches of Joseon and China's history and reality as well. It was about this time when the in-depth research on the Western scholarship and Catholicism was developed into a religious pursuit. It was also this time when

Jeong Yak-yong (1762~1836) and Dasanchodang
Jeong Yak-yong was born in the same year when J. J. Rousseau published *The Social Contract, Or Principles of Political Right* in Europe. Jeong once wrote that it was the people who would enthrone a king and it was the people who held the right to dethrone him. In the 18th and 19th centuries he was one of the most representative scholars of the time and was able to integrate all the researches and activities of the progressive intellectuals into a unified narrative of his own. He authored more than 500 books including *Gyeongsaeyupyo* and *Mokminshimseo*, which contained propositions for effective administration of local and central governments. The picture on the right is the house named "Dasanchodang," where Jeong Yak-yong spent most of his time in his 18 years of expulsion. Because there was a large tea field, he created a pen name 'Dasan' for himself, which means 'Tea everywhere.' The house is located at Gangjin of the Jeollanam-do province.

Qing's advanced technology and then promote businesses and commercials in Joseon, began to flourish.

Jeong Yak-yong and Park Je-ga, and King Jeongjo

The ideas of Park Je-ga and Jeong Yak-yong which were supported by King Jeongjo are very much worth noticing.

Park Je-ga argued that the respect of frugality caused reduction in people's consumption, and also the disappearance of once-developed spectacular technologies. He also argued that Joseon should not hesitate to encourage consumptions and develop technology. He also contended that it was necessary to accept others' advanced technology and civilization in order to make a country wealthy and powerful.

However, the major interest of Jeong Yak-yong was somewhat different. He witnessed the majority of farmers not being able to free themselves from poverty. So he wanted to promote a countrywide reform which could change the whole society. He did acknowledge the significance of accepting new technology like Park Je-ga, but on the other hand he supported political and social reforms, anchored with a countrywide land reform as a top priority project.

Jeong Yak-yong's idea of strengthening the royal authority and reforming the entire system had supports of all the Namin scholars. However, the Noron faction which was the main stream force inside the government opposed such ideas, criticizing them to be too radical and dangerous. Park Je-ga also faced similar objections. Some of his ideas were shared by a few Noron faction members, yet his view of Qing differed from the others, as they saw Qing as a mere group of barbarians.

In 1800, after the death of King Jeongjo, the balance maintained among factions was once again disrupted. The Noron faction which had been in power accused the Namin members of being brainwashed by the heresy called Catholicism. Park Je-ga's pragmatism was also rejected. In order to make Joseon a truly civilized country, the Noron members thought that they had to prohibit Catholicism, and they argued "Rejecting heresy means upholding the value of Neo-Confucianism." However, their outdated argument hindered the progress of the Joseon society significantly.

Park Je-ga (1750~1805)
He suggested the abolition of the class system because he believed that doing so was necessary in order to develop the society, and that the idea of discrimination between ranks and classes in terms of occupation should be overcome. He was one of the most representative scholars of the "Bukhak" School. He emphasized the importance of developing technology and suggested to do so by increasing exchanges with Qing. He demanded the expansion of international trades, and visited Qing four times as a governmental envoy.

Manseokgeo Reservoir
Manseokgeo was completed in 1795. Its construction was the centerpiece of King Jeongjo's agricultural reforms, and the facility itself largely contributed to the development of farming in Korea. King Jeongjo constructed a large-scale national farm near the reservoir.

The Hwaseong City and the Manseokgeo Reservoir, King Jeongjo's New City Construction Project

In 1794, the construction of the Hwaseong fortress (actually, a walled-town city) began. It had been 400 years since the Joseon Dynasty established its capital at Seoul. King Jeongjo intended to construct a new city that could compete with the capital in its size and functions.

Not far from the south of Seoul, there is Hwaseong (now the Suwon). King Jeongjo relocated the grave of his belated father, crown prince Sado, to this city.

In Hwaseong, a large, temporary residence for the king was built, along with shops for foreign merchants and houses for commoners. At the north side of the city, a large scale reservoir was constructed along with an official farm in which advanced agricultural skills could be experimented. King Jeongjo issued a special order that he would appoint anyone to the government, regardless of their classes, if they demonstrated potentials in farming.

In the fall of 1796, the construction of a beautiful and overwhelming fortress that surrounded the city of Hwaseong was finally complete. Inside the fortress, merchants formed a center of commerce, and innovative farming techniques were experimented outside of the city.

Hwaseong

The construction of the Hwaseong fortress was completed in 1796. A temporary palace and office buildings were erected at the center, and this new city was surrounded by walls. The parameter is 5,744m long, and the size of the area is 188,048m². Most of the structures inside the city have been maintained for over 200 years. Based on the construction report (Hwaseong seongyeok eugwe) that was printed after the initial completion of the city, all features of the Hwaseong fortress were recently restored, exactly as it was originally built. In December 1997, it was registered as a World Cultural Heritage.

❶ **Paldalmun** This is the south gate of Hwaseong. Jeong Yak-yong, the designer of this city, carefully studied domestic and foreign methods of building a walled town. Chinese bricks were used for the first time when this gate was built.

❷ **Shinpungru (Haenggung)** The Haenggung is a temporary palace in which the king stayed while visiting the city of Hwaseong. The picture is Shinpungru, the front gate of the Hwaseong Haenggung. The Hwaseong Haenggung was damaged during the Japanese occupation period when it was used for another purpose, but later restored between 1989 and 2003.

❸ **Banghwasuryujeong** It is a place built to defend the northeast side of the city. 'Banghwasuryujeong' means a beautiful pavilion erected for the people to appreciate the flowers and willow trees. And due to its spectacular scenic view, it is now representative tourist site. Outside the fortress, there is an artificial pond named "Yongyeon," which houses water transported from the Suwoncheon stream.

❹ **Bongdon** In case of emergencies such as an enemy invasion or other sorts of national crises, smoke and fire were used respectively during the day and night to inform people in oher areas of urgent situations. There are remains of chimneys and fire holes (bricks were used in building them) as well as the building which was used for the military personnel's residence.

3

The People's Uprising

The old system becomes the subject of reform

King Yeongjo and King Jeongjo left a legacy of king-centered politics and a strengthened royal authority. However, serious problems emerged when several in-law relatives of the royal family began abusing power in the name of the royal family. A few families that carred names of Andong Kim and Pungyang Jo led most of the political operations, without the consent of the others.

The provincial governments were also in trouble. As the authority of regional officials grew more powerful, the local autonomy became vulnerable to the power, and moreover, there was no safety devise that could restrain the corrupted officials. As checks and balances collapsed, and measures that reflected the opinions of the people in dynastic policies through discussion and debates were nullified, politics in the government became nothing but a gross hindrance to the overall development of the society.

Selling governmental positions became a common practice and was soon followed by the exploitation of greedy and selfish officers who paid a considerable amount of money for those seats and got eager to get compensated. The city merchants who had accumulated a little wealth, and the farmers who were able to secure some financial ability to spare, became the target of such exploitations. In the

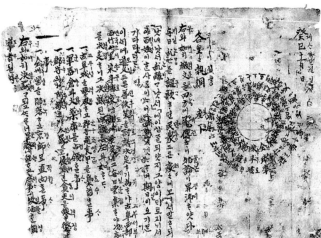

Bowl-shaped Notice of Appeal
People who stood up against the tyranny of corrupted local officials wrote an announcement to call more people and have them participate in the uprising. As can be seen in the picture, it was intended to hide the identity of the leading figures by listing all the participants' names in a circular fashion. For this reason, it is called a 'Bowl-shaped Notice of Appeal.' Inside the picture is a similar document that was created at the time of the Gobu Civilian Insurrection that broke out in 1894.

meantime, the impoverished peasants who were not able to afford keeping a piece of land, came to the point that they could not bear the burden of high taxes any longer. Jeong Yak-yong described the situation: "All farmers without means of feeding themselves are thinking of revolt." And according to a "Bowl-shaped Notice of Appeal," anyone invited to join such uprising actually cheered at the prospect of revolt, saying that the situation around them was such a mess that it was only good to have social disruptions.

Hong Gyeong-rae died and became a legend

In 1811, the whole country was suffering from famine, so the impoverished scoured the streets looking for food. In December of that year, a large scale uprising took place in the Pyeongan-do province. The financially collapsed Yangban figures whose chance to serve government had been blocked led the revolt. And the merchants who had gone out of business due to exploitations also joined the revolt. In addition, the homeless people participated in the uprising as well.

Hong Gyeong-rae led the revolt declaring "We will raid into Seoul, execute the corrupted high-ranking officials, and make a new world." In a short time, the revolt army swept the whole Pyeongan-do province, and people supported them everywhere. The capital was thrown into a state of panic. For four months, the rebel army fought the well-trained soldiers sent from the central government. Those who did not participate in the revolt observed the battles unfolding.

In April of 1812, the base of the revolt army, the Jeongju castle was demolished and all the rebels who fought there were slaughtered. However, in 1816 and 1817 another person who identified himself as Hong Gyeong-rae raised another revolt. The rumor that the Hong Gyeong-rae figure who was killed at Jeongju was not the 'real' one continued to spread. We can see that he died and became a genuine legend. It was the eager wishes of the people looking for a heroic figure to come that made him a truly legendary character.

Sunmuyeongjindo (part)
The Sunmuyeong soldiers were sent to oppress the peasants' uprising that occurred in the Pyeongan-do province. In the picture, behind the wooden barricade, we can see officers organizing their troops to get ready to attack the people in the Jeongju fortress. This uprising lasted for about four months, and ended when the Jeongju fortress fell. The soldiers sent to repress this rebellion killed most of the men in town, excluding women and children.

Appearance of Foreign Ships

The news that Qing was largely defeated in the first China-England war (1840~1842), and the rumor that the allied armies of England and France trampled on the capital of Qing in the second battle of the China-England War (1856~1860) spread out in Joseon. Along with this news, the ships of western countries showed up at the coast of Joseon, and Catholicism as a belief that conflicted with the virtues of Confucianism caused insecurity in the Joseon society.

People are the Heaven

While the people were thinking about revolutions, the conservative literati in power prohibited discussions of social reforms, saying that they should prohibit heresy and persistently uphold Neo-Confucianism. Studies on the Westerners and their religions were totally oppressed, and progressive ideas and the people who supported them were ousted from the government altogether.

However, political ideas demanding reforms rapidly spread throughout the people. Some said that a person with the last name Jeong would demolish the Joseon Dyanasty. While others believed that Mayata Buddha would come to reconstruct the world. Another rumor that was widely believed was that Hong Gyeong-rae was still alive.

The fervent desire wishing for a new society grew even bigger, as the people became more desperate to escape from their suffering. Also, the increased number of Catholics and unknown foreign ships navigating the seas of Joseon made the people more frustrated and perplexed.

In the 19th century, the ideas of the people were integrated into a religion named Donghak. In 1860, Choi Je-wu established this new religion, and argued "People are divine like the heaven." He also argued that if one continued practicing Donghak, that person would be able to have an opportunity to live

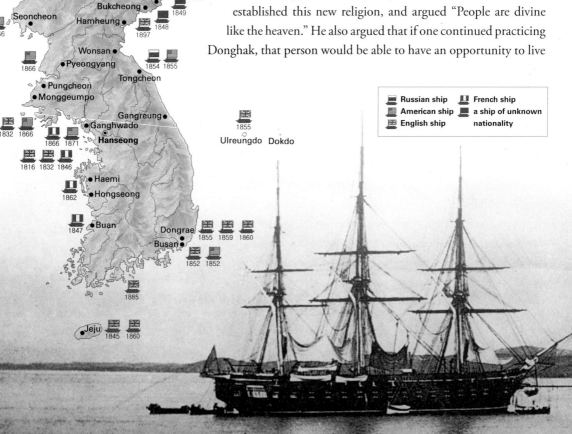

Russian ship   French ship
American ship   a ship of unknown
English ship   nationality

A foreign ship
The American ship, Colorado, that appeared in the coastal waters of Namyang in 1871.

in a new world, and lead a life that would be much better than the one he or she was leading.

Unfortunately, Choi Je-wu was considered as a heretic figure and was executed by the government. Nonetheless, the teachings of Donghak continued to be practiced by his followers. 30 years later, they stood up again to fight for the opening of a new world.

The people proclaim they are the main characters in history

As the public's awareness of things developed, they continued opposing the unfairness of the official power in the government. Some directly appealed to the king or high-ranking officials about the wrong-doings, while others posted writings to accuse the corrupted Yangban figures. Autonomous local organizations named 'Hyanghwe' worked in groups to have their requests answered by the government.

In February 1862, the people's demand became intense in Jinju, and their desire to overthrow the old system grew stronger than ever. Farmers protested against unfair taxation and executed the local officers who forcefully collected too much taxes. In essence, they reformed the local tax system. The Jinju protest spread throughout the country, and as a result, similar protests occurred in 37 Gun or Hyeon areas, during the year of 1862 alone. Alongside the Gyeongsang-do province, similar activities continued in the Jeolla-do and Chungcheong -do provinces as well.

Though the central government promised to reform the tax system, no change was ever made. Nevertheless, the people declared that they were the owners of the society. Now they were ready to make the world their own world.

Choi Je-wu (1824~1864)

He was a poor Yangban figure, but had studied Neo-Confucianism since he was young. He created a new religion by accepting various traditional ideas on the basis of the Confucian view, and integrating them with Catholicism. He liberated his own two female slaves, accepted one of them as his daughter-in-law, and adopted the other as a daughter. We can see that he had a revolutionary attitude against discrimination of class and gender.

1862 (Imsul) Year Peasants' Uprisings

In 1862, the peasant uprisings that first arose in Danseong and Jinju in the Gyeongsang-do province grew. In the same year there were uprisings in almost half of the regional towns and villages existing in the south side of the Korean Peninsula. This period is called as the "Age of People's Uprisings." Although most uprisings occurred separately from village to village, some villages were allied with neighbors. Occasionally, the Yeongnam people would participate in the Chungcheong-do provincial uprisings as well.

▲ Baekdusan

Hamheung

Hwangju

Gwangju

Jeongan
Gongju
Eunjin
Igsan Gaeryeong
Jeonju
Buan
Hamyang
Hampyeong
Suncheon
Jangheung

Hoedeok
Sangju Andong
Seonsan
Geochang
Milyang
Jinju Changwon
Nambae
Ulsan

Jeju

Joseon's Folk Paintings, Strikingly Reflecting the Daily Life

The Woman Wearing Jeonmo by Shin Yun-bok
Size 28.2×19.1cm.

As a Korean, if one gets a remark saying that he or she has no sense of shame, it is regarded as a critical comment that requires one to feel ashamed of his or her own despicable behaviors. Koreans have always valued a frugal life style, with a good manner based on the Confucian behavioral codes. They always tried to practice all the required manners. Although they were sometimes blamed for placing too much emphasis upon superficial formalities, Koreans considered cultivating one's mind by keeping manners as very important. For this reason, all the portraits of the Yangban figures feature a very serious look.

Contrary to the wealthy Yangban figures, most of the commoners were too busy working to focus on manners and to follow certain rules. Most people who were engaged in farming and handcrafting only wished that they would have a better life with no needs to worry about meals, and that their hard life would be paid off by their honest sweat. A new style of painting, which was called 'folk painting,' depicted the daily lives of the commoners with profound empathy.

At the center of such paintings, there were ordinary people portrayed as main figures: women picking wild vegetable, or working farmers. Smithies and markets were drawn as well. Children, the elderly, and attractive young ladies with embellishments appeared as major characters. Moreover, paintings that used women as their subject and paintings that dealt with sexual themes began to appear as well.

The painters themselves might have dreamt of a new world. They might have dreamt of a society in which secular values were not oppressed, workers were treated fairly, and women were free from discrimination. Perhaps by observing the characters described in folk paintings, we could look into the very changes that were happening at the time.

❶ Rice Threshing painted by Kim Hong-do

Kim Hong-do was an official artist at the Dohwaseo office, and he was well known for his sphere of influence that led to the opening of a new era of landscaping pictures and folk paintings. His painting skills were so remarkable that he was authorized to draw a portrait of King Jeongjo. He depicted the features of commoners' lives and their emotions. Most importantly, he left a number of folk paintings that adopted sarcasm to ridicule the reality. In this picture the look of farmers who are sweating to thresh the grains from the straw, contrasts with the arrogant Yangban figure who is smoking a cigarette with a pipe in a very leisurely way. Size 39.7×26.7cm.

❷ Horse Shoeing by Jo Yeong-seok

Jo Yeong-seok (1686~1761) who was a scholar and painter in the later Joseon period was known for opening a new era of "the Painting in the Literacy" in the field of landscaping pictures and portraits. The picture depicts a horse shoeing scene in which a horse was laid on its back with four legs tied to the wooden poles. While a man pressed the horse with a stick to hold it, the other man is hamming the nails on the horse shoes. The looks of the horse clenching its teeth and the man biting his lower lip and hammering the horse shoe are impressive. Size 36.7×25.1cm.

On the Way to the Market by Kim Hong-do
Size 39.7×26.7cm.

1863 ~ 1896

1866
Joseon defeated the invading French fleet that attempted to occupy Seoul. ("Byeonginyangyo")

1868
A political movement that occurred in Japan in 1868 resulted in the formation of a centralized government system which adopted an aggressive 'Westernization Policy.' ("Meiji Restoration")

1871
Joseon defeated the invading American fleet. ("Shinmiyangyo")

1876
Joseon signed the Ganghwado Treaty, promising to open a trade relationship with Japan.

1882
A military insurrection brought down the government which was promoting the country's opening to the world. ("Imogullan")

1884
A political coup to establish a modern governmental system in Joseon, modeled after the Japanese reform, occurred. ("Gapshinjeongbyeon")

1885~1887
Soon after Joseon established a diplomatic relationship with Russia, Britain occupied Geomundo (Is.), breaching international law. ("Geomundo incident")

1894
Farmers united with the religious organization of Donghak, and led people's uprisings throughout the country.

1894~1895
Japan won the First Sino-Japanese War. International competition over the Korean Peninsula and China became tenser than ever.

1894~1896
The Gabo-year Reform was propelled by the progressive Joseon officers supported by Japan.

1896
As the king fled to the Russian legation in order to escape Japan's threats, the pro-Japanese cabinet was dismantled.

IX Joseon at a Turning Point

Western countries invaded Joseon. Qing and Japan also attempted to rule Joseon. Confronting foreign power was a complicated task, and uniting internal order was also not that easy. Although the people's way of thinking and interests of their own were all different according to their classes, a united Joseon was the only option that would allow the country to maintain its own independence. Progressive officials pushed forward a reform in 1884 and 1894, and in 1894 the Donghak peasants also led a revolution of their own. Yet, such efforts unfortunately had to clash with each other, and that made the task of creating a united Joseon much harder. Could there have been any other way?

Jemulpo Open Port Until 1883 this area was a quiet fishing town. Yet, due to its vicinity to Seoul and its distinguished political and economical importance, a number of foreigners actively visited here and established a presence. Compared to the old scenary filled with straw-roofed houses, those foreign visitors added another look to the area.

Ports of All Three East Asian Countries Opened

Qing, Japan, and Joseon signed on commercial treaties with Western countries from 1840s to 1870s. However, all these three countries had to make an agreement on unequal treaties, which granted Western countries extra-territoriality and acknowledged those countries' privileges in trade activities as well. Thus, all three countries became part of the world economy in a very disadvantaged way from the very beginning.

Qing was invaded twice by Western countries and was severely defeated, and that forced China to sign quite unfair treaties. In order to reform the society which was becoming increasingly chaotic, a popular movement called the "Taiping Rebellion" was organized, which was followed by the "Yangmu Movement" that was a reform promoted by the Chinese government.

Since Japan had been forced to sign a treaty with the United States in 1854, the Japanese government countinued to establish commercial treaties with various Western countries one by one. Low-ranking warriors who opposed the Bakuhu authorities that had opened up its ports chose to revolt and established a new national system, only to employ a full-fledged Westernization Policy later. ("Meiji Restoration")

Joseon was placed in a dilemma due to multiple pressures imposed from outside. Not only was it invaded by France and the United States, but it also had to protect itself from the advances of Qing and Japan which intended to assure their security by sacrificing Joseon. Opening its own ports was a tough task and a risky decision that the Joseon people had to make.

1840
Qing signed an unequal treaty with Britain, after being defeated in the Opium War. (The Treaty of Nanjing, 1842)

1844
Qing signed unequal treaties with the United States and France.

1854
Japan established a diplomatic relationship with the United States and Russia.

1857~1860
The allied army of Britain and France invaded Qing again. Russia mitigated the dispute and arranged an agreement, and received Maritime Province of Siberia from Qing.

1858
Japan signed unequal treaties with the United States, Russia, Britain, France, and Holland.

1866~1871
Joseon was invaded by France and the United States.

1876
Joseon succumbed to Japan under diplomatic pressure and signed an unequal treaty. (The Treaty of Ganghwado)

Guangzh

The Treaty of Ganghwado signing (1876)
Japanese appeared in the coast of Joseon and provoked a military conflict. In the following year, more troops landed on Joseon, demanding Joseon to choose between a war and opening of its ports. As Joseon signed the treaty with Japan, the modernization process began.

• Beijing
• Tenjin

Gangwhwado • ● Hanseong(Seoul)

Tokyo ●

● Nagasaki

● Nanjing

The Treaty of Amity and Commerce (the U.S–Japan)
In 1853, naval fleet of the United States threatened Japan and forced them to choose between a war and opening of its ports. In the following year Japan signed an unequal treaty, in order to maintain peace (The U.S.- Japan Peace Treaty). After the signing in 1858, Japan fully opened up its ports, and also the entire country.

The Treaty of Nanjing signing
Soon after Qing prohibited the British merchants' selling of onium, Britain invaded Qing demanding the guarantee of free trades. Qing agreed to pay a huge amount of indemnity to Britain, open its five ports, and hand over Hongkong to Britain as well.

Opium War (1840~1842)
England invaded Qing demanding free trades, as Qing prohibited the opium trade. As a result, defeated Qing was forced to sign an unequal treaty. Chinese ships destroyed by the British fleet can be seen in the picture.

1

The Old System at Risk; Joseon Seeks Reforms

Joseon refuses to form an amicable relationship with the West

> Western barbarians invaded our land. If we do not fight, then we would have to make treaties with them and become friends with them. Befriending the Western barbarians would mean selling out our own country. This was documented in 1866 and inscribed on a monument which was erected in 1871.

The contents inscribed on this Cheokhwabi monument made it very clear that the Westerners were nothing but barbaric invaders, and also clear that anyone who would call for an amicable relationship with the West should be severely punished. It shows us the firm nature of Joseon's foreign policy at the time.

1871 was the year when Joseon defeated the American invaders. In April of that year, American ships appeared at Ganghwado (Is.), an entry point to the Seoul capital, requesting the establishment an official trade relationship. As Joseon rejected their offer, the American fleet invaded Joseon under the justification of 'attempting to form a peaceful treaty.' History records this incident as the "Shinmiyangyo."

Earlier than that in 1866, a large fleet of the French navy invaded Joseon, as they were attempting to force Joseon to sign a trade treaty, under the guise of investigating the death of a French priest who

Shinmiyangyo
In 1871, the admiral of the United States' Asian Fleet invaded Ganghwado of Joseon, with five warships manned by total of 1,230 naval and army soldiers. The Gwangseongjin Battle of June 11th was the fiercest one. The death toll amounted to about 400 people, yet the Joseon soldiers continued to confront them courageously, and the U.S. fleet had to withdraw. This picture shows the American soldiers at Gwangseongjin who took the flag featuring the letter "Su," which was the symbol of the commanding officer.

was killed by the Joseon government for illegal missionary work. However, Joseon refused to let them in, and defeated them eventually in a battle that we now refer to as the "Byeonginyangyo."

Nations of the West: recognized as invaders

Since the 17th century, the Western world and its civilization were continuously introduced to Joseon. In fact, the first contact was not in any way hostile. In the beginning phase of their relationship, many Koreans considered the Western culture as a source of information that should be studied and explored. In other words, the people actually welcomed the introduction of the Western civilization, without seeing them from a biased view.

However, those who studied the Western world encouraged other people to explore the world of Christianity as well, and it started to clash with the traditional value system of Confucianism since the latter half of the 18th century. In response, people started to express concerns and display caution. And since the 19th century when persecution of Catholics became quite intense, the technological aspects of the Western civilization came to be considered as dangerous as well. Koreans were very much concerned about the possibility that the spreading of Catholicism might result in more invasions from foreign countries in the future.

The international situation in the 1840s only aggravated such concerns. The fact that China was defeated in the Opium War, and that Japan was forced to open its borders by the U.S. forces only added worries to Koreans.

And proving the Koreans' worries were indeed legitimate, the Joseon Catholics who were being oppressed actually dared to request France to send a troop to make a military attack. The French counsel Bellone stationed in Qing swore in 1866 saying that "The day the Joseon king executes a French missionary will be the last day of the Joseon Dynasty... I will discuss the matter of occupying Joseon and enthroning a new king with our king." The Westerners did not have much respect for the Asians, and clearly showed no shame in invading them.

The ruling class which had been considering Neo-Confucian values as the ultimate ideal to be upheld, and Westerners who approached Joseon with a military force, were two major factors that prevented Koreans from developing a new world.

Cheokhwabi
This monument was erected in 1871. It clearly states that exchanges or trades with Westerners are strictly prohibited, in the memories of battles fought with foreign countries in 1866 and 1871. The Joseon people called these two invasions from the French and the Americans as "Byeonginyangyo" and "Shinmiyangyo." "Yangyo" means 'disturbances caused by the Western barbarians.'

Defense against foreign invasions and internal reforms

The bureaucrats were painstakingly looking for a solution, as they began to realize the seriousness of the threats made by foreign powers. Some claimed that they should implement an even harsher isolation policy, prohibiting all the Joseon people from conducting foreign trade activities with the Westerners, whereas others said that all Catholic believers should be restrained and monitored so that they would not have the chance to ally themselves with the Westerners and betray their own people.

But the officials in power had more serious concerns. In case of civilian unrests, like the ones with the magnitude of the peasants' revolt of 1862, there would be no way to protect Joseon from foreign invasions with sufficient defenses. They were well aware of Qing's recent submission to the Britain-France allied forces' invasion, which occurred when Qing was having severe internal troubles due to the Taiping Rebellion of peasantry uprising (1851~1864).

Then, as the Korean people were facing a significant crisis, Regent Heungseon Daewongun, Yi Ha-eung took control of the Joseon government, as his son ascended the throne succeeding King Cheoljong. This young king was King Gojong (reigned from 1863 to 1907), and he was still too young to govern the country himself, so his father practically ruled Joseon for the time being.

Heungseon Daewongun reorganized the bureaucratic system and put the king at the center of power. Then, he reconstructed the Gyeongbokgung, in an effort to establish the king's authority once again. He also reformed the tax system that had long been burdening the people. In addition, he purged the government of corrupted officials and removed some of the Yangban figures' autonomous privileges so that they could no longer exploit the people arbitrarily. All these efforts were to essentially reduce the gap between the general population and the royal family.

Heungseon Daewongun Yi Ha-eung (1820~1898) and the Gyeongbokgung
As the father of the king, he remained in executive power for about 10 years as the regent of Joseon. He tried to stop the regional officials' and wealthy local power's exploitations of the general population, and by reconstructing the order of society he intended to establish a channel through which people could directly communicate with the king. He also tried to protect Joseon from foreign invasions by establishing a centralized governing power.

The policy of pursuing national prosperity and strong defense

A firm anti-foreign policy was supported by the people. The provincial literati strongly opposed the idea of negotiating with Westerners, as they considered them too barbaric to understand the noble culture of the Joseon Dynasty. People also voluntarily participated in fights against foreign forces.

In order to defend the country, the Joseon government needed to train a powerful army and be ready to maintain alert status for an extended period of time. A powerful royal authority, a strong fiscal situation, and also levying of new taxes were necessary. This meant the emergence of a new policy which emphasized national prosperity and defense above all else, replacing the idea of upholding ideal Confucian politics that valued a stable society more than anything else.

However, such new policy soon faced challenges. The ruling Yangban class disagreed on strengthening royal authority, and called for an even broader theocracy and stronger local self-governing. Meanwhile the people opposed the overall increase in taxes, and eventually turned their backs on Heungseon Daewongun.

Others even voiced their opinions, saying exchange and trades with foreign countries were no longer an option but a reality. They believed that expansion of trades and embracement of new technologies would bring prosperity to the country, as they were convinced that the period in which China was the center ended, and that an era in which all countries would have to contend with each other was at dawn.

Around the time when people withdrew their support to Heungseon Daewongun, his son finally became an adult. King Gojong declared that he would directly involve himself in the governing of the country. The father had to withdraw from power, and accordingly, his policies were revised.

Park Gyu-su (1807~1877)
He served in several important official positions. Through his two visits to Qing, he became well aware of the international trends of the time and reform movements that were in progress inside Qing. In order to confront Western countries, he claimed that Joseon should adopt policies of the industrialized civilizations. He argued that Joseon should encourage international exchanges and take aggressive initiatives in developing diplomatic relationships with other countries.

'Yangban' Confucian Students' Opposition to the Opening of Ports

Yi Hang-ro was one of the Confucian scholars who most strongly supported Daewongun's policy of prohibiting trading with the outer world, but he also criticized Daewongun's construction of the Gyeongbokgung.
The reasons why the Confucian scholars opposed the opening of ports to other nations are well documented in a letter of appeal that was sent to the king from Gi Jeong-jin (1798~1879) in 1866.

> "They are so bothering because they want to annex us (Joseon). They also want to take our country from us and enslave us and our culture. They want to take our wives and daughters, and want to make us barbarians who know nothing of decency and integrity. Opening of the country and allowing them free passage would only be accommodating such intentions, and it would be much harder to return to things as they were. In two or three years after the country's opening, the entire population would turn into Western people. And then, who would be serving you and whom would you be leading?"

Yi Hang-ro (1792~1868)

Ganghwado, the Beginning of the Modern History of Korea

In August 1866, a French admiral named Rose of the Far East Naval Fleet sailed through the Hangang to measure routes that would reach the capital city of Seoul, and concluded that "If we successfully occupy Ganghwado, that would mean occupying the capital itself, so just as Qing finally succumbed to us right after the demolition of its capital, Joseon too would have no other choice but to accept our offer." One month later he attacked the Ganghwado with 1,000 marines soldiers aboard total of seven warships.

Ganghwado is closely located to both Seoul (capital of Joseon and today) and Gaeseong (capital of the late Goryeo). It was also the temporary capital of Goryeo for many decades during the Mongol invasions of the 13th century. Even during the 17th century when Joseon was preparing a war against Qing, designating the island as the dynasty's new temporary capital was once again considered.

During the Joseon period many products that were collected as tax were transported to Seoul by sea, and Ganghwado was essentially an entry point for such traffic. The French invaded here in 1866 and so did the Americans in 1871. The Japanese warships invaded here as well in 1875 and 1876, and that led to an inequitable treaty between Joseon and Japan.

Ganghwado was a place that served the capital well, but it also suffered a lot because of that very function. Valuable historical records and genealogical records of the royal family have been in custody here. In the 1860s and '70s many people gave their lives for defending the capital.

Two "Yangyo" Invasions

France and the United States invaded Joseon, requesting the opening of its ports, in order to initiate trade. Ganghwado where fierce battles took place is now considered a place that symbolizes the time of turmoil that existed in modern Korean history.

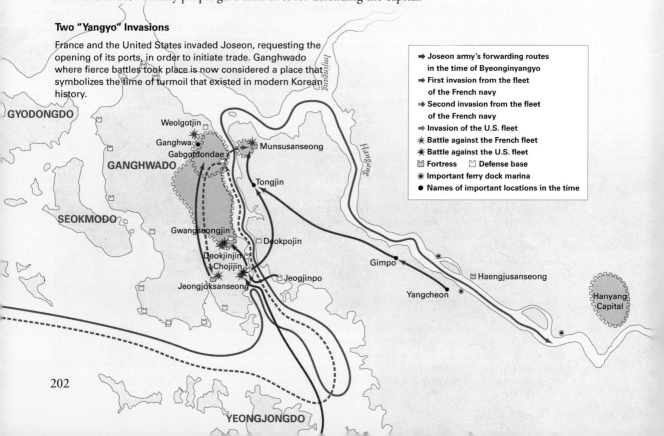

Legend:
- Joseon army's forwarding routes in the time of Byeonginyangyo
- First invasion from the fleet of the French navy
- Second invasion from the fleet of the French navy
- Invasion of the U.S. fleet
- Battle against the French fleet
- Battle against the U.S. fleet
- Fortress   Defense base
- Important ferry dock marina
- Names of important locations in the time

GYODONGDO

Weolgotjin
Ganghwa
Gabgotdondae
GANGHWADO
Munsusanseong

Tongjin

SEOKMODO

Gwangseongjin
Deokpojin
Deokjinjin
Chojijin
Jeogjinpo
Jeongjoksanseong

Gimpo
Haengjusanseong
Yangcheon
Hanyang Capital

YEONGJONGDO

Ganghwabujeondo (Map of Ganghwado)

❶ **Woegyujanggak** Important royal documents were stored here, and it was looted by the French soldiers in 1866. Although France promised to return a number of books that they had pillaged, it has not kept its promise yet.

❷ **Gwangseongjin and Yongdudondae** In 1871, a fleet of American warships invaded Ganghwado. The Joseon soldiers fought to their death and eventually forced the American soldiers to withdraw. The U.S. lieutenant commander Shulay recalled this time and said, 'Such gallant soldiers, determined to fight for their families and nation, are hard to find elsewhere.'

❸ **Jeongjoksanseong** A renowned place that once housed genealogical records and historical items of the Joseon Dynasty's royal family. The Joseon army defeated the French navy here. After that, the French decided to withdraw.

❹ **Yeongjongdo** Korea's largest international airport is here. However, this place was massively destroyed due to the Japanese invasion of 1875. Japan invaded Ganghwado's shore in 1875, deliberately staged a standoff and a military clash with the Joseon soldiers. Next year they forced Joseon to sign a far-from-impartial treaty under a military threat.

2

Joseon Joins Modernized Countries

Opening ports

In 1876, Joseon signed its first international treaty with Japan. It was the first modern treaty that Korea ever signed according to the international law system of the modern era. The treaty began with the clause that affirmed Joseon's independence: "Joseon is an independent nation, of which sovereignty is equal with Japan's." (The Byeongja-year Treaty of Amity)

Although the treaty acknowledged Joseon and Japan as equal countries, and with this treaty both parties agreed to cooperate with each other in inviting a better future for both countries, Koreans do not consider this treaty to have been beneficial to each other at all. The treaty was a product of continued threats of invasion, and it included all those unfair conditions such as extraterritorial rights, that had similarly been forced upon Japan when it made a treaty with Western countries itself.

Japan disguised its ambition by defining Joseon as 'an independent nation' in the first provision, but Joseon had already been an independent nation. Although the Sino-centric international order required Joseon to have a Tributary-Appellation relationship with China, it never lost its independence in terms of internal administration and diplomatic policy. The reason that Japan put in the clause of Joseon's independence nonetheless was to fend off China's previous influence over Joseon. Yet, such

The Forced Treaty of Ganghwado
Since the Meiji Restoration, Japan had been preparing to invade Joseon. They firmly believed that doing so would ensure the safety of Japan from foreign powers. In 1876, Japan demanded Joseon to negotiate a diplomatic relationship, while threatening Joseon with a large Japanese fleet. Forced to make a choice between a war and a treaty, Joseon reluctantly agreed to sign the Ganghwado Treaty, under the name of 'renewing a diplomatic relationship that had already been existing.' This picture was taken while the treaty was being negotiated, and it shows Japanese troops assuming a threatening position with their modern weapons outside the Yeonmudang (hall). The Yoenmudang was where soldiers who guarded Ganghwado were trained.

attempt made Qing more concerned over its level of influence that it had upon Joseon. The competition over ruling Joseon between Qing China and Japan was the major factor that hindered the progress of Joseon's own reforms at the time.

"Let's learn Western technology and civilization"

Although Joseon adopted a conciliatory policy in dealing with Japan with the Ganghwado treaty, the Joseon's foreign policy was not immediately changed because there was a major objection to the treaty itself, and the Yangban figures and governmental officials' level of caution against Japan and the Western world was still very much high.

Then, after Joseon sent two official envoys to Japan in 1876 and 1880, the atmosphere changed. The officials started to seek for some new changes. They also acquired new information regarding the new world order through Qing, which ensured them it was imperative to learn Western technology and culture without hesitation. They became aware of the gap that existed between Joseon and other countries, and thought if Joseon allowed them to trade, then they would also agree to refrain from unconditionally invading Joseon.

In 1880 the Joseon government finally decided to implement an open policy, as it wished to preserve the country by enhancing its diplomatic relation with Western countries and forming a balance of power among powerful nations. Also, by adopting an active policy of importing new technology, the Joseon government wished to enforce its military and economic power. In order to take further steps of promoting such decision, the Joseon government established "Tongligimuamun," a special office built to implement the new reform policy, which reviewed and carried out the reform plans of foreign affairs, military, and industry. Establishing a modern military system was pushed forward as well, along with sending observers and students abroad.

In the meantime, Joseon's domestic reforms in the area of politics was falling behind. The ruling class remained intact, and officials' corruptions continued. Instead of seeking for the people's consent, policies were forcefully imposed upon them.

Although sufficient time and efforts were required until the new policy bore its fruit, those who could not receive financial supports as before, immediately arose in the opposition of the new policy. While people's

Kim Gi-su (1832~?)
Soon after the Ganghwado treaty was signed, he was dispatched to Japan as an official envoy. He led a large group of representatives. After he returned, he introduced the changed nature of Japan to the Joseon people, thus providing them with an opportunity to view Japan from an entirely new perspective.

Reports from the Envoys
In 1880, Joseon dispatched a large number of researchers to Japan, in order to collect information needed in promoting the Open-door Policy. They analyzed the situation in Japan from a variety of perspectives. However, as there was also a strong opposition to such efforts, these researchers were secretly dispatched, and analyses reports they filed were never widely read.

Choi Ik-hyeon (1833~1906)
In 1876, he led the movement of demanding not to open ports to Japan, even at the cost of a war. He opposed trades and exchanges with other countries. He also organized an army to confront the Japanese force, when Japan heightened its aggressiveness in 1895 and 1905.

support to the government was stalling, the opposing forces soon became organized. The Open-door Policy of the new government was garnering only limited supports.

Which one should we choose, Western civilization or the Asian culture?

The Open-door Policy stirred guite a controversy over the issue of whether Joseon should establish an amicable relationship with the U.S. The dispute initiated in the bureaucratic society quickly developed into a clash between the government and the literati society.

Those who opposed such relationship claimed that judging from America's unjustified attack on Joseon that happened ten years ago, it had to be carefully monitored. They also believed the relationship with the U.S. would affect open policies to other countries as well, and then heretic Western religions, philosophies, and customs would swarm into Joseon. Those who considered a Confucian society as the most idealistic one perceived the situation as a serious challenge upon their cultural history.

However, King Gojong once said, "Between the powerful and the weak (countries), the gap is already too large. If we do not accept their technology, how could we stop them from looking for an opportunity to harm us or willfully humiliating us?" This is an argument that asserts, in order to preserve independence, it is imperative to sign treaties and accept technology.

In 1881, the literati population protested openly in front of the palace, requesting that the Open-door Policy be abandoned. They also promoted a large scale petition campaign.

Modern army 'Byeolgigun,' first organized in 1881
Most of the money spent in organizing a modernized army came from the salaries of laid-off 'old army soldiers', or portions of the salaries of soldiers who had to endure unfair treatments. Later for that reason, the traditional soldiers who joined the 1882 revolt attacked the Byeolgigun force and the Japanese military trainers.

Soldiers protesting the Open-door Policy

The government's Open-door Policy that had been maintained precariously, was dramatically abolished due to the military insurrection of 1882.

In June of 1882, soldiers stationed in Seoul mutinied. As they were never paid for the last 13 months, infuriated soldiers organized a mutiny to raid the storages, and to execute governmental officials who were in charge of such despicable acts. They also occupied the palace, requesting that the Open-door Policy be nullified and a nationwide political reform be implemented. We now refer to this insurrection as the "Imogullan."

Corrupted bureaucrats were the ones who provided the excuse for the revolt. But the revolt was also a product of a crisis caused by financial deficits of the government. New policies required a large amount of money, yet the revenue remained the same. Problems were bound to happen.

In the aftermath of this incident, Heungseon Daewongun was restored to power, as King Gojong asked for his help in subduing the military rebellion. Heungseon Daewongun tried to dramatically weaken the Open-door Policy and was willing to go back to the old system. But soon he failed to maintain his hegemony, when Qing China sent its troops into Joseon to intervene in Joseon's internal affairs. As Qing's troops marched into Joseon, Japanese troops also landed on Joseon soil. Competitions between Qing and Japan were indeed a hindrance that blocked the independent actions of the Joseon people.

Imogullan
Due to a financial crisis in the government, which was caused by the establishment of the modern army, the 'old army' soldiers were laid off without being paid. So they armed themselves and staged a revolt (1882). They not only killed major governmental officials who endeavored to promote the country-opening policy, but also attacked the Japanese legation and killed the Japanese military trainers. The picture describes the Japanese escaping the legation with their flag. Later Japan forced Joseon to sign the Jemulpo Treaty, while threatening Joseon with four warships and demanding Joseon's official apology and also compensations for damages done to the Japanese in 1882. This treaty also officialized the presence of a Japanese army inside Joseon, in the name of guarding the Japanese legation.

3

Radical Reforms Attempted

"Let us reconstruct the nation!"

On December 4th of 1884, the day the modern postal administration of Joseon was launched for the first time, a banquet was going on till late at night. And then suddenly, it ended in bloodshed. A small group of reformers had decided to remove the conservative figures (who had always opposed reforms) from the government, and managed to grasp power. We now refer to this incident as the "Gapshinjeongbyeon."

Those who led the coup were young radical bureaucrats, including Kim Ok-gyun and Park Yeong-hyo who had developed an amicable relationship with King Gojong. These progressive reformers seized the palace and persuaded the King to announce measures for reforms. Their reform plans included confirming Joseon's sovereignty by severing the subordinate relationship with Qing, separating the royal authority from governmental administration, establishing a modern form of bureaucracy by hiring officials based on one's ability instead of one's lineage, making changes in taxation, and reforming the fiscal system, etc.

Though confrontation with Qing was inevitable, they did not quite prepare themselves for it. And

The leaders of Gapshinjeongbyeon
These leaders sought for a countrywide reform, modeled after the Meiji Restoration of Japan. Reorganization of the governmental offices, abolition of the class system, reforms in education, appointment protocols and the tax system, and the promotion of a modern industry, were some of their major agendas. From the left are Park Yeong-hyo, Seo Gwang-beom, Seo Jae-pil and Kim Ok-gyun.

the promised Japanese support was insufficient to say the least. On the third day of the coup the Qing forces seized the Joseon palace. The coup leaders were either killed or had to flee to Japan.

Later Kim Ok-gyun reminisced the day as follows; "Joseon's reform is so urgent that another single day must not pass. If we delay the reforms, then it would no longer be the same Joseon that we have today."

Qing claims its suzerain over Joseon

In 1882, two years prior to the Gapshinjeongbyeon, the relationship between Joseon and Qing had already dramatically changed due to the military revolt. Qing immediately sent a large number of troops to suppress the revolts, as the Joseon government hastily appealed to China for military support. Qing deeply involved itself in the internal affairs of Joseon by recommending a diplomatic adviser and a financial advisor, with the intention of keeping Joseon as a sort of vassal state.

As Qing's intervention continued to grow, Japan's own plan to occupy Joseon also continued to develop. Japan stationed its troops in Joseon under the pretense of guarding its own people. Japan also endeavored to build a pro-Japanese power inside Joseon.

Western technology added to the spirit of the East

While Joseon's independence was jeopardized by the interference of Qing and Japan, Joseon people strived to accept new technology and culture

Hanseongsunbo
The first newspaper of Korea that was published in 1883. It was issued every ten days. It was an official newspaper and also a magazine (bulletin) that informed people of all governmental affairs. It was written exclusively in Chinese letters. Publication stopped for a year because the facility was destroyed by the Gapshinjeongbyeon coup. Later publication resumed under a new name *Hanseongjubo*. 17cm in width, 24cm in length. It was made of 24 pages.

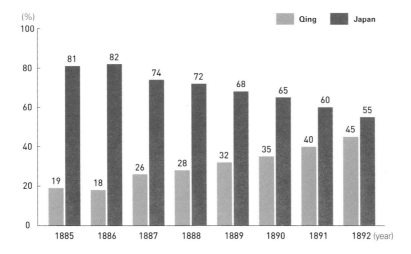

Joseon's international trade structure
After the 'old army' soldiers' revolt, Qing forced Joseon to sign a treaty that would allow Qing and Joseon people to freely trade on sea and in land. The treaty also defined Joseon as the vassal state of Qing. By this treaty, a formal set of regulations regarding trades between Joseon and Qing was established. The Qing merchants who benefitted more from this treaty actively expanded their business in Joseon. This graph shows the percentage of trades conducted between the Koreans and Qing merchants, and the Koreans and Japanese merchants, since Joseon's opening of ports. We can see that the First Sino-Japanese War must have broken out of their competitions against each other, over the Korean Peninsula.

from the outside. However, Joseon's transition process to a modern country was hampered due to insufficient fiscal funds. Qing stationed its troops in Joseon and controlled the finance of Joseon.

Regarding the speed and measures of reforms, the opinions of the progressive faction were divided into two groups. While discussing their position toward Qing and Japan and addressing the issue of lack of finance, the ones who advocated a gradual change, the so-called 'Moderate,' believed that modernization should not proceed at the cost of the cultural values of the Orient that had been upheld by both Joseon and Qing for many years. They thought that a certain level of protection from a stronger country like Qing would be inevitable, in the midst of all those international competitions.

On the other hand, others who were in support of radical reforms believed that they must reconstruct the whole country by wholeheartedly adopting and embracing Western technology as well as the Western legal system. They concluded that their worst enemy was Qing, so they decided to promote more cooperation with Japan.

The differences between these two groups eventually led to the coup d'etat in 1884, which ended in only three days. The radical party was wiped out, and the moderates had to endure a long cold political period. The coup which pursued the independence of Joseon ironically came to bolster the position of Qing.

Adopting a modern postal system
Due to Gapshinjeongbyeon's dismal failure, the adoption of a modern postal system was delayed for a while. The photo to the left is the post man who was hired in 1895 to deliver mails for the first time in Korea. He carried a postal bag on his shoulder, holding an umbrella in his right hand, and a cigarette pipe in his left hand. The photo to the right is the new modern postal office (Wujeongguk) that was about to be opened.

Britain's occupation of Geomundo; Will Joseon be able to maintain its sovereignty?

As a result of the coup in 1884, the hostilities between China and Japan somewhat alleviated. However, neither country was in support of Joseon to proceed with its own reforms.

Being afraid of the Korean Peninsula's becoming an international battle-field, Joseon strived to strengthen itself by organizing a strong army and by making a balance among multiple interests and ambitions of many foreign countries. As part of such efforts, Joseon established a diplomatic relationship with Russia in 1884. However, in 1885, in protest of such relationship the British occupied the peaceful island of Geomundo located in the southern region of Joseon (the "Geomundo Incident," 1885–'87). This incident, which spawned from Russo-English hostilities, clearly demonstrated the potential role that Joseon could play in the middle of various international conflicts.

Amidst these affairs, the Joseon people came to support the idea that Joseon should obtain a diplomatic position of complete neutrality, warranted by various neighboring countries. Nevertheless, such neutrality was only possible with the withdrawal of China, and without diplomatic power it was impossible to begin with. In order to obtain such power, Joseon's reform policies had to show some notable progress, but those reforms were still in their early stages.

English soldiers' graveyard
For 22 months, England illegally occupied Geomundo, which they named Port Hamilton during the time. Under the name of keeping the Russians in check, they sent six warships and two transport vessels to Geomundo. The picture shows the graveyard of English soldiers who died at the island.

Introduction of new ideas and things
After the Gapshinjeongbyeon, efforts to develop industries and adopt a new education and medical system went underway. The Joseon government invited teachers from other countries and established Yugyeonggongwon to teach Western knowledge and foreign languages to the Korean people. The government also established national farms to conduct experimental tests of new agricultural technology, and built factories of machine production and textile manufacturing. To the left is a photo of a teacher and students at Incheon Public Foreign School (1898). The photo to the right is the building of Jeonhwanguk, which was the currency manufacturing facility.

4

Clashes Between "Revolution from the Bottom" and "Reforms from the Above"

The year of 1894, diverging fates: three nations of East Asia

The drive to open doors to foreign influences and the initiation of reform policies rekindled all the volatile dangers that had been surrounding the internal structure of Joseon. With the opening of doors to foreign trades, rice exportation increased tremendously and the lives of farmers were seriously threatened. The price of grains fluctuated frequently, and the governmental officials exploited the people by manipulating price differentials. Those who were successful in rice trades became wealthy land owners, while many farmers had to struggle with the rising prices of rice. In extreme cases, they lost their land and became tenant farmers for other people.

The financial crisis caused by new policies resulted in the increase of taxes. The cronies of the royal family created a structural corruption inside the bureaucratic system, and with the outdated taxation system, it exploited the peasantry population even more.

The 1890s began with the insurrection of farmers demanding a definite dissolution of the old system. The Donghak Peasantry War (1894) was one of them.

Jeon Bong-jun (1855~1895) and his house
The peasant uprising was led by the Donghak leaders such as Jeon Bong-jun, Son Hwa-jung, and Kim Gae-nam. In 1892 and 1893, they arranged huge assemblies in Seoul and other cities, demanding political reforms and resistance against foreign enemies.
Jeon Bong-jun was an intellectual peasant who taught the village children and represented the people's suffering and difficulties. As the religious Donghak spread throughout the peasants pretty rapidly, he became a member of an organization to reform the Joseon society. The picture to the left is Jeon Bong-jun arrested. The house of Jeon Bong-jun is in Jeongeup of the Jeollabuk-do province.

The Donghak Peasantry War and the First Sino-Japanese War

Soon after the Donghak Peasantry War broke out, Qing and Japan, intent upon expanding their respective influences over the Korean Peninsula, dispatched their armies. Japan sent a large army to Joseon, intending to wage a war with the Chinese. Japan, which had carefully prepared for such conflict for a very long time, won the First Sino-Japanese war. As a result, Japan took over the Liatung Peninsula and Taiwan, and collected a substantial amount of restitutions. With this war, Japan occupied major cities of Joseon and began to dominate Joseon.

QING

Shenyang
Neuzwang
Guryeonseong
Amnokgang
Dandong
Hwawon
Euiju
Lushun
Dalian
▲ Baekdusan Dumangang
Haeyangdo
Pyeongyang
Wonsan

➡ Advance Routes of Qing troops
➡ Advance Routes of Japanese troop
✳ Battle fields between Qing and Japan
⬤ Operations of the first peasantry troops
➡ Paths taken by the first peasantry troops
⬤ Operations of the second peasantry troops
➡ Paths taken by the second peasantry troops

War ended due to Japanese victory (1895. 2. 16.)

Weihaiwei

Conflict between Qing and Japanese Fleets (1894. 6. 23.)

JOSEON

Incheon
Hanseong
Chuncheon
Hangang
Pungdo

Yellow Sea

East Sea

Confrontation between Qing and Japanese Armies (1894. 6. 27.)

Ulleungdo

Seonghwan
Gongju
Ugumchi
Nonsan
Daejeon
Gobu
Samrye
Okcheon
Jeongeup
Taein
Yeonggwang
Jeonju
Jangseong
Sunchang
Naju
Daegu
Haenam
Gangjin Jangheung

Busan

Jeju-do

JAPAN
Shimonoseki
Hiroshima

Signed Treaty of Shimonoseki (1895. 4. 17.)

The farmers, revolting to invite an equal society

In January 1894, peasants in the Jeolla-do province's Gobu area staged a riot demanding that corrupted government officials be punished. Seizing control of the district office, the farmers released prisoners and distributed grains amongst each other, as such grains had unjustly been taken from them. A revolt of the people had indeed begun.

The Gobu Revolt progressed in a manner slightly different from that of the civilian riots that had occurred in over sixty different places during the previous year. The revolt leaders had already, since the previous year, come to the decision of "Destroying the Gobu fortress, crushing Jeonju (the center of the Jeolla-do province) and head for Seoul."

In March of 1894, armed farmers from many regions of the Jeolla-do province including Gobu, began to gather at Baeksan of Buan. Convinced that they would not be able to make any meaningful difference even if they did succeed in getting rid of some wicked officials, they finally initiated a full-scale revolt which literally means "revolution of mind." Filled with determination, the farmers crushed the government's newly trained army dispatched from Jeolla-do and the capital, and conquered the entire Jeolla-do region and liberated countless districts in less than a month.

Baeksan Uprising (historical recording paint)

In March 1894, residents of several villages staged an allied uprising. Thousands of farmers gathered together at Baeksan, and announced that they rose to correct the wrongdoings of the government. They identified themselves as 'righteous soldiers.' "This movement is to behead the wicked officers inside and drive the foreign invaders out. People who are suffering from the Yangban figures and wealthy land owners, and low-ranking officers oppressed by local governors, are all our brothers. We urge you to stand up, and make your voice heard right now at this very moment."

Revolution and anti-revolution

As the peasants' revolts spread quickly, the government was consumed with panic, and went as far as requesting troops to be dispatched from China. Having been waiting for such an opportunity to expand its influence over Joseon, China dispatched a large army which was immediately followed by a dispatch of a large Japanese army as well. The unrelenting determination of the farmers met with foreign troops marching into their country.

As a stage had been set for a collision between China and Japan inside Joseon, the peasantry army accepted the government's proposal for a negotiation. A cease fire was temporarily agreed upon under the condition that the farmers would cease all military actions, in return for the government's promise to honor their demands. It was May of 1894.

For several months, revolutionists and anti-revolutionists coexisted in the same region. In every district, farmers established self-regulating offices that were called Jibgangso,■ and dismantled the old system from the very basis. Corrupted officials were exiled, documents that certified the Nobi servants' status were burnt, and rotten noblemen and wealthy figures were punished. Huge debts accumulated due to high interest rates were all dismissed, and campaigns began for fair distributions and cultivations of lands. A new world was on their doorstop, just as they all dreamt for a long time.

However, the government became more and more anti-revolutionist in its stance. The government demanded that both armies of China and Japan be disbanded immediately, but Japan, having been training their army over the past decade with China as the imaginary foe, refused to do so. In June of that year, Japan usurped the royal palace and forced the Joseon government to establish a new regime. They intended to justify their invasion of Joseon, with the implementation of a new Joseon domestic reform. They also ambushed the Chinese forces stationed in Joseon. Hence the First Sino-Japanese War finally broke out (1894).

In August of that year, Japan, having achieved overwhelming victories over China at sea and land, began to prepare for the suppression of the peasantry army, and even requested military support from the newly established Joseon government, in a full-forced act of anti-revolution.

Reforms from the above

The new Joseon government, established with the support of Japan, was formed of those who had earlier agreed to promote the Open-door Policy. Until January of 1896, various policies were set in motion. The Japanese

Japanese troops landing on the Incheon Harbor
Under the name of supporting the Joseon government in its suppression of the people's uprisings, Qing entered the Chungcheong-do province. However, from the beginning Japan sent troops to Seoul, in anticipation of a Chinese-Japanese conflict in the near future. The picture shows Japanese troops landing on Incheon, the nearest port to Seoul.

■ Jibgangso A voluntary organization of the peasants who led reforms

agenda of staging a foundation for invasion and the reformists' intentions of constructing an independent people's nation were complexly intertwined in the process.

In the Autumn of 1894, the peasantry army rose once again, opposing the Japanese invasion and implementation of a new government. However, the new government, while acknowledging some of their demands, in fact cooperated with Japanese forces to suppress the peasantry army by force. Even many local literati figures joined the suppression. In November of that year, raising the flag of independence and reform as well, the peasantry soldiers from across the country gathered together and stood against the allied forces in a fight for their own destiny. But in the end, they were unable to achieve victory.

Since June of 1894, the new government set forth policies for establishing a new national order, modeled after the modern nation-building process of Japan. They tried to dissolve Joseon's relationship with China, enforce a separation between the king and the state, adopt a parliamentary cabinet system, abolish the class system and the state examination system, strengthen public education, and encourage the use of the Korean alphabet, Hangeul.

Their "new nation" project met with a strong resistance from the inside. The royal family firmly denounced all the attempts to diminish royal authority, and the nobility class were not receptive to the idea of abolishing the class system or changing the regulations related to their hair styles and attire. As the new government had earlier slaughtered the peasantry army

Kim Hong-jip (1842~1896) and the Gungukgimucheo
Kim Hong-jip travelled to Japan as an envoy in 1880. In June 1894, he was appointed as prime minister of the new government and led reforms until February 1896.
To the right is the picture of a meeting inside Gungukgimucheo, which legislated reform policies for three months from June 25th to October 1st, 1894.

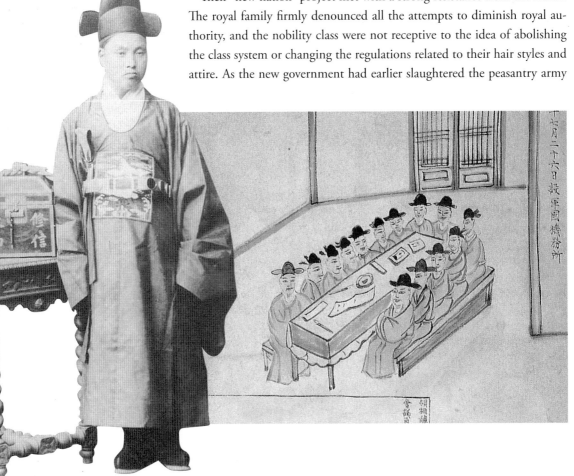

with the Japanese, support from the farmer class was not to be expected.

The people's opposition to a modernization process dependent on foreigners

The new government of 1894 only depended upon Japan for its reforms. As Joseon's dependence upon Japan increased, so did the intervention of Japan in all Joseon matters.

And as those reforms progressed, anti-government and anti-Japanese sentiments continued to grow among the people. The royal family began to use the competition between Russia and Japan in its own efforts to establish another new government. Accordingly, the Japanese invaded the palace and responded in savage violence, butchering the queen of Joseon.

However, opposition against the pro-Japanese government continued to rise, and so did the armed struggles against Japan. Survivors of the Peasantry War and those who were once thought of as their enemies, members of the nobility class, began to cooperate. They called themselves the Army of Justice (Patriotic Soldiers), and began their struggles in numerous areas. We now call them the Eulmi Patriotic Soldiers' battles of 1895.

In February 1896, the sitting 'new' government was destroyed by a coup d'etat that the royal family itself had staged. King Gojong who had earlier fled to the Russian legation in the fear of getting killed ("Agwanpacheon"), ordered the new government to be overthrown. Although the king saved his life by taking a refuge at the Russian legation, the sovereignty of Joseon was seriously damaged.

Japanese troops in front of the Russian legation
In protest of Agwanpacheon, Japan demanded King Gojong to return to the palace, while positioning cannons in front of the Russian legation. Japan also stationed a number of soldiers in Seoul, even after the First Sino-Japanese war. Japan was indeed the biggest trouble on the way to Joseon's independence.

The ordinance prohibiting hair topknots
The new government which led the "Gabogyeongjang" reforms abolished the traditional lunar calendar and accepted the solar calendar. It also required people to change their traditional style of clothes such as hats and formal robes. Although such orders were acceptable to a certain degree in terms of practicality, frugality, and sanitary reasons, there were strong oppositions to this forceful change that ordered people to abandon a long time tradition.
The picture shows us a scene in which a man's topknot is being forcibly cut off. One of the documents on the right is the order of the king, which indicated that king himself cut his topknot and therefore all people would have to cut their topknot as well. The other document is a public notice that they should confront the ordinance to keep their tradition.

The Joseon's Image Reflected on the Westerners' Views, and the Western World in the Eyes of the Joseon People

Soon after Joseon opened its ports to foreigners, the number of foreign visitors dramatically increased. Of course, the people from Qing and Japan were the largest block of visitors. Among the Westerners in Korea, Americans were a majority, and most of them visited Joseon for missionary works. Through them, Joseon's features began to be actively relayed in the Western world, while the Western culture was introduced to the Joseon people as well.

In the Westerners' views, Koreans were neither "the people with a unique civilization in East Asia" nor "the people who had five thousand years of splendid tradition and history," as the Koreans believed themselves. To the people from industrialized countries, Korea was viewed as a rather old or mysterious country.

The number of visiting Western missionaries significantly increased due to the spread of Protestant churches. Having established several churches, many missionaries also operated schools and medical facilities. For this reason, Christianity was often identified as an equivalent of the entire modern civilization. Koreans who came to know Christianity through the Western people presumed that modernization could indeed be accomplished by means of Christianization. Churches opposed the discrimination of classes and genders, and also let the Joseon people accept new customs of funeral and ritual.

However, most people believed that Christianity was having a negative impact upon the Korean traditions and their efforts of maintaining sovereignty. In China, where Christianity and foreigners were identified as an 'invasion force,' the Boxer Rebellion broke out in 1900. Those "Boxers" wanted to drive all the foreigners and Christians out of their country.

Having lost its sovereignty to Japan in 1910, the people of Joseon became to observe the world through the eyes of Japan, and the world also came to examine Joseon from the Japanese perspective. Therefore, not only to the Westerners in Joseon but also to all the Westerners in general, Joseon was viewed with the distorted images that were created through the lens of Japan.

There were a number of American missionaries among the Westerners. In 1884 H. N. Allen (1858~1932), who came to Joseon as a doctor of the American legation, and H. G. Underwood (1859~1916) and H. G. Appenzeller (1858~1902) and Mary Scranton (1834~1909), were the most representative ones. The missionaries carried out their missions for Koreans through medical or educational activities. Gwanghyewon, which Allen established with the support of the government (later its name changed to Jejungwon) was the very first western-style hospital in Korea. In the meantime, Underwood (Yonhi College), Appenzeller (Baejae Hakdang), Scraton (Ehwa Hakdang) established private schools. There were also many missionaries who involved themselves in businesses in order to create profits, or figures who were affiliated with the royal family using their own alien status. As a part of the 19th century Evangelism, Christianity spread out in Korea, and contributed to form a Korean tradition of Protestantism that generally put more emphasis upon individual salvation than social participation.

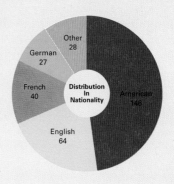

305 Westerners (including family members) residing in Seoul in 1912: nationality and occupation

❶ **Door to door missionaries** Evangelization and missionary activities were carried out in a way of looking for girls in villages.
❷ **Baejae Hakdang** Aphenzeller taught two students in 1885, but next year when King Gojong wrote the sign Baejae Hakdang, the number of students increased.
❸ **Jejungwon** Jejungwon was a national hospital that was opened in 1885, and it was run by American missionaries like Allen. Administration and management were mostly taken care of by the Joseon people.

1897 ~ 1921

1897
The Joseon Dynasty changed its title to the 'Great Han Empire.'

1899
A sovereign constitution was established, which also legally established an absolute monarchy system.

1904~1905
Japan and Russia battled over the hegemony in East Asia. Japan won the war with supports from U.K. and U.S.

1905
The Eulsa-year Treaty that took away Joseon's rights of independent diplomacy was forcefully signed. Armed struggles against the Japanese continued, while a series of patriotic enlightenment projects continued as well in the forms of building schools and establishing media activities.

1910
The Great Han Empire was annexed by Japan.

1914~1918
World War I began in Europe and spread throughout the world.

1917
The Russian revolution occurred, and the first Socialist government was born.

1919
Countrywide independent movements continued to develop, and the Korean Provisional Government in exile was organized, joined by various independent movement factions.

1920
Independence Army that had been fighting the enemy outside the Korean Peninsula demolished the Japanese troops several times.

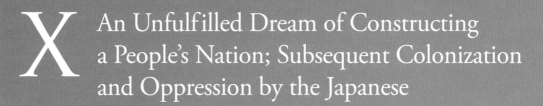

X An Unfulfilled Dream of Constructing a People's Nation; Subsequent Colonization and Oppression by the Japanese

In 1910 the Great Han Empire was forced to agree with Japan's annexation of Korea. This meant that the Great Han Empire would be dismantled, and the Joseon people's efforts to construct an independent nation would be put on hold for an indefinite period of time. It also meant all civil freedom would be denied.

Koreans' resistance against the Japanese imperial authorities was not only meant to construct an independent nation but also to terminate monarchism that had lasted for thousands of years and replace it with a democratic republic system. The Provisional Government of the Republic of Korea too did not try to resurrect the Great Han Empire but establish a newly born Korea that would be run by a democratic republic system.

Dongnimmun (Independence Gate) Dongnimmun was built with the funds raised in the spirit of self-reliance and independence. And such heightened sense of independence led to the foundation of the Great Empire of Han. This gate is located at the Independence Park in Seodaemun, Seoul.

Imperialists' Invasion and the Colonized Joseon

Even in the midst of foreign invasions, the Joseon people's struggle to build an independent nation continued. In the time of crisis, with the Korean sovereignty under attack, they chose to unite and fight the invaders.

However, it was beyond their abilities to defend themselves alone from the invasions of powerful Western nations and from Qing and Japan's intervention in Korean affairs. Their reform efforts were thwarted and discouraged. As a result, Joseon became a colony of Japan in 1910.

During the Japanese ruling, the Joseon people suffered heavily. Their rights as human beings were ignored and violated. They had to receive education which was designed to degrade their own history and culture.

The Joseon people continued to fight the Japanese imperialists, in order to regain independence and found a democratic nation, in which all individuals would be regarded as owners of the nation. It was also an effort to renew the political systems and cultural traditions of Joseon.

Russia-Japan Peace Treaty (Treaty of Portsmouth, September 1905)
"Russia acknowledges Japan's huge interest in the Korean Peninsula and agrees that Joseon should be rendered a protectorate of Japan."

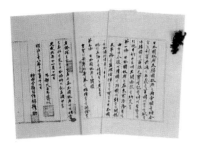

Eulsa-year Treaty Document without either a title or a signature
There was neither endorsement of the Emperor nor signs of delegation to the ministers. No title was found either. The emperor refused to endorse this treaty signing and was forced to resign in 1907.

1894 The First Sino-Japanese War; the Donghak Peasantry War; the Gabo Reform

1895 The Eulmi-year Incident (Assassination of the Joseon Queen)

1897 Establishment of the Great Han Empire

1904 The Russo-Japanese War

1905 The Eulsa-year Treaty

1910 Deprivation of Sovereignty

1911 The Xinhai Revolution

1914 World War I (~1918)

1915 Japan joins World War I

1919 March 1st Movement; Foundation of the Provisional Government of the Republic of Korea; May 4th Movement in China

1912 Organization of the Chinese Communist Party

The Russo-Japanese War and the Eulsa-year Treaty

Around the time of the Russo-Japanese War, which lasted from 1904 to 1905, the alliance between Britain and Japan was strengthened, and new negotiations proceeded between Japan, U.S. and Russia. Through these negotiations Japan was allowed to rule the Korean Peninsula and South Manchuria, while recognizing Russia's authority of occupation in northern Manchuria. The United States and Britain also acknowledged Japan's ruling of Joseon, in order to consolidate their respective rulings over the Philippine Islands and India. In November of 1905 the Japanese imperialists forced Korea to sign a treaty, which included references to Japan depriving Korea of its diplomatic functions, and Japan's institutionalizing of its intervention in Joseon's internal affairs. Based on this treaty, which was pretty much incomplete considering the minimum requirements of an international treaty, Japan began to deprive Korea of its sovereignty.

First battle scene between Russia and Japan in Korea
French newspaper *Le Petit Parisien* (Apr. 17th 1904).

Japanese troops created an atmosphere of fear, in the night before the Eulsa-year Treaty.

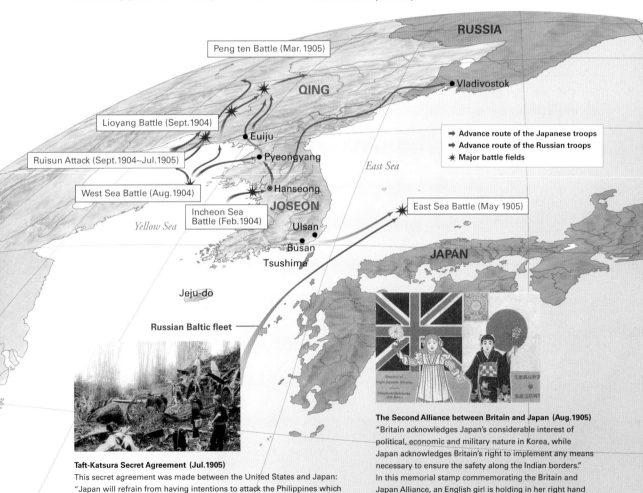

Peng ten Battle (Mar. 1905)

RUSSIA

QING

● Vladivostok

Lioyang Battle (Sept.1904)

● Euiju

● Pyeongyang

East Sea

→ Advance route of the Japanese troops
→ Advance route of the Russian troops
✳ Major battle fields

Ruisun Attack (Sept.1904~Jul.1905)

West Sea Battle (Aug.1904)

◉ Hanseong

JOSEON

East Sea Battle (May 1905)

Incheon Sea Battle (Feb.1904)

Ulsan ●

Yellow Sea

● Busan

Tsushima

JAPAN

Jeju-do

Russian Baltic fleet

Taft-Katsura Secret Agreement (Jul.1905)
This secret agreement was made between the United States and Japan:
"Japan will refrain from having intentions to attack the Philippines which is now occupied by the United States; on the other hand, the United States recognizes the legitimacy of Japan's rendering of Korea as one of its protectorates, in the light of recent results of the Russo-Japanese War."

The Second Alliance between Britain and Japan (Aug.1905)
"Britain acknowledges Japan's considerable interest of political, economic and military nature in Korea, while Japan acknowledges Britain's right to implement any means necessary to ensure the safety along the Indian borders."
In this memorial stamp commemorating the Britain and Japan Alliance, an English girl is holding in her right hand a chrysanthemum, a symbol of the Japanese emperor, and a Japanese girl is holding in her left hand a rose, a national flower of Britain. They are also holding hands.

1

Last Reform of the Great Empire of Han (Daehan Empire)

Establishment of the "Great Empire of Han"

At 2a.m., on October 12, 1897, a ritual to the heavens was performed at the Hwangudan altar which was brightened by thousands of lanterns. It was the coronation of King Gojong, in which he made himself the emperor of the Great Empire of Han (The "Daehan Empire"). This ceremony was performed in hopes of maintaining Korea's status as an independent country and protecting its own sovereignty.

The proclamation of the Great Empire of Han was made possible thanks to the efforts of the government and the people alike. Two years before in 1895, King Gojong proclaimed that he officially terminated the traditional relationship that Joseon had had with Qing, and launched a country-wide campaign joined by civilians and governmental officials to commemorate its independence from Qing. At the time the Dongniphyeophoe (Independence Club) began to publish *The Independence* newspaper (Dongnipshinmun) and built the Dongnimmun (Independence Gate) with a series of fundraising. In February 1897 as King Gojong returned to the palace from the Russian legation, the independence campaign reached its peak. Both Japan and Russia promised not to invade Joseon. The coronation cer-

East Asia in the Late 19th and Early 20th Century

After the First Sino-Japanese war, the competitions among imperial countries to occupy East Asia intensified. In 1894, Japan occupied Taiwan. In 1897, Germany seized the Kiaochow Bay in China. In 1898, Russia, England, and France colonized parts of China as well. All kinds of either amicable or hostile relationships among these countries only increased the level of uncertainty regarding East Asia's fate. During the time Joseon was deprived by these imperial nations of its economic rights over mining, forest development, construction of telecommunication and railroads.

emony was carried out under this kind of international atmosphere.

The movement for constructing a people's nation gains momentum

However, the road to independence was distant and full of trials. Japan and Russia which officially promised the independence of Joseon conducted secret deals regarding the options of splitting up the Korean Peninsula. They even contemplated upon the option of Japan occupying Joseon in exchange of Russia's ruling Manchuria.

However, this kind of crisis invited more vigorous efforts from the Korean people to secure their own sovereignty. Civilians and governmental officials participated in the organization of the Dongniphyeophoe(Independence Club) and the Hwanggukhyeophoe(Imperial Society), and things that were unimaginable before started to happen.

The class system was already outdated, and a modern bureaucratic administration was established. Some officials who were born from a commoner family rose to the highest bureaucratic positions of the Great Empire of Han. Also, modern education contributed to producing a number of high-ranking officials. The idea that the Koreans all belonged to a unilateral lineage that came from the same forefather was duly promoted, and many songs named as the 'national anthem' were newly introduced as well. It was also about this time when the Taegeukgi flag began to be widely used. And movements for building companies and schools became more active in pursuit of independence.

King Gojong in the German military uniform (1852~1919)
King Gojong and the cronies of the royal family intended to implement a political system somewhat similar to that of the Russia's Tzarist system that delegated all power to the emperor. During the "Gwangmu Reform" which lasted from 1897 through 1904, the authority and jurisdiction of the royal family over dynastic governance was significantly strengthened in terms of finance and national projects, rivaling other ordinary bodies inside the government.

Hwangudan
'Hwangudan' was an altar where kings performed rituals to heavens, and in East Asia, only emperors were allowed to perform ritual ceremonies to the Heaven God. The altar was built in the place of Nambyeolgung where Joseon's officials used to welcome Qing's delegates. The declaration of the Great Empire of Han's foundation was made here as well, and we can see that it was to propagate and proclaim that Joseon was finally able to establish a new relationship with China.

"Dongniphyeophoe" and "Manmingongdonghoe"

It was Dongniphyeophoe which pioneered first to lead all those changes. Dongniphyeophoe was organized by intellectuals and bureaucrats who wished to reform the society, and the Club argued that the society must wholeheartedly embrace Western technology, institutions and religion.

This organization built the Independence Gate, published *Dongnipshinmun*, and also arranged large scale discussion meetings to let the public understand its agendas. The Independence Club anticipated that Russia would become the most powerful threat in the forseeable future, so it launched public rallies called the "Manmingongdonghoe (Convocation of Thousands of People)" as part of their efforts to put Russia under check. The Independence Club also continued to claim the civil rights of the Joseon people and initiated a Democratic movement requiring the organization of a national assembly in 1898.

However, there were many others who thought the leadership of the emperor had to be secured first in order to speed up the process of strengthening the country. Conservative bureaucrats, circuit merchants and Confucian intellectuals were those who supported the emperor. They organized the "Imperial Society," and called themselves the imperial guard of the emperor. They also objected to the movement of organizing a national assembly.

Dongnipshinmun (Korean version; English version)

According to the Korean Newspapers Publication plan established during the Gabo Reform period, Seo Jae-pil first founded *Dongnipshinmun (The Independence)* in 1896. Three pages were printed in Korean and one page was in English. Later the newspaper separately published a Korean version and an English version. In the beginning it was published every other day, three times a week. On July 1st of 1898, it changed into a daily newspaper. Due to financial difficulties, the publication stopped on December 4th, 1899. Today the media industry of South Korea celebrates April 7 as 'Newspaper Day,' in commemoration of the day on which *Dongnipshinmun* was first published.

Dongnimmun

Dongnimmun, the Independence Gate was established at the place where Joseon used to welcome the Qing's envoys. The money needed to construct this gate was collected by fundraising movements by people who eagerly sought for their own independence. Those who participated in the fundraising became major members of the Independence Club.

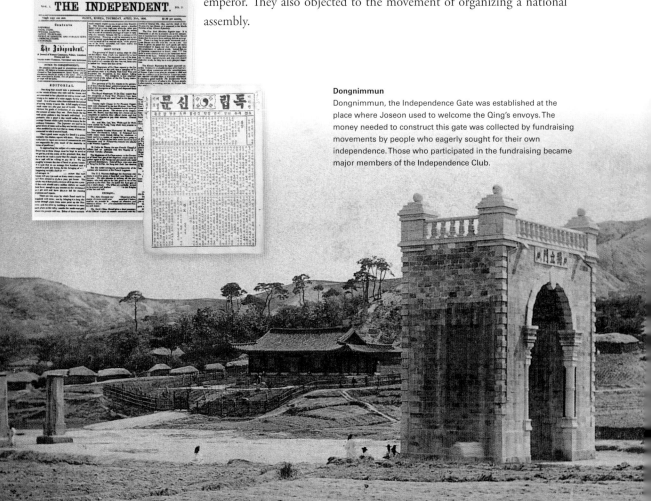

Failure of the last reform for the establishment of a People's Nation

In 1899, the Great Empire of Han announced the so-called "Constitution of the Great Han Empire," which dictated that the emperor of the Great Han Empire held administrative, legislative, judiciary, and military power over the country. It was the emperor's victory over the long-continued argument requiring a national assembly. Since then, the emperor led the "Gwangmu Reform" aiming for the country's modernization.

The government increased its military investments and put a lot of efforts into nourishing a modern industry. In order to learn new technology, the government sent students abroad and established modern institutions for education inside the country. It also conducted a country-wide land survey in order to increase revenue and sustain relevant administration.

Yet, the emperor's efforts had its own limits. Even with a deteriorating financial condition, the government still had to invest 30% of its budget into military expenses, and the reform efforts were still not producing the desired effects.

Because of the memory of a compromised sovereignty, the "Gwangmu" government which experienced crucial damage from a depriviation of sovereignty not only tried hard to maintain a neutral position between Japan and Russia, but also struggled to develop amicable relations with the U.S. and European countries. However, since all the countries that participated in seizing East Asia considered their own interests as a top priority, the attempts of the Great Han Empire were prevented from advancing to its goal.

Taejeonggwan Document
In 1906, Japan ignored Joseon's territorial claims and added Dokdo to the list of their territories. Although Japan claimed that it simply declared its ownership over an uninhibited island, Joseon had been recognizing Dokdo as its own territory in the official gazette for a long time. This document was a letter from the Taejeonggwan office, the highest organization of Japan at the time, written in response to the query of the foreign ministry. It clearly declared that "Be aware that Dokdo is not a part of Japanese soil."

Dokdo
Dokdo is an island located in the southeast of Ulleungdo (Is.) This island has been a part of the Korean territory since the 6th century. The Empire of Han claimed its territorial rights over the north part of the Dumangang in its negotiations with Qing over border issues. And in 1900, Joseon reaffirmed that Dokdo was part of its territory through a royal mandate. Through such process the Korean borders on land and sea were officialized in a modern term.

Modern History at the Gyeongungung Palace and the Jeongdong Street

The Deoksugung Palace (Gyeongungung), which is located at the center of the metropolitan city of Seoul, was originally the house of Prince Weolsandaegun, an elder brother of King Seongjong. During Imjin-waeran in the 1590s, the Gyeongbokgung was burned down, so the Deoksugung was decided to be used as a temporary residence for King Seonjo. Later, in this place the King Gwanghaegun government was orverthrown and the enthronement of King Injo took place. And in the 1890s, King Gojong promoted here his last reform effort right upon his return from the Russian legation in 1897, and resided here until he died. In the east side of the palace there was the Hwangudan where the ceremony of the 40th anniversary of King Gojong's coronation (and his ascension to the Emperor seat) was conducted. In its west side there were a number of foreign legations and a town of residences built for foreigners. The Seokjojeon (hall) at the Deoksugung once again served its historic role as a space for the U.S. and Russia Joint Commission meeting, which was held to decide the future fate of the Korean Peninsula.

❶ **Deoksugung** Its original name was Gyeongungung. But later it was changed to 'Deoksu' in hopes of King Gojong's longevity after he resigned from the throne. Later, most of the palace was destroyed by the Japanese. At the center of the picture is the Junghwajeon (hall), and to its left is the Seokjojeon (the East residence).

❷ **The Jeongdong Church** An American minister named Appenzeller built the Jeongdong Church near the Deoksugung. Many foreign legations gathered there, and many foreigners began to reside near the church as well. The Jeongdong street was full of foreign atmosphere, and thus named "a Miniature of the Western World."

❸ **The old Russian legation building** Being threatened by Japanese troops, King Gojong fled to the Russian legation in 1896 and stayed there for more than a year. During that time foreign countries' intervention in Korean affairs was intensifying. This picture is the watchtower of the old Russian legation.

❹ Hwanggungwu at Hwangudan Hwangudan is the place where King Gojong was enthroned as the Emperor of the Great Empire of Han. However, today a subsidiary building named Hwanggungwu and a monumental stone-drum built in commemoration of the 40th anniversary of King Gojong's coronation are the only things left. In 1913, the Japanese government turned this sacred place where heavens used to be worshipped, into a hotel.

❺ Jungmyeongjeon In November 1905, the Japanese summoned all the ministers here and threatened them to sign the so-called Eulsa-year Treaty. Though King Gojong sternly refused to endorse such an unfair treaty, Japan made Korea its protectorate state anyway with threats.

2

Joseon's Confrontation Against the Japanese Invasion

"Today, we cry out in lamentation!"

Last time when Marquis Ito Hirobumi visited Korea, naive Korean people welcomed him saying "He has been saying all the time that he would serve the continuation of peace among the three countries in East Asia. So by coming here he must be intending to propose methods for Korean independence." However, it is so difficult to figure out the truth in this world! Far from what we expected, how dare can Ito Hirobumi suggest such unfair five provisions in the treaty? This treaty indicates not only the division of our country but also that of the three Asian countries. Where does his true intention lie? However, since our almighty emperor sternly refused to agree with the treaty, we presume that the Marquis as well must have known that those provisions were unacceptable to the Korean people. Alas! All those Joseon ministers who are no better than dogs and pigs! They have betrayed their own people by pursuing their own interests. They gave away four thousand years of tradition and a five-hundred year old dynasty to the others. They sold out this country in fear of false threats and delivered Joseon's 20 million countrymen to be enslaved by others… – *Hwangseongshinmun,* November 20, 1905

Jang Ji-yeon (1864~1920)
He was a Confucian scholar, but he believed that traditions needed to be recreated and reinterpreted, and that new cultures from the outside should be embraced as well. He joined the Independence Club and conducted a campaign for the recovery of Korean sovereignty through media as the president of *Hwangseongshinmun* since 1902. To the right is his editorial titled as "Shiilyabangseongdaegok (Today, we cry out in lamentation!)" for condemning those governmental officials who betrayed their own country by agreeing to sign the Eulsa-year Treaty.

The above editorial, "Shiilyabangseongdaegok" which was written in frustration by Jang Ji-yeon reveals how Korea was forced to become a protectorate state of Japan. The meeting was held at the Gyeongungung which was surrounded by Japanese soldiers. This treaty was declared effective without the emperor's (King Gojong) agreement or endorsement. The U.S., Britain, and Russia all withdrew their legations from Korea and acknowledged the legitimacy of this treaty which deprived Joseon of its diplomatic rights.

The Great Empire of Han became a protectorate state of Japan

Imperial Japan continued its efforts to make Joseon its own protectorate. Japan started the Russo-Japanese War in 1904, and as the war broke out, Japan stationed a large number of troops in Korea and demanded the Joseon government to assist Japan's war efforts, pledging that Japan would fully support Joseon in its escaping from Russia's influence. Japan also insisted that Joseon should consult Japanese consultants in the future in making all kinds of diplomatic or financial decisions, arguing that such consultation would ultimately facilitate Joseon's own efforts of modernization. When the war was over, Japan forced Joseon to sign the Eulsa-year treaty.

After signing of this treaty, Japan intervened in every aspect of Korean governance. All their promises for Joseon's independence and modernization turned out to be a lie because Japan excluded the Koreans from administrating national affairs to build a colonial government of and for Japan.

Japanese soldiers guarding the Daeanmun gate of the Gyeongungung while the Eulsa Treaty was being forcefully signed
In the midst of the Russo-Japanese War, Japan mobilized a large scale of army and stationed them in Seoul. To force the signing of an unfair treaty which deprived Joseon of its diplomacy, the Japanese had their army surround the palace. The main gate of the Gyeongungung in which the emperor's office was located, is seen in the back in the picture.

However, things did not turn out as the Japanese anticipated; angry Koreans united to fight against the Japan rule, regardless of their regions and classes.

Outburst of anti-invasion struggles

As the Japanese exploitation became worse and more aggravating, the Koreans' resistance against it intensified as well. They confronted the Japanese with weapons, and they also launched political movements to gather national strength and carry out reforms.

After the treaty of 1905, Koreans initiated movements to nullify that illegitimate treaty. Some Koreans fell into despair and committed suicide, while merchants closed down their business and students refused to attend school. Confucian literati figures signed up for the petition movement for independence and the passionate youth began to execute a minor number of the national traitors. All these people gathered to become one against the Japanese, while overcoming the difference between themselves.

Yet, the treaty remained unchanged. The Japanese authorities took away the Korean sovereignty one by one. In response to that, bursts of violent clashes evolved into armed struggles over time, and the independence movements gradually transformed into a well-organized and continuous movement to strengthen the country.

An Jung-geun and Ito Hirobumi

After Ito Hirobumi, the ex-prime minister of Japan, forced the Koreans to sign and accept the Eulsa-year Treaty, he was appointed as the first Governor General and led the task of annexing Korea. Ito claimed that the Yellow people (like those in Asia) should unite to protect themselves from the westerners' invasion. An Jung-geun who had continued to fight Japan in armed struggles assassinated him. An argued that peace in Asia would only come when the three nations of East Asia would support one another; however, Japan attempted to rule Joseon with brutal oppression. The photo is a poster of the movie that depicted the life story of An Jung-geun. This shows how much he has been loved by the Korean people. To the right is Ito Hirobumi who is introduced in the history text book of Japan.

나의 전쟁은
이제부터 시작이다!

도마
안
중근

www.komaahnjoongkeun.co.kr

❶憲法発布式(錦絵、憲政記念館蔵)　明治天皇が内閣総理大臣の黒田清隆に憲法を授けているところ。

❷伊藤博文　長州藩(山口県)出身。大久保利通の死後は、政府の中心となった。

大日

第1条
　天皇之
第3条
　カラス
第4条
　治権ヲ
　依リ之
第11条
第13条
　及諸般
第29条
　二於テ
　ノ自由

追究❸

大日本帝国憲法

憲法の発布

政府は、憲法
文らをヨーロッパに派遣した。伊藤
の強いプロシア(ドイツ)の憲法を参
に着手した。それとともに、立憲政
かかり、1885(明治18)年に内閣制度
代の内閣総理大臣となった。また、1
制・町村制と府県制・郡制が発布し
いに整えられていった。

Struggling for freedom with their lives at risk

I saw the guns they were holding. Among the six guns that they held, five of them were different kinds. But none of them seemed to be in very good condition. They were people ensured of an unavoidable death in hopeless battles. However, when I looked at the soldier standing to my right, I saw courage in his eyes, and a smile of confidence as well. That was when I had a certain realization. It might have been my mistake to pity them. Even though their method of expression could have been flawed, at least they were instilling a patriotic valor in the minds of their countrymen. They spoke that, believing that they were doing something worthwhile, "We are probably going to die anyway, but it is better to die as a free man than to live as a Japanese slave." — F. A. Mckenzie, *Korea's Fight for Freedom* (1920)

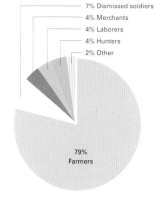

Source: *"Research on the History of Independence Movements"* by Park Seong-su

Former occupations of the Righteous Army soldiers

The provincial Yangban figures, most of whom were landlords, stepped forth to assist the armed struggle. Confucianism which had always valued self-discipline and an ethical life, and wealth and social influence, formed a foundation for their struggle.

The majority of the soldiers were anonymous commoners. Resistance forces led by farmers or hunters also began to emerge. When the old army of Korea was forced to disband in 1907, many soldiers joined the so-called Righteous militias.

The Righteous militias that operated in small numbers mainly targeted Japanese soldiers, policemen, corrupted governmental officials cooperating with Japan, and those who became wealthy by exploiting the Korean people. In 1907, the people organized a United Righteous Army and launched an assault on the capital Seoul.

The struggles of the Righteous Army were most active between 1908 and

Anti-Japanese Righteous militia
The struggles of the Righteous militia rose again in 1904, but later since 1909 it became much tougher to maintain the fight. In 1909 the Japanese troops brutally attacked the Righteous Army soldiers all over the Jeolla-do province where the activities of the Righteous Army were most active. This incident is known as the "Southern Campaign." Countless Righteous Militia soldiers were arrested or shot to death. Survivors either went underground to continue their activities or did not have any other choice but to flee across the border.

1909. For two years, they battled the Japanese troops more than a thousand times. Their attacks hampered Japan's speedy colonization of Korea.

The Japanese colonial government organized a large number of troops to attack the Righteous Army forces. They surrounded and burned down whole villages, committing ruthless massacres. However, one of the Righteous Army soldiers once said: "we do not give up fighting because the enemy is powerful; in any circumstance we will fight with all our heart and strength." Like this, the Righteous Army soldiers did not stop their life-risking struggles.

From the emperor's subjects to citizens

The educated and wealthy also rose to restore the strength of Korea with all possible ways available to them. It was their conclusion that Korea lost its sovereignty due to their weakened national strength. So, they thought the most urgent thing to do in recovering sovereignty was to develop certain capabilities that would allow them to sustain their own independence.

The "Self-Strengthening Society" (Daehanjaganghoe) and the "New People's Association" (Shinminhoe) were organized as part of the Koreans' efforts to recover their own sovereignty. Furthermore, intellectuals established schools in order to educate their own people and continued to disclose and propagate the harsh reality of the Japanese occupation through media and newspapers. They built modern industries and educated technologies. Many private schools were open at the time, and this shows the people's passion for education and desire for unification. Many organizations and individuals established schools and developed textbooks so as to spread out modern knowledge, and to organize the will of the people.

In addition, the women's participation in official activities became more prevalent. They organized female educational boards to open and administrate Girl's high schools and colleges. As a result, the number of Girl's schools gradually increased. In addition, the women's involvement in raising funds to pay debts to Japan was nothing less than remarkable.

Although some people believed that Korea should receive instructions from Japan in order to modernize itself, and some of them even believed that it would be better to merge the two nations into one, the majority of Koreans were strongly determined to fight against the Japanese invasion.

They began to identify themselves as citizens who were the owners of their own country, unlike the subjects to be ruled. It was at that point when

The Japanese record of the amount of money collected through the National Debt Compensation Movement (1907)
In 1907, the National Dept Compensation Movement called for the paying off of all debts that the Koreans owed to Japan. It was necessary to do so for Joseon, to discontinue its economic subordination to Japan. Men stopped drinking and smoking while women sold their own jewelry, in order to raise funds to pay off the debt. This movement was sort of "revived" during the recent foreign exchange crisis of 1997, in the form of a "Gold Collection" movement.

researches on the Korean language and Korean history became so active. Ju Shi-gyeong studied the Korean language, while Shin Chae-ho and Park Eun-shik studied history, and with their studies they all proved that the Koreans had been a tightly-knit community with a distinguished culture and language. Na Cheol also founded the Daejonggyo religion, which worshipped the great forefather of the Korean people, Dangun.

With all these efforts, the modern Korean race was born, as a cultural community distinguished from others, and as an alliance of equal individuals struggling to regain their sovereignty from the Japanese rule.

The Foundation of Modern Democracy

Even in the danger of being deprived of its sovereignty, many intellectuals newly interpreted the Korean tradition of endeavoring to develop their own creative culture so as to make it a basis of maintaining Korean people's independence.

Ju Shi-gyeong (1876~1914), and his Korean language and literature research
He believed that studying and using the Korean language and letters was the most important thing to do, in order to preserve the Korean language, not to mention the Korean spirit, while educating new ideas to the people.

> The most important thing to do in preserving one's national foundation is to preserve the country's words and letters. If we do not cultivate our words and letters, the national foundation would have no choice but to weaken. When our national foundation deteriorates, it would be impossible to recover the national power as well. So it is urgent to encourage people to study our spoken and written language and correct wrong usages of it so that it could be widely used in the future. —Ju Shi-gyeong, Gugeomunjeon (1908)

Shin Chae-ho (1880~1936), and his research on the Korean history
He was the leading figure in the efforts of raising people's spirits through historical research and writing activities. By writing biographies that introduced heroic characters in the Korean history to the Korean people of his time, he appealed to the people that all Koreans had to become anonymous heroes themselves. He also put the Korean race at front and center of his studies.

> History of a country is a record that documents both its times of prosperity and deterioration. If we discard our race, there would be no history, and if history is discarded, the people would not value their own country...Today with Nationalism we need to crush all people's ignorance, and with the concept of a nation we need to educate the young people... —Shin Chae-ho, Doksashinron (1908)

Na Cheol (1863~1916) and Daejonggyo
He was a Confucian scholar who worked as a government official in the Great Empire of Han. Later he organized a group of assassins to eliminate the five infamous officials who betrayed the Korean people by signing the Eulsa-year treaty. Attempting to discard the Confucian tradition which had been considering China as the center of world civilization, he founded the Daejonggyo religion which was designed as a national religion based upon the Dangun figure. Dangun was a symbol of the Koreans' independence from China, and their resistance against Japan. The Daejonggyo religious order argued that "all Asian nations are one and the same."

3

Joseon, a Colony of Japan:
Distorted Modern History of Korea

Joseon became a Japanese colony

On August 29, 1910, the Japanese military government announced the following treaty as signed; "The king of the Great Han Empire handed over the sovereignty of Korea to Japan entirely and permanently." Japan said that the king agreed to all of the conditions of annexation with an understanding that it was inevitable for him to sign, and that the Joseon government only added an article which dictated "Japan guarantees the security of the Joseon royal family." However, many Koreans lamented on hearing that declaration and found themselves determined to make that day the beginning of a new period, full of fierce struggles.

> The birds and creatures weep and the mountains frown
> The world of roses of Sharon is now ruined
> I close my book under the autumn night lamp and reminisce
> It isn't easy to live the life of a learned in this world. —*Jeolmyeongshi* (Poem of Death) by Hwang Hyeon

A waving Japanese flag in front of the Geunjeongjeon
A picture of a Japanese flag waving in front of the Guenjeongjeon in the Gyeongbokgung, the symbol of the Great Empire of Han. The so-called 'treaty of annexation' was signed on August 22, 1910, yet the Japanese authorities officially announced it 7 days later, because they feared the uproar of the Koreans.

Japan declared its annexation of Korea after it massacred 17,688 Koreans who joined the Righteous Army forces and apprehended an even larger number of Koreans under similar charges. All Korean organizations were dismantled and dismissed. Even the organizations which supported the annexation were not an exception and they were forced to disband as well. All magazines and newspapers published in the Korean language were forced to close their business and a number of private schools were closed down as well. Moreover, the Japanese military government censored all textbooks, curricula, and scrutinizing of the teachers' actions became common.

The annexation indicated not only the extermination of the Great Empire of Han, but also a crushing blow to the Koreans' long time struggle for establishing their own independent republic; it also meant the void of the freedom of citizens, and disappearance of media and schools that were accomplished through struggles.

A corporal punishment device
"Taehyeong," a form of a punishment: the naked rears of a criminal, lying on his or her stomach on the straw mat with both of his or her wrists and ankles shackled, were beaten continuously (Joseon Taehyeong Order I, 1912). This barbaric punishment was completely abolished in Joseon in the 19th century, but it was revived by the Japanese Governor-General office. Of course, this punishment was only used in punishing Koreans.

A despotic ruling of the Japanese military government

Once the Japanese annexation of Korea was declared, the Great Empire of Han disappeared. From then to 1945, the physical terrains of Joseon became a part of Japan. Japan propagated that there were no more Koreans, and all Koreans were now Japanese subjects. However, no Joseon person agreed to such rule; moreover, no rights that were equal to the Japanese were given to the Koreans.

Instead of the emperor of the Great Empire of Han, it was the Japanese Governor-General office to be in charge of ruling the Koreans. The of-

Construction of the Governor-General Office building
The Japanese authorities demolished many valuable Korean cultural heritages. They tore down parts of the main palace Gyeongbokgung, and built the Japanese colonial government building there, in order to remove the sight of the main palace entirely out of the Koreans' view. (But fortunately it was not completely dismantled.) The Great Empire of Han, the sole representative of Korean sovereignty, was not strong enough to resist the Japanese invasion and was unable to play a pivotal role in obtaining independence again. The royal family was able to receive a minimum privilege in exchange of its submission to the Japanese imperialists, but most people who struggled for the recovery of their sovereignty did not want the resurrection of the royal family afterwards.

fice constituted laws that would be applied to the Koreans, and organized judges for the Korean courts. There were no Korean organizations; all powers were diverted to the office.

The Governor-General was selected from the Japanese military officers in the service. They instituted strict and harsh military regulations and punishments that might as well be applied to soldiers in war, in ruling the Koreans. Japanese military policemen and armed soldiers administered these regulations.

Since the Japanese annexation of Korea in 1910, many Joseon people were ruthlessly exposed to barbaric violence. Under the inspection network which was practically a web of Japanese police, no Koreans had freedom. Furthermore, no freedom of meeting and association, speech or press was given to Korean people.

Violence forged under the justification of modernization

The Governor-General's ruling system was established upon the Joseon people's suffering. The office took over power, then confiscated and nationalized the properties of the royal family, and gained immense profits through exploitation of other national resources. The Governor-General office also increased taxes, and even made new taxes which adopted the Japanese tax system. The budget deficit that was about 20% of the budget of 1910 was resolved in 1919.

Land Survey Operation
The Japanese authorities surveyed lands throughout the country from 1912 to 1918. They measured the lands in Joseon based on the Japanese land system, officially registered them, and then reconfirmed ownership of those lands.

The most crucial project designed to cover all the expenses of the Japanese colonial government was the Land Survey Project. Since 1912, the colonial government conducted surveys on land ownerships, along with sizes and prices of all those lands. In the process, many lands that belonged to farmers came to be registered as national treasure, and the colonial government collected more money by levying taxes upon lands according to their own prices.

The Governor-General ordered to use the modern terms to survey property ownerships of the lands. As a result, all the traditional rights of farming became deprived. In order to cultivate the same land they used to grow crops on, they had to make new contracts with the landlords as tenant-farmers. Taking advantages of that, the landlords made contracts that required more proceeds. The tenant farmers found themselves in a situation in which they had to beg for the landlords' favor to continue farming.

Under the slogan of agricultural reform, the Japanese Imperial authority forced the farmers to cultivate specific crops and instructed specific methods for farming. Also, the Cooperation Ordinance (1910) dictated that whoever planned to establish a business in Joseon must obtain permission from the Governor-General office or otherwise it could be disbanded.

The modernization which was forced by the Japanese rule was more likely a systematization of violence.

The Oriental Colonization Company
In 1908, the Japanese authorities established the Oriental Colonization Company to support and facilitate Japanese migration to Korea. Most of the lands that had belonged to the Governor-General office were resold to this company at a very cheap price, and this company then re-endorsed these lands to the Japanese people. In the process the Oriental Colonization Company produced a number of Japanese landlords, and the company itself became the largest landlord and exploiter of farmers throughout Joseon.

4

Establishment of a Provisional Government of the Republic of Korea

Persistent struggles in the darkness

We as Koreans pledge before God and the Heavens to dedicate our lives to taking back our sovereignty from the Japanese. In case we do not achieve independence in our own generation, we will let our children continue the fighting against Japan until the very day the Japanese are completely driven off our soil and we take back our sovereignty.

The above pledge was issued by the Daehangwangbokhoe community which was organized in 1915 by those who were involved in the Righteous Soldier Movement and the intellectuals who had been actively participating in the movement for strengthening national capabilities. In order to regain Korean sovereignty, this organization trained armies outside of Korea and raised funds inside the country to support such activities. Although most of its leaders were executed in 1918 when the network of Daehangwangbokhoe was uncovered, there were other organizations that were not discovered; thus Koreans' resistance movements were able to be continued in China and Russia, in the regions where the Japanese imperial authorities were not able to reach.

Due to barbaric violences and the web-like inspection network, the time of silence seemed destined to continue. However, the resistance did not stop, and in the near future a massive explosion of resistance was about to break out.

Seodaemun Prison
This prison, where many Joseon people who led the Korean Independence Movement were tortured or executed, was built by the Japanese in 1908. In 1995, it was decided to remodel the building and turn it into a museum, in order to celebrate the 50th anniversary of Korean Independence. 3 years later it was reopened under the name of the "Seodaemun Prison Memorial," in 1998. Among the exhibitions, there are recreations of prison cells, watch towers, and the execution site, and there is also a comprehensive exhibition hall.

The great outburst, the March 1st Movement

The burgeoning of the explosive March 1st Movement became active in 1917. In Russia, a socialist revolution broke out, and with World War I the colonies of stronger nations were "redistributed," and that became a catalyst for the national movements of all those occupied countries. Finally, the Principle of Self-determination was declared by the U.S. and revolution-ized Russia: "All people have rights to decide their future." A warmer season for all the colonies seemed to be on its way.

In 1917, Independence Movement activists working outside the Korean Peninsula proclaimed the "Declaration of Unity," and took a great leap in Independence Movements by calling for the ultimate unity among them-selves. From 1918, a Declaration of Independence was claimed in vari-ous places, and diplomatic activities of appealing for Korean independence was initiated. Finally on March 1st of 1919, well-organized demonstrators carried out a ceremony for Korean independence in more than ten cities nationwide simultaneously.

> We hereby proclaim the independence of Korea and the liberty of the Korean people. We announce to the world our own will to uphold the great cause of equal human rights, and we are determined to pass this sacred duty on to our descendants. We urge them to maintain the Korean government and the pride of the Korean race. *– The Declaration of Independence* (1919)

Philadelphia Hurray Protest Marching
The March 1st Movement continued wherever Koreans resided. The Korean students at Tokyo and students in regions above the Korean Peninsula such as Jiandao and the Maritime Province did so as well. Also, the Korean people who resided in the United States held the Independence Ceremony as well. They arranged meetings and street rallies to inform Japan and the international society of the Korean situation and the necessity of Korean Independence. The picture shows the Koreans' marching in a street rally which was held in Philadelphia on May, 1919.

March 1st Movement

The "March 1st Movement" refers to a series of demonstrations which continued throughout the country for two months since March 1st, 1919. More than 1,500 street protests are recorded. Among the 232 Joseon administrative districts, 227 places witnessed demonstrations. Regardless of their social class, it was a nationwide Korean struggle.

- ● **Large scale uprising sites**
  (over 10,000 participants and more than 15 rallies)
- ● **Small scale uprising sites**

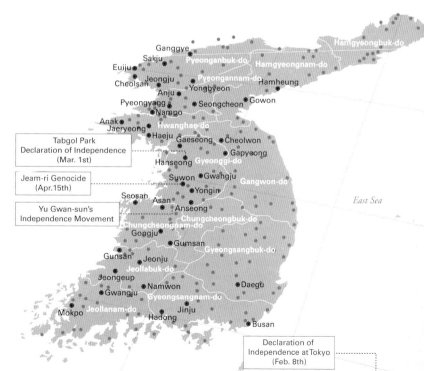

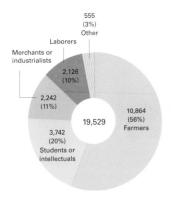

555
(3%)
Other

Laborers

Merchants or
industrialists

2,126
(10%)

2,242
(11%)

19,529

10,864
(56%)
Farmers

3,742
(20%)
Students or
intellectuals

Occupations of those who were
arrested for joining the March 1st
Movement

After performing the ceremonies of the Declaration of Independence, crowds rallied peacefully on the street requesting independence, holding the Taegeukgi flags in their hands. The Taegeukgi flag which had to be kept hidden for the last decade came out to the streets, and the sound of cheers thundered the earth and heaven.

The protest spread across the country instantaneously. Although the first round of demonstrations was initiated in large cities, they gradually expanded to provincial areas, in medium and small cities. The movement triggered by the younger population and also the religious leaders came to involve people from all classes including farmers and laborers. The thundering sounds of cheers and hurrays burst out in every area where Koreans resided, even outside of the Korean Peninsula.

Provisional Government of the Republic of Korea is born

Those who led "The Manse Movement" were going to "appeal" for independence to both Japan and the international society upon their declaration of independence. However, the crowds did not count on Japanese generosity or the international society's conscience.

Many people participated in the demonstrations because they could not accept the Japanese rule. They resisted the unforgivable violence by employing numerous methods. Although they failed in achieving independence, they were able to create a huge milestone toward a greater victory.

In March, when the people's protests were still continuing, the first Korean Provisional Government was founded inside the Maritime Province of Siberia. In April, two other provisional governments were established in Shanghai and Seoul respectively. Many Koreans celebrated the foundation of the provisional governments, expecting them to bring such declaration to reality in the end. Not before long, all those provisional governments

Main members of the Provisional Government
In September 1919, all the provisional governments that had been organized in various regions were united under the Provisional Government of the Republic of Korea. A temporary body of legislature was established. Yi Seung-man who was an activist in the United States was designated as President, and Yi Dong-hwi who had been fighting in Jiandao and the Maritime Province was appointed as Prime-minster. The third person from the left in the front row is Kim Gu, the sixth person from the left in the second row is Yi Dong-hwi, and the person next to him is Yi Seung-man (Syngman Rhee).

大韓民國三年一月一日
臨時政府及臨時議政院新年祝賀式紀念撮影

were united into one, and declared that they would achieve independence and construct an entirely new Korea, with a provisional set of constitutions.

> 1st article: The Republic of Korea is a democratic republic.
> 2nd article: The Provisional Government of the Republic of Korea governs Korea according to the decisions of the Provisional body of legislature.
> 3rd article: The people of the Republic of Korea are equal regardless of their sex, class, wealth, and rank
> — Provisional Constitution was proclaimed on April 11, 1919.

Hong Beom-do (1868~1943)
Hong Beom-do who once was a gunner participated in the Righteous Army activities and finally joined the Korean Independence Army. Later he moved to Russia and became a Communist to fight against the Japanese.

Armed anti-Japanese resistance rages

Even though the Declaration of the Independence Movement had stirred up the entire country, it was ultimately quelled in front of the ruthless violence of Japanese rule. As a result, many people crossed the borders out of patriotic passion to challenge the Japanese in new, yet unexplored ways. There were many people who willingly sold their property to purchase weapons to supply soldiers of the Independence Army.

The March 1st Movement revived the armed resistance, which had remained stagnant since the Righteous Militias' defeat. Manchuria served as the center of the armed resistance. The Independence Army frequently crossed the border and attacked the Japanese soldiers. The Japanese stationed their military to suppress the Independence Army.

In 1920, the Independence Army under the leadership of Hong Beom-do and Kim Jwa-jin won a monumental victory against the Japanese military. Hong Beom-do engaged in military actions against the Japanese troops, which attacked the main base of the Independence Army (the "Bongodong Battle"). After this victory, three Japanese army divisions entered China to support their force in Manchuria. They clashed with Korean troops, but they were defeated due to a successful strategy of Kim Jwa-jin and Hong Beom-do which lured them to be trapped in the mountainous area. About 1,200 Japanese soldiers were killed in this battle (the "Cheongsanri Battle").

Kim Jwa-jin (1889~1930)
He was the son of a large landlord, but he served in the enlightenment movement and then joined the Independence Army. Until 1930, he actively involved himself in the Nationalist movements in Manchuria, and kept distance between himself and Communism in his entire life.

However, these two victories resulted in aggravating the Japanese aggression further in Manchuria, and more severe interventions in Manchurian affairs made the Koreans' resistance much more difficult. However, the vast area of Manchuria remained as an important base for the anti-Japanese movements until the Japanese Imperialists were completely driven out of it.

Taegeukgi and the National Anthem: Wishes for Independence

Until the East Sea is dried and Mt. Baekdusan is worn away, God watch o'er our land forever!

Live long Our Korea!

Roses of Sharon, thousand miles of our country filled with splendid rivers and mountains! Guarded by her people, ever may Korea stand!

The Korean national anthem along with the flag "Taegeukgi" were made as official symbols of Korea in 1948. In fact, the Korean national anthem and the "Taegeukgi" flag had been kept in the Koreans' hearts for a long time.

In 1883 the flag was officially used for the first time. As a matter of fact, the Joseon Dynasty had sometimes used the symbol of Taegeuk when they conducted exchanges with various Chinese dynasties. And then, around 1882 when the Korean people's foreign exchanges with other countries became much more active, the Taegeukgi flag was officially made, and the next year it was raised in all public offices throughout the country. From the 1890s when Koreans were aspired to achieve their independence, various anthems were composed by schools and newspaper companies. In 1902, the Great Empire of Han appointed its anthem which begins with the following lyrics; "May the heaven king help our emperor."

When Koreans faced danger of losing their sovereignty, they changed the subject of lyrics of the Korean anthem, from "emperor" to "the people of the Great Han." At first Yun Chi-ho wrote lyrics to the melody of the old Scotland folk song, "Auld Lang Syne." Later in 1936, when An Ik-tae composed an anthem song to the lyrics, the Korean anthem which we now have today was finally made.

After Koreans lost their sovereignty, the use of the Korean anthem and flag was completely prohibited. For such reasons the Korean people came to love them even more than before. Also, they turned into symbols representing the independent spirits of Koreans. As Korea restored its sovereignty in 1945, the Korean flag Taegeukgi and the national anthem were all revived.

❶   ❷   ❸

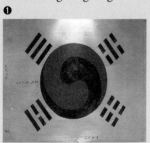 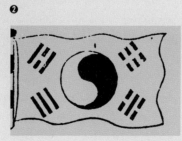 

❶ **The first Taegeukgi** The white background symbolizes peace, and the Taegeuk figure composed of red and blue circles symbolizes the source of two principles in the universe. The overall Taegeuk figure indicates harmony between such dual cosmetic properties: the harmony of yin and yang. And the 'trigrams' which seem to be surrounding the Taegeuk figure symbolize "prosperity." This design was adopted from a trigram inside the "Book of Changes."

❷ **Taegeukgi flag printed in Dongnipshinmun** Around the time when the foundation of the Great Han Empire was declared, people became more and more aware of the idea of all the Korean people sharing the same brotherhood, and they became more and more interested in figures and images that could represent such brethren identity of their own.

❸ **Go Gwang-sun's Taegeukgi** A line saying "Bulwonbok," which meant "not before long, independence will be achieved," is written on the flag that was owned by a Righteous Army leader named Go Gwang-sun (1848~1907). To the Koreans who were struggling for their independence, Taegeukgi was like the country itself envisioned in their hearts.

Music note of the Korean National Anthem that was written by An Ik-tae (1906~1965)

The first national anthem

It was first written in 1902, which was the 40th year of King Gojong's reign. The pictures show the cover of the book that contained the National Anthem, and lyrics written in Korean. It begins with the line "May the heaven king help our emperor."

1922 ~ 1945

1922~1923
The Nationalists organized a movement to enhance the national strength. Such efforts were mainly made of raising funds for promoting industry and founding universities.

1923~1924
Farmers and laborers began to be more actively organized. In 1925 the Joseon Communist Party was founded, under the slogan of class liberation and national independence.

1926
A massive protest for independence was held upon the day of funeral arranged for the Great Han Empire's last emperor Sunjong (the "June 10th Movement"). The next year appeared the organization of the Shinganhoe community, a product of cooperation between the Nationalists and Communists.

1931
In 1931 the Japanese occupied Manchuria. From the following year, the Korean and Chinese soldiers joined strength in fighting the Japanese army in Manchuria.

1937
As Japan attacked China in 1937 and German attacked Poland in 1939, the whole world was plunged into chaos.

1938
In 1938 the Joseon Righteous Militia of young Korean men living inside China was organized. In 1940 the Korean Restoration Army was established and continued to fight the Japanese.

1941
As Japan launched an attack upon America at Pearl Harbor, Hawaii, the Pacific War began. The Provisional Government of the Republic of Korea at Chongqing in China announced a national foundation decree and declared war against Japan. Next year the Joseon Righteous Army was established inside Northern China.

1943
The representatives of the U.S., Britain and China publically authorized the independence of Korea after the surrender of the Japanese Empire (the Cairo Conference).

1944
Yeo Un-hyeong and others domestically organized the "Korean Government Foundation Alliance" and tried to bring the early demolition of the Japanese Empire.

1945
In 1945 soon after World War II ended, Korea was liberated.

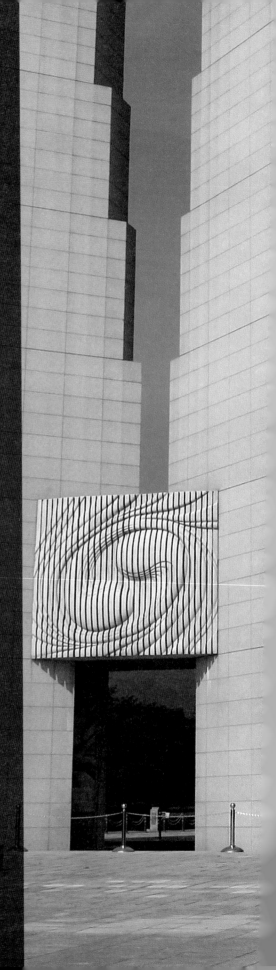

XI Koreans' Preparation for Liberation

"By holding elections we will have people freely and equally join the government. By adopting a national ownership system we will make equal distributions of economic interests. We will have all the people attend schools with the public fund. We will ensure the Koreans' right of determining our own fate in and out of the country. We will eliminate all kinds of unequal relationships between peoples and nations…" (Founding Principles)

The process of struggling against the Japanese imperialists was also a time seeking ways to found a new country for the Korean people.

The Independence Memorial Hall of Korea   The Independence Memorial Hall of Korea is located in Cheonan of the Chungcheongnam-do province. It opened in 1986. All kinds of historical materials, which show us the suffering that the Korean people had to endure, and their endless efforts for independence, are in exhibition. The tower erected in the front of the Memorial hall is the "Gyeoretap (Monument to the Nation)," which resembles the shape of bird's wings that are about to soar and the hands of a praying person.

World War II and the Korean Independence Movement

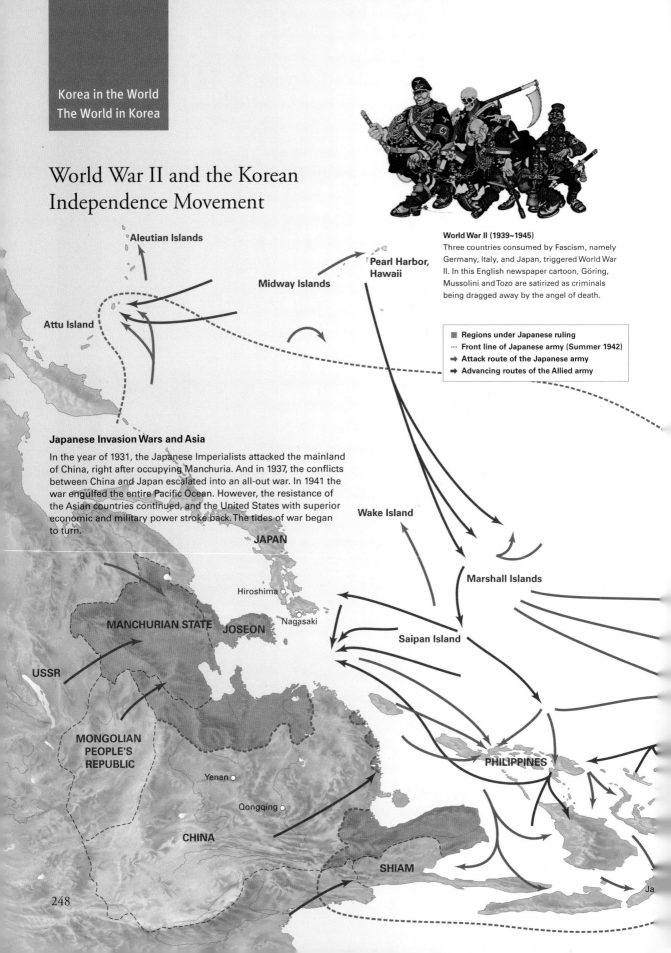

World War II (1939~1945)
Three countries consumed by Fascism, namely Germany, Italy, and Japan, triggered World War II. In this English newspaper cartoon, Göring, Mussolini and Tozo are satirized as criminals being dragged away by the angel of death.

Aleutian Islands

Pearl Harbor, Hawaii

Midway Islands

Attu Island

- ■ Regions under Japanese ruling
- ⋯ Front line of Japanese army (Summer 1942)
- ➡ Attack route of the Japanese army
- ➡ Advancing routes of the Allied army

Japanese Invasion Wars and Asia

In the year of 1931, the Japanese Imperialists attacked the mainland of China, right after occupying Manchuria. And in 1937, the conflicts between China and Japan escalated into an all-out war. In 1941 the war engulfed the entire Pacific Ocean. However, the resistance of the Asian countries continued, and the United States with superior economic and military power stroke back. The tides of war began to turn.

Wake Island

JAPAN

Marshall Islands

Hiroshima

Nagasaki

MANCHURIAN STATE **JOSEON**

Saipan Island

USSR

MONGOLIAN PEOPLE'S REPUBLIC

Yenan

Qongqing

CHINA

PHILIPPINES

SHIAM

Ja

The leaders of the Yalta Conference
At the Yalta Conference held in February of 1945, it was agreed that Russia would join the war against the Japanese. In the photo, we can see British Prime Minister Churchill, U.S. President Roosevelt and Soviet Leader Stalin from left to right.

Nuclear bombing at Nagasaki in Japan (below)
The United States dropped nuclear bombs at Nagasaki and Hiroshima, with the intention to end the war before the Soviet Union join the war. With only two nuclear bombs, approximately 300,000 people were killed in the blink of an eye.

Due to World War II, the world was in turmoil in 1941. Battles were continuing in Europe and Asia at the same time. In Europe, since Hitler invaded Poland in 1939, Germany occupied most of Europe and the northern part of Africa and even invaded Russia. In the meantime, in Asia the Imperial Japanese started a war against the United States and succeeded in expanding its power to Southeast Asia through a series of invasions.

The Japanese Imperialists promoted a notion of forming "the Great Asian Community" to confront European power, thus justifying its invasion wars. In response to such justification, the allied forces of the United States, Britain, and China attacked regions occupied by the Japanese troops, while Koreans also built its own Independence Army to fight against the invaders in cooperation with the allied armies.

Koreans concentrated their efforts upon conducting activities inside China where 80% of the Japanese soldiers were stationed. Making Chongqing and Yanan the center of their efforts, military units were organized to resist Japanese ruling alongside with Chinese forces. Also, before the full-fledged attack of the Allied Forces was launched, they received special training to secretly enter Korean territory. In addition, they dispatched special units to the battle field of Myanmar where Britain and Japan were fighting in support of the Allied Forces' war effort. The triumph of the Allied Forces was also the victory of the Koreans who fought against Fascism and Japanese ruling.

New Guinea

Korean Independence soldiers in training
Koreans and the Chinese cooperated in their fighting against the Japanese ruling. The photo shows Korean Independence soldiers in training.

1

Development Without Development:
People Are Tired

Exploiting the colony under the name of development

During World War I, the Japanese economy flourished with its production of military supplies and weapons. However, after the war the economy entered a recession. Japan also started to face serious issues of food shortages and riots caused by low agricultural productivity. Japan decided to solve its economic problems by exploiting its own colony, Korea.

In the beginning of the 1920s, the Japanese Empire abolished the Cooperation Ordinance which had been regulating the number of Japanese companies established in Korea with the approval of the Japanese Governor-General, in order to encourage more Japanese corporations to invest in the Korean market. The tariff barrier between Korea and Japan was dismantled as well. The markets were merged, and Japanese capital and commodities continued to flood into Korea.

Such initiative did stimulate the activities of the Korean corporations as well. However, such corporations remained as only small or mid-sized ones in the fields where the Japanese were yet to enter. It was difficult for the Korean corporations to have a competition with the Japanese ones well facilitated with more advanced technology and their government's support.

Korean laborers working in a mine
According to Japan's industrialization policy of its colonies, which was implemented in the late 1920s, power plants, mines and fertilizer plants were developed inside the northern areas of the Korean Peninsula. However, as industrialization proceeded, labor hours for the Joseon people became longer while their wages continued to decrease.

After the 1930s, the amount of Japanese capital in Joseon increased exponentially. The Japanese wished to keep their land as the more advanced industrial zone, while establishing Joseon as a transit area for the Japanese to transport things from Manchuria, which was the area for growing crops and producing raw materials.

The industrialization of Joseon was closely related to the war efforts of Japan. Japan developed electrical sources in Joseon in order to industrialize it, taking advantage of the inexpensive land price of Joseon, and exploited mineral resources. As many Japanese began to invest their capital into the operations of Japanese industries located in the northern part of Korea, the region quickly developed into a center for heavy industries such as metal and chemical industries.

Throughout the 1930s, the number of manufacturing industries rapidly increased. However, most of the owners and executive officers of the industries in all areas were Japanese. And the capital was owned by the Japanese. In order to increase the Japanese owners' profits, Korean workers were only paid a meager wage, without any kind of minimum security or compensations. Developments were made, but these developments were irrelevant to improving the lives of the Koreans. In fact, such developments was merely another form of exploitation of the Korean people.

The landlord system of the Japanese colonial government

In 1920, the Japanese authorities began to carry out a large-scale plan to increase rice production. They improved reservoirs and distributed fertilizers and seeds of new-type rice. Accordingly, in the 1920s rice production did rise in quantity.

However, other than a few landlords, a majority of the Korean tenant farmers' lives were not changed, as those tenant farmers had to submit more than 50% of what they harvested to their landlords as rent payments, fertilization costs, and union fees for irrigation. The lives of other independent farmers remained the same as before. In many cases, the independent farmers whose land sizes were too small to make a living became tenant farmers. In the meantime, the total amount of land mass occupied by landlords continued to increase during this period of increased rice production. With the Japanese authorities' support, Japanese landlords continued to thrive, and by 1935, 18% of Korean rice paddy fields went over to the Japanese landlords.

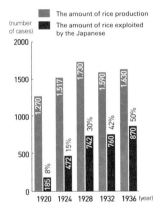

A comparison between the amount of rice produced and the amount that was exploited by the Japanese

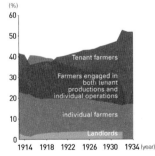

Composition of the farmer population during the Japanese occupation period

The amount of rice transported to Japan increased more rapidly than that of rice produced. Rice production was commercialized by the landlords, and most of the rice sold to Japan was collected from the tenant farmers. The Japanese government supported the landlord system in order to ship more rice to Japan. The outcry of the suppressed Korean farmers was totally ignored.

Three different faces of the colonized Korea

The Japanese occupation changed the appearance of the Korean society. Many Korean farmers who were robbed of their land chose to leave their homes in order to find new jobs. Ports, mines, and other labor markets in cities were always crowded with such people.

As modern industries began their operations, the number of laborers working at stores and factories increased. The number of foreigners who were mainly Japanese also dramatically increased.

Seoul, the center of colonized Korea, which came to have a population of over 1 million by the 1930s, was vividly demonstrating such changes. A Japanese residential area located in downtown Seoul overflowed with fancy stores and electric street lights, lit up the night as if it were day. Also in Jongno, the traditional marketplace maintained its own vitality, filled with affluent Koreans and merchants. However, around the outskirts of Cheonggyecheon, which ran between the Japanese residence area and the Korean market street, people who left their farms and were eventually pushed into the city continued to live in misery, and as a result, a large-scale slum area was formed. While the Japanese were leading the prosperity of a capitalistic civilization and the opulent Koreans were pursuing a changed lifestyle throughout the city, the indigent individuals were living a miserable life in huts. These three new faces were common not only in Seoul but throughout the Korean Peninsula.

Two different looks of Seoul
In the 1930s, Seoul continued to develop features of its own, as a modern city. In the left is the look of Chungmuro street in the 1920s. At Namchon, which was today's Myeong-dong and Chungmuro streets of Seoul, there were many Japanese stores in business. Yet, behind these streets poor people lived in huts and were forced to endure dreadful living conditions, as we can see from the picture in the right.

Nationalism and Socialism

The changing society demanded a new response from the Korean Nationalists. So, the Korean Nationalists developed new ideas and actions.

After the declaration of independence in 1919, many Koreans believed that in order to achieve independence the most urgent matter at hand was to grow national competence. People promoted Korean enterprises in order to grow economic competence and independence of the Korean economy, and promoted university foundations and establishment of night classes for the working class.

Many Koreans turned to Socialism for new hopes and prospects. Inspired by the Russian Revolution and the anti-Imperialism movement in Russia, many Independence activists, students, and intellectuals voluntarily accepted the Socialist ideas.

They believed that Socialism was an ideological weapon that could liberate the oppressed class of farmers and laborers. Yet, they were also Nationalists, as they considered the Japanese people to be the Capitalistic class and Koreans as the Proletariat class, and in the end regarded the Korean independence as a priority above all else.

Since the mid-1920s, while competing with each other, the Nationalists and Socialists also decided to cooperate with each other in order to achieve independence. And at the same time, a new kind of movement which argued to accept the Japanese rule and then find ways to bolster their strength appeared. Yet, in case of the latter, considering the fact that the Japanese authorities did not acknowledge any kind of political rights of the Joseon people, it only served to legitimize the Japanese rule and policies. In order to enhance the lives of the Koreans, the distorted system of order established by the Japanese had to be destroyed first. Independence from the Japanese was the ultimate foundation that could invite competence and prosperity of the Korean people.

The movement of encouraging national production and consumption
"Let's use what we make." The movement which was arranged and promoted under this slogan was supported and joined by many Koreans. The photo in the left is an advertisement paper encouraging the use of national products, which was funded and issued by the Gyeongseong Textile Company. The photo in the right is a cotton roll made in Joseon, called as "Taegeukseong."

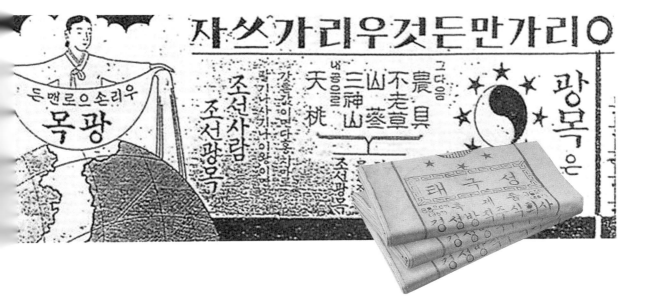

2

Emergence of Social Movements

Uprisings of tenant farmers spread like wildfire

On October 21, 1924, *The Dong-A Ilbo* newspaper reported that 76% of the people living in the fertile farmlands of the Jeolla-do province were not having three meals a day (23.6% had only one meal a day; 45.2% had two meals a day). In the meantime, the total gross of annual income of the farmers living at the Gangseo Farm of the Pyeongannam-do province was reported as 514 won, while the total amount of their annual expense was 547 won. This article which reported a 33% deficit, obviously shows the difficult lives of farmers who could not free themselves from financial deficits.

Farm rent amounted to 50% of the entire harvest and occupied the largest portion of people's annual expenses. Of course, there were many people who had to pay even more, and in the meantime, many people continued to lose even the opportunity to cultivate their lands. As the landlord system was reinforced by the Land Survey Operation of the Japanese authorities, rent fees were raised and cultivation rights were sequestered throughout the country.

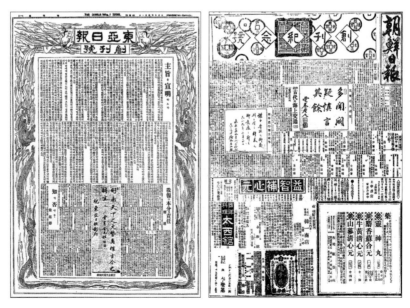

The foundation of The Dong-A Ilbo and The Chosun Ilbo newspapers (1920)
Facing serious resistance from the Korean people with the March 1st Movement (1919), the Japanese imperial authorities implemented a new policy that partially recognized Koreans' freedom of speech, along with the freedom of the press, assembly, and association. Due to this policy shift, several Korean newspapers were founded, and various organizations were formed to promote active social movements in the 1920s. This picture shows the first issues of *The Dong-A Ilbo* (left) and *The Chosun ilbo* (right), the two major Korean newspapers that were founded in 1920.

In 1920, the first labor organization in Korean history, the Joseon Labor Communion, was formed. Its objective was to stand against unjust demands of the Japanese and to create a front of mutual assistance among Korean laborers. The majority of farmers also became more active, in the attempt to protect their rights to live. The farmers fought against the unwarranted raising of rents and removal of their cultivation rights. The Tenant Farmers' Union and the Farmers' Union were formed as tools of protest.

In July of 1922, the Joseon Labor Communion announced a proclamation stating "Tenant farmers unite!," aggressively supporting the struggle of farmers. Mainstream social movements led by the enlightened figures and followed by the general public who were determined to fight began.

Farmers organized regional parties and aggressively allied with each other to fight for their cause. Although most struggles ended with the triumph of the landlords backed by Japanese police, their cause continued to grow and their awareness of their own rights continued to increase.

Tenant farmers' strike at Amtaedo
Amtaedo is an island located inside the Jeolla-do province. When a pro-Japanese landlord who owned most of the rice fields in the area attempted to collect high-rated tenant fees from the farmers, the farmers arranged a 'starvation to death' alliance in 1924, launched a series of tenant disputes, and achieved their own victory against the landlord.

Beginning of the modern labor movements

A colonial industrialization gave birth to a modern labor force in Korea. However, the labor laws of the Japanese government which were designed to protect the Japanese wage workers were not applied to the situations of the Korean laborers. Most Korean laborers had to endure more than 12 hours of labor a day with incredibly low wages, and needless to say, suffered from racial discrimination.

Laborers in the same regions and companies united to fight the violence and exploitation of the capitalists. The Japanese government mobilized police forces to subjugate the protests, but the oppressed laborers formed regional and national alliances in defiance of such subjugation.

The Wonsan General Strike (1929), which began when a Japanese director of a petroleum company assaulted a Joseon worker, was a typical example of emerging Korean labor movements under the Japanese rule. The movement began with laborers demanding the termination of the Japanese director and the improvement of labor conditions, but the protest quickly inflated into a fight joined by all Wonsan laborers and businessmen. This protest was supported by laborer organizations throughout the country and also throughout laborer unions on the international level as well. Although the protest itself was brought to its knees by Japanese police and capitalists, this incident showed very well why workers decided to fight, and how they must fight in the future.

Shinyeoseong (New Women)
In the 1920s, magazines for women started to be published. Such magazines featured various forms of literature that promoted women's intellect and enlightenment, and those entries often included articles that dealt with the theme of 'women's liberation.'

Active social movements in various classes

The students and youths of colonized Korea continued to breathe energy into social movements and Nationalist movements. Students voluntarily organized book clubs where they pragmatically studied the realities and future prospects of their country. Through a series of collective withdrawal from classes and attendance in public demonstrations as well, they resisted colonial education in their own way. The younger generation that spanned across all kinds of classes, organized youth groups and stood at the forefront of Nationalist and Socialist movement.

Women began to form collectives to throw organized movements as well. Women who received modern education refused to withstand the paternalistic order of the society and defined themselves as 'new and improved' modern women. As the number of working women continued to rise, female labor movements gradually grew and expanded as well. The Children's Day was first enacted, and the Youth Movement displayed another step forward with the publication of children's magazines.

The Baekjeong figures who were still discriminated against even after the abolition of classes organized the "Hyeongpyeongsa" organization, which meant "Equality" demanding the abolishment of prejudice and discrimination against them.

The "Hyeongpyeong (Equality)" Movement
"Hyeongpyeong" referred to a scale that was used by the Baekjeong figures (butchers), yet it was also a word that symbolized the people's will to create a world of equal beings. The Baekjeong figures who had been suffering severe discrimination by others organized a community named "Hyeongpyeongsa" in 1923 and started their own campaign of class liberation. The community grew to become a national organization joined by 400,000 members, and engaged itself in movements of nationalist independence and class abolition.

The Birthplace of the World's Children Movement
Bang Jeong-hwan (1899~1931), who was the pioneer of the 'Children Movement,' claimed that children should be respected as individuals. This monument is located in Jongno-gu, Seoul, in front of the Central Chapel of the Cheondogyo order.

Rising Nationalism

Due to the Japanese policies on religion, many religious organizations and believers became supportive of the Japanese government, but national religious activities remained in action. The Cheondogyo order which succeeded the Donghak school and Christianity played a pivotal role in the March 1st Movement. And the Daejonggyo order, a religion that worshipped Dangun as the forefather of Korea rose up in armed struggles against the Japanese. In addition, Won-Buddhism was created by integrating Korean ideas into Buddhist beliefs, and philosophical efforts were made to integrate Korean traditions into Christianity as well.

The Korean Language Movement, which encouraged researches upon the Korean language and also promoted the language's wide distribution throughout the country, was set in motion in order to counter the Japanese policies which forced the Japanese language upon the Korean people. It was around this time that the "Hangeul Day" was enacted and the Korean language's spelling rule was revised. In opposition to the 'colonial history' that was being taught to the Korean people in order to rationalize the Japanese occupation of Korea and distort Korean history beyond repairs, a Nationalist academia of history was established to help people understand the Korean history correctly, independently, and progressively. Also, literature depicting the Korean sentiments enthusiastically prospered as well.

While accepting new cultures and new products, Koreans developed a modern spirit by integrating their efforts to advance their traditional virtues with their passion for social and national movements.

Cheondogyo Chapel
Cheondogyo, the successor of the Donghak school, was one of the leaders of the March 1st Movement. The order published several kinds of magazines such as *Gaebyeok* (Daw of Cilization), *Shinyeoseong* (New Women), *Eorinyi* (Children), and *Nongmin* (Farmers). Through such publications the order promoted both cultural and social movements. The picture is the Cheondogyo Central Chapel constructed in 1921.

Distorted Korean history books
The Japanese authorities published Korean history books that contained distorted images and interpretations of the Korean history, as part of its ruling policy of the Korean Peninsula. Prevailing inside such books were prejudiced arguments claiming that "Koreans are not able to develop their own country," or "The Koreans only have a low-grade nature."

Nationalist history books
These books were written from the Koreans' Nationalistic perspective. They revealed the Japanese invasion of Korea and emphasized the independent nature of Korean history and the fine culture of Korea.

3

Emergence of Various Nationalist Movements

The stirring of East Asia

In November of 1921, the U.S. strived to create a new international order in East Asia with the help of England and Japan. Until February of the following year, the U.S. led the signing of several treaties. As Europe withdrew from East Asia, America emerged as the new key player and the Imperialistic rule of Japan seemed to have secured stability. The Washington Consensus initiated the East Asian version of the Treaty of Versailles.

It seemed that under the cooperation of America, Japan, and England, East Asia had become stable. But in the 1920s East Asia was once again disturbed with the reform movements that emerged from the bottoms of the societies. As the Koreans commenced a full scale 'Declaration of Independence' Movement, the Chinese continued their anti-Japanese efforts with their own May 4th Movement. Koreans established a provisional government and actively engaged in armed struggles against the Japanese, while the Chinese organized a revolutionary Nationalist party, Kuomintang, creating foundations for a

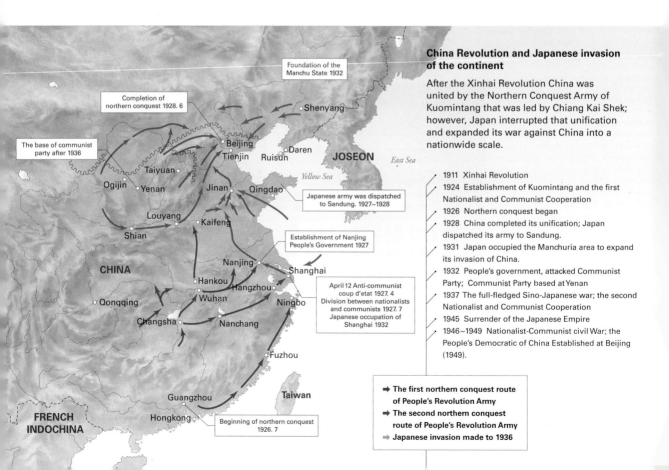

Foundation of the Manchu State 1932

Completion of northern conquest 1928. 6

The base of communist party after 1936

Japanese army was dispatched to Sandung. 1927~1928

Establishment of Nanjing People's Government 1927

April 12 Anti-communist coup d'etat 1927. 4
Division between nationalists and communists 1927. 7
Japanese occupation of Shanghai 1932

Beginning of northern conquest 1926. 7

Shenyang
Beijing
Tienjin Ruisun Daren
Taiyuan
Ogijin Yenan Jinan Qingdao
Louyang
Kaifeng
Shian
CHINA
Nanjing
Hankou Hangzhou Shanghai
Qonqqing Wuhan Ningbo
Changsha Nanchang
Fuzhou
Guangzhou Taiwan
FRENCH INDOCHINA Hongkong

JOSEON
East Sea
Yellow Sea

China Revolution and Japanese invasion of the continent

After the Xinhai Revolution China was united by the Northern Conquest Army of Kuomintang that was led by Chiang Kai Shek; however, Japan interrupted that unification and expanded its war against China into a nationwide scale.

- 1911 Xinhai Revolution
- 1924 Establishment of Kuomintang and the first Nationalist and Communist Cooperation
- 1926 Northern conquest began
- 1928 China completed its unification; Japan dispatched its army to Sandung.
- 1931 Japan occupied the Manchuria area to expand its invasion of China.
- 1932 People's government, attacked Communist Party; Communist Party based at Yenan
- 1937 The full-fledged Sino-Japanese war; the second Nationalist and Communist Cooperation
- 1945 Surrender of the Japanese Empire
- 1946~1949 Nationalist-Communist civil War; the People's Democratic of China Established at Beijing (1949).

➡ The first northern conquest route of People's Revolution Army
➡ The second northern conquest route of People's Revolution Army
⇨ Japanese invasion made to 1936

long-term struggle. Having succeeded in a Socialist revolution, Russia also supported East Asia's anti-imperialist movements.

Especially, the Chinese people's revolution played a decisive role in the overall anti-imperialist efforts throughout East Asia. Kuomintang which was organized by Sun Wen in 1924 led the unification movement of China, while the Chinese Communist Party established in 1921 also expanded its power rapidly. At times the Communist Party and Kuomintang did cooperate, and when China was united by the latter it emerged as a powerful force which could stand against Japan that had been dreaming to invade the mainland all the time.

Nationalist movements diverging in various directions

Many Koreans were dismayed when they heard the news that the U.S. had acknowledged Japan as one of the three most powerful countries in the world. As a result, some abandoned their engagements in the Nationalist movements, and some people even began to argue that instead of achieving independence right now the Koreans would be better off trying to gain more strength and international recognition for the time being. However, the Korean Nationalist movement continued to receive either support or inspiration from the revolutionary efforts of China, and from Russia, which was assisting anti-imperialist movements in several areas.

Na Seok-ju's Bombing Incident
The picture shows an issue of *The Dong-A Ilbo* that reported a person named Na Seok-ju (1892~1926) threw a bomb to the Oriental Colonization Company in December 28, 1926.

Especially China became the base of operations for the Nationalist movements of the Koreans, as their homeland was already occupied by the Japanese. Korea exchanged personnel, materials, and ideological resources with China, and continued their efforts in both China and Korea.

In Shanghai, there was the Provisional Government of the Republic of Korea which was organized with various oversea groups dedicated to the Korean independence. And in Manchuria, the Korean Independence Army trained its troops in preparation for the armed struggles against the Japanese.

Also, many anarchists waged violent struggles against the Japanese in both China and Korea. The Euiyeoldan organization in China was one of the most representative groups of the time. It assaulted Japanese government offices inside Korea, numerous times.

As Nationalist movements continued to diverge in many directions, debates regarding their methods and also the look of the new nation which would inevitably come after the liberation, became more active.

Making the "National Solitary Party"

Since 1926, those involved in the Nationalist movements initiated the "National Solitary Party" movement, in hopes of overcoming the Koreans' own differences in ideologies and achieving independence. This movement which continued in and outside of Korea led to the foundation of the Shinganhoe organization, which became the most powerful anti-Japanese party of the time. Even in the regions of China, efforts to unify all the relevant parties become more active.

Shinganhoe was founded in Seoul in 1927. Nationalists and Socialists together established firm principles designed to achieve political and economic independence. For four years, Shinganhoe established many regional offices, which played a substantial role in protecting the socio-economic interests of the Koreans and raising the people's awareness of their national identity.

Cooperative measures were also actively taken in Manchuria. Various independence movement organizations merged with the Joseon Revolutionary Party and the Korean Independence Party, and both of them organized military regiments to fight the Japanese.

The cooperation between the Nationalists and Socialists hugely contributed to the task of preparing the new, independent Korean government that would have to come in the future. Principles of the Provisional Government of the Republic of Korea were also established in the early 1940s as part of such endeavors.

By holding elections we will have people freely and equally join the government.
By adopting a national ownership system we will make equal distributions of eco-

Reports of the establishment of zzthe Shinganhoe organization
Shinganhoe announced its own platform of agendas, designed to accomplish the Korean people's political and economical liberation from the Japanese, and to unite the Korean people with the exclusion of opportunists. Its main policies included seeking for freedom of media, meetings, publication and organizations, as well as the abolition of bad (cruel) laws and torture, opposition to the Japanese migration, and boycotting unjust taxation.

June 10th Movement
In 1926 inside Seoul, wherever the last emperor Sunjong's funeral parade passed by, the crowd joined demonstrations arranged against the Japanese.

nomic interests. We will have all the people attend schools with the public fund. We will ensure the Koreans' right of determining our own fate in and out of the country. We will eliminate all kinds of unequal relationships between peoples and nations… – Founding Principles

Another outburst of "Hurray for Korean Independence!"

Sentiments of cooperation and unification were born out of the anti-Japanese movements, and in return, such sentiments provided the overall efforts of those movements with momentum that would allow them to spread throughout the country.

It was the 1926 rally that created an atmosphere of cooperation. Timed at the funeral of King Sunjong, the last emperor of the Great Han Empire, Socialists and uncompromising Nationalists organized Korean students and citizens for a full scale movement of declaring independence. On June 10th, once again, the streets of Seoul were overwhelmed by shouts of "Hurray for Korean Independence!" (the June 10th Movement). Shortly after this movement, Shinganhoe was founded.

In 1929, student movements became more intensive and spread out even more, with the support of social organizations including Shinganhoe. In November of that year, by organizing a massive rally, the students of Gwangju demanded that Japan abolish racial discrimination and discontinue distorted colonial education (the Gwangju Student Movement). Shinganhoe notified the public of the students' efforts, and soon the news spread throughout the country. In winter the same year, major cities like Seoul and Gwangju again witnessed the independence movements gaining more power and momentum.

Gwangju Students' Resistance against Japan

On October 30, 1929, an incident in which a Japanese student harassed a Korean female student triggered a clash between a group of Korean students and that of Japanese students. Soon after this incident was unfairly taken care of by the police, school and media altogether, a large-scale protest erupted in Gwangju on both November 3rd and November 12th, with cooperations of many schools. Another round of protests ensued as well in more than 200 schools throughout the country, supporting the cause of the original student demonstration and requesting the termination of student oppression in general. The number of students who were expelled from the school due to their participation in the protest mounted to approximately six hundred. In the left is the Dong-A Ilbo newspaper issue that reported the incident, and in the middle is the picture of Park Jun-chae who was a 2nd grade student of Gwangju Common High School and initiated the fight as his own sister was the one harassed by the Japanese students. In the right we can see the monument which was erected to commemorate the Gwangju Student Resistance Movement.

4

Founding a Nation While Fighting Against Fascism

Colonial Fascism and the sufferings of Koreans

In 1931, Japan occupied Manchuria. Six years later Japan waged a war on China. In 1941, it attacked the United States and invaded Southeast Asia, which initiated the Pacific war. In this period, Japan mobilized its own people and also the people of the colonies in its war efforts, under the name of preventing the proliferation of Communism and consolidating the unity among Asian countries to respond to the Western threat. As a result, Fascism engulfed Asia.

As Japan implemented the National Mobilization Law and the Major Industry Controlling Law, it forced all Koreans into battlefields. Many Koreans were arrested and sent to ammunition factories or mines, where they were enslaved and sentenced to toil in death-like labor. Many young men were drafted and killed in the battlefields, and many Korean women as well were sent to the battlefields as Comfort women and were forced to live as sex-slaves.

Most of the industrial activities focused more and more upon the production of military goods. Since

Kidnapped
This is a picture which described the memories of an elderly female who was kidnapped by the Japanese authorities and was forced to serve as a "Comfort woman" (sexual slavery) of the Japanese military during the war.
These Korean "Comfort women" were drafted to 'serve' the Japanese soldiers, and the ones who survived the Pacific War returned home after the war. In Korea today there are approximately one hundred survivors, and since 1992 about ten-plus elders have been living together at the "House of Sharing." Although they have been demanding an official apology of the Japanese government by protesting in front of the Japanese embassy every Wednesday, Japanese officials have been ignoring such actions.

the beginning of the Pacific War, Japan continued to suffer from lack of resources and materials, while its national economy was collapsing. In the end, Japanese initiated a controlled economic policy and resorted to pillaging of even the most bare necessities of the Korean people.

The Japanese upheld Fascism as their social ideology as it rationalized the purpose of their battles. All Koreans were required to pledge their unconditional loyalty to the Japanese emperor everyday. The use of Korean language and Korean history education were banned and prohibited. Moreover, Japan forced Koreans to change their names into Japanese versions of such names. Even the slightest opposition was suppressed, and the society became a one large barrack.

Confrontation of Koreans against the Japanese in alliance with the Chinese

Koreans along with the Chinese carried out a series of anti-Japanese movements. In 1932, when a Korean Yi Bong-chang threw a bomb at the Japanese emperor and shocked the entire Japanese society, and when Yun Bong-gil hurled a bomb that killed many Japanese soldiers and a high-ranking Japanese officer in China, the Chinese applauded their courage.

There were countless incidents where Koreans cooperated with the Chi-

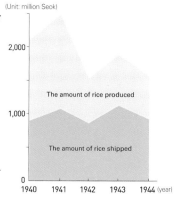

(Unit: million Seok)

The amount of rice produced

The amount of rice shipped

The amount of rice produced, and the amount of rice delivered to Japan
After the Second Sino-Japanese War in 1937, the Japanese imperial authorities exploited Korean agricultural products in order to supply themselves with materials necessary for their war efforts. They collected agricultural products from farmers by force and newly implemented a 'Distribution System.' About half of the Korean agricultural products were delivered to the Japanese government. Other than grain, the Japanese set delivery quotas for leather and iron as well.

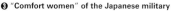

❶ Pledge of being the Emperor's citizens
The Japanese imperial authorities made various forms of barbaric demands to the Korean people, in an attempt to obliterate the Korean spirit and culture so that they could recruit more Koreans who would willingly fight for Japan. Koreans were required to pledge their loyalty to the Japanese emperor as an imperial citizen, every day. They had to pay respect to the emperor and his ancestors as well. Also, the use of the Korean language was banned, and the Koreans were forced to adopt Japanese versions of their original names, by the law.

❷ Forced draft
From 1939 to 1945, Japanese imperial authorities mobilized more than one million Korean laborers for mining, construction works, and munition factory operations. Under the supervision of the Japanese military, Korean laborers were treated as slave laborers. And to hide such dark secrets, the Japanese never hesitated to resort to mass killings. Furthermore, the Japanese drafted about 300,000 Korean soldiers by force.

❸ "Comfort women" of the Japanese military
In 1944, the Japanese imperialists announced the 'Comfort Women (sexual slavery) Duty Ordinance', and forcefully drafted Korean women over the age of twelve and under forty, to be sent to the battlefields. Korean women were harshly driven to work at munition plants as well, and they were taken to China or even Southeast Asia to serve as either laborers or sexual slavery. More than half of the 200,000 souls who were drafted by the Japanese authorities as Comfort women were Korean women. To conceal one of their most heinous crimes, the Japanese Imperialists committed mass genocide, or left those women on the battlefields.

nese to fight against the Japanese army. Right after Japan occupied Manchuria in the early 1930s, the Joseon Revolutionary Army and the Korean Independence Army allied with the Chinese to defeat the Japanese army. In 1936, Korean and Chinese Communists organized the Northeast Anti-Japanese Allied Army. The Anti-Japanese Allied Army staged attacks along the border of Manchuria, leaving significant damages to the Japanese forces, and then advanced into Korea, hurting the Japanese even further.

In Manchuria, the anti-Japanese military struggle became more difficult in the late 1930s. However, a part of the Korean Independence Army moved to the mainland China and Russia to continue fighting the Japanese military.

The army to advance into the country ("Gungnaejeongjingun")
One unit of the Korean Restoration Army was trained by OSS (Office of Strategic Services) in early 1945 to stage a guerrilla war inside Korea, and was about to be sent into the Korean Peninsula. However, the plan was put on hold when the Japanese Imperialists surrendered in August, and as a result, this army had to return to China upon the moment they arrived in Seoul.

Koreans struggled until the Day of Liberation

The anti-Japanese armed struggle remained active on Chinese soil. In 1937, as the Second Sino-Japanese War began, Koreans living in China insistently joined armed conflicts.

Kim Won-bong organized the Korean Revolutionary Party and established the Joseon Militia Army (1938). Also the Provisional Government organized the Korea Restoration Army (1940). Later the Korean Restoration Army, after assimilating part of the Joseon Militia Army, attacked the Japanese troops with the support of the Chinese Kuomintang party.

Meanwhile, a part of the Joseon Militia cooperated with the Chinese Communist Party to fight against the Japanese. They were placed under the jurisdiction of the Joseon Independence Alliance and continued to fight until the Japanese surrendered. The Korean Independence Army continued their fights in Russia as well, with the Russians' support.

As Japan neared its own defeat, it became increasingly desperate. However, sensing that the day of independence was not too far ahead, the Korean struggles for independence became more intense than ever before. In 1944, the Nation (Korean Government) Foundation Alliance was formed by people like Yeo Un-hyeong. On August 15th of 1945, Japan finally surrendered. The Japanese occupation, and a long bloody war, finally ended.

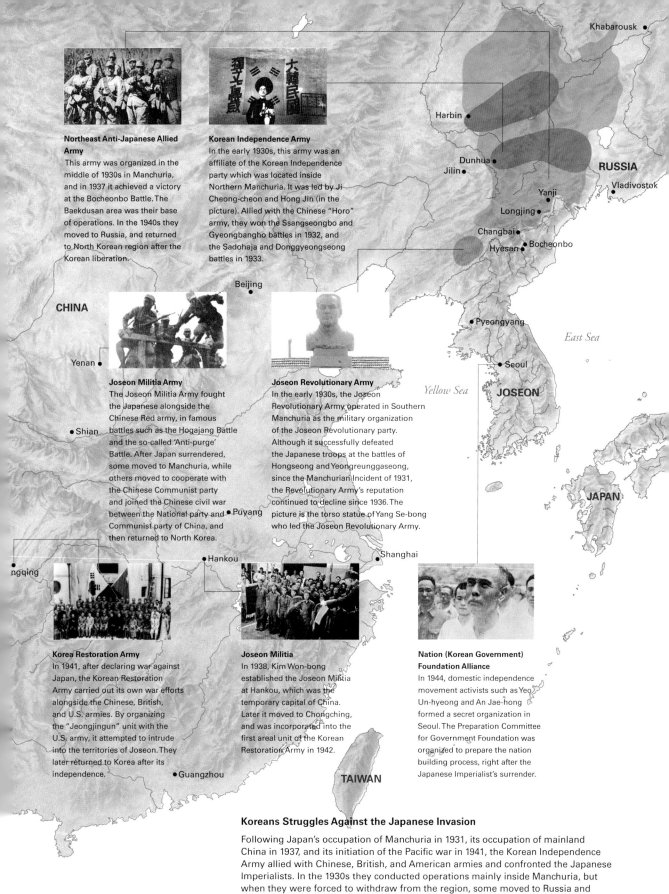

Northeast Anti-Japanese Allied Army

This army was organized in the middle of 1930s in Manchuria, and in 1937 it achieved a victory at the Bocheonbo Battle. The Baekdusan area was their base of operations. In the 1940s they moved to Russia, and returned to North Korean region after the Korean liberation.

Korean Independence Army

In the early 1930s, this army was an affiliate of the Korean Independence party which was located inside Northern Manchuria. It was led by Ji Cheong-cheon and Hong Jin (in the picture). Allied with the Chinese "Horo" army, they won the Ssangseongbo and Gyeongbangho battles in 1932, and the Sadohaja and Donggyeongseong battles in 1933.

Joseon Militia Army

The Joseon Militia Army fought the Japanese alongside the Chinese Red army, in famous battles such as the Hogajang Battle and the so-called 'Anti-purge' Battle. After Japan surrendered, some moved to Manchuria, while others moved to cooperate with the Chinese Communist party and joined the Chinese civil war between the National party and Communist party of China, and then returned to North Korea.

Joseon Revolutionary Army

In the early 1930s, the Joseon Revolutionary Army operated in Southern Manchuria as the military organization of the Joseon Revolutionary party. Although it successfully defeated the Japanese troops at the battles of Hongseong and Yeongreunggaseong, since the Manchurian Incident of 1931, the Revolutionary Army's reputation continued to decline since 1936. The picture is the torso statue of Yang Se-bong who led the Joseon Revolutionary Army.

Korea Restoration Army

In 1941, after declaring war against Japan, the Korean Restoration Army carried out its own war efforts alongside the Chinese, British, and U.S. armies. By organizing the "Jeongjingun" unit with the U.S. army, it attempted to intrude into the territories of Joseon. They later returned to Korea after its independence.

Joseon Militia

In 1938, Kim Won-bong established the Joseon Militia at Hankou, which was the temporary capital of China. Later it moved to Chongching, and was incorporated into the first areal unit of the Korean Restoration Army in 1942.

Nation (Korean Government) Foundation Alliance

In 1944, domestic independence movement activists such as Yeo Un-hyeong and An Jae-hong formed a secret organization in Seoul. The Preparation Committee for Government Foundation was organized to prepare the nation building process, right after the Japanese Imperialist's surrender.

Khabarousk

RUSSIA

Harbin

Dunhua **Jilin**

Vladivostok

Yanji

Longjing

Changbai

Hyesan **Bocheonbo**

Beijing

CHINA

Yenan

Shian

Pyeongyang

East Sea

Seoul

Yellow Sea

JOSEON

Puyang

JAPAN

Hankou

Shanghai

ngqing

Guangzhou

TAIWAN

Koreans Struggles Against the Japanese Invasion

Following Japan's occupation of Manchuria in 1931, its occupation of mainland China in 1937, and its initiation of the Pacific war in 1941, the Korean Independence Army allied with Chinese, British, and American armies and confronted the Japanese Imperialists. In the 1930s they conducted operations mainly inside Manchuria, but when they were forced to withdraw from the region, some moved to Russia and others moved to China, where they continued their war of independence. Many secret organizations were formed and continued their activities inside Korea as well.

Historic Hall of the Seodaemun Prison, and the Independence Memorial Hall of Korea

The Japanese occupation brought enormous suffering to the Koreans. The people who dared to confront the Japanese Imperialists to accomplish independence had to endure much more excruciating pains as well.

Koreans protested against the Japanese imperialists with a variety of methods in and out of the country. Koreans confronted the invasion of the Japanese Imperialists, to maintain peace and also to regain their own sovereignty that was taken away from them.

At the Historic Hall of the Seodaemun Prison in Seoul (www.sscmc.or.kr/culture2), tragic scenes of torturing Korean patriots who participated in the independence movement can be viewed. Various efforts that were made in the process of obtaining independence are also presented at the Independence Memorial Hall of Korea (www.i815.or.kr) at the Cheonan region in the Chungcheongnam-do province.

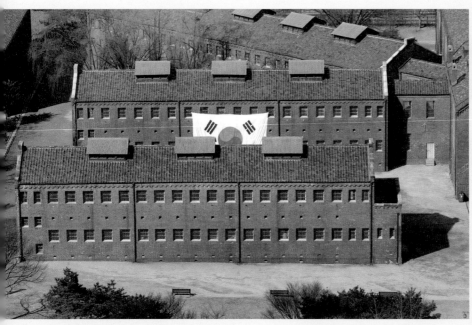

Historic Hall of the Seodaemun Prison
This is the place where countless Korean patriots were detained since it was opened in 1908. Even after the liberation it continued to be used as a prison until 1987, and later, in order to promote a spirit of independence among the younger generations of Korea, the facility was totally renovated. In 1998, it reopened as the Historic Hall of the Seodaemun Prison.
❶ **Monument of Commemoration** ❷ **Execution Ground** ❸ **Solitary Confinement**

266

The Independence Memorial Hall of Korea
This Hall was built with a national fundraising that began in August 1982, and also with the government's cooperation. It was first opened in August 15, 1987, and in 1995, the "Hill of Hopes for Unification" was newly constructed. In this Hall, there are various exhibitions regarding the Koreans' efforts toward independence, and there are also various displays of historical evidences to such efforts. Research activities and education are also supported.

There are seven exhibition rooms at the Independence Memorial Hall of Korea. There are four rooms where various types of independence movements can be seen, and there are other rooms that display the Korean traditional culture and the Koreans' national movements that were dedicated to the cause of modernization. In the 7th room, visitors can experience the past as well.

The inside of the Independence Memorial Hall of Korea

Migration of Koreans During the Occupation: Koreans Overseas

In 2005, the number of Korean immigrants exceeded six million. Those immigrants are currently residing in approximately 170 different countries. Many Koreans immigrated during the Japanese occupation and during the industrialization period. During the Japanese occupation period the Koreans left the country for mostly financial reasons, or for political exiles, or for studies abroad.

When Japan surrendered in 1945, there were about 4 million Koreans residing in Manchuria, Japan, China, and America, which was about one sixth of the total Korean population at the time. The ratio was relatively high compared to 1.5~2% of the Indian migrant population and 2% of Chinese migrant population.

After achieving independence, most Koreans remained in their adopted countries. Then since the 1960s, another wave of Korean migration took off. For the purpose of learning or working, Koreans moved to America, Germany, and South America, and they formed Korean communities in these countries. As the Korean economy developed, the Koreans' international activities have become more active than before, and the number of Koreans residing abroad has increased as well.

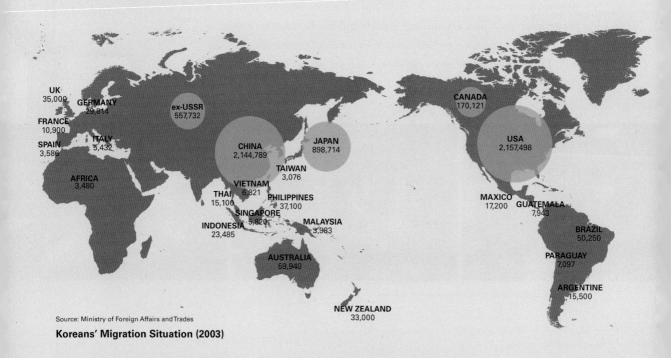

Source: Ministry of Foreign Affairs and Trades

Koreans' Migration Situation (2003)

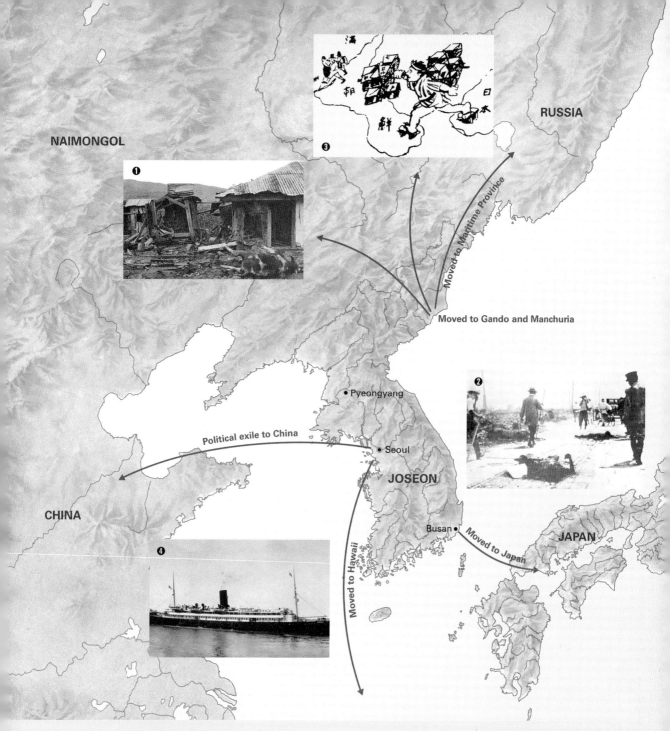

RUSSIA

NAIMONGOL

❸

❶

Moved to Maritime Province

Moved to Gando and Manchuria

• Pyeongyang

❷

Political exile to China

⊛ Seoul

JOSEON

CHINA

Busan •

JAPAN

Moved to Japan

❹

Moved to Hawaii

Koreans' Migration Situation (1890~1930)

❶ **Gando Disaster (1920)**
As the Korean Independence Army actively worked for Korean independence along the border, Japan mobilized a large portion of its troops to Gando. In three or four months since October 9th, they burnt down Korean villages and indiscriminately massacred Koreans everywhere. For 27 days (from October 9th to November 5th), official records indicate that approximately 13,469 Koreans were killed. However, in reality much more Koreans were either injured or killed.

❷ **Genocide committed against Koreans during the Gwandong earthquake**
An earthquake of a 7.9 magnitude occurred in Japan in September 1923. This earthquake hit densely populated areas such as Tokyo and Yokohama. In this chaotic situation, the Japanese imperialists intentionally spread out the rumor of Korean riots, in order to justify their ruthless genocide of the Koreans.

❸ **"Who is coming and who is going"**
A Newspaper editorial cartoon depicting the Koreans' migration to Manchuria, driven by the Japanese. (*The Dong-A Ilbo*, October 10th, 1927)

❹ **The Ship Gallic, with the first generation of Korean immigrants headed for Hawaii on board (1903)**
On December 22, 1902, the first wave of Korean immigrants to Hawaii was launched, as Koreans left the Jemulpo port by boarding a Japanese ship headed for Japan. They then transferred aboard a Gallic ship at Kobe, and arrived at Hawaii on January 13, 1903.

1945 ~ 1960

1945

Right after the liberation of 1945, the Nationalist movement leaders took their step in rebuilding the country by organizing the Preparation Committee for the National Foundation. However, the Soviet forces marched to the north of the 38th parallel line while the U.S. military imposed authority upon the south of the Korean Peninsula.

1946

In 1946, in order to discuss establishing an independent government of Korea, the first meeting of the Joint Commission between the U.S. and USSR was held, but not much accomplishment was made. Yi Seung-man argued that South should build a separate government of its own. Seriously concerned about the prospect of division, Yeo Un-hyeong promoted the movement of a Joint Cooperation between the Left and the Right.

1947

Truman Doctrine was declared. Conflicts between the U.S. and USSR continued, and the second meeting of the joint commission between the two countries ended without achieving anything.

1948

On May 10, 1948, a separate election was held in the south of the 38th parallel line. In July, Constitutions were legislated, and on August 15th, the government of the Republic of Korea was established. Meanwhile, in the north of the 38th parallel line, the Democratic People's Republic of Korea was established in September 1948.

1949

In 1949, the Chinese Communist Party won the Chinese Civil War, and the People's Republic of China was founded.

1950~1953

The Korean War broke out with the North Koreans' attack, and continued for three years. The war left Koreans with irrevocable damages. Right after the war ended, the ROK-US Mutual Defense Agreement was made.

1954

In 1954, the Korean Constitution was revised for the second time to allow Yi Seung-man to make his ruling permanent. Jo Bong-am who was a candidate for presidency was executed after being framed as a spy.

1958

In 1958, a cooperative union system for farming and individual businesses was established in North Korea, and it meant the emergence of a Socialist economic system.

XII The Establishment of a Democratic Republic and the Country's Division

남북철도연결구간 열차시험운행
2007. 5. 17

On August 15th of 1945, Korea was liberated from the cruel occupation, and three years later it founded a democratic republic. However, no one expected that such independence would be followed by a division of the country. No one at the time could have imagined that the 38th parallel line would divide the Korean people into two different political systems. The two governments could not tolerate each other, so they fought a fierce war that lasted for three years. The separation of the peninsula became a reality, and a lasting division finally occurred after almost 1,300 years of unification.

Restoration of the Gyeongeuiseon Railroad The division that accompanied Korea's liberation also led to a disconnection in railroad operations between the South and the North. This picture shows the railroad finally reconnected for test operations, and trains being readied for trial runs again, as South and North reconciliation has been proceeding.

Conflicts During the Cold War Period

After the end of World War II, the United States and the Soviet Union rose as two super powers of the globe. With their newly established presence, the world was divided into two realms, Capitalism and Communism, with the U.S. and USSR at their respective centers. These two powers collided with each other everywhere in the world.

The ensuing Cold War cut the world in half and divided Europe into East and West. Vietnam was divided at the northern 17th parallel, while Korea was divided at the 38th parallel.

With the Cold War, the inner dynamics of East Asia significantly shifted. A civil war between the Nationalist Party (Kuomintang) and the Communist Party broke out in China. As a result, the People's Republic of China was established in the mainland with a communist system, while the Nationalist Party withdrew to Taiwan. In the meantime, Japan came to play a pivotal role in the overall anti-communist efforts supported and controlled by the United States.

The Cold War also hugely affected the Koreans' destiny. It played a key role in creating "Two Koreas." The Korean Peninsula became a frontline of conflicts between Communists and Capitalists and one of the most sensitive areas in the world.

Cold War and Asia

The Cold War meant more than it was to the Asians, including the Koreans. Countries that had long maintained unity were divided, and countless people had to endure excruciating pain, or be killed during wars.

■ USSR and its allies in 1958
■ U.S. and its allies in 1958

Japanese Self-Defense Army

USSR

MONGOLIA

JAPAN
1945 Occupied by the United States
1951 Recovery of its sovereignty
1951 Signing of the U.S. and Japan
Security Treaty
1954 Organization of a Self-Defense
Force

1948 Foundation of the Democratic
People's Republic of Korea
1950 North Korea's invasion of South
Korea

NORTH
KOREA

SOUTH
KOREA

1945 U.S. Military administration imposed
1948 Foundation of the Republic of Korea
1950~1953 Korean War

Foundation of the People's Republic of China

CHINA
1949 Foundation of People's
Republic of China;
The Republic of China
withdrew to Taiwan

Korean War

PHILIPPINES
1951 Signing of a mutual defense
treaty between the United
States and Philippines
1968 Communist revolts
1972~1978 Civil War

1953~1974 Civil War

EAST
PAKISTAN
MYANMAR
LAOS
NORTH
VIETNAM
1945 Foundation of the Democratic
People's Republic of Vietnam
1954 Vietnam divided into North
and South
1965~1975 Vietnam War

THAI

CAMBODIA
SOUTH
VIETNAM

1972~1974 Civil War between the
Communist Khmer Rouge
and non-Communists

MALAYSIA
1948~1960 Communist uprising,
led by the Muslims

Vietnam War

1

Upon Liberation, the Process for Building a Nation Accelerates

Preparations for founding a nation

On August 15, 1945, Japan surrendered unconditionally to the Allied Forces, and that finally brought an end to the war. Japan's defeat meant the independence of Korea, since in 1943 the leaders of America, Britain, and China held a conference at Cairo to discuss the situation of post-war Asia and promised the independence of Korea: "In due course, Korea shall be free and independent." (1943, Cairo Declaration)

Koreans welcomed the day of independence with delight and also tears. Korean flags, which had been hidden in people's houses, stormed the streets, and the shouting "Hurray for Korea's Independence!" trembled the earth and heavens.

Soon after being liberated, Koreans began to passionately prepare for the reconstruction of their own government. One of the first leaders who called for the creation of a new nation was Yeo Un-hyeong. He had been preparing to establish a new country by organizing the Nation Foundation Alliance, and he immediately launched the Preparation Committee for the National Foundation, and was handed

The Korean people welcoming their liberation
On August 15th of 1945, the Japanese Imperialists declared "unconditional surrender," and on the next day 20,000 prisoners who had been locked in police stations and prisons throughout the country were released. A wave of joy for liberation completely engulfed the country.

over the Governor-General office's jurisdictions. The Committee was joined by many national activists. There were 145 branches of the Committee established throughout the country.

The Committee aspired to found an independent country and also a democratic government, and declared the foundation of the Joseon People's Republic on September 6, 1945. All the regional branches were transformed into 'People's Committees.' This was two days before the U.S. military forces established their presence in Korea.

The U.S. and USSR Forces occupied Korea and divided it into two

It was the Korean and Chinese Nationalist movements that mostly fought the Japanese prior to 1941. Then in 1941, the United States of America emerged as the new leading force of the Allied Forces, and in 1945 the Soviet Union finally joined the Allied Forces as well. And after the war ended, America, China, and Russia created a new world order.

The United States was the most influential one, and it attempted to place Korea under a trusteeship for a certain period of time, since they needed a pro-American government in Korea. The Soviet Union also marched into the Korean Peninsula to establish a pro-Russian government and was ready to accept the trusteeship as an alternative option. And in the meantime, Koreans' wishes to establish their own government were mostly ignored.

The United States and the Soviet Union respectively occupied the southern and northern areas of the 38th parallel, under the justification of dis-

The U.S. flag hung at the Joseon Governor-General office building
Instead of the Japanese flag, the American flag was posted at the building. According to the agreement with Soviet Union, the United States which occupied the south part of the 38 parallel line came with the authority to rule it until a new government was fully founded. The flag was an indicator to the reality of Korea, which was still not able to achieve full independence, within the Cold War atmosphere.

The 38th Parallel line that ran across roads and villages
The 38th parallel line resulted in random divisions in the Koreans' lives. It was a wall that divided the Korean Peninsula into two, as it literally cut through villages, roads, and fields.

arming the Japanese troops. As military governments were established in both regions, not only the People's Republic, but also the Provisional Government of the Republic of Korea which had fought the Japanese for decades, all turned out to be powerless organizations, unauthorized by the U.S. and USSR.

The military governments of the U.S. and USSR needed Korean supporters. Recognizing the domestic situation of political affairs as favorable to its interest, the Soviet Union decided to support the People's Committees that had been organized from below. On the contrary, the U.S. decided to employ many policemen and officials who had worked for the Japanese Governor-General or the Japanese Empire in general.

Confrontations between the Left and Right: hindrance to founding a single government

Following the liberation of Korea, many patriots returned home. Yi Seungman and Kim Gu who led the independence movements in America and China respectively also came back to Seoul, Korea. In the meantime, Kim Il-seong and Kim Du-bong who used to work for independence in USSR and China made their political ground in Pyeongyang of North Korea. In both north and south of the Korean Peninsula, numerous political parties and associations were organized.

However, the leaders were divided, between people who wanted a Democratic government and people who wanted a Socialist state. In the wake of

Aggravated confrontation between the Left and the Right
Facing the conclusions made at the Moscow Conference of Foreign Ministers, the Rightists opposed the trusteeship (left), while the Leftists argued that the establishment of a temporary government (right) was the top priority. Disagreement soon turned to aggravating conflicts, which ultimately inhibited genuine efforts to establish a unified government from going forward.

all those division even anarchism was recommended. In addition to that, the leaders did not have the experience of working together inside the same organization.

In December 1945, the Moscow Conference of Foreign Ministers from the three countries (U.S., U.K., USSR) was called to discuss the procedures for Korean independence. It was decided that the U.S. and USSR would form a joint committee and launch a Korean provisional government, and that total of four countries, U.S., U.K., USSR, China and the Korean Provisional government would discuss the issue of trusteeship.

Koreans were divided over the decision of the Moscow Conference, as people on the Right who called themselves as Nationalists opposed the trusteeship, while people on the Left which was composed of mostly Socialists believed that accepting the decision would be helpful in achieving an early independence. The Right criticised the Left for selling the country over to Russia, while the Left argued that dismantling the 38th parallel and establishing a political and economic unity between the North and South was more urgent.

As Pro-Japanese conservative groups joined the anti-trusteeship movement, the Left called for the removal of pro-Japanese elements and the promotion of land reform. The conflicts between the Left and Right only became worse. The establishment of a unified republic in the Korean Peninsula was becoming increasingly difficult.

Kim Il-seong (1912~1994)

An Jae-hong (1891~1965)

Yi Seung-man (Syngman Rhee) (1875~1965)

Park Heon-yeong (1900~1955)

Yeo Un-hyeong (1886~1947)

Kim Gu (1876~1949)

The confrontation between the Left and the Right concerning the issue of building a new nation

In the north side of the 38th parallel line the Soviet Union army marched, while in the south side the U.S. army supporting the Rightists was stationed. The Left and the Right disagreed with each other over the ways to construct a new nation. Kim Il-seong became the first Prime minister of the North while Yi Seung-man was elected as the first President in the South. An Jae-hong and Yeo Un-hyeong who were considered as neutral parties sought for ways that could unite the Left and the Right in cooperation, but even such efforts were not able to prevent the division of the country. Kim Gu refused to participate in the South Korean government as he was still arguing for a unified government. Park Heon-young who led the Socialist movement in the south later became the Vice premier of North Korea.

2

Establishment of the Republic of Korea

Beginning of the division

When the war ended, all Japanese troops withdrew from Korea. However, the Korean economy was still in trouble. Almost half of the remaining industries built by the Japanese and their technology shut down due to not only lack of engineers and material supplies but also disconnection of marketing routes. Also, the situation in which 79% of the heavy industry was located in the north, while 70% of the light industry located in the south, caused some serious problems for both parts of the Korean Peninsula.

Social stabilities could only be acquired with a swiftly founded government and a conclusive and extensive reform plans in place. But both the U.S. and USSR, which wanted a government helpful to their own agendas, were pretty much passive in helping out the Korean reforms, and their presence only drew Koreans further away from their fellow brethren.

The provisional government of the North, under the leadership of the People's Committee, carried out land reforms by liquidating pro-Japanese properties and nationalizing all industry. Also they pro-

The first meeting of the Joint Commission between the United States and the Soviet Union (left)
According to the decisions made at the Moscow Conference, the Joint Commission between the United States and the Soviet Union was held for the first time in Seoul. This meeting ended without results, due to a large gap in opinions regarding the organization of a provisional government. This is the picture taken on March 20th of 1946, at the Commission meeting which was held at the Deoksugung.
Committee of Cooperation between the Left and the Right (right)
As the Joint Commission failed to reach a consensus in the first meeting in 1946 and Yi Seung-man argued the establishment of a separate government, Yeo Un-hyeong and Kim Gyu-shik organized the Committee of Cooperation between the Left and the Right to alleviate the tension between the South and North and thus find a way to build an independent, unified nation. This picture was taken at the second meeting of the Committee of Cooperation held after Yeo's death.

claimed laws ensuring the rights of laborers and the equality between men and women. As the North Korean government continued to stabilize itself, many 'Rightists' in the north who disagreed with all these policies fled to south across the 38th parallel.

The changes in the North put a lot of pressure upon the South. The Rightists in the South who were rather generous toward pro-Japanese figures and passive in punishing them, untied themselves under the name of anti-Communism. Thus, they demanded that a government only for the South be founded to lead the struggle against Communism in the North.

In the fall of 1946, the struggles of impoverished farmers and laborers of the South intensified. Eventually, their struggles turned into a resistance against the U.S. military government, which in turn suppressed the protest and decided to oppress the activities of the Leftists.

In this chaotic situation of confrontation between the North and the South, the Leftists and Rightists who were concerned about the prospect of a permanently divided nation, like Yeo Un-hyeong of the Preparation Committee and Kim Gyu-shik who had worked for the Provisional Government, tried hard to establish a unified government inside Korea. However, their efforts of demanding cooperation between the Leftists and Rightists, and negotiations between the U.S. and USSR failed to accomplish a unification between the South and North.

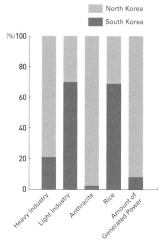

Source : Survey Department of Joseon Bank
Annual Economic Report of Joseon, 1948

Comparison of the economic structures of the 38th parallel's South and North at the time of liberation

Intensification of the Cold War

Although the second meeting for the U.S. and USSR Joint Commission opened in 1947, it was difficult to anticipate fruitful results in the first place, as the confrontation between these two countries had been internationally intensifying. While more Socialist countries were emerging in Eastern Europe as the Soviet Union contributed to their liberation, and political parties leagued with Communism were showing rapid progress in Western Europe, the U.S. provided economic support to Western European nations with the Marshall Plan. In the same year, the establishment of separate governments in Germany was decided, as the country was already occupied in division.

Arrested people in the 4.3 Incident
As the general election in 1948 was approaching, the people of Jeju-do arose with weapons, opposing the idea of establishing a separate government only in South Korea. The police and soldiers counteracted such people's actions, and in the process about one ninth of the civilians living in Jeju-do were killed.

Proclamation Ceremony of the Republic of Korea
On May 10 of 1948, a general election was held in South Korea, and following the legislation of Constitutions on July 17th, the Republic of Korea was established on August 15th. In North Korea, the Supreme People's Committee held an election to adopt a Constitution, and accordingly the Democratic People's Republic of Korea was born on September 9th.

Establishing the Government of the Republic of Korea

In 1947, as the Cold War intensified, the United States and the Soviet Union were confronting each other in numerous places in the world. And their conflicts greatly affected Korea's future destiny.

In the end of 1947, America brought the Korean issue to the United Nations. The UN General Assembly tallied votes and decided that nationwide elections under the supervision of the UN be held throughout the country. The Soviet Union refused to endorse the decision, arguing that the elections should be held after the withdrawal of foreign troops from Korea. Then, the UN decided an election to be held only in South Korea.

By that decision, the division of the country became a reality. Kim Gu and Kim Gyu-shik visited Pyeongyang and had a meeting with the North Korean leaders. In the meantime, residents of Jeju-do, vetoing the idea of a South Korea-only election, staged a fierce protest which led to the death of countless people. Yet, a general election was held in South Korea as planned on May 10, 1948, and 198 Assembly members were elected.

The legislative and judicial branches of government were formed and a Constitution was enacted. Finally on the 15th of August, the establishment of the Republic of Korea was proclaimed. And following it in the north, the establishment of the Democratic People's Republic of Korea was proclaimed.

Yi Seung-man was elected as the President of the Republic of Korea to lead South Korea on the basis of a Capitalist economy, while North Korea

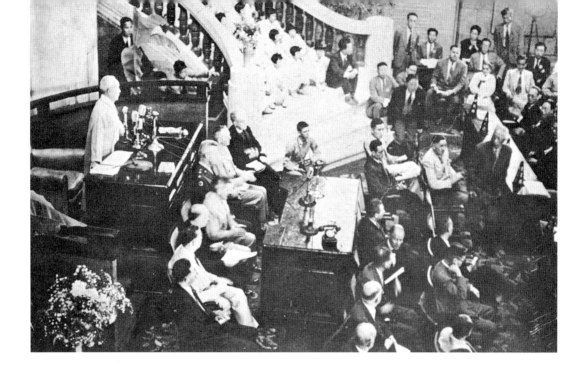

formed the Democratic People's Republic of Korea on the basis of the system of Socialism, under the leadership of Kim Il-seong.

A division after 1,300 years of unification

The Republic of Korea "is the fruit of our efforts to rebuild our independent nation, succeeding the great spirit of independence of the March 1st Movement…, will secure equal opportunities for everyone in all areas including politics, economy, society, and culture by establishing a democratic system…, will promote our people's equal improvement in life internally, and externally… will secure safety, freedom and happiness of us and our descendants…" (excerpts from the First Constitution). In this respect, the Republic of Korea was a successor of the Provisional Government of the Republic of Korea, and was the crowning achievement of movements that strived for the foundation of an independent nation.

However, the Republic of Korea was founded at the cost of the peninsula's own unity. The Korean Peninsula was finally divided, after having remained unified for 1,300 years. The 38th parallel was a tentative line that was drawn between the North and South to disarm the Japanese troops, yet it eventually became the dividing line of South and North Korea. Koreans did not have the power to oppose the decision of the U.S. and the Soviet Union as they were too powerful to confront, and now the 38th parallel line was about to cause a more tragic incident that changed the fate of the entire Korean race.

The First National Assembly (that created the Constitution)
In South Korea, on May 10th a general election was held to elect 198 lawmakers, and on May 31st the First Assembly was held. Since the objective of this meeting was to create a Constitution, this particular assembly is also called the "Constitution Assembly."

3

Outbreak of the Korean War

The anti-Communist system established by the Yi Seung-man administration

Farm lands are to be equally distributed to peasants (article 86) ... Industries such as transportation, communication, finance, insurance, electricity, irrigation, water and gas are to be operated by the government for the benefit of the public (article 87). Special Laws may be legislated to punish malicious anti-national activists (article 111)... – The First Constitution

In liberated Korea, all people expected reforms of this kind. Soon after the government was established, Koreans demanded their implementations. The National Assembly enacted the Land Reform Law and the Punishment Law on Anti-National Actions.

Yet, landlords and pro-Japanese Koreans resisted against these actions in various ways. Yi Seung-man, who seized power with the support of the Hanguk Minjudang (Korean Democratic Party) which represented the landlord class and pro-Japanese officials and policemen, fell into a dilemma.

In the end, Yi Seung-man decided to protect his supporters, and in order to do that, he found his political justification in anti-Communism. To eliminate all Communists he protected the pro-Japanese policemen, and finally he obstructed the National Assembly's efforts of accusing pro-Japanese activities.

Special Committee of Investigation and Punishment of those who acted against the Korean people
In 1948, the National Assembly made a law to punish those who acted against the Korean people. The Special Committee of Investigation and Punishment of those who acted against the Korean people, a Special Prosecutor Office and a Special Court were all organized to accuse pro-Japanese sympathizers. The picture shows the pro-Japanese Koreans entering the court.

Punishments of anti-national perpetrators were discontinued, and anyone who were labeled as a Communist or 'bbalgaengi' (a "commie" or "reds") were not even granted with basic civil rights.

Since 1950, land reforms were conducted in the way of purchasing and distributing lands at a certain cost. Since the majority of the farmers in the South wished redistribution of the farm lands, the Yi government initiated the land reform to obtain popularity. However, the reform was done incompletely, and as a result, the living conditions of the farmers were not that much enhanced. However, the disappearance of the landlord system was indeed an accomplishment.

South and North plunged into a civil war

As much as the Yi Seung-man government wanted to be recognized as the sole government of the Korean Peninsula, it was still a government only representing half of the peninsula. And North Korea was facing the same problem. So, before one of them was destroyed, they were to remain as mere half-governments. In that regard, one could say that they were destined to go to war.

The North Korean government established a strategy to accomplish unification through war, and since 1949 it prepared a war, considering the Communists' triumphs in China and the United States' withdrawal from the South to be advantageous to their plans.

The North Korean government's officials visited Mao Zedong and Stalin to seek cooperation in the war and confirmed allied relationships with

Farming Lands Reform
With the Land Reform Order issued in 1950 in South Korea, about 550,000 Jeongbo (5,454,548,000m²) of lands were re-distributed to the poor farmers. Due to this order, the landlord class finally disappeared from South Korea.

Kim Il-seong visited USSR
In April and May of 1950, Kim Il-seong visited USSR and China, where he received promises of support from Stalin and Mao, and their agreement on the Korean War as well.

❶ North Korea's invasion of South Korea
On June 25th of 1950, the North Korean army invaded South Korea with an all-out attack. They occupied Seoul in three days. It only took three more months to push forward and take over most of the South Korean region, except for a few areas of the Gyeongsang-do province like Daegu and Busan.

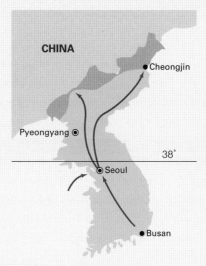

❷ Participation of the United Nations army
The United States called for a UN Security Council meeting, which eventually made a decision for the UN army to join the Korean War. The UN army successfully carried out the Incheon Landing Operation on September 15th of 1950, and advanced to Seoul on the 28th of September. On October 13th they marched to Pyeongyang, across the 38th parallel line and advanced to the Amnokgang by the end of October.

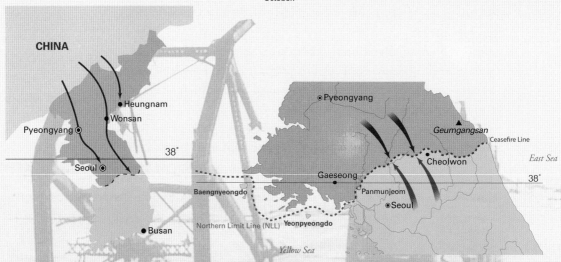

❸ Chinese army's intervention
As the allied forces marched to the north, on October 25th Chinese troops joined the Korean War. As the Chinese intervened in the war, the situation was reversed. The UN forces had to withdraw from Seoul, but it re-approached the areas near the 38th parallel line in early 1951.

❹ The Military Line set up according to the Armistice Agreement
As the war ended, according to the Armistice Agreement made on July 27th of 1953, the war's frontline of the time became the military line of division between South and North. Each army withdrew 2km from the line and agreed to make the buffer zone de-militarized.

- ➡ Forwarding Routes of the North Korean Army and Chinese Army
- ➡ Forwarding Routes of the United Nations Army
- ▒ Occupied Area by the North Korean Army
- ▒ Occupied Area by the United Nations Army

Korean War and the Irrevocable Damage

The final division of the Korean Peninsula proceeded through total of three steps. First, in 1945 the 38th parallel line was drawn as the U.S. and USSR armies stationed themselves in south and north of the Korean Peninsula. Then in 1948 separate governments were established in north and south respectively. Finally, in 1950 with the Korean War, division was made complete, with international recognition. The Korean War lasted three years and tragically resulted in a harsh sense of rivalry against each other and anti-democratic political situations in both South and North Koreas.

them. North Korea also brought home the North Korean troops serving for the Chinese Communist Party to strengthen its own military.

In the spring of 1950, the hostility between the North and South escalated more than ever. While North Korea prepared for war under the slogan of "Complete Occupation of the Country Land," South Korea asserted "Unification by Pushing Forward to the North" and reinforced its anti-Communism policy. Antagonism between the two grew to the extent that they spread out propaganda fliers rebuking each other, and clashes near the 38th parallel line became far more frequent.

Outbreak of war

On June 25, 1950, North Korea started a war by pushing forward the 38th parallel. In mere three days, Seoul was seized. And in three months the North Korean army pushed forward to the southeast tip of the Korean Peninsula. Forceful unification by North Korea seemed almost complete at this point.

In response, the U.S. actively joined the fight for South Korea, from the very beginning of the war. America's justification for fighting in the Korean Peninsula was to protect a Democratic country from Communist invasion. Also the United Nations reprimanded the invasion and thus agreed to send the UN forces composed of 16 nationalities to Korea with the U.S. at the helm. The war between the North and South turned into an international war.

On September 15, 1950, the U.S. forces successfully completed the Incheon Landing Operation as a sudden attack. As the U.S. forces initiated their attacks, the tides of war indeed turned, and not much time was given for the North Korean army to retreat to the north. The allied forces of the Republic of Korea and the United Nations pushed the North Korean troops across the 38th parallel line, and by winter reached the Amnokgang. In two months, the allied forces occupied most of the northern region of the 38th parallel line. The North Korean government faced the risk of losing its regime.

However, when China entered the war, once again the situation was reversed. China not only considered North Korea as their comrade country to which they were allied in their fights against the Japanese, but was also worried that the collapse of North Korea would threaten their own security.

China joined the war by sending huge militia troops. Although the Soviet Union did not officially participate in the war, it actively supported North Korea and China. Now the Korean War developed to become a war that represented the animosity of the international Cold War.

In early 1951, Seoul was once again seized by the allied forces of North Korea and China. Then the allied UN forces once again pushed them back above the 38th parallel line, yet this time they were unable to gain further ground to the north. In the beginning of the war, the South Korean army retreated all the way to the southern end of the peninsula, then pushed forward all the way up to the north. Yet in the end, they all found themselves back to where it first started.

As the war continued for three years, the two Koreas came to realize that it was no longer possible to unify the peninsula by force. In 1951, the Soviet Union proposed a cease-fire. Yet, with animosity running high, negotiations took much longer than anticipated. And in the meantime, many young people lost their lives in battles.

Damages by the war, and atrocities committed against civilians

The Korean War resulted in a considerable number of casualties and deaths in addition to destruction of many mountains, fields, and cities. Approximately 150,000 Korean soldiers, 35,000 UN soldiers, 520,000 North Korean militia and hundreds of thousands of Chinese soldiers were killed. The number of casualties and people who were lost was too large to be counted.

During the war many civilians were terribly victimized. The number of civilians' death amounted to almost one million people. A large number of people were victimized due to repetitive bombings. Moreover, both Koreas killed a huge number of civilians. In the beginning of the war, the South Korean army, while retreating, massacred civilians who were in favor of the Communists. And later, when the North Korean army occupied such towns they also executed many people who were not supportive of Communism. And when the front line of the war moved toward the north, once again many people who were believed to be in favor of Communism were killed.

Even civilians themselves killed each other. While front lines were moving between south and north, and the Leftists and the Rightists took turns to occupy towns and villages day and night, people killed each other believing the victims were their enemies. The financial loss was incredible. 50.5% of the factory facilities were destroyed. 1.7 times the GNP of that time, the amount of 412.3 billion won, was lost due to the war. The whole peninsula turned into a total ruin.

The fire ceased, however...

On July 27, 1953, the U.S., North Korea, and China signed the cease-fire treaty. Although shooting was stopped, it was not yet the complete end of war, as the cease-fire negotiations failed to lead to a peace negotiation.

A meeting between political leaders, which was planned to be held in 3 months, was never opened. In 1954, the Geneva Meeting also failed to suggest a peaceful resolution; the South asserted that under the supervision of the United Nations the South and North should vote together for a unified government. Yet, the North claimed that a general election should be held after the United Nations army completely withdrew.

After 1954, there was no further discussion on unification. Since then until now, the Republic of Korea's Army and the U.S. armed forces have been facing the North Korean army. The 'truce line' that replaced the 38th parallel still remains in tension.

The above picture shows Seoul demolished after the war, and the bottom picture shows the condition of Pyeongyang.

Armistice Agreement
In June 23 of 1951 the Soviet Union suggested to have a cease-fire meeting, and as a result, on July 10 at Gaeseong a meeting was held. Due to disagreements on the established military line, the monitoring organization, as well as exchanges of prisoners of war, reaching a conclusion was delayed. It was July 27 of 1953 when representatives of North Korea, China, and the United Nations army all signed the agreement. South Korea did not sign the agreement as it opposed the cease-fire.

DMZ; from the Days of the 38th Parallel to the Restoration of the Gyeongeuiseon Railroad

The Demilitarized Zone divides the Korean Peninsula in half. In the zone, there is an area created by the Military Demarcation Lines (MDL), established 2km to the north and the south respectively. This is the place where South Korea and North Korea continue to confront each other, in quite a different situation as implied from the word "Demilitarized Zone."

As Japan surrendered in 1945, the U.S. and USSR stationed troops in the south and north of the 38th parallel line respectively. The 38th parallel line was replaced by the Demilitarized Zone according to the agreement of the cease-fire meeting in 1953. This 248km DMZ line which begins at the Yeseonggang (R.) and the mouth of the Hangang in the west, travels through Panmunjeom to the south of Gaeseong. It passes Cheorwon and Geumhwa and reaches Goseong on the East coast, completely dividing the Korean Peninsula.

Joint Security Area
The Joint Security Area is a designated place where both South and North Koreas manage in cooperation to take care of works that should be done. Armistice meetings and South-North meetings are held here. The fact that Korea is the only divided nation on Earth can be obviously seen here.

In the DMZ area there are only two residential areas such as the Daeseongdong Freedom Village in the South and Pyeonghwachon in the North. Since no one can enter the DMZ, it has become home to many rare animals and plants. Also there are check points and observation stations manned by the South and North Korean troops.

To the Koreans, the DMZ is a line of division that exists between brothers and sisters as well as husbands and wives. Yet, since the 1990s, as the Korean people's inclination for unification increased, the line of division continued to gradually fade out.

A road was opened and led to the initiation of Geumgangsan tours, and the Gyeongeuiseon railroad was restored after all those years of separation. Koreans are all waiting for the day when the DMZ line would collapse and they would finally be awarded with the unification they deserve.

❶ College students' movement for Unification
In 1989, Yim Su-gyeong participated in the 13th World Young Students'
Festival held at Pyeongyang as the representative of South Korea's
National Association of University Student Representatives. She returned
to the South through Panmunjeom with Mun Gyu-hyeon, a member of
Catholic Priests Association for Realization of Justice.
❷ Cooperate chief executive officer's visiting North with a herd of cattle
In 1998, Jeong Ju-yeong, one of the most representative chief executive
officers of South Korean cooperates, visited his home town in North Korea
with trucks full of cattle.
❸ South-North experimental operation of the railroad
On May 17 of 2007, the Gyeongeuiseon line and the Donghaeseon
line were restored, and a train finally crossed the cease-fire line in an
experimental operation which was not possible for the past half century.
❹ The president walking over the 38th parallel line
Around 9 a.m. on October 2 of 2007 the South Korean President Roh Moo-
hyun walked across the 38th parallel line to participate in the South-North
Summit in Pyeongyang.

4

Divided into Two Nations

Formation of a divided nation

After the cease-fire was put in place, South Korea and the U.S. signed a mutual defense treaty. Also in 1951, the Japanese and the Americans agreed to conclude a treaty of alliance. As a result, Korea, the U.S., and Japan constructed an alliance, while North Korea, China, and the Soviet Union created an alliance as well. Although the war was over, the Korean Peninsula was still the battleground between the former and the latter.

As multiple Cold War fronts between the North and South and between the Soviet Union and the U.S. forged upon the Korean Peninsula, despotic regimes were established in both South and North Koreas. Under the slogan of Anti-Communistism, South Korea named the North as a puppet government of Communism, while the North condemned the South as a mere instrument played by the U.S. They also united the people under their ruling, with slogans like "Marching toward north (South Korea)" and "Liberation of the South (North Korea)."

Resisting their own government was difficult for the people of the two Koreas. In the South, the Yi Seung-man regime continued to extend its despotic ruling with the support of policemen and gang members. He even executed a major opposition leader by setting up a political trap claiming he was a Communist spy, who only argued the necessity of a peaceful unification. In the North, Kim Il-seong forged a strong power base of his own by first eliminating all of his political foes who challenged his absolute power. By 1956, he monopolized power in the North.

The scene of trial for the Jinbodang (a progressive party) Incident
Jo Bong-am who was the Presidential candidate of the Jinbodang, is standing in court. As the first minister of the Agricultural Department, Jo Bong-am dared to confront the ruling power of Yi Seung-man and ran for the election. He criticized the government's policies and showed different perspectives on the unification policy. He was unjustly accused of espionage, sentenced to death, and soon executed.

In 1953, when the Korean War ended, Koreans had to rebuild their countries from ashes. It was also the beginning of Korean modern history. The division of the South and North resulted in confrontations between China and Japan as well as the United States and the Soviet Union. The South and North exchanged hostility while building their own despotic regimes.

North Korea establishes a Socialist regime

Most of the production facilities and factories in the North Korea were destroyed completely by the war. The government led reconstruction of those facilities, and bases for production were newly established. In the wake of all those efforts, the Socialist system was founded.

In 1954, the North Korean government implemented a Three-year People's Economy Development Plan. It was meant to develop agricultural production and production of necessities and shortages while investing finite resources to heavy industries as a priority. Most of the foreign aids that came from fellow Socialist countries were invested in that area as well.

The first Five-year period (Economy) Development Plan (1957~1960) was initiated in 1957 and continued with the establishment of a Socialist political system. By 1958, all agricultural areas were reorganized under the system of cooperative unions. Socialism was also adopted in business and industries. As its relationship with the USSR deteriorated and financial support from both the USSR and China reduced, a policy of self-reliance was initiated, and economic campaigns such as the "Cheollima Movement" were launched to encourage competitions among workers.

In 1961, upon the completion of two economic development plans, the fourth General Assembly of the Joseon Labor Party was held in Pyeongyang. North Korea invited foreign leaders of the Communist countries and

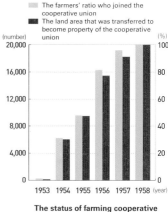

The farmers' ratio who joined the cooperative union

The land area that was transferred to become property of the cooperative union

The status of farming cooperative unions

Collective farms
North Korea declared the implementation of Socialist economic policies as it continued to rebuild the society from ashes. Regarding farming, the North Korean people adopted a Socialist system of "collective farming", and as a result, by the end of 1950, most of the land was transformed to become "collective farms."

proclaimed that it had completed construction of the foundation for Socialism.

Market economy system reinforced in South Korea

Meanwhile, South Korea developed its own Capitalist economy. In November of 1954, the Yi Seung-man government amended the constitution to drastically revise the principle of industry nationalization, and subsequently the government sold all liquidated properties from the Japanese Imperialists to civilian corporate buyers. As a result, in South Korea the concept of 'Jaebeol' (a major house in control of a fleet of industries and businesses) came to emerge. They accumulated enormous wealth by purchasing all the liquidated assets at a relatively low price.

South Korea's Capitalist economy grew considerably fast thanks to the financial support of the U.S., which considered South Korea as its anti-Communism base in Asia and continued to support it with financial aid. The total amount of financial aids exceeded 50% of the GNP of years between 1954 and 1961. Also it was equivalent to the amount of 40% of the total government taxes of years between 1957 and 1960.

The U.S. financial aids to South Korea solved the food shortage problem of the South and furnished supplies to the military system. Provision of wheat, cotton, sugar, and raw materials contributed to the development

Foreign aid materials being piled at the Busan port
The United States of America offered development aids to South Korea according to the Agreement on Aid between the Republic of Korea and the U.S. of 1948. Particularly, as the Agreement on Surplus Agricultural Products Cooperation was made in 1955, approximately 203 million dollars worth of surplus farm products were shipped to South Korea from 1956 to 1961.

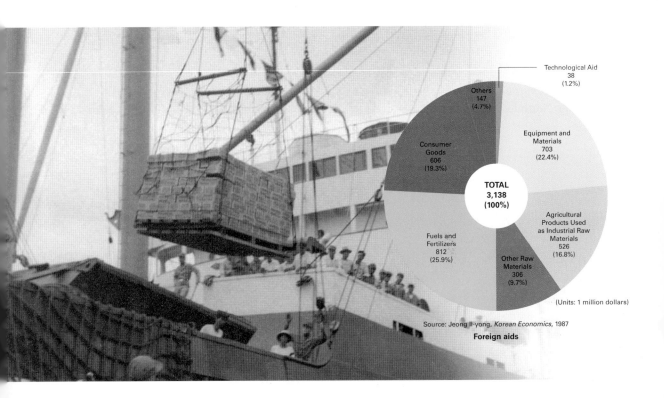

Technological Aid 38 (1.2%)

Others 147 (4.7%)

Equipment and Materials 703 (22.4%)

Consumer Goods 606 (19.3%)

TOTAL 3,138 (100%)

Agricultural Products Used as Industrial Raw Materials 526 (16.8%)

Fuels and Fertilizers 812 (25.9%)

Other Raw Materials 306 (9.7%)

(Units: 1 million dollars)

Source: Jeong Il-yong, *Korean Economics*, 1987

Foreign aids

of light industry in South Korea. But they also led South Korea into a long-term stagnation in terms of agricultural production and made South Korean economy very much dependent upon foreign countries' support.

After the war, in the north a Socialist government based on communal properties and thus a controlled economy was established, while in the south a Capitalist government was formed emphasizing free market competitions and private enterprises. The Korean people came to live under two different governments.

Competing dictatorships between South and North

South Korea and North Korea had been competing in a hostile relationship for ten years since the end of the war. Although the situation was soon reverted, in the beginning the economic development of North Korea was ahead of that of South Korea, as the North Korean government pushed forward the Socialist construction plans with mass mobilization while the South relied on foreign aids. As competitions continued, South and North became more estranged than before.

The confrontation between South and North brought about sharp military competitions and outspoken expressions of animosity; yet, the Korean Peninsula remained relatively stable. The division existed as part of an international order (the Cold War), and the authorities of South and North bound their people with the propaganda and prospect of forceful unification in the future. Unsecured peace was maintained on the Korean Peninsula, with fear of another potential war.

There were many similarities existing in both South and North Koreas. Both of them adopted Nationalism, yet as part of a very anti-National strategy. Their slogans of (antagonistic) unification, their despotic systems, process of economic developments, and the methods of mass mobilization systems were quite the same. The existence of an enemy became a necessary condition for one's survival.

South and North Koreas in the 1950s both emphasized the importance of national security. Legitimacy issues between South and North only promoted extreme levels of Nationalism, which ignored the values of a liberal and democratic society, with a diversified citizenship blossoming inside an international community of common sense. Common people from both sides had to suffer from oppressive dictatorships. The most important task for the Korean people was to accomplish a democratic nation.

The Differences and Similarities Between Two Koreas

The Korean people formed a united country through Shilla's unification of the three kingdoms and the reunification by Goryeo. However, cultural differences and alienated sentiments were developed due to the war that divided Korea into South and North.

The disparities between South and North are most evident in terms of politics and the economy. The difference between the Socialistic centralization of authority in the North and the Democratic establishment of South has bred differences in social life itself. Furthermore, the socialistically planned economy of North Korea and the Capitalistic establishment of South Korea brought about contrasts in economic life as well.

In North Korea where its people are constantly watched and controlled, a rather monotonous and concise social order can be seen compared to South Korea, due to Socialistic structuring of the region. A culture of large assemblies and crowd-gathering events forced by the government were developed. In the meantime, the 'Juche ("self-determining, self-relying, self-sustaining")' Ideology of North Korea allowed for the preservation and recreation of Korean traditions such as Hangeul or many other seasonal customs.

The culture of South Korea was heavily influenced by the U.S. and the Western world. The war forced the Korean society to be flooded with Western culture, and in the process of urbanization and industrialization the traditional culture of Korea continued to vanish. Koreans have been sensing a possibility of losing their own traditions and continued to make efforts in combining Korean traditions with Western culture, to create an entirely new culture.

The external differences between Southern and Northern cultures are as great as their differences in political ideologies. However, despite the disparities, they maintained a sense for a 'uniform culture' that had taken shape over thousands of years prior to the country's division. In spite of all those years of separation, Koreans still speak a single language and enjoy the same traditions side by side. Koreans consider New Year's Day and Chuseok (Thanksgiving) to be the most important holidays and share the same moral beliefs founded upon the teachings of Confucianism and Buddhism. Most importantly, Koreans share a notion of homogeneity, as they believe that they are all part of the same race and the same national culture.

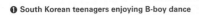

❶ South Korean teenagers enjoying B-boy dance
B-boy dance, which refers to part of the hip-hop culture formed in New York, attracted tremendous popularity among the Korean youngsters. A Korean B-boy team won the World's Best B-boy battle in 2006, and was the only team invited to perform on the Eve of the Beijing Olympic Games in 2008.

❷ North Korean art performance 'Arirang'
In North Korea, mass gymnastic games or audience card section performances are often held in a stadium. The picture shows an 'Arirang Performance,' in which more than 100,000 people participated.

❸ Pyeongyang street in North Korea
❹ Jongno District in South Korea

1960 ~ 2010

1960
Yi Seung-man Dictatorship was overthrown in the April Revolution, and the 2nd Republic was established.

1961
A group of military officials led by General Park Chung-hee staged a coup d'état and seized power.

1962
An industrialization process led by the government began with the 1st Economic Development Plan.

1971
Hostility between the United States and China was mitigated a bit. China joined the UN.

1972
In both South and North Koreas, new Constitutions were introduced, in order to secure unconditional power for the rulers.

1980
The May 18th Democratic Movement erupted in Gwangju against the military regime. In the following year, the 5th Republic was founded with former Military leaders at the helm.

1987
The June Democracy Movement demanded a direct presidential election and democratic reforms, and ultimately resulted in the collapse of the military authoritarianism, Vigorous labor movements gave birth to many democratic labor unions.

1988
The 24th Olympic Games were held in Seoul. 13,304 athletes and sports officials from 160 countries participated.

1989
Reunification of Germany was followed by the collapse of Eastern European Socialist countries. The Soviet Union collapsed in 1991.

1997
South Korea experienced economic turmoil due to foreign currency shortage. This year also marked a peaceful governmental transfer from the ruling party to the opposition for the first time.

2000
A summit meeting between leaders of South and North Koreas was held in Pyeongyang for the first time since the division of the Korean Peninsula. The second summit meeting was held in 2007.

XIII Changing Korean Peninsula, Dynamic Korea

The 24th Olympic Games were held in major cities of Korea, including Seoul, from September 17th to October 2nd of 1988. South Korea became the second country to host the Olympic Games in Asia, and the 16th in the world. South Korea became well known to the world, mostly because of its dynamically changing image which stemmed from its dramatic economic developments and democratic accomplishments. 13,304 athletes and officials from 160 countries participated in the Seoul Olympic Games.

Seoul, Myeong-dong in May 2010 We can see the energetic nature of the Republic of Korea, from each of the faces of all the lively people on the street.

People's Power in the 1980s and the June Democracy Movement

In the late 1980s, the people power erupted in many places in the world. Mass societies of citizens formed in the wake of industrialization and urbanization, fiercely resisted anti-humanist and anti-social despotism.

People's power in Asia succeeded in having their voice heard and also achieving democracy. They exploded in the Philippines and South Korea in particular, where democratization movements had long continued to bring down despotism.

In February of 1986, the Philippine people overthrew the Marcos government that had been ruling the nation for 21 years. In June of the following year the Korean people toppled the despotic government as well. In Thailand the May Bangkok Protesters confronted the military coup d'état in order to defend democracy.

People's power was also acknowledged in Eastern Europe. The people of East Germany, Poland, Hungary, Czechoslovakia, Bulgaria, and Rumania founded democratic governments.

The June Democracy Movement of South Korea in 1987 was a great turning point for the Korean people. Although Koreans' wishes to build their own independent nation were discouraged by the Korean War and the ensuing division, they continued to solve problems of poverty through economic development. And they did not give up their dream of establishing a democratic republic in which people would be the owner of their own country. Triumphs of this anti-despotism struggle based upon economic developments and the thirst for democracy are now contributing to the overall task of overcoming the peninsula's division and thus creating a commonwealth nation.

88 (Eighty eight) Movement (1988)
A large scale protest joined by citizens, students, and priests broke out in Myanmar on August 8 of 1988, when the entire Asian region was striving for democracy. However, this protest did not succeed in creating a democratic government that would replace the existing regime supported by the military. Although the number of votes supporting the democratic factions outnumbered that of votes supporting the military government, in an election that was held in the second year since the military coup, the military government nullified its result by suppressing the protesters with bloody violence. Since this protest, oppressive ruling has been continuing, with total denial of any kind of a democratic procedure.

1986
February Revolution in the Philippines; Taiwan organized an anti-government opposition party.

1987
June Democratic Protest in South Korea; Taiwan Martial Law was cancelled.

1988
Myanmar 88 Movement; Foundation of a People's government in Pakistan

1989
A large scale Liberation movement in China: Tiananmen Square Protests

1990
Democratization of Mongol in high gear

1992
Military government of Thailand withdrew due to the May Struggle.

June Democracy Movement (1987)

Tiananmen Square Protests (1989)
Protests led by university students in Beijing who demanded the ending of corruptions and democratic reforms continued for about two months. Nearly one million students and intellectuals participated in the protests, but the Chinese government suppressed it through military power in June 1989.

SOUTH KOREA

CHINA

Democratization Movement in Taiwan (1986)
The democratization movements of South Korea and the Philippines made a great impact on Taiwan, where despotic ruling of the Kuomintang party had long been continuing. Influences from the February Revolution of the Philippines and the June Democratic Protest of South Korea contributed to the Taiwan people's forming of an opposition party, which succeeded in nullifying the martial law that had lasted for forty years. After that, organizing parties was legalized, and the system of direct voting in presidential elections was also adopted.

TAIWAN

May Struggle (1992)
Since March 1992, anti-military government protests occurred in many large cities such as Bangkok. In May, the military government fired at the protesters and the bloodshed led to angry citizens' eruption, which forced the government to be more susceptible to the citizens' demands. In a general election that was held in September the same year, the law which had earlier legitimized the military intervention in politics was completely abolished.

PHILIPPINES

MYANMAR

THAILAND

February Revolution (1986)
Marcos who had become president in 1965 declared martial law to enlist the military in sustaining his own power. Since then, he remained in power for more than twenty years. In 1986, when he attempted to extend his term through a fraudulent election, the Democratic factions organized a nationwide alliance under the slogan of 'Overthrowing Despotism.' As a result, they succeeded in founding a democratic government.

Asian Democratization of the 1980s

During the Cold War period, despotic governments in the Asian region prevailed under the name of anti-Communism and economic developments. Yet, as all confrontations generated by the Cold War started to subside, such governments were no longer able to secure their own legitimacy. Students and laborers who had been at the center of all those democratic efforts united with the urban middle class and led democratization struggles into a new direction. Asia in the 1980s was a hotbed for democratization efforts.

1

Industrialization Picks Up Pace in South Korea

The Democratic Revolution of April 19th, and the Military Coup on May 16th

In April 1960, a fever of revolution spread throughout South Korea. Infuriated and frustrated by twelve years of Yi Seung-man's despotic regime, civil protests continued to take place as Yi attempted to extend his term once again by amending the Constitution.

Though Koreans at times submitted to the violent oppression of power, they protested against dictatorship through the act of voting. The Presidential election in 1956 particularly threatened the Yi Seung-man administration. So he tried to remain in power through a rigged election in 1960. In April 1960, students and civilians gathered to demonstrate demanding the nullification of the rigged election and resignation of Yi Seung-man. The demonstration shook the entire nation, and the Yi Seung-man administration eventually fell (April 19th Revolution).

Soon a democratic election was held and the Second Republic was born. With the birth of a new republic, Koreans expected the realization of democracy and economic justice while pursuing diplomatic negotiations with North Korea toward a peaceful unification.

However, the newly established republic collapsed before it could make any significant accomplish-

▲ **May 16th Military Coup**
On May 16th, 1961, a group of young military officers under command of a major general named Park Chung-hee staged a coup d'état. They took over the government and brought down the Second Republic which was established after the April 19th Revolution.

◄ **April 19th Revolution**
On April 19th 1960, Korean people rose up in protest, demanding an investigation of the rigged election of March 15th, and the resignation of President Yi Seung-man.

ment. A military regime seized power through a coup d'éta (May 16th Military Coup), only one year after the April Revolution. The new regime proclaimed a military administration, advocating anti-Communism and swift economic developments.

Promotion of the Economic Development Plan

Park Chung-hee proclaimed a military administration, promising an end to disorder and a beginning of an economic development. The first Five-year Economic Development Plan (1962~1966) began in 1962, and the second five-year Economic Development Plan ensued in 1967. Evolved in the process was the Korean-style development model, in which the government proactively involved itself in the operations of the market.

The government made efforts to obtain more foreign capital and aggressively enforced financial policies by founding a government-owned bank. The capital generated from these sources was distributed to strategic industries according to the priorities set by the government. Companies which borrowed money with low interest rates responded with aggressive investments and expansion of their pools of oversea buyers.

These companies mainly manufactured and exported light industrial products such as textiles, shoes, and plywood, made from raw materials purchased abroad. In the mid-1960s, steel and petrochemical industries took off and became an integral part of the industrialization process. Accumulation of investments and the support from cheap and abundant labor force led to a rapid growth in industries. The Koreans of this generation were armed with high self-esteem, diligent work ethics, and a penchant for

Steel Industrial Complex in Pohang
Pohang Steel Company, which was founded to develop heavy industries in 1968, hugely contributed to Korea's economic development by manufacturing steel products with imported raw materials.

(%)

—○— Attendance rate: from elementary school to middle school
—●— Attendance rate: from middle school to high school
—○— Attendance rate: from high school to college

Percentage of school attendance
The school attendance rate in Korea was higher than that of other countries of similar economic size. The number of students who attended middle and high schools rapidly increased in the 1970s and 1980s, and since the 1990s the number of college students dramatically increased.

The amount of export reaches $10 billion
The Korean government promoted a strategy for economic development that was focused upon building an export-oriented industry. The industry accomplished $10 billion worth of export in 1977. The amount of export in 1995 was more than $100 billion.

learning, and came to witness the transformation of their own country during their lifetime.

Korea, an industrialized nation

Industrialization that began in the 1960s continued in the 1970s. The third and fourth Economic Development Plans that took place from 1971 to 1981 were similar to those of the 1960s, as they all continued to promote an export industry led by the government.

Furthermore, there were striking developments in heavy chemical industries. The government newly designated total of six major fields, steel, machinery, shipbuilding, electronics, petrochemical, and nonferrous metal as 'strategic industries,' and aggressively developed them. The Pohang Iron Complex, the Ulsan Petrochemical Complex, the Changwon Combined Machinery Complex, the Yeocheon Combined Chemical Complex, the Gumi Electronics Complex were all developed around this time period.

As heavy industries grew, general exports reflected that as well. The number of manufacturing industries increased dramatically, and the portion that heavy industries occupied among them grew much bigger.

City population had multiplied while the number of workers involved in agricultural and fishery industries noticeably decreased. The populace was drawn to larger cities like Seoul, as new industrial cities were constructed around there. In 1979, OECD (Organization for Economic Cooperation and Development) classified Korea as a "newly industrialized country."

Petrochemistry Complex in Ulsan
The construction of Ulsan's Petrochemistry Industrial Complex began in 1967 and was completed in 1972. It houses oil refineries as well as petrochemical liaison factories. Thus, it formed a huge industrial complex, with the automobile industries nearby.

The Gyeongbu Expressway
The construction of the Gyeongbu Expressway started in 1968 and was completed in 1970. It became the first expressway that connected Seoul with Busan. This expressway, with a total length of 417 kilometers, serves as the main industrial artery that links the metropolitan area of Seoul with the Yeongnam region industrial complexes. Thanks to this expressway, it became possible for the South Koreans to visit anywhere in the country and engage in business, in the scope of a single day.

Free Trade Zone of Masan
The Free Trade Zone of Masan was designed in 1970 by the government. It offered various tax benefits to the companies which housed their plants and offices in Masan.

Miracle on the Hangang, Ups and Downs

In the 1960s and '70s, the Korean economy had grown so rapidly and in such a magnitude that the world had begun to call it the 'Miracle on the Hangang.' However, many problems were still brewing underneath the facade of a rapid growth.

The Korean government reestablished a normal diplomatic relation with Japan without receiving any form of an apology or reparations for Japan's 36-year colonial rule of Korea, on the pretext of raising funds for the economic development of the country. The Korean government also had to send a number of Korean youths to the Vietnam War.

Large business enterprises grew rapidly while small and mid-sized enterprises along with the consumers were often excluded from the concerns of the government. By placing priority on building major businesses' competing capabilities, the government often neglected the rights of laborers and oppressed the labor movements. Furthermore, agricultural workers did not receive proper compensation, as 'price ceilings' were required to keep food prices low enough for the laborers in the cities.

The damaged pride of the country, an economic development that continued rather not democratically, and a growth that was accomplished without sharing what was achieved, invited questions to the real purpose of an economic development. Students continued demonstrations demanding the realization of true nationalism and democracy while laborers were continuously asking for economic equality.

Jeon Tae-il (1948~1970)
On November 13 of 1970, Jeon Tae-il, a laborer who worked at the Seoul Pyeonghwa market, committed a suicide by burning himself to death. He did so to argue that the working conditions of laborers who had been suffering from low wages and overtime working while being forced to silence under the shadows of rapid economic developments must be improved. This incident became the turning point for the entire labor movement. The picture is his statue built in front of the Pyeonghwa market, which is located at the Cheonggyecheon 5th street and was also the very place where he sacrificed himself.

Protest against 'the Korea-Japan Pact'
On June 22nd 1965, the Korean government signed the 'Korea-Japan Pact' and established a formal relationship with Japan. Protests continued throughout the country in opposition of the idea of reconciliation with Japan that colonized Korea for 36 years.

Dispatching troops to the Vietnam War
The Korean government dispatched its troops to Vietnam. The number of dispatched soldiers mounted to approximately 300,000 from 1965 to 1973, as the war became very fierce. In exchange of dispatching the troops, the United States provided Korea with both economic and military aids.

Environmental pollution
Rapid industrialization which proceeded without preparation or caution beforehand caused severe environmental pollutions of water, air, and soil. It made many people suffer from illness without even knowing the exact reasons.

Metropolitan City:
the New Image of Today's Seoul

In the middle of the city of Seoul there flows the beautiful Hangang. Since the Joseon Dynasty built its capital at Seoul, it has been the center of politics, economy, and culture of the country for the last 600 years. Many cultural heritages in Seoul exhibit the traditional culture of Koreans. Now Seoul is a modernized city full of skyscrapers, subways, and cars. Seoul is the center for administration, finance, information, and cultural activities. The total resident population of Seoul is over 10 millions today, but when its satellite cities included, the total population reaches up to about 25 millions, which is about 50% of the total population of the Republic of Korea.

Seoul is the living proof of Korea's economic growth. 20% of the total GDP is produced in Seoul. Also more than 50% of the total finance and banking are concentrated in the city of Seoul, and more than 40% of IT industries are located in Seoul as well.

Seoul is one of the three mammoth cities in East Asia along with Beijing and Tokyo. Seoul is the center for consumer markets, facilitating airports, express train stations, bus terminals, and ports which connect East Asia to the world. As South Korea became part of the international economic axis in terms of industries, banking, and information, Seoul is now connected through the Incheon International airport to numerous areas of East Asia and the world in a fast and effective manner.

The Expansion of Administrative Districts of Seoul

4km radius of Hanseongbu

Hanseongbu

The picture of Seoul taken in the 1900s

Extended in 1911

The picture of Seoul in 1930s

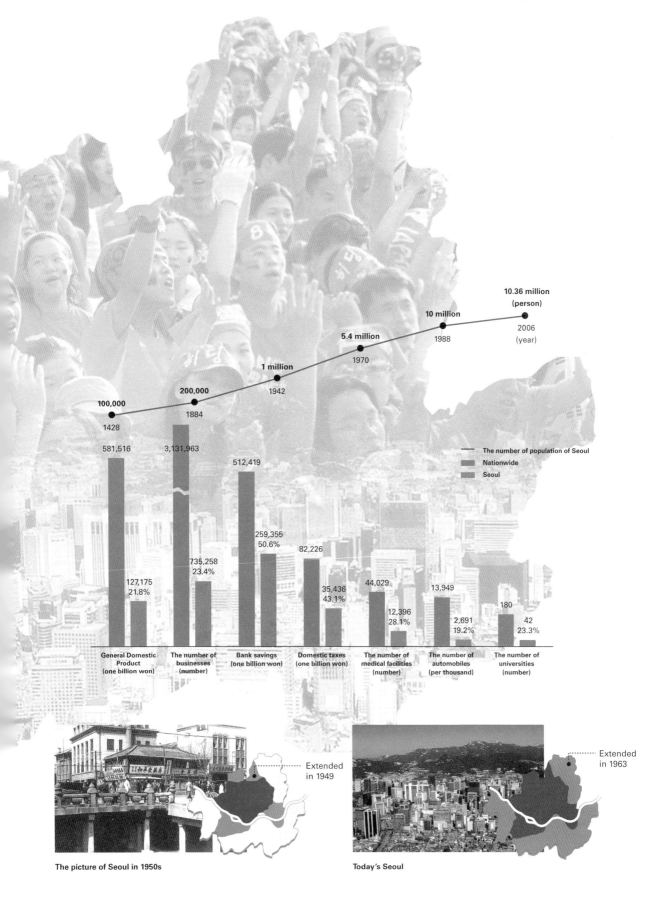

10.36 million
(person)
2006
(year)

10 million
1988

5.4 million
1970

1 million
1942

200,000
1884

100,000
1428

The number of population of Seoul
Nationwide
Seoul

581,516

3,131,963

512,419

259,355
50.6%

127,175
21.8%

735,258
23.4%

82,226

35,436
43.1%

44,029

12,396
28.1%

13,949

2,691
19.2%

180

42
23.3%

General Domestic
Product
(one billion won)

The number of
businesses
(number)

Bank savings
(one billion won)

Domestic taxes
(one billion won)

The number of
medical facilities
(number)

The number of
automobiles
(per thousand)

The number of
universities
(number)

Extended
in 1949

Extended
in 1963

The picture of Seoul in 1950s

Today's Seoul

2

Accomplishment of Both Industrialization and Democracy

Park Chung-hee seeks for Military Authoritarianism

As his convictions of modernizing the country and escaping underdevelopment succeeded to some degree in producing positive results, Park Chung-hee managed to win the Presidential elections twice in a row. However, he attempted to seize power for an indefinite amount of terms, and he did so by manipulating the Constitution.

In 1972, he forcibly dismissed the National Assembly and enacted a new constitution, namely, the "Yusin (New) Constitution," with the support of the military and the police. It allowed the President to nominate one-third of the national representatives and suspend certain laws that were legislated by the National Assembly. The Yusin Constitution put an end to direct presidential elections.

The government oppressed all democratization movements and even put people to death under the name of law. However, the movements for democracy led by infuriated university students continued to rock the country, and civil activist groups composed of intellectuals and religious figures began to emerge and stand up against dictatorship.

❶ A Presidential election held at a gymnasium (1972)
The Electoral College of 5,000 representatives elected the President of Korea under the 'Yusin' political system. The Electoral College representatives were not allowed to reveal which specific candidate they were in support of.

❷ The Bu (Busan)-Ma (Masan) Resistance
In the fall of 1979, a huge demonstration joined by numerous citizens and students rose up to demand the abolishment of the Yusin system and the restoration of democracy. These demonstrations broke out in the cities of Busan and Masan. The protesters in both cities were subjugated by the military.

❸ October 26th Incident
On October 26th 1979, President Park Chung-hee, the symbol of the Yusin system, was assassinated. The picture is a scene in which Kim Jae-gyu, head of the Korean CIA at the time, was recreating the moment that he shot the President.

Democratization Movements engaged

The so-called 'Yusin system' came to an end in 1979. The fight against dictatorship was fierce, and laborers continued to fight for their rights to live. The civilian resistance that erupted in Busan and Masan in October 1979 in particular, had a substantial impact on the fate of the Yusin system.

Arguments for a partial democracy within the Yusin system began to develop. Then, the head of National Intelligence, Kim Jae-gyu, suddenly assassinated the president, Park Chung-hee. With his death the Yusin system, a system which was completely dependant upon the absolute authority of a single ruler, came to an end as well.

Though many Koreans expected that democracy would come soon, it was discouraged by "the New Military faction," ■ another group of military officers led by Chun Doo-hwan. The factions within an overgrown military seized power by staging another coup d'état on December 12th.

With the establishment of another military authority, the Korean society once again had a tough time. However, civilians and students in Gwangju demonstrated for ten days beginning upon May 18th, 1980, demanding the disbandment of the new military authority and restoration of democracy (the May 18th Democratization Movement).

The new military force squashed civilian protests and consolidated its power. As a result, in 1981, Chun Doo-hwan became the 7-year term president after enacting a new constitution, similar to that of the Yusin Constitution. The fifth Republic began like this.

■ **The New Military faction** This 'New Military faction' refers to yet another military faction which staged a coup d'état on December 12 of 1979. They had been gathering colleagues through the secret 'Hanahoe' organization inside the military, and soon after the assassination of Park Chung-hee they took control of the government.

❶ **December 12th Military Coup d'état (1979)**
A group of military leaders who had been deeply involved in politics since the May 16th military coup staged a coup d'état once again. Chun Doo-hwan and Noh Tae-woo, two leaders of the coup, later became Presidents. The picture shows the tank that was driven to the Central Governmental building at Gwanghwamun by the coup d'état force.
❷❸ **May 18th Democratic Movement (1980)**
The citizens of Gwangju stood up against the fully armored military troops. More than 200 people were killed, including 25 soldiers. Approximately 3,000 people were injured.

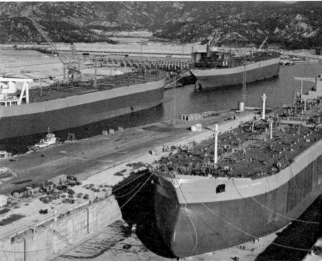

An automobile factory in Ulsan and a shipyard in Pohang in the 1980s
Ulsan and Pohang are located in the southeast part of the Korean Peninsula and have developed into huge industrial complexes since the 1980s.

Accomplishing an 'Industrial Revolution'

In 1979, the year of Park Chung-hee's demise, the Korean economy fell into a crisis, as the investments in heavy chemical industries that continued with the government's deliberate support had been showing repeats and excess. Many enterprises went out of businesses, and for the first time in 20 years the economic growth rate began to back paddle.

The Chun Doo-hwan administration tried to overcome this problem by means of enormous financial support, forceful mergers and liquidations, and also by opening up the Korean economy even more. As a result, the overall role of the 'Jaebeol' houses in the national economy was expanded. Also, in the name of strengthening the competitive capabilities of the business, the government continued to put stronger restrictions upon the labor movements.

With events that took place from 1986 to 1988, Korea began to take the shape of a modern, industrialized country. The so-called phenomena of "Three lows," which referred to low interest rates, low oil prices, and 'low (underrated) dollars,' provided favorable opportunities for the Korean economy and allowed rapid growth of it. Shipbuilding, automobile production and construction industries led to a rapid accumulation of capital, and the economic growth rate exceeded 12% per annum. Also, industrial technology progressed dramatically and became less and less dependant upon foreign technology and capital.

Changes became evident in societal structures as well. The 'Jaebeol' houses acquired more influence and became the leading power of the society, while the number of laborers increased and its movement organizations became more active. The number of white collar office employees also increased greatly. With the labor class and the democratic movement hand in hand, a new level of a civilized society began to take form.

The June Democracy Movement, the first steps towards Democracy

Massive labor struggle in Ulsan
Democratic labor unions were organized in many large corporations since the June Democracy Movement. The picture is a protesting labor force in Ulsan, in the fall of 1987. Ulsan is one of the leading industrial cities in Korea.

From the beginning of the 1980s, democratization movements considerably grew. Countless students and civilians held demonstrations in the streets, demanding justice against those responsible for the 1980 Gwangju massacre. Laborers engaged in labor movements as well. Students, intellectuals, and laborers came to form a unified front, and political parties also joined the democratization movement since 1985.

In 1987, the Great Democratic Alliance was created in opposition of the Chun Doo-hwan administration. Democratization movement groups that united under the 'People's Campaign Headquarters for Achieving a Democratic Constitution' held massive demonstrations demanding the amendment of the Constitution. The demonstration which began on June 10th, lasted for about 20 days, and millions of civilians and students stood against the police shouting out for democracy, and finally secured their victory, in what we now call the "June Democracy Movement" of 1987.

After military despotism retreated, laborers threw themselves into a struggle to form a democratic labor union. Especially, the male laborers in big corporations stood together to form democratic labor unions, and office workers and professionals organized labor unions.

Finally, the era of military authoritarianism was ended. The Korean people held a free election and successfully hosted the 24th Olympic Games, with their pride in having accomplished both industrialization and democracy.

- The places of June 10 Protest
- The places of Both June 10 and June 26 Protest

Chuncheon
Seoul
Bucheon · Seongnam
Incheon · Anyang · Wonju
Suwon
Taebaek
Cheonan · Cheongju
Gongju · Andong
Daejeon · Gimcheon · Yeongcheon
Gunsan · Daegu · Pohang
Iksan · Geochang · Ulsan
Jeonju
Jeongeup
Jeju · Gwangju · Jinju · Changwon
Seogwipo · Muan · Gwangyang · Masan · Busan
Suncheon
Mokpo · Yeosu
Wando

Sites of Demonstrations Arranged on June 10th and June 26th

Protestors with neckties in the June Democracy Movement
Many office workers participated in the June Democracy Movement, along with students and members of non-governmental organizations.

3

North Korea: the Socialist Country Hits a Wall

Establishing 'Socialist industrialization'

The economy in North Korea had been steadily growing as a result of the Seven-Year Plan (1961~1967) that was implemented in 1961. The percentage of national income controlled by industry increased from 25% (1956) to 65% (1969), and led to the successful establishment of a Socialist industrialization. As a balance between light industry and agriculture was achieved, the living standard of the people was enhanced as well.

Since the 1960s, mass production of Polyvinyl Alcohol brought huge shifts to the apparel industry and not to mention people's clothes, and production of food also increased. New cities were built and modernized residences were provided to the rural areas.

With the provision of free medical care, expansion of free and mandatory education, the national welfare system continued to develop. With the establishment of institutes such as nurseries and pre-schools, the nation began to take responsibility for child rearing as well.

The Statue of the Cheollima Campaign
"Cheollima" refers to a legendary horse that was known to have run so swiftly that it could make a thousand-ri (0.4km) travel a day. The Cheollima Campaign was adopted as an important strategy that would facilitate the five-year Economic Development Plan which was initiated in 1957. With shortage of technology, capital, and materials, North Korea pursued a policy to mobilize all available labor forces in order to achieve economic development. Although the ultimate goal of the Cheollima Campaign was to increase the overall production, the campaign was not a mere mobilization movement that would only serve economic development. It was also used as a political propaganda to promote multiple ideas that would guide the society.

Attempting to apply the "Juche" Ideology to the entire society

> The Socialist Constitution of the Democratic People's Republic of Korea is a Kim Il-seong legislation of the ideology and accomplishments behind the building of the country.

The Socialist Constitution which was established in 1972 argues that Socialism and "Kimilseongism" are the same things. It underlines an absolute trust in the Joseon Labor Party in regards to the nation-building process led by Kim Il-seong's leadership and achievements in the anti-Japanese struggle. In accordance with this constitution, Kim Il-seong was able to position himself as the head of state and to secure ultimate power. After 1967, "Kimilseongism" became the fundamental policy of their party, namely the 'Juche' Ideology.

In 1974, spreading of this ideology throughout the party and the population was proposed as a fundamental goal of the government. Kim Il-seong's life and struggle during his anti-Japanese movements became a model from which all people should learn.

Nominated as the only successor of this leader in 1974, Kim Jeong-il, Kim Il-seong's son, secured an

Administrative Districts in North Korea

North Korea has two directly-controlled municipal cities including Pyeongyang, and nine provinces. The total land size is 122,762km², and the total population is 23.3 million (as of 2008). The overall size of North Korea is larger than that of South Korea, while the population is about half of that of South Korea. Because of the mountainous geography, North Korea is enriched with underground resources, yet it also experiences more difficulties in food production.

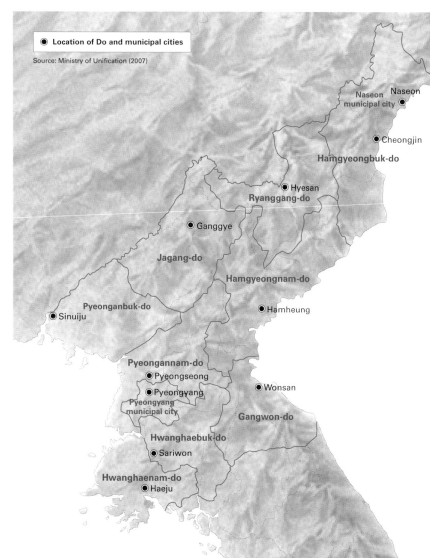

● Location of Do and municipal cities

Source: Ministry of Unification (2007)

Naseon / Naseon municipal city

Cheongjin

Hamgyeongbuk-do

Hyesan

Ryanggang-do

Ganggye

Jagang-do

Hamgyeongnam-do

Pyeonganbuk-do

Hamheung

Sinuiju

Pyeongannam-do

Pyeongseong

Wonsan

Pyeongyang

Pyeongyang municipal city

Gangwon-do

Hwanghaebuk-do

Sariwon

Hwanghaenam-do

Haeju

indomitable authority within the party in 1980. From here on, Kim Jeong-il was referred to as the 'beloved leader,' and actually led the nation through all of its matters of great consequences.

The planned economy meets a wall

As the Juche Ideology and a notion of unity around the leader were emphasized, the North Korean system operated with relative stability. Any thoughts or imagination beyond the frame of Juche Ideology were suppressed. People's criticism against the party and their raising questions to the supreme leader or the party were not accepted in any condition.

Then, the 1950s' and '60s' "successful economy," which strengthened the people's belief in their leader and the party, came to face a test. In the 1970s, the North Korean government promised complete victory of Socialism through achieving "sovereignty, modernization, and the advancement of science in the people's economy."

However, the technology that should have acted as the core of this promise met various obstacles. In 1979, the GNP per person was $1,920, which was higher than that of South Korea ($1,636) at the same year. However, in the beginning of the 1980s, the economic growth slowed down and the second Seven-year Economic Development Plan (1978~1985) did not reach its goal. At this time, the Socialism in Eastern Europe which had been providing North Korea with raw materials and foreign capitals began to subside. North Korea did not anticipate that at all.

The expected improvement of the public's living standards began to reach its limit as well. The economic policy of self-sufficiency, and the stagnation in technological developments, did prevent the industry from achieving competitive capabilities on the international stage. Exports grew difficult

Pyeongyang, the center of North Korea
Pyeongyang, which was destroyed during the Korean War totally transformed into a well-planned city which now reflects a Socialist ideology. The Daedonggang flows through the center of the city, and there are major buildings standing in its vicinity.

and problematic, and that led to a decrease in incoming foreign currency, which also led to periodic halts in imports of resources, energy, not to mention foreign state-of-the-art technology.

In the beginning of the 1980s, the economic growth considerably slowed down. North Korea instituted the Joint-Venture Company Act (1984) to allure foreign resources and implemented a new policy that gave incentives to business activities. However, policies of economic management that had been established in the 1950s were generally maintained, so the results of this new act were negligible.

"Let us live by our own ways"

In 1989, East Germany collapsed and Germany became one. And following the Eastern Socialist nations, the Soviet Union finally fell in 1991. Massive demonstrations kept going inside China.

Such changes gravely alarmed North Korea. Especially as the friendly cooperative relationships with their "Socialistic brothers" came to an end, North Korea fell into a deeper economic crisis. The procurement of petroleum and raw materials, and exports in general, all faced serious difficulties. And with the shortage of electricity, factory operations became increasingly demanding.

The North Korean leaders intended to break free from this crisis by propagating the slogan of "Let us live by our own ways." Pointing out that the collapse of Communism in Eastern Europe was because of the Capitalistic countries' attacks and also wrong management of the ruling parties, they claimed that they could preserve their Socialist system if they united both the party and the people with their leader at the center.

To overcome the economic crisis, they took various actions to invite foreign investments. And with military tensions declining, they also made positive steps toward talks between South and North Koreas' high-ranking officials. The relationship between them, which had been formed through war and competitions, was finally beginning to change.

Kim Il-seong (right) and Kim Jeong-il (left)
Kim Jeong-il (1942~), the current leader of North Korea, was designated as an official successor to Kim Il-seong in 1974, and has ever since made important decisions for national policies.

4

The Korean Peninsula Changing, South and North Getting Closer

The Republic of Korea after the June Democracy Movement

Right after the June Democracy Movement, in a democratic atmosphere, South Korean people held a presidential election and also an election to select national representatives. As the opposition parties failed to unite behind a single candidate, the victory of the presidential election was given to the candidate from the "new military" regime, but still, the opposition party won by great margin in the election for the national representatives. A new era of democracy was truly imminent, and no one could stand against that.

In the 1992 presidential election, Kim Young-sam who had long served as a leader of the opposition party then made a startling compromise with the politicians from the "new military" regime, and was elected as President. The Kim Young-sam administration then accused and punished former presidents of the military faction with charges of treason. Also, the administration contributed to the 'rooting'

❶ **President Kim Young-sam (1993~1998)**, who had served for a long time as a national representative and leader of the opposition party, was elected as President after shifting sides and joining the ruling party. The Kim Young-sam administration called itself as the "Civilized Government," arguing that the "Military president era" was finally over.

❷ **President Kim Dae-jung (1998~2003)** escaped death twice under the Park Chung-hee and Chun Doo-hwan administrations. As the first President who came from the opposition party, Kim Dae-jung declared his government as the "People's Government," which referred to the coming of a true dawn of a democratic era.

❸ **President Roh Moo-hyun (2003~2008)** has long been involved in civil rights movements as a lawyer. After he was elected with the support of the younger generation, he emphasized the importance of the people's participation in the operation of national affairs, and he also claimed to advocate the concept of a "Government, Participated."

❹ **President Lee Myung-bak (2008~)** has been a legendary character in the Capitalist society of South Korea. He began his career as an employee, but later became a chief executive officer. He also served as a national representative and was later elected as Mayor of Seoul.

Geneva Agreement between North Korea and the United States of America (1994)
An agreement was made between the United States, which attempted to prevent North Korea from developing an atomic bomb, and North Korea, which requested a peaceful state of security in the Korean Peninsula. According to the agreement, North Korea agreed to abandon plans to develop atomic bombs, in exchange for the constructions of two nuclear power plants in North Korea and the provision of 500 thousand tons of heavy oil per year. Both countries agreed to establish completely normal political and economical relationships.

of democracy in the people's daily life, by adopting the election of local governments.

Korean Peninsula in crisis

As North Korea attempted to develop atomic bombs in 1994, the Korean Peninsula was faced with a prospect of war. The United States of America demanded that North Korea cease the development of atomic bombs immediately. The relationship between South and North hit a wall and intergovernmental talks were frozen. North Korea rejected the U.S. demands and asked for a peace treaty first. In the meantime the U.S. once planned to attack North Korea's atomic facilities.

As talks between North Korea and the U.S. resumed, and a summit meeting between South and North Korea was prepared, the crisis of a war dissolved. But the sudden death of Kim Il-seong, accompanied by a heavy flood and a subsequent drought caused yet another crisis for North Korea. Thousands of people were not able to receive food rations, and some even crossed the border to escape from starving.

In 1997, South Korea faced an economic crisis as well. The financial calamity that had begun in Southeast Asia caused a sudden foreign currency crisis for South Korea. South Korea requested an urgent aid to the International Monetary Fund, which demanded a merciless economic restructuring.

This economic crisis devastated the entire society. The economic growth decreased sharply, recording −6.7% (1998), and the unemployment rate

Gold Collection Campaign (1997)
As the economic crisis was aggravated, a campaign to collect gold, in which people voluntarily took out their gold sitting in their closet and donated them to the authorities, in order to enable the government to buy more foreign money.

which had been below 3% reached up to 8.6% (1998). A lot of business enterprises filed bankruptcy, and the national income declined in half.

Two South-North Summit Meetings

Kim Dae-jung, a long time opposition party leader, was elected as President in the 1997 Presidential election, which was also the time of economic crisis. For the first time in history, a peaceful transfer of power was carried out, from the ruling party to its opposition. And 5 years later, Roh Moo-hyun who had long served as another key member of the democratic movements was elected as President.

During their service as President for the past 10 years, the South Korean government pushed consistent policies geared toward reconciliation and cooperation between South and North. During this period, in North Korea Kim Jeong-il was chosen as the supreme leader, and he as well tried to open up the society to address the crisis of its social system.

A summit meeting was held in Pyeongyang in June of 2000. Both leaders of South and North Korea, Kim Dae-jung and Kim Jeong-il, agreed to expand their trades and cooperation in all areas, as they found a common consent for policies and principles toward a reunification of the Korean Peninsula. In 2007, President Roh Moo-hyun crossed over the demilitarized zone, a symbolism of division, on foot and held a 2nd summit meeting with Kim Jeong-il.

Families that were scattered around South and North were able to meet, and South Koreans were allowed to visit North Korea's major sightseeing sites. The political, economic, and cultural exchanges between South and North Korea expanded exponentially. Both South and North athletes

South and North Korea Summit talk (2000)
Kim Dae-jung, the President of the Republic of Korea and Kim Jeong-il, the chairman of the Defense Committee of the North Korea, shook their hands at the Sunan airport of Pyeongyang. It was the first Summit talk ever made after a 55-year division.

Gaeseong Industrial Complex
At Gaeseong, a suburban city near the cease-fire line in North Korea, South and North worked together to construct a world-class industrial complex. Construction began in 2002, and it now operates with the South Koreans' technology and capital and the North Koreans' labor combined.

Production of LCD televisions and semi-conductors
According to OECD statistics, South Korea's information and communication technology ratio in its entire industry shows the highest figure among member countries of OECD. The amount of productions in Memory conductors, LCD televisions, and cellular phones is ranked 2nd in the world, and the distribution of super-fast internet access, an integral part of IT infrastructure, shows a top-class level in the world. These pictures show workers producing LCD TVs (left) and semi-conductors (right).

marched together in the international games, the roads and railroads that had been disconnected for a long time were linked again, and economic cooperation increased even more.

Koreans remain optimistic on future prospects

Even though both South and North Koreas had been through several hardships, circumstances on the Korean Peninsula have been getting better. Efforts toward a peaceful settlement regarding the North Korean atomic bomb issue began to show signs of resolution within the frame of South and North talks, North Korea and the U.S. talks,▪ and the six-party talks. The economic crisis in North Korea that led to social system crisis had been somewhat overcome.

The South Korean economy continued to grow despite economic difficulties. Following the foreign currency crisis, the growth rate continuously recorded over 4% annually in general, as the information and telecommunication industries, automobile production and shipbuilding industries continued to grow and develop.

In the fields of shipbuilding and semi-conductor production, South Korea is the international front runner. It is also the second in cellular phone production, the 5th in automobile production and the 6th in steel manufacturing (according to the 2008 index). The amount of General Domestic Product ranked 13th in the world, and the overall scale of Koreans' international trading also joined the league of world's best.▪

The prospect of resolution for the North Korean issue is still murky at best, and it is also difficult to anticipate the future fate of the Korean economy. Nonetheless, a majority of Koreans remain optimistic about their future, as they have already gone through a lot of crises, while achieving extraordinary changes and accomplishments.

▪ **The six-party talks** In order to solve the nuclear issues of North Korea, the six party talks were held on August 27, 2003. Participating nations are South Korea, North Korea, China, Russia, Japan, and the United States.

▪ According to the report of 2008 "The Republic of Korea in the World," South Korea ranked first place in the number of working hours, second place in labor productivities, third place in the savings' ratio, in number of patent registrations and in number of students studying in the U.S, and also the seventh place in R&D investment. South Koreans were able to make a great leap and overcome many crises, with their diligence in study and work and their savings which were deposited for the future.

The Korea Peacekeeping Forces (left)

The Republic of Korea joined the United Nations together with the Democratic People's Republic of Korea in 1991. Both Koreas became a member of the UN in the 43th year of their respective governments' foundation. Since then, South Korea participated in the United Nations' peacekeeping operations many times. The picture shows the soldiers of the Korea Peacekeeping Force, who were sent to Lebanon in 2007.

Ban Ki-moon (1944~) (right)

A professional diplomat of Korea, Mr. Ban has been serving as the UN Secretary General since January 2007.

Korea and the Koreans, achieving dynamic changes

Industrialization in South Korea was accomplished on the basis of export-industries that were promoted by the government, and such economic openings were accompanied by continuing economic growth. Thus, many South Korean business enterprises expand their activities and move their production facilities overseas as well.

Many Koreans left the country to study abroad, or embarked upon business activities, and some of them even settled down there. Around the year 2000, new cultural trends like the so-called 'Hanryu' ("Korean waves") began to evolve, due to popular South Korean culture that captured the attention of many Asian countries.

The South Korean economy had grown through, not only exports, but also imports as well. Foreign businesses which sought to move production facilities here in Korea increased, and the number of foreigners who sought jobs inside Korea gradually increased as well.

Dynamic changes in South Korea continued by the people's creative adoption of foreign cultures. Historical experiences of the people of the U.S. and Japan, and their studies and knowledge in particular, had huge influences upon the changes that occurred inside the South Korean society.

Outside Korea, the number of those who can speak Korean and are related with Koreans through bloodlines, is close to about 6 million around the world. According to a consensus done in 2009, it appears that the total number of foreigners in South Korea is over 1.1 million. Their lives and cultures are being integrated into the daily lives of Koreans.

A prospect of the future

In the winter of 2007 and the spring of the following year, elections for the president and national representatives were held. South Koreans elected Lee Myung-bak, whose campaign slogan called for 'A First-class Korea,' while the ruling party that led the expansion of democracy, and reconciliation and cooperation between the South and North Koreas for the last 10 years, was defeated. 20 years have passed since the June Democracy Movement, and the administrations that regarded themselves as democratic governments for 10 years came to an end. And the South Koreans are now standing at a turning point.

The year of 2010 marks the 100th year since Korea was deprived of its sovereignty by the invasion of Imperialist Japan, and the 60th anniversary of the Korean War which led to devastation of the country and a division that cut the Korean Peninsula in half. The South Koreans have always been working hard under the idea of "development first, reunification later," or "growth first, distribution later," yet they always longed for democracy and peace as well. And now, as one chapter of the Korean history that was full of dynamic changes are finally bookended, they are facing a new chapter unfolding.

Koreans ask themselves what kind of future they should work toward, and they try to find answers from the past. Its long history, along with the experiences of the recent 20th century, is a treasure chest of knowledge that could be utilized in imagining new futures. Looking back at the path we have traveled until now, we Koreans attempt to discover new paths that have not yet been pursued or realized in the present.

"Dreams come true"
This card section was performed by the Korean supporters "Red Devils," during the 2002 Korea-Japan World Cup semi-final match between Korea and Germany. Koreans' enthusiasm and willingness for a better future is reflected in this phrase.

One Million Foreigners, Various Nationalities Inside Korea

According to a Korean government report, the total number of foreigners residing in South Korea as of May 1st 2009 reached the number of 1,106,884 people, equivalent to 2.2% of the total registered residents (49,593,665). This number includes those who have no Korean nationality and have stayed more than 90 days (925,470), those who obtained the Korean citizenship (73,725), such as the immigrated women for marriage, and the children of foreign residents (107,689).

The foreigners in Korea have rapidly increased since 1993. In this year, for the first time, the foreign internship system was enacted so that foreign workers from different countries were allowed to settle in the domestic labor markets as major industrial labor forces.

Among them, foreign workers ranked at the top of 52%, followed by marriage immigrants (11.4%) and study-abroad students (7%). According to their nationalities, 56.5% of Chinese including Chinese Koreans, 21.2% of Southeastern Asians, 5.4% of the US citizens, 3.9% of Southern Asians, and 2.4% of Japanese ranked in number.

Main Foreign Villages in Seoul

Philippine Street

Jongno-gu

Seodaemun-gu

Nepalean Street

China Town

Hyehwa-dong

Russia-Central Asia Village

Itaewon Tourists District/Muslim Street

Jung-gu Changshin-dong

Yeonhi-dong

Dongdaemun

Gwanghi-dong

Mongol Tower

Itaewon

Yongsan-gu

Japan Town

Dongbuichon-dong

French Seorae Village

Guro-gu

Yenben Street

Banpo-dong

Seocho-gu

Garibong-dong

Also, it appears that most of them resided in the metropolitan area (65.2%) which has more jobs, including 30.3% in Seoul, 29.3% in Gyeonggi-do, and 5.6% in Incheon. In total of eleven self-governing local bodies, foreign residents were reported to be occupying more than 5% of the total population. Such areas include the metropolitan area, Gangseo-gu in Busan, Eumseong and Jincheon in Chungcheongbuk-do, and Yeongam in Jeollanam-do, etc.

❶ Mosque at Itaewon in Seoul
There is a Mosque, Central Masjid, at Itaewon in Seoul. It was built in 1976 on a site that was provided by the Korean government with funds that were donated from Muslim countries. There are ten more Islam temples in Korea.

❷ Incheon China Town
These streets were first formed when Incheon harbor was opened in 1883. Korean and Chinese cultures coexist here. There are about 500 Chinese-Korean residents, and the entire area became a famous tourist site filled with Chinese food and culture.

❸ Itaewon in Seoul
Due to its proximity to the United States Army base it became a famous shopping area for foreigners. In the 1960s, about 40 foreign embassies and a large residential area for diplomats were developed, and ever since the entire area has become a place for tourist attraction, international shopping and entertainment.

❹ Village Without Borders, at Wongok-dong in the Ansan City
This village was formed when many foreign workers at the Ansan Industrial Complex settled in. There are approximately 60,000 foreigners from over 50 different countries residing here. 150 foreign stores are housed throughout the Wongok-dong area. Living here are many Chinese-Koreans from China, workers from Southeast Asian countries including Vietnam, and Central Asia such as Uzbekistan.

Aichi Prefectural Ceramic Museum, Japan 103_Dish with patterns of Pomegranate Baekje Culture Institute 51_The Royal Tomb of King Muryeongwang Baek Seung-jong 291_Collective farms Buyeo National Museum 34_Remains excavated at Songguk-ri, Buyeo area 59_Baekje incense burner made of gold and copper Cheongju National Museum 92_A vase with bird patterns 107_Goryeo ink stick 123_Jikji Printing blocks and a photographed edition Chion-In, Japan 109, 114_ Mireukhasaenggyeong Byeonsangdo Gimhae National Museum 47_The Gaya Pottery Gongju National Museum 51_Golden ornaments Gyeongjijeon, Jeonju 134_Yi Seong-gye Gyeongju National Museum 44_Gold crown 77_Glass, Jewel sword 84_Juryeonggu 88_A bone container with a shape of a tile-roofed house Haeinsa, Hapcheon 123_The Tripitaka woodblock Kagami Jinjya, Japan 127_Suweoul Gwaneumdo Kim Ho-seok 184_Jeong Yak-yong (offered by Gangjin City) Kim Ji-hong 295_South Korean teenagers enjoying B-boy dance Kim Sung-chol 36_Hwasun Dolmen Park in Jeollanam-do 37_North style Dolmen, South style Dolmen 48_Janggunchong 68_Muyeorwangreung 80_Seokguram 84_Anabji 89_Tile-roofed house 96_Mireukjeon at Geumsansa 108_Village shrine 128_ Songgwangsa 130-131, 135_The Geunjeongjeon hall at Gyeongbokgung 135, 150-151_Jongmyo 136_Seonggyungwan 148_The statue of King Sejong 159_Hakgujae and Jirakjae, Suweolru the front gate of Dodong Seowon 166_Site of the Mandongmyo Shrine 177_Bangye Seodang 187_Hwaseong, Paldalmun, Banghwasuryu- jeong 210_Wujeongguk 220-221_Dongnimmun 229_The Jeongdong Church, Hwanggungwu at Hwangudan, Jungmyeongjeon 261_Monument of Gwangju Stu- dent Resistance Movement Kim Soon-duk (House of Sharing) 262_〈Kidnapped〉 Kobe City Museum, Japan 49_Chiljido 175_Travel route of the Joseon Tong- shinsa emissaries Korea Army Museum 160_Dongraebu Sunjeoldo Korea Democracy Foundation 307_May 18th Democratic Movement (offered by Kyunghyang Shinmoon) Kwon Tae-gyun 20-21_Danyang Geumgul 25_Hand axe found at Jeongok-ri, Yeoncheon-gun, Gyeonggi-do province 30_A portrait of Dangun 31_Sehyeong Bronze Daggers 33_Myeongdojeon 38_Scene of harvesting 39_Songpyeon, Family paying respect to their ancestors' graves 40-41_Onyeo- sanseong 52_Tombs of Goguryeo 58_Gukdongdaehyeol 62-63_Babsang, Process of Making Soy Sauce, Gimchi, Bulgogi, Bibimbab 64-65_Munmudaewangam in the Front Sea of Gampo, near Gyeongju 68_Kim Yu-shin 71_The underwater tomb of King Munmuwang 76_Traces of log barricades at Cheonghaejin 77_A statue of a military officer at Gwaereung 79_Budo, Gameunsatab, Yeonggwangtab 83_Iljumun, Cheonwangmun, Yeonhwagyo, Chilbogyo, Cheongungyo, Baegungyo, Buddha, Seokgatab, Dabotab 86_Castle of gentry 102_Porcelain Expositions 110-111_The Gyeongpango storage facility where the "Triptaka Koreana" 129_Roof-tile carved with wishes 133_Angbuilgu 135_Sajikdan, Sadaemun 146_Nongsajikseol 158_Dosan Seowon 159_Munseonggongmyo, Ganghakdang, Jangseogak 167_So- hak 169_Yeolnyeomun 175_The Journal of Hamel 180_Tangpyeong monument 184_Dasanchodang 189_Sunmuyeongjindo 203_Woegyujanggak, Yongdudondae, Jeongjoksanseong 212_Jeon Bong-jun's house 227_Dokdo 228-229_Deoksugung, The old Russian legation building 237_A corporal punishment device 240_Seo- daemun Prison 246-247_The Independence Memorial Hall of Korea 256_The Birthplace of the World's Children Movement 257_Cheondogyo Chapel 268_Histor- ic Hall of the Seodaemun Prison, Monument of Commemoration, Execution Ground, Solitary Confinement 267_The Inside of the Independence Memorial Hall of Korea 321_Mosque at Itaewon in Seoul, Incheon China Town, Itaewon in Seoul, Village Without Borders, at Wongok-dong in the Ansan City Lee Young-lan 129_Buddha's Birthday, Yeondeung Procession, Tabdori 296-297_Seoul, Myeong-dong in May 2010 303_Jeon Tae-il Lee Heon-jong 27_Siberian comb-patterned clay pot Lee In-mi 89_Straw-roofed house, Ondol and 'Maru' Leeum, Samsung Museum of Art 95_Goryeo's Gold-plated Bronze Grand Pagoda 99_Ajibdo- daeryeon 183_Inwangjesaekdo Metropolitan Museum of Art, USA 92_A three-drawer chest with Dangcho patterns Ministry of Culture, Sports and Tourism 290_ The scene of trial for the Jinbodang Incident 292_Foreign aid materials being piled at the Busan port 303_Dispatching troops to the Vietnam War Modeoksa, Cheongyang 206_Choi Ik-hyeon National Archives and Records Administration, USA 275_The U.S. flag hung at the Joseon Governor-General office building (offered by NOONBIT Publishing Co.), The 38th Parallel line that ran across roads and villages National Museum of Korea 27_Comb-patterned clay pot at Am- sa-dong, Seoul 29_Mandolin-shaped bronze daggers 37_Things found with dolmens 61_Baekje Gwaneumsang, National Treasure No. 83: A Sitting Golden/ Bronze Maitreya statue 89_A miniature of a cooking fireplace 92_A blue celadon incense burner with carved patterns of seven treasures 103_Melon-shaped celadon vase, Grayish blue-powdered celadon with patterns of peony vines, White celadon vase, White pot with blue-lined patterns of clouds and a dragon 105_Dragon- engraved bronze Buddhist bell 113_The Gyeongcheonsa Pagoda 118_Samguksagi, Samgukyusa 121_Yi Je-hyeon 122_Goryeo's metal types of Chinese letters 124_ Cheonsan Daeryeobdo 143_Waegwando 147_White Celadon Bowl 153_Cheonja Chongtong, Hwangja Chongtong 154_Gosagwansudo 167_Shinhaeng 179_Sang- pyeongtongbo, Taepyeong Seongshido 181_Straw Mat Weaving 192_The Woman Wearing Jeonmo by Shin Yun-bok 193_Rice Threshing by Kim Hong-do, Horse Shoeing by Jo Yeong-seok, On the Way to the Market by Kim Hong-do National Palace Museum of Korea 180_Portrait of King Yeongjo Newsbank Image 39_ An express bus terminal crowded with people heading for their home towns 278_The first meeting of the Joint Commission between the United States and the So- viet Union 282_Special Committee of Investigation and Punishment of those who acted against the Korean people 295_Jongno District in South Korea 300_April 19th Revolution 303_Protest against 'the Korea-Japan Pact' 312_Pyeongyang 313_Kim Il-sung and Kim Jeong-il Ojukheon & Gangneung Municipal Museum 156_Yi Yi Park Jong-jin 94_Wanggeonwang 101_Yeongtongsa at Gaeseong Pusan National University Museum 37_Red polished pottery Pyeongyang Chosun Art Museum 137_Nosangalhyeondo Ryukoku University, Japan 142_Honilgangriyeokdaegukdo Jido Sakyejul Publishing Ltd. 46_Susan-ri Mural Painting (Re- stored graphics) Samsung Electronics 317_Production of LCD televisions and semi-conductors Sannomaru Shozokan, The Imperial Household Agency, Ja- pan 120_Monggoseubraehwoisa Seoul National University Kyujanggak Institute for Korean Studies 133_Cheonsangyeolchabunya Jido 135_Doseongdo 138_Jo- seonwangjosillok, A Sacho material containing records of King Injo's reign 145_Yongbieocheonga, Samganghaengshildo 203_Ganghwabujeondo Son Seung-hyun 28_Cheomseongdan 44_Daereungwon Tenri University, Japan 86_Choi Chi-won The Andong-Soju and Traditional Food Museum 113_Sojugori The Indepen- dence Hall of Korea 223_First battle scene between Russia and Japan in Korea, Japanese troops created an atmosphere of fear, in the night before the Eulsa-year Treaty 233_Anti-Japanese Righteous Militia 234_The Japanese record of the amount of money collected through the National Debt Compensation Movement 238_Land Survey Operation 239_The Oriental Colonization Company 241_Philadelphia Hurray Protest Marching 242_Main members of the Provisional Govern- ment 249_Korean Independence soldiers in training 256_The "Hyeongpyeong" Movement poster, Children's day poster 257_Nationalist history books 263_Forced draft The Korean Christian Museum at Soongsil University 133_Honcheoneui 177_Bronze globe The National Folk Museum of Korea 112_Jokduri The War Memorial of Korea 153_Stone ball Tokyo National Museum, Japan 92_lacquer ware products inlaid with mother-of-pearl material featuring chrysanthemum patterns University of Tokyo Faculty of Letters, Japan 75_A Dragon Head 81_Double Statues of a Sitting Buddha Yokohama History Museum, Japan 27_Japa- nese "Jomon" clay pot Yongin City 155_Shimgok Seowon Yonhap News Agency 32_The Cheongcheongang 39_A memorial service for the ancestors 70_Goryeo- yeong 148_The beauty of Korean letters 171_Ancestral ritual at the temple 270-271_Restoration of the Gyeongeuiseon Railroad 273_Japanese Self-defense Army, Korean War 274_The Korean people welcoming their liberation 288_Joint Security Area 289_College students' movement for Unification, Cooperate chief execu- tive officer's visiting North with a herd of cattle, The president walking over the 38th parallel line 294_South and North Korean athletes marching together 295_ North Korean art performance 'Arirang' 306_October 26th Incident 307_December 12th Military Coup d'état 309_Protestors with neckties in the June Democra- cy Movement 315_Gold Collection Campaign 316_South and North Korea Summit talk, Gaeseong Industrial Complex 318_The Korea Peacekeeping Forces, Ban Ki-moon Yu Eun-kyung 112_Korean bride in the traditional wedding ceremony

A Korean History for International Readers

What Do Koreans Talk About Their Own History and Culture?

First Published 15 November 2010

Author | The Association of Korean History Teachers (전국역사교사모임)
Translator | Michelle Seo (김문희)
Adviser | Lee Kang-hahn

Publisher | Kim Hag-won
Chief Manager | Lee Sang-yong
Chief Editor | Sun Wan-kyu
Editor | Choi Se-jeong, Park Jung-sun
Text Design | AGI Society
Cover Design | Minjinki Design
Mapping | Kim Kyeong-jin, Im Geun-Sun
Photography | Kwon Tae-gyun, Kim Sung-chol

Published by | Humanist Publishing Group Inc.
Registered | 5 January 2007 No. 313-2007-000007
Address | 564-40 Yeonnam-dong, Mapo-gu, Seoul, Korea 121-869
Tel (+82) 2-335-4422
Fax (+82) 2-334-3427
Website | www.humanistbooks.com
E-mail | humanist@humanistbooks.com

ⓒ The Association of Korean History Teachers, 2010

ISBN 978-89-5862-363-2 03900
      978-89-5862-364-9 (set)